Statistics and Econometrics:
Methods and Applications

Orley Ashenfelter

Princeton University

Phillip B. Levine

Wellesley College

David J. Zimmerman

Williams College

John Wiley & Sons, Inc.

ACQUISITIONS EDITOR	Leslie Kraham
ASSOCIATE EDITOR	Cindy Rhoads
MARKETING MANAGER	Charity Robey
SENIOR PRODUCTION EDITOR	Norine M. Pigliucci
COVER DESIGNER	Madelyn Lesure
PRODUCTION MANAGEMENT SERVICES	Suzanne Ingrao
COVER ART	Dana Spaeth/SuperStock

This book was set in Times Roman by Pine Tree Composition.

This book is printed on acid-free paper. ∞

ISBN-10: 0-470-00945-4
ISBN-13: 978-0-470-00945-1

Printed in the United States of America

10 9 8 7 6 5 4

This book is dedicated
to our wives, Ginna, Heidi, and Susan.
O.A., P.L., D.Z.

Preface (or *Frequently Asked Questions*)

How is this book different from other econometrics texts?

We regularly teach introductory econometrics, but we have never been satisfied with the choice of textbooks that we confront. As empirical economists, we want a book that shows our students how to do econometrics and conveys the excitement of applied work. Our goal in this book is to display both the methods of econometrics **and to show the excitement of econometric applications.** To accomplish this goal we provide econometric applications in every chapter, even when covering topics like probability, where they are sometimes not expected. These applications address important, real world questions.

Why is it important to include credible applications in an econometrics text?

In our own research, we have relied heavily on econometric tools to provide believable answers to important issues relevant to both public and private decision-making. Economic analysis is often capable of providing theoretical predictions regarding the direction of a particular relationship but it cannot tell us the magnitude of that relationship. Is the demand curve steep or flat? Just how much do wages rise with education? For other questions, economic analysis cannot even tell us the direction of the relationship. Does labor supply rise with an increase in the wage? Does a merger that reduces competition and creates efficiencies lead to higher or lower prices? Even important questions outside the purview of economic analysis often require estimates of the impact of one variable on another. Does student performance improve with smaller class sizes? Our desire to answer questions like these motivated us to conduct our own econometric analyses, and we have written this book in an attempt to motivate our students to do the same thing

Does this book provide a rigorous introduction to econometric methods?

Our focus on real world questions does not diminish the need to understand the technical intricacies of a sophisticated econometric analysis. The credibility of econometric research relies upon whether or not it was conducted in an appropriate manner. Research that addresses an important topic but that does not display a mastery of the technical components of the analysis is of little value. Therefore, we also intend to present a rigorous introduction to econometric techniques.

What topics are covered in this book, and why were they chosen?

In the development of this book, there were two fundamental decisions that we made regarding the coverage of material. First, we had to make a choice between a book that covered all potentially relevant material and a book that focused on only the topics we considered most important. Some texts in econometrics treat more topics than we do and serve a useful purpose as a reference. We have chosen to limit the topics covered in this text to those that we address in our courses. From our experiences in teaching econometrics, we have found that those books that provide encyclopedic coverage of the field overwhelm students. When students read the book they find so many topics that were not covered in our lectures that they tend to ignore the book all together! The book that we have written has largely been developed straight from our lecture notes, so we teach virtually all the material in it. We sought to present the material in such a way that faculty can cover a particular topic and simply assign students to "read all of Chapter 12." Similarly, problems at the end of chapters are designed more like problem sets than as exhaustive lists of questions that cover all the topics in the chapter.

The second important decision we had to make was where to begin and end our coverage of material. Some colleges and universities teach a one-semester course in econometrics that begins with basic probability theory and ends with regression analysis. The curriculum at other institutions includes a two-semester sequence. Probability and statistics is covered in the first semester and regression analysis, including more sophisticated topics like time series and panel data methods, are covered in the second semester. We have chosen to write a book that is flexible enough to cover both types of instruction. For those who teach all the material in one semester, coverage could begin at the beginning of the book and end when the instructor runs out of time (perhaps with multiple regression in Chapter 12). Alternatively, in a two-semester sequence, the first half of the book (through, say, Chapters 9 or 10 on simple linear regression) could be covered in the first semester and the remainder in the second semester. Of course, the second semester would have to review the basics of probability and statistics, so we have provided Appendix A1 to facilitate that process. Thus, even if the first semester of a two-semester course is taught in another department, instructors could assign Appendix A1 followed by the material in Chapters 9 through 18 for a self-contained treatment of the second semester's material. For those who choose to use this book for both semesters of the two-semester sequence, students will appreciate the ability to buy a single book.

ACKNOWLEDGMENTS

As with any endeavor that requires extensive inputs of time and energy, this book could not have been completed without the significant assistance of others. Perhaps most important, we are extremely grateful to our students, who have helped us understand what works and what does not work in an econometrics class. They have also been invaluable as test cases for draft versions of the book, helping us locate sections that needed improvement. We have also benefitted greatly from the input of our colleagues, who both helped refine the material covered and provided suggestions and data for some of the applications (which are often contained in boxes). The comments of many reviewers have also been of tremendous value. Our thanks go to all of the following individuals:

Richard J. Agnello
University of Delaware

Joseph G. Altonji
Northwestern University

Samru Altug
University of York

Richard T. Baillie
Michigan State University

Jere R. Behrman
University of Pennsylvania

Anil Bera
University of Illinois–Champaign

Mitali Das
Columbia University

Cresenta Fernando
Brandeis University

Yee-Tien Fu
Stanford University

Pedro Gozalo
Brown University

B. E. Honore
Princeton University

Eric Jensen
College of William and Mary

Shakeeb Khan
University of Rochester

Subal C. Kumbhakar
State University of New York–Binghamton

Byung Joo Lee
University of Notre Dame

Lee Ohanion
University of California at Los Angeles

Tom Potiowsky
State Economist, State of Oregon
Portland State University

Peter Toumanoff
Marquette University

M. Daniel Westbrook
Georgetown University

Zhijie Xiao
University of Illinois at Urbana–Champaign

In addition, we thank our editor at John Wiley & Sons, Leslie Kraham, as well as publisher, Susan Elbe, associate editor, Cindy Rhoads, and marketing manager, Charity Robey. Finally, this book could not have been completed without the continuous support and encouragement of our families.

Author Biographies

Orley Ashenfelter is Joseph Douglas Green 1895 Professor of Economics at Princeton University. His areas of specialization include labor economics and applied microeconomics, econometrics, and the analysis of dispute-settlement systems. He has been Director of the Office of Evaluation of the U.S. Department of Labor (1972–73), a Guggenheim fellow (1976–77), the Benjamin Meeker Visiting Professor at the University of Bristol (1980), a Fellow of the Center for Advanced Study in the Behavioral Sciences (1989), and the Meyer Visiting Research Professor at the New York University School of Law (1990). He edited the *Handbook of Labor Economics* and was Editor of the *American Economic Review*. He is Co-editor of the *American Law and Economics Review*. His current research includes the evaluation of the effect of schooling on earnings, the impact of dispute resolution systems on wages, and the valuation of safety risks.

Phillip B. Levine is an associate professor of economics at Wellesley College, a research associate at the National Bureau of Economic Research, and a Faculty Affiliate of the Joint Center for Poverty Research. He has also served as a senior economist at the White House Council of Economic Advisers. Phil received a BS degree with honors from Cornell University in 1985 and a PhD from Princeton University in 1991. He has been a member of the faculty at Wellesley since then. His research has largely been devoted to empirical examinations of the impact of government programs and social legislation on individuals' and firms' behavior. Topics include: (1) the impact of imperfect experience rating in the unemployment insurance system on firms' layoff behavior, (2) whether welfare recipients move between states because of differences in welfare generosity, and (3) the impact of abortion legalization on fertility behavior.

David J. Zimmerman is an associate professor of economics at Williams College, director of the Williams Project on the Economics of Higher Education, a research associate at the Institute for Research on Poverty at the University of Wisconsin-Madison, and a participant in the National Bureau of Economic Research's programs on education. He has served as a researcher at the World Bank, a lecturer at Princeton University, and as a visiting scholar at the University of Toronto and the University of Wisconsin–Madison. David received his Bachelor of Commerce degree from the University of Toronto and a Masters and PhD from Princeton University. He has been on the faculty of Williams College since 1991. He has written extensively on a diverse set of topics including welfare reform, abortion legislation, the economic returns to education, and social and economic mobility. His current research is focused peer effects and inequality in American higher education.

Brief Contents

Contents

Chapter 1

Introduction

1.1   WHAT IS ECONOMETRICS?

It might seem surprising, but it is difficult to precisely define *Econometrics*. This is largely because the scope of its application is very large. Econometricians (the people who "do" econometrics) come in many varieties. Econometricians might be interested primarily in evaluating the efficacy of different public policies targeted at alleviating poverty. Or, they might be interested in building elaborate mathematical models that are used to predict the future course of the economy. Sometimes they are interested in the creation of new data sets. At other times they might be developing new statistical methods to tackle a difficult empirical problem. Some econometricans are number crunchers—spending hours each day in front of a computer. Others work primarily with pen and paper, deriving equations based on theoretical reasoning. The literal definition of econometrics is "measurement in economics." It is the *empirical* arm of economics. A useful working definition is:

> Econometrics is the application of statistical methods to problems that are of concern to economists.

But, alas, even this definition is not quite perfect since the tools used by econometricians are useful well beyond the disciplinary boundaries typically associated with economics. Econometric models have been used to analyze the effects of free agency on baseball salaries, to predict the quality of new batches of wine well before they are ready for consumption, and to estimate the impact of reduced class size on student performance. So, it is worth noting that the tools you will learn in this book are broadly applicable.

Generally speaking, econometrics is primarily interested in three activities:

1. Quantifying economic relationships
2. Testing competing hypotheses
3. Forecasting

1.1.1 Quantifying Economic Relationships

Economic theory seldom provides answers with the level of precision required for the judicious implementation of policy. Supply and demand curves are ubiquitous in introductory economics courses. But, you soon learn that the outcomes of many policies are tied to the *magnitude* of the slope of the supply and demand curves. We often need to know *elasticities* before a practical analysis can begin. A classic example involves the consequences of raising the minimum wage. Typically, it is asserted that such a policy will cause employers to reduce employment while also encouraging more workers to enter the labor market—resulting in unemployment. The magnitude of the effect, however, depends crucially on the slopes of the relevant labor supply and labor demand curves. Theory does not tell us the magnitude of these slopes. Econometric analysis attempts to fill this gap.

The techniques employed in econometrics help economists to deal with an important problem that is almost omnipresent in applying economic theory: Often it is not possible to conduct randomized experiments. In the "lab" sciences we might measure the effect of a drug by randomly assigning some people to a treatment group that receives the drug and others to a control group that does not. We could then follow the participants and measure differences in their lifespan or whatever outcome is of interest. Any difference in the outcome between the treatment and the control group might reasonably be attributed to the drug. Similarly, social scientists would often (at least in the name of science) like to be able to use experimentation. But, it is often difficult or impossible to do so. It might be informative to randomly assign different policies to different groups of otherwise similar people and gauge the effect. Indeed, there are probably many situations where such a strategy should be followed but is not. In practice, however, we often simply see different policies and different outcomes. The people exposed to different policies may or may not be much alike—making it difficult to ascribe any differences in their outcomes to a particular policy. Econometric methods help us proceed with quantifying causal relationships when we do not have the luxury of a formal experimental approach.

1.1.2 Testing Competing Hypotheses

Frequently, economists advance different theories purporting to explain how the world works. Importantly, the effectiveness of policy will often depend on which theory is correct. The impact of a tax cut on consumer spending, for example, depends on understanding the appropriate model of consumption behavior. Simple Keynesian models relate consumer spending to *annual* disposable income. Other theories relate consumer spending to *lifetime* income. If the first model is correct, a reduction in taxes will increase current disposable income and have an impact on current consumption. If the second model is correct, a tax reduction could have a much smaller impact on consumption, particularly if the tax cut is regarded as a one-shot deal with little impact on lifetime earnings. An appropriate fiscal policy must distinguish between these models. Econometric analysis attempts to fill the gap.

1.1.3 Forecasting

Researchers are often interested in forecasting the future values of economic variables. They may want to forecast the future levels of inflation, or unemployment, or the stock market. Forecasting the future viability of the social security system, for example, relies on forecasting the number of program beneficiaries and the amount received per benefi-ciary along with the number of workers and the amount they contribute. Forecasting contributions would involve forecasting the earnings of workers in the labor force—po-tentially for several years in the future. This might involve estimating the trend in labor productivity over time. Again, econometrics attempts to provide the information needed to conduct such analyses.

1.2   THE USE OF MODELS

As we have seen, economists use *models* to describe real-world processes. Models are sim-plified depictions of reality and often take the form of an equation or set of equations that de-scribe some economic setting. A market for apples, for example, might be characterized by a supply and a demand curve and the resulting equilibrium where quantity supplied equals quantity demanded. The macroeconomy might be described using an aggregate demand and aggregate supply curve. But, how do these models relate to the empirical models developed by econometricians? One important difference is that economic theories are usually *deter-ministic*. For example, if we specify consumption spending to depend on income, then once income is known, consumption is also known with certainty. More formally, if *consumption spending$_i$* = *f(income$_i$)* where *i* indexes different individuals, then once we know the appro-priate functional form (theory may or may not help us here) and *income,* then we know the level of consumption spending. It is deterministic. Ah, if only life were so simple. If we could model *everything* then perhaps all would be deterministic, but from the practical van-tage point of econometrics we accept randomness. We accept the fact that people or firms or countries that look very similar in a variety of measurable dimensions may still behave dif-ferently. We simply cannot control for all the differences that might exist. For example, people who have similar levels of income are very likely to differ in their consumption pat-terns. This suggests that empirical models of consumption spending include a *stochastic* or *random* component. Or, more basically, we allow an error term to enter into our model. Formally, *consumption spending$_i$* = *f(income$_i$)* + ε_i. The error term, ε_i, allows individuals with the same level of income to have different levels of consumption spending. For some people the error will be positive—they will consume more than the typical person with a given level of income. For other people the error might be negative—they will consume less than is typical at that income level. Our model will require us to specify the nature of the error terms. In essence, an econometrician takes a world that is not deterministic—that is, a world characterized by randomness—and attempts to quantify this randomness. We will discuss this in greater detail later in the book, but typically we assume that the mean or av-erage error is zero. This being the case, our deterministic theory is then reinterpreted as telling us not how each and every individual's consumption behaves when income changes, but rather how the mean or average of consumption varies with income. This is an important distinction, and one that is necessary to move from the world of theory to the world of econo-metric models and data.

1.3   TYPES OF DATA

Data (the plural of *datum*: from the Latin word for "given") provide the pieces of infor-mation that we use in conducting an econometric analysis. They provide the raw material we need to quantify economic relationships, to test competing theories, or to construct forecasts. They are the inputs required for any empirical investigation. Data may be described as a set of *observations* on one or more *variables*. For example, we might have information on the variable "income," or "age," or "grade in the econometrics course" for a number of people. Each occurrence for a variable is called an *observation* for that variable. For example, Bill Smith might provide an observation of $12,000, 36, B+ on these three variables (income, age, grade).

Data come in different formats. There are three basic structures to the data used in the practice of econometrics. These data types are referred to, respectively, as cross-sectional, time series, and panel data.

1.3.1 Cross-sectional Data

Cross-sectional data provide information on a variety of entities (individuals, firms, countries, etc.) at the same point in time.

Example 1

Observation	Person	Income	Age
1	Lucy Smith	$56,000	26
2	Bill Jones	$14,000	22
3	Howard Lincoln	$144,000	46

In this data set we have one observation for each entity (person) for the variables income and age.

Example 2

The *Current Population Survey* is a monthly survey of 50,000 households in the United States. The survey, which has been conducted for over 50 years and is designed to be nationally representative, is the main source of information on the state of the labor force for the U.S. population. The survey provides information on a variety of variables including employment, hours of work, and earnings. Information from this survey forms a cross-sectional data set that is used each month to calculate the official unemployment rate.

1.3.2 Time Series Data

Time series data provides information for the same entity (e.g., individual, firm, country, etc.) at different periods in time.

Example 1

Observation	Person	Year	Income
1	Lucy Smith	1996	$56,000
2	Lucy Smith	1997	$58,000
3	Lucy Smith	1998	$61,000
4	Lucy Smith	1999	$62,500

In this data set we have four observations on one entity (the person Lucy Smith) for one variable (income) at different periods of time (i.e., the years 1996–1999).

Example 2

Each year the *U.S. Department of Commerce* assembles data on the U.S. *Gross Domestic Product (GDP)*. The following is a time series data set for *GDP* (measured in millions of dollars) for the years 1990–1998.

Observation	Year	GDP (in $millions)
1	1990	5,803.2
2	1991	5,986.2
3	1992	6,318.9
4	1993	6,642.3
5	1994	7,054.3
6	1995	7,400.5
7	1996	7,813.2
8	1997	8,300.8
9	1998	8,759.9

1.3.3   Panel (or Longitudinal) Data

Panel or *longitudinal data* is a combination of cross-sectional and time series data. A panel data set provides information on a variety of entities (e.g., individuals, firms, countries, etc.) at different periods in time.

Example 1

Person	Year	Income
Lucy Smith	1996	$56,000
Bill Jones	1996	$14,000
Lucy Smith	1997	$58,000
Bill Jones	1997	$16,000
Lucy Smith	1998	$61,000
Bill Jones	1998	$17,500
Etc.	Etc.	Etc.

In this data set we have data on two entities (Lucy Smith and Bill Jones) for different periods of time (i.e., the years 1996–1998). So, we might say we have a time-series of cross sections.

Example 2

The *National Longitudinal Survey of Youth, 1979* is a panel data set comprised of a nationally representative sample of 14- to 22-year-olds. The survey was conducted annually between 1979 and 1993 and biannually from 1994 onward. In the first year there were 12,686 participants, most of whom have remained in the sample over time. The survey provides information on a large number of variables including income, marital and fertility history, assets, educational attainment, job training, and so on.

1.3.4 Data Sources

There are a large number of data sources that are useful for conducting economic analysis. Many are gathered by the government, some by nongovernment organizations (e.g., the World Bank), some by research organizations, others by individual researchers. A good source to learn the range of data resources available to economists has been compiled by Bill Goffe in *Resources for Economists on the Internet* and can be found on the World Wide Web at http://rfe.wustl.edu/Data/index.html.

1.4 CONDUCTING AN EMPIRICAL PROJECT

Now that you have a general idea of what econometrics is all about, it is probably useful to think about how, in broad terms, you would proceed with an empirical project. The following are five steps you are likely to follow.

1.4.1 Pick a Topic

First you have to decide what it is you are going to research. What is it that you want to know? Do you want to estimate a demand elasticity? Do you want to determine whether a training program for low-skilled workers has "worked"? Do you want to forecast future CO_2 emissions in third-world countries? Obviously there are an infinite number of things you might want to know. But, at this stage in the process you should aim to answer two questions with great clarity:

1. What question are you asking?
2. Why is it important?

For example, if you are investigating whether a training program for unskilled workers has worked, you must be very clear about what it means to have "worked." Do you mean they have higher wages? Lower unemployment rates? Higher "job satisfaction"? It is also often useful to describe why you think your question is important. What are the implications of your answer? Would your findings suggest a market failure? Or, would they suggest a particular policy response?

How do you get started? You might identify a topic of interest by reading the newspaper. Often, topics that are underresearched or poorly understood are marked by vitriolic disagreement. You might also use the classification system developed by the *Journal of Economic Literature*. This journal provides summaries of research papers for a variety of topics. You might find yourself gravitating toward topics related to fiscal policy, or economic growth, or social welfare. More basically, you might simply be a little introspective. What topics do *you* find interesting? What questions capture *your* imagination?

1.4.2 Learn What Others Have Learned about This Topic

Once you have identified a topic that you believe is interesting, you should spend some time learning what others have done on that topic. There are a variety of places to turn and we will mention only a few that are particularly helpful. First, you might turn to the online index *Econlit,* which provides a searchable database for research done in economics. Another useful source is the *Social Science Citation Index.* This index will let you learn which authors have cited a particular study in their own work. This helps you to track which papers seem to be seminal to the literature in which you are interested. Which papers seem to be cited time and time again? You might also check the *National Bureau of Economic Research* (www.nber.org), which publishes current working papers on a variety of topics. Again, the *Journal of Economic Literature* provides helpful summaries of a wide range of economic research. After spending a few hours with these resources you will begin to get a feel for the intellectual "lay of the land" for the topic you have chosen.

1.4.3   Have an Empirical Strategy

At this juncture, you are going to have to think more carefully about how you will do your econometric analyses. Are you quantifying some relationship, testing a theory, or generating a forecast? Often the empirical exercise can be framed simply as: X affects Y. You have to decide what Y is, what X is, and the nature of their relationship. But, as a first step you will need data that include Y and X. Hopefully your investigation of the existing literature will have been helpful on this score. At this point you will likely apply the methods you will learn in this book. You will gather data and use the appropriate econometric techniques. You may compare means, estimate regression models, and so on. It might be useful to imagine yourself as Sherlock Holmes. There is a question you are trying to answer and you carefully and creatively bring a variety of evidence to bear in doing so. But, that is jumping ahead. We will learn more about the options available for your empirical strategy in the chapters that follow. That, after all, is what the book is about.

1.4.4   Interpret Your Results

Once you have implemented your empirical strategy on actual data you will need to interpret your results. What do they tell you? Are the results clear or ambiguous? Do they shed light on what is or is not appropriate policy? Can the results be generalized beyond the context implicit in your study? Are the results robust? Do small changes in your empirical approach or the way you classify your data have a noticeable effect on your results? At this point you should be candid. You are trying to answer a question. You are *not* trying to prove *your* prior point of view on the matter. Be scientific. Report what you find with nothing up your sleeve.

1.4.5   Write a Report

To write your report you can simply describe the first four steps you have taken. State the question you are addressing and why it is important. Summarize the appropriate existing literature. Describe how you will tackle your problem empirically. Summarize your data, including the variables used and any restrictions you imposed in selecting your sample. Outline your econometric strategy. Interpret your results with a focus on the question you initially posed.

1.5 OVERVIEW OF TEXT

This book provides a self-contained introduction to the study of econometrics. Chapters 2 through 8 provide a brief yet complete introduction to mathematical statistics. Chapters 9 through 18 focus on regression models and their extensions. Appendix A at the end of the book provides a summary of the statistical chapters (2 through 8) and serves as a bridge between the two halves of the book. Students who have already studied statistics may find this appendix a useful review before moving on to later chapters. Statistical tables are given in Appendix B at the end of the book. Finally, each chapter provides a problem set to be used in practicing what was learned in that chapter. Econometrics is best learned by practice.

Chapter 2

Basic Probability Theory

2.1   INTRODUCTION

In this chapter we introduce the tools of probability theory. Probability theory forms the logical foundation of statistical inference, a key topic in later chapters. We begin with some basic definitions.

2.2   BASIC DEFINITIONS

2.2.1   Random Trial

A *random trial* is an experiment or activity where (1) a number of different outcomes are possible and (2) the outcome that will prevail in a given trial is uncertain.

Examples

1. Games of chance provide many excellent examples of random trials. The act of rolling a die, drawing a card from a deck, or spinning a roulette wheel are all examples of a random trial. In each case, we do not know what the outcome will be until we actually conduct the experiment.

2. A researcher asks randomly selected individuals whom they will vote for in an upcoming election. Again, different responses are possible and the response received varies from person to person.

3. A bottle of 10-year-old wine is opened. Will the wine be good? Uncertainty prevails until the experiment is completed.

4. A sprinter runs a 100-meter race. The exact time that it will take him or her to complete the 100 meters is uncertain.

2.2.2 Basic Outcomes

A *basic outcome* is the outcome associated with a particular random trial.

Examples

1. You might get a 4 when you roll the die or draw a queen of spades from a deck of cards.
2. A selected individual reports that she is voting Democrat.
3. The bottle of wine is absolutely first-rate.
4. The sprinter breaks the world record, finishing the race in 9.70 seconds.

More generally, we denote the different possible outcomes of the random trial as o_i where the subscript i indicates the number of the trial. For example, if on the first toss of a die we get a 3 and on the second toss we get a 4, then $o_1 = 3$ and $o_2 = 4$. Notice that outcomes may be *qualitative* (e.g. "Democrat" or "Republican") or *quantitative* (i.e., numerical). Quantitative outcomes can in turn be *discrete* (i.e., a few different possible outcomes like the roll of a die) or *continuous* (i.e., an infinite, or practically infinite, number of different possible outcomes like the sprinter's time). For the time being we will restrict ourselves to discrete outcomes. We will consider continuous outcomes in the next chapter.

2.2.3 Sample Space

The *sample space (S)* is the set, or list, of all possible basic outcomes from the random trial.

Example

If we toss one die, then the sample space is given by $S = \{1,2,3,4,5,6\}$. More generally, if there are N possible basic outcomes from the random trial, then $S = \{o_1, o_2, \ldots, o_N\}$. The outcome of the random trial must be one of the outcomes in the sample space.

APPLICATION 2.1 | *Nothing Better to Do?*

How about rolling a die 20,000 times to see if it is "fair?" That's what R. Wolf did and reported in an 1882 journal article. Here's what he found:

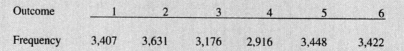

Outcome	1	2	3	4	5	6
Frequency	3,407	3,631	3,176	2,916	3,448	3,422

SOURCE: Example 131 (p. 98) in Hand, D.J., F. Daly, A.D. Lunn, K.J. McConway, E. Ostrowski (eds.), *A Handbook of Small Data Sets*. London: Chapman and Hall, 1994.

2.2.4   Event

An *event* is a subset of basic outcomes of the sample space. We say an event "occurs" if any of the basic outcomes comprising the event occurs. An event differs from an outcome in that it may include more than one outcome.

Example

If event A is comprised of tosses of the die exceeding 2, then $A = \{3,4,5,6\}$.

2.2.5   Venn Diagrams

Basic outcomes, events, and the sample space can be depicted using a Venn diagram. The sample space is represented by a rectangle and events are usually shown as circles or parts of circles. In this Venn diagram, there are two events, A and B, that overlap, indicating that some of the outcomes in A are also in B.

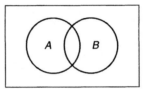

2.3   SET THEORY

Since events are conveniently shown as sets of outcomes, the language and tools of set theory are very useful for the development of probability theory. In this section we introduce some mathematical notation useful in working with sets.

2.3.1   Unions, Intersections, and Complementation

Sets can be combined in different ways to form new sets. Denoting two events as A and B, we have the following basic set operations.

Complementation

A' is the *complement* of A and contains all of the basic outcomes not in the set A.

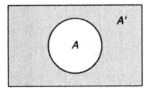

Example

If $S = \{1,2,3,4,5,6\}$ and $A = \{3,4,5,6\}$ then $A' = \{1,2\}$. (Note: When you read A' you can verbalize it as "*not A*.")

Union of Events

The *union* of A and B, written $A \cup B$, is the event whose outcomes belong to set A or set B, or both.

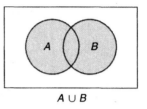

$A \cup B$

Example

If $A = \{3,4,5,6\}$ and $B = \{2,3,4,5,6\}$ then $A \cup B = \{2,3,4,5,6\}$. (Note: When you read $A \cup B$ you can verbalize it as "*A or B*.")

Intersection of Events

The *intersection* of set A and set B, written $A \cap B$, are the events whose outcomes belong to both set A and set B.

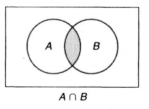

$A \cap B$

Example

If $A = \{3,4,5,6\}$ and $B = \{2,3,4,5,6\}$, then $A \cap B = \{3,4,5,6\}$. (Note: When you read $A \cap B$ you can verbalize it as "*A and B*.")

Mutual Exclusivity

Two events A and B defined over the sample space S are said to be *mutually exclusive* if they have no outcomes in common; that is, if $A \cap B = \phi$, where ϕ is the null or empty set.

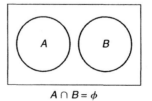

$A \cap B = \phi$

Example

If $A = \{3,4,5,6\}$ and $B = \{2\}$, then $A \cap B = \phi$.

Another way of indicating that two sets are mutually exclusive is to say that their Venn diagrams are nonoverlapping.

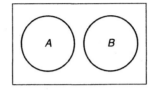

Partition

A set of events A_1, A_2, $A_3 \ldots A_N$ *partitions* the sample space if the events are mutually exclusive (that is, $A_i \cap A_j = 0 \; \forall_{i \neq j}$) and together they cover all of S (that is, if $\bigcup_{i=1}^{N} A_i \equiv A_1 \cup A_2 \cup A_3 \ldots A_N = S$).

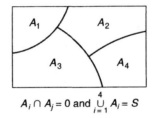

$A_i \cap A_j = 0$ and $\bigcup_{i=1}^{4} A_i = S$

Examples

If $S = \{1,2,3,4,5,6\}$ then $A_1 = \{1,2\}$ and $A_2 = \{3,4,5,6\}$ partition S. Notice that the two events are mutually exclusive and their union contains all of the outcomes in S. We will use the notion of a partition in later derivations.

2.3.2   Some Rules for Set Operations

Unions, intersections, and complementions of sets follow several algebraic rules and we describe some of them here. Venn diagrams can be used to verify all of these rules, but in this discussion we show only those for which verbal descriptions are too cumbersome.

Commutative Rules

   1. The union of A and B equals the union of B and A: $A \cup B = B \cup A$.
   2. The intersection of A and B equals the intersection of B and A: $A \cap B = B \cap A$.

It does not matter the order in which we take the union or intersection of two sets.

Idempotency Rules

1. The intersection of A with itself is A: $A \cap A = A$.
2. The union of A with itself is also A: $A \cup A = A$.

If two sets are identical, then their union is the same set and their intersection will rule out every event within the set.

Rules for S and ϕ

1. The union of A and the null set is A: $A \cup \phi = A$.
2. The union of A and the sample space S is the entire sample space S: $A \cup S = S$.
3. The intersection of a set A and the null set is the null set: $A \cap \phi = \phi$.
4. The intersection of a set A and the sample space S is the set A: $A \cap S = A$.

Combining a set with an empty set leaves the original set, and combining a set with all possible outcomes leaves all possible outcomes. Alternatively, there is no overlap between a set and the empty set, and the overlap between a set and all possible outcomes is the original set.

Involution Rules

1. The complement of the complement of A is A: $A'' = A$.
2. The complement of the null set is the entire sample space S: $\phi' = S$.
3. The complement of the sample space S is the null set: $S' = \phi$.

Those outcomes not in the set comprised of the outcomes not in a set A are the outcomes that are in A (describing this rule requires us to violate rules of grammar against using double negatives!). If an outcome is not in the null set, it must be in the sample space. If it is not in the sample space, it must be in the null set.

Complementation Rules

1. The union of A and its complement is the entire sample space: $A \cup A' = S$.
2. The intersection of A and its complement is the null set: $A \cap A' = \phi$.
3. The complement of the set comprised of the union of A and B is the same as the intersection of the complement of A and the complement of B: $(A \cup B)' = A' \cap B'$.
4. The complement of the set comprised of the intersection of A and B is the same as the union of the complement of A and the complement of B: $(A \cap B)' = A' \cup B'$.

The set of outcomes either in a set or out of a set represent all the possible outcomes. No outcome is both in a set and out of a set. The third and fourth rules are best seen using a Venn diagram. For example, the third rule is shown below.

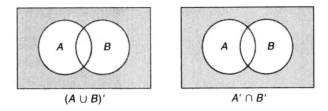

$(A \cup B)'$ $A' \cap B'$

Associative Rules

     1. $A \cup (B \cup C) = (A \cup B) \cup C$ and

     2. $A \cap (B \cap C) = (A \cap B) \cap C.$

Distributive Rules

$$A \cap (B \cup C) = (A \cap B) \cup (A \cap C) \text{ and } A \cup (B \cap C) = (A \cup B) \cap (A \cup C)$$

Venn diagrams provide a useful tool to show that each of these rules is true. More formal proofs proceed by showing that any basic outcome that is in the left-hand side of the equation is also contained in the right-hand side of the equation and vice versa.

2.4   PROBABILITY

The next step in our development of the basics of probability theory is to assign to each basic outcome in the sample space a value called its *probability,* which is a measure of how likely it is that that outcome will result when we conduct the random trial. This section will provide a discussion of some basic properties of probability.

2.4.1   Fundamental Postulates

The probability of an event occurring is simply the sum of the probabilities of the basic outcomes underlying the event. That is: $P(A) = \sum_A P(o_i)$. Common sense suggests that the "probability" we assign to an event A should satisfy certain basic postulates. As formulated, these postulates apply to discrete sample spaces. First probabilities should be non-negative. Impossible events will have a probability of zero, but no lower. The closer the probability is to zero the less likely it is the outcome will occur. Second, since S contains all possible outcomes (one of which must occur), we require the probability of S to be 1. That is, some outcome must occur. Finally, the probability of the union of a set of mutually exclusive events should simply be the sum of the probabilities of the events. More formally we write these basic postulates as:

     Postulate 1. $P(A) \geq 0.$

     Postulate 2. $P(S) = 1.$

     Postulate 3. If the set of events $A_1, A_2, A_3 \ldots A_N$ are N mutually exclusive events then:

$$P(A_1 \cup A_2 \cup \ldots \cup A_N) = P(A_1) + P(A_2) + \ldots + P(A_N)$$

Note: We will sometimes use the *summation operator* to simplify the notation associated with summing. Briefly,

$$\sum_{i=1}^{N} x_i = x_1 + x_2 + \ldots + x_N.$$

For example, we can use it to rewrite axiom 3 as:

$$P(A_1 \cup A_2 \cup \ldots \cup A_N) = \sum_{i=1}^{N} P(A_i)$$

Example

In the newspaper you often read of seemingly amazing things happening. For example, you might read that John Doe was struck by lightning twice during his lifetime. Is this really quite so amazing as it appears? Or, is it actually quite a likely event? To answer, you must note a critical distinction. It might be quite unlikely that one particular person would get hit by lightning twice, but it might not, in fact, be so unlikely that *someone* gets hit twice by lightning in their lifetime. And, of course, it is that someone (John Doe) who makes it into the newspapers. To see the issue more clearly, suppose the odds of getting hit by lightning twice are *p*—where *p* is doubtless a very small number. But, in the United States, the odds of *someone* getting hit twice by lightning is

$$P(me \cup you \cup John\ Doe \cup \ldots) = p + p + p \ldots$$

if we assume everyone has the same odds of being struck twice. With a large population and enough time, this outcome is not quite so unlikely as you might first think.

2.4.2   Results

Several additional results can be deduced from these three basic postulates.

Result 1. Let A and B be two mutually exclusive events defined over S. Then: $P(A \cup B) = P(A) + P(B)$. If A and B are mutually exclusive, then the probability that both A and B occur is the sum of the probabilities that A occurs and B occurs. Note that result 1 holds only for mutually exclusive events and is a simplification of Postulate 3. The result is easily seen by looking at the Venn diagram where the two events have no overlap since they are mutually exclusive.

Example

Suppose we roll a die. What is the probability that we will get a 2 or a 6? Since $P(2) = P(6) = 1/6$ and since these events are mutually exclusive (only one can happen on a given roll of the die), we have $P(A \cup B) = 1/6 + 1/6 = 1/3$.

Result 2. $P(A') = 1 - P(A)$. That is, the probability that A does not occur is 1 minus the probability that A occurs.

Proof. Follows from $P(S) = 1 = P(A \cup A') = P(A) + P(A')$.

Example

The probability it will not rain is simply 1 minus the probability that it will rain.

Result 3. $P(\phi) = 0$. That is, impossible events have a zero probability.

Proof. $P(\phi) = P(S') = 1 - P(S) = 0$.

Result 4. If $A \subseteq B$, then $P(A) \leq P(B)$ (where the symbol, $\subseteq$, is read as "is contained in"). That is, if all of the basic outcomes in A are also in B, then the probability of B must be at least as large as the probability of A.

Proof. If $A \subseteq B$, then $B = A \cup (B \cap A')$ (which is easily seen in a Venn diagram), and so $P(B) = P(A) + P(B \cap A') \geq P(A)$ since $P(B \cap A') \geq 0$.

Result 5. $0 \leq P(A) \leq 1$.

Proof. This follows from the fact that $\phi \subseteq A \subseteq S$ and result 4.

Result 6. $P(A \cup B) = P(A) + P(B) - P(A \cap B)$. This result indicates that the probability of observing A or B is the sum of the probabilities of observing either A or B less the probability that they both occur. In effect, we subtract the intersection from the sum to avoid double counting. Notice that result 6 is a generalization of result 1 and is true whether or not the events A and B are mutually exclusive. Result 6 simplifies to result 1 if A and B are mutually exclusive, since then $P(A \cap B) = 0$.

Proof. Notice that A and $A' \cap B$ are mutually exclusive events. Further, $A \cup (A' \cap B) = (A \cup A') \cap (A \cup B) = S \cap (A \cup B) = (A \cup B)$. Thus, $P(A \cup B) = P(A) + P(A' \cap B)$ as these events are mutually exclusive. Also, $P(B) = P(B \cap (A \cup A')) = P(B \cap A) + P(B \cap A') = P(A \cap B) + P(A' \cap B)$, implying $P(A' \cap B) = P(B) - P(A \cap B)$. Thus, $P(A \cap B) = P(A) + P(B) - P(A \cap B)$.

Example

Suppose 50% of economists read the *New York Times*, 65% read the *Wall Street Journal*, and 30% read both. What is the probability that a randomly selected economist reads at least one of the two newspapers? We are told that $P(A) = .5$, $P(B) = .65$, and $P(A \cap B) = .3$. We are asked to determine the probability of an economist reading A or B or both, that is, the union. From result 6 we know $P(A \cup B) = .5 + .65 - .3 = .85$.

Result 7. $P(A \cup B) = 1 - P(A \cup B)' = 1 - P(A' \cap B')$. That is, the probability of A or B occurring is 1 minus the probability of "not A" and "not B" occurring.

Result 8. If the set of events $A_1, A_2, A_3 \ldots A_N$ *partitions* the sample space, then for any event B: $P(B) = P(B \cap A_1) + P(B \cap A_2) + \ldots + P(B \cap A_N)$. Note: We may write this using summation notation as

$$P(B) = \sum_{i=1}^{N} P(B \cap A_i)$$

In other words, if we added the probabilities of observing all the common outcomes between B and each of the partitions of A, we would get the entire probability of observing B. Therefore, if we partition the sample space into A and A', then we can use result 8 to write $P(B) = P(B \cap A) + P(B \cap A')$. We will use this result below.

2.4.3 Interpretations of Probability

While the probability postulates and results listed above show how we can manipulate probabilities, they do not tell us how we should actually assign probabilities to events. For example, suppose you toss a coin. What is the "probability" of getting a head? You probably answered .5, but what logic did you follow in responding? Historically, three major interpretations of probability have been advanced: the *classical*, *frequentist*, and *subjective* interpretations of probability.

Classical Interpretation

Suppose a random trial has N mutually exclusive outcomes, each of which is equally likely to occur. If event A occurs in N_A of the outcomes, then the probability of event A occurring is:

$$P(A) = \frac{N_A}{N}$$

Example

The toss of a coin has $S = \{head, tail\}$. If the event A is defined to be "heads," then the number of mutually exclusive outcomes is 2 and the number of outcomes associated with event A is 1. Thus, assuming heads and tails are equally likely we would have: $P(A) = 1/2$.

The chief problem with this definition of probability is that it is circular. To make it operational the outcomes must be "equally likely to occur." The notion of "equally likely" is, however, itself a statement about probabilities.

Frequentist Interpretation

If a random trial is repeated a large (infinite) number of times under identical conditions, then $P(A)$ is given by the fraction of the time that A occurs in the random trial. Thus, $P(A)$ is simply the long-run empirical relative frequency of the outcome A. More formally:

$$P(A) = \lim_{n \to \infty} \left(\frac{n_A}{n} \right)$$

where n is the number of times the trial is conducted and n_A is the number of times that event A occurs.

Example

In the coin-toss example the frequentist definition would assert $P(A) = 1/2$, because a coin that is tossed a large number of times under identical conditions yields heads about one-half of the time. Thus, the probability is derived from repeating the experiment of tossing the coin many times under identical conditions.

The freqentist approach provides an extremely fruitful way to conceptualize many of the issues we will be considering in this book. Often we will make use of a *conceptual experiment* where we ask you to imagine what would happen if we actually did repeat a given experiment a large number of times under identical conditions. Many powerful results can be obtained from such reasoning. It should also be noted that with modern computers it is often possible to have the computer simulate experiments very quickly and record the results. We will discuss this approach later in the book when we consider Monte Carlo simulations. That said, the principal difficulty with applying this approach to probability is that sometimes it is simply not possible to conduct repeated trials in a controlled setting. Questions such as: "When will the war end?" or "Will I get promoted tomorrow?" are not amenable to frequentist calculations. Also, the observed relative frequency derived from a finite number of repetitions can deviate from the true probability that would (in principle) be obtained from repeating the random trial an infinite number of times. Indeed, while interned during World War II, John Kerrich, a South African mathematician, flipped a coin as many as 10,000 times! While the fraction of times he got heads was not exactly .5, it did get closer and closer as the number of trials increased. The frequentist faith is that the fraction would converge to .5 if the number of trials continued forever.

Subjective Interpretation

People often make probability assessments based on their intuition or "gut feelings." Such personal or subjective definitions of probability assert probabilities on the basis of personal beliefs concerning the particular situation. As such, subjective probabilities ascribed to events will differ from person to person. If these subjective measures are logically consistent, they can provide a functional basis for probability theory. The subjective approach to probability is particularly useful in situations where "equally likely" outcomes do not exist and repeatable experiments are not feasible.

2.5   CONDITIONAL PROBABILITY

Often we are interested in knowing the probability that an event will occur given that we know another event has already occurred. Suppose we have two events A and B. Associated with these two events are four possible outcomes: $A \cap B$, $A \cap B'$, $A' \cap B$, $A' \cap B'$. In the first outcome both A and B occur. In the second outcome only A occurs. In the third outcome only B occurs, and in the last outcome neither A nor B occurs. Suppose we know that B has occurred. Then we know that either $A \cap B$, or $A' \cap B$ has occurred. In only the first of these two outcomes ($A \cap B$) does A occur. Letting $P(A|B)$ denote the probability of A occurring given B has occurred, we have:

Result 9. Let B be an event such that $P(B) > 0$. Then, the *conditional probability* that event A occurs given that event B is known to have occurred is given by the ratio:

$$P(A|B) = \frac{P(A \cap B)}{P(A \cap B) + P(A' \cap B)} = \frac{P(A \cap B)}{P(B)}$$

This result can easily be depicted with a Venn diagram. Draw events A and B as overlapping circles.

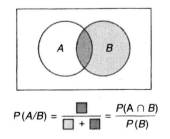

$$P(A/B) = \frac{\blacksquare}{\square + \blacksquare} = \frac{P(A \cap B)}{P(B)}$$

Since we know event B has occurred, we know that some outcome in event B's circle occurred. The question, then, is what fraction of the time will an outcome in event A also have occurred? This will simply be the ratio of the intersection of events A and B to the whole area for event B. That is, it is the fraction of the time that A occurs when B has occurred.

Examples

1. Suppose we toss a die and are told the number was even. What is the probability that the number was 2? Thus, we want to know $P(2|even)$. Intuitively, we know the relevant sample space is now $\{2,4,6\}$ and 1/3 of these outcomes is a 2. More formally,

$$P(2|even) = \frac{P(2 \cap even)}{P(even)} = \frac{P(2)}{P(2 \cup 4 \cup 6)} = \frac{P(2)}{P(2) + P(4) + P(6)},$$

which is simply equal to $(1/6)/(1/2) = 1/3$ as above.

2. In a classroom poll, 20 out of 50 women and 12 out of 40 men oppose a campus policy. A ballot drawn at random indicates opposition. What is the probability it was cast by a man? Intuitively, we know that a total of 32 people opposed the policy, of which 12 were men. Thus, the probability of it having been cast by a man is 12/32. More formally,

$$P(man|oppose) = \frac{P(man \cap oppose)}{P(oppose)} = \frac{12/90}{32/90}$$

which is $12/32 = \dfrac{3}{8}$.

APPLICATION 2.2   *Me? Cheat? I Would Never Do (or, at Least, Admit to) That*

This is a trick to try to get responses to sensitive questions. You ask a respondent to flip a coin, and choose to answer question (A) nonsensitive or (B) sensitive according to the result (which is *not* revealed to the interviewer). Then:

$$\%yes \approx p(\%yes|nonsensitive) + (1 - p)(\%yes|sensitive)$$

The point is that saying "yes" should be less difficult with this method. The estimate of the response in the population to the sensitive question is:

$$\%yes|sensitive = \frac{\%yes - .5(\%yes|nonsensitive)}{.5}$$

where we have assumed $p = .5$, where p is the probability of getting a head, which, on average, will be .5.

Example:

Princeton students were asked about whether they (A) had ever attended a religious service in the last year, or (B) had ever seen in-class cheating. A separate survey showed $\%A = 60\%$. The survey found $\%Yes = 39.2\%$. The *estimate* of the percent seeing violation of the honor code is thus

$$\frac{39.2 - 30}{.5} = 18.4\%$$

Notice that we may use result 9 to express the probability of A and B occurring as the probability of A occurring given B occurs times the probability that B occurs. That is:

Result 10. $P(A \cap B) = P(A|B)P(B)$.

We may also use result 9 to modify result 8, yielding:

Result 11. If the set of events $A_1, A_2, A_3 \ldots A_N$ *partitions* the sample space, then for any event B:

$$P(B) = \sum_{i=1}^{N} P(B|A_i)P(A_i)$$

A simple case of result 11 occurs when we use result 8 and partition the sample space into A and A'. Then result 11 simplifies to:

Result 12. $P(B) = P(B|A)P(A) + P(B|A')P(A')$.

2.6 BAYES' THEOREM

Bayes' theorem provides an extremely useful application of conditional probabilities whereby knowledge that event B has occurred is used to revise (update) the probability that event A has occurred.

Result 13 (Bayes' theorem). If A and B are two events with $P(A) > 0$ and $P(B) > 0$ then

$$P(A|B) = \frac{P(B|A)P(A)}{P(B|A)P(A) + P(B|A')P(A')}$$

Proof. From the definition of a conditional probability and result 10 we have

$$P(A|B) = \frac{P(A \cap B)}{P(B)} = \frac{P(B \cap A)}{P(B)} = \frac{P(B|A)P(A)}{P(B)} = \frac{P(B|A)P(A)}{P(B|A)P(A) + P(B|A')P(A')}$$

where we make use of result 12 in writing the denominator.

Example

Consider the problem of testing for a particular disease. Let A be the event that the person has the disease and B be the event that the test indicates they have the disease. Suppose the odds of having the disease are 1 in 10,000. If you have the disease, the test will correctly indicate you have the disease 90% of the time and 10% of the time will indicate you do not have the disease (i.e., a "false negative"). However, if you do not have the disease the test will mistakenly indicate that you do have the disease 1 in 1000 times (i.e., a "false positive") and will correctly indicate you do not have the disease 999 in 1000 times. Now, suppose you have taken the test and it indicates you have the disease. What are the odds you really have the disease? Let's first use some of the notation of conditional probability to indicate what we know. We have been told that $P(A) = 1/10,000$, and so we know $P(A') = 9999/10,000$. Also, $P(B|A) = .9$ and $P(B'|A) = .1$. Finally, $P(B|A') =$

| APPLICATION 2.3 | *You Gotta Relent if it's 95 Percent. Or Do You?* |

Many firms would like to be able to implement mandatory tests for illegal drug use among their employees. Indeed, in 1986, the Reagan administration, by Executive Order, gave government agencies the authority to conduct urine tests for illegal drug use on all new employees. Bayes' theorem provides an important tool for analyzing such policies. In situations where illegal drug use is not widespread and where the tests used to a certain usage are inaccurate, then an unacceptably large number of nonusers may be falsely accused of using drugs on the job. But, at what point are such tests accurate enough? In 1987 a bill introduced to the New York Senate indicated that screening tests of this sort must "have a degree of accuracy of at least ninety-five percent." But, according to Bayes' theorem, the effectiveness of such a requirement would depend on the prevalence of drug use in the working population. Suppose both false positives and false negatives meet the requirement of being accurate 95% of the time. Further, suppose 5% of the working population indulge in illegal drugs. In this case, only half of the people indicated to be drug users would, in fact, be drug users.

SOURCE: Finkelstein, Michael O. and Bruce Levin, *Statistics for Lawyers*. New York: Springer Verlag, 1990.

$1/1000$ and $P(B'|A') = 999/1000$. We are asked to calculate $P(A|B)$. Using Bayes' rule we have

$$P(A|B) = \frac{.9 \times 1/10,000}{(.9 \times 1/10,000) + ((1/1000) \times (9999/10000))} \cong .08 \text{ or } 8\%$$

Intuitively, suppose you have 1,000,000 people being tested. Of those, we would expect 90 to have the disease and 999,910 to not have the disease. Of the 100 with the disease 90 would test positive. Of the 999,900 who don't have the disease, 999.9 would test positive. Thus, we would have $100 + 999.9 = 1099.9$ people testing positive, of which only 90 would actually have the disease. Again, the fraction with the disease who tested positive would be 90/1099.9 or about 8%. Notice that this surprisingly low figure is being driven by both the rarity of the disease and the errors in testing.

We can generalize Bayes' rule to allow for several possible mutually exclusive outcomes.

Result 14. Suppose the set of events $A_1, A_2, A_3 \ldots A_N$ *partitions* the sample space. If $P(A_j) > 0$ and $P(B) > 0$, then

$$P(A_j|B) = \frac{P(B|A_j)P(A_j)}{\sum_{i=1}^{N} P(B|A_i)P(A_i)}$$

2.7 INDEPENDENCE

Conditional probabilities deal with evaluating the probability an event will occur given we know another event has occurred. Sometimes, however, the fact that one event has occurred conveys no information at all about whether another event will occur. When the occurrence of one event provides no information about the occurrence of another event, we say the two events are *statistically independent*.

APPLICATION 2.4	*They Say It's Hot, but It's Probably Not*

Often when we observe a streak of successes, we attribute it to skill and prowess. Sometimes people refer to this as the "hot hand." The basic principles of probability, however, tell us that even if events are statistically independent, we would still observe streaks in their outcomes. One should attribute causality to the streak only if we can reject statistical independence. In other words, only if subsequent success is greater than we would have predicted if the outcomes were statistically independent can we attribute it to a hot hand.

This problem frequently appears in discussions about sports and investing; a streak is identified and people claim that the player or mutual fund manager has a hot hand. For instance, consider the 10,000 or so funds rated by Morningstar, the leading mutual fund research firm. Suppose that in any given year a fund has a probability of 0.5 of providing an annual investment return that is greater than the market average. If annual returns are statistically independent, then one would expect that over a five-year period, $0.5^5 = 3.125\%$, or about 313 funds would outperform the market in each of the five years. One could point to any one of those funds and claim its manager has a hot hand. Unfortunately, if the outcomes are truly statistically independent, that fund has no greater chance that it will outperform the market next year than any other fund. For instance, Bogle (1994) reports in his study of almost 700 mutual funds that "a top 20 fund's performance in one year has no systematic relationship to its ranking in the subsequent year" (p. 86). This may explain the frequent mutual fund disclaimer that "past performance is no guarantee of future results."

Sporting events provide another example where hot hands are often claimed. Consider a basketball player who sinks several shots in a row. Some may claim that he is "in the groove," "shooting the ball with confidence," or is "on fire." Again, one needs to test these claims against the alternative that the streak is just a random event that may result in response to statistically independent trials. Tversky and Gilovich (1989) tested this hypothesis using data from nine players on the Philadelphia 76ers during the 1980–81 basketball season. They found that the likelihood of making a shot after a previously made shot was no different than that following a missed shot.

SOURCES: Bogle, John C. *Bogle on Mutual Funds: New Perspectives for the Intelligent Investor.* New York: Richard D. Irwin, 1994.

Tversky, Amos and Thomas Gilovich, "The Cold Facts About the 'Hot Hand' in Basketball." *Chance*, Vol. 2, No. 1 (1989), pp. 16–21.

Result 15. Two events (*A* and *B*) are *statistically independent* when $P(A|B') = P(A)$. Alternatively, since

$$P(A|B) = \frac{P(A \cap B)}{P(B)}$$

Result 16 provides an alternative expression for independence.

Result 16 (Multiplication Rule). Two events (*A* and *B*) are *statistically independent* when $P(A \cap B) = P(A)P(B)$. This result follows directly from the relationship that

$$P(A|B) = \frac{P(A \cap B)}{P(B)}$$

and Result 15.

Example

Suppose 1 in 20 people are rich and 1 in 5 people have red hair. What is the probability that a randomly selected individual will be rich and have red hair? Assuming red-haired people are no more likely to be rich than anyone else (that is, rich and red hair are independent), then $P(\text{rich} \cap \text{red hair}) = P(\text{rich})P(\text{red hair})$, which is $(1/20)(1/5) = 1/100$. To see the simple logic in this, suppose you randomly selected 100 people. Typically, 5 would be rich and 1 of the 5 would have red hair. Thus, 1 in 100 would be rich and have red hair.

The multiplication rule can be expanded to the case of multiple independent events.

Result 17. If A_1, A_2, A_3,...A_N are independent events then $P(A_1 \cap A_2 \cap A_3 \cap...A_N) = P(A_1)P(A_2)P(A_3)...P(A_N)$.

Example

Suppose you have applied to three graduate schools: A, B, and C. The odds of getting into A are 20%, into B are 40%, and into C are 60%. What is the probability you get accepted at all three schools? Assuming the selection process is independent, the odds are $(20/100)(40/100)(60/100) = .048$.

Notice that the concepts of independence and mutual exclusivity are very different. If A and B are mutually exclusive then $P(A \cap B) = 0$, whereas if A and B are independent then $P(A \cap B) = P(A)P(B)$. Intuitively, if A and B are mutually exclusive, then if B occurs we know that A did not occur. Thus, the occurrence of B provides useful information about A, indicating that the two events are not statistically independent.

2.8   PROBLEMS

1. Is it true that $P(A \cap B/B) = P(A/B)$?

2. In each of the following random experiments, describe the sample space S for the experiment. Then use your intuition and experience to assign a value to the probability p of each of the events A occurring.

   a. The toss of an unbiased coin, where the event A is "heads."

   b. The draw of a card from a standard deck of cards, where the event A occurs if a club is drawn.

   c. The cast of two unbiased dice, where event A occurs if the roll is less than 5.

3. Suppose one card is drawn at random from a standard deck of cards. (What is the sample space S?) Define a number of events as follows:

   $A = \{x: x \text{ is a jack, queen, or king}\}$

   $B = \{x: x \text{ is a 9, 10, or jack, } and \ x \text{ is red}\}$

   $C = \{x: x \text{ is a club}\}$

   $D = \{x: x \text{ is a diamond, heart, or spade}\}$

   Find the following probabilities:

   a. $\Pr(A)$

   b. $\Pr(A \text{ and } B)$

   c. $\Pr(A \text{ or } B)$

   d. $\Pr(C \text{ or } D)$

   e. $\Pr(C \text{ and } D)$

4. Suppose you are playing in a championship basketball game. There are four seconds left in the game and your team is losing by two points. You have the ball and call a time out. You have two choices. You could try for a three-point play to win. The odds you succeed are .3. Or, you could go for a two-point play and force the game to go into overtime. The odds of making the two-point play are .5. Suppose the odds of winning in overtime are .5. Which option would you choose?

5. The probability a beginning golfer makes a good shot if he selects the correct club is 1/3. The probability the shot is good with the wrong club is 1/5. In his bag are four different clubs, only one of which is correct for the shot he is about to make. Sinc the beginner knows practically nothing about the choice of the proper club, he selects a club at random. He chooses a club and takes a stroke. What is the probability he got off a good shot? Given that he got off a good shot, what is the probability that he chose a wrong club?

6. A recent graduate has submitted his application to the World Bank for a position in the Young Professional Program. He knows the Bank hires 4% of its applicants. Only some of the applicants receive an interview. It is known that among all the applicants hired 98% receive interviews, the other 2% being related to Division Chiefs! Furthermore, among all applicants *not* hired only 1% are interviewed. Our recent graduate was just called for an interview and asks you to tell him the probability that he will be hired. What do you tell him?

7. Suppose you have applied to three graduate schools: *A*, *B*, and *C*. The odds of getting into *A* are 20%, into *B* are 40%, and into *C* are 60%. What is the probability you get rejected at all three schools? Get accepted to at least one school?

8. An economist wants to know what fraction of workers in a factory sometimes smoke marijuana on the job. She collects a random sample of 100 workers. To allay their fears she conducts the investigation indirectly. Each worker is assigned a number between 00 and 99. Anyone whose number is between 00 and 69 is asked to answer *yes* or *no* as to whether they sometimes use marijuana on the job. The other workers must answer *yes* or *no* to a trivial question such as "Do you ever wish you won a lottery?" The results were as follows: 44% of the responses were *yes*. What fraction would we estimate answer *yes* to the marijuana question?

9. Monty Hall (the host of *Let's Make a Deal*) has presented Fred with the choice of three doors. Behind two of the doors are "booby prizes." A new car is behind the other door. Fred selects a door (#1, for example). Monty then shows him a booby prize behind one of the unselected doors (#2, for example). Monty then offers Fred the chance to switch from his original selection to the unopened, unselected door (#3 in our example). Should Fred switch? (Aside: This is a very famous problem and was the subject of a front-page *New York Times* article some years back.)

10. A college newspaper at a prestigious Ivy League school published a fact stating that last year the graduate school admitted 500 men and only 380 women, despite the fact that 2000 applicants of each gender applied for admission. On this basis, the newspaper charged that women were being discriminated against in the admissions process.

Buried in the last paragraph of the article is a quote by a university official claiming that every department in the university has a higher acceptance rate for female than for male applicants. For instance, in arts programs only 10% of the male applicants were admitted while 12% of the female applicants were admitted. In the sciences, 30% of the male applicants were admitted compared to 40% of the female applicants. The breakdown of applicants to each program type is as follows:

	Male	Female
Arts	500	1500
Sciences	1500	500

a. Using the information above, complete the following table:

	Male		Female	
	Applied	Admitted	Applied	Admitted
Arts				
Sciences				
Total				

b. Does it appear that the claim by the university official is true? That is, do women appear to be admitted at a higher rate in each program type?

c. How do you reconcile these findings with the overall lower acceptance rates for women? Is sex discrimination occurring or not?

Chapter 3

Random Variables and Probability Distributions

3.1   INTRODUCTION

In the previous chapter we introduced the notion of a random trial (experiment), the resulting outcomes, and the assignment of probabilities to these outcomes. But some of the outcomes we discussed, like the outcome of a coin toss, are qualitative in nature, and it is often more convenient to work with outcomes that are quantitative. In this chapter we develop the notion of a random variable that assigns a number to each basic outcome in the sample space. We then consider the assignment of probabilities to each value assumed by the random variable. We start with some basic definitions.

3.2   BASIC DEFINITIONS

3.2.1   Random Variables

A *random variable* is a function or rule that assigns a real number to each basic outcome in the sample space.

Examples

1. Suppose our random trial consists of flipping a coin three times and recording the outcomes as "heads" or "tails." Then, $S = \{$HHH, HHT, HTH, HTT, THH, THT,

TTH, TTT}. Notice that the basic outcomes are nonnumerical. We define a random variable X that assigns the number of heads to each outcome in the sample space. Then, $X(\text{TTT}) = 0$, $X(\text{HTT}) = X(\text{THT}) = X(\text{TTH}) = 1$, $X(\text{HHT}) = X(\text{HTH}) = X(\text{THH}) = 2$, and $X(\text{HHH}) = 3$.

2. Continuing with example 1, we could create a new random variable $Y = X^2$. The new random variable Y assumes the square of the number of heads in three flips of the coin. Since X takes on the values 0,1,2, and 3, Y will take on the values 0,1,4, and 9.

Thus, the random variable takes the different basic outcomes o_i and assigns them a number $X(o_i)$. Notice that the domain of the random variable X is the sample space and the range of X is the real number line. Ironically, a random variable is neither random nor a variable but is rather a function that maps the elements of the sample space S to the real number line. It is only "random" in the sense that the value it assigns to a basic outcome is not determined until the random trial is actually conducted and the basic outcome determined. That is, its value changes from trial to trial and uncertainty prevails in advance of the trial as to what outcome will occur. Random variables greatly facilitate statistical analysis in that they provide a numerical description of the outcomes of the random trial. It is much easier to work with (add, subtract, multiply, and divide) numbers than with nonnumerical entities like HHH.

Often our basic outcomes are already numeric in nature. For example, if our random trial involves asking randomly selected individuals their incomes, then we receive a number in response. In this instance we may simply define our random variable to assume the same values as the basic outcomes, like income levels, themselves. Alternatively, we might still want to define a random variable that assigns different numbers to these outcomes. For example, we might define X to equal 1 for people with incomes over $100,000 (i.e., the "rich") and zero otherwise.

3.2.2 Discrete and Continuous Random Variables

A random variable that takes on a limited number of distinct values is called a *discrete* random variable.

A random variable that takes on an infinite number of values over a continuum is called a *continuous* random variable.

Examples

1. In our coin-toss example above, X takes on one of four values: 0,1,2, or 3. Thus, X is a discrete random variable.

2. If our random trial involves randomly selecting individuals and asking them their height (i.e., X = height), then a virtually infinite number of responses are possible since height can be measured in arbitrarily small units. Thus, X might be treated as a continuous random variable.

Obviously the distinction between continuous and discrete random variables is somewhat arbitrary. We could, for example, measure heights to the nearest inch, in which case there would be a fairly large, but not infinite number of different possible outcomes.

Sometimes, however, it is analytically advantageous to treat variables like height, income, temperature, time unemployed, and so forth as continuous, even though in a strict sense (at least with currently available measurement tools) they are discrete. For example, it would be possible, though quite cumbersome, to list all of the distinct values for income in the United States. Deciding whether to treat a variable as discrete or continuous really depends on which is a more useful characterization for the task at hand.

3.3   PROBABILITY DISTRIBUTION FOR A DISCRETE RANDOM VARIABLE

3.3.1   Assigning Probabilities

The fact that discrete random variables take on a limited number of outcomes allows us to create a list of these outcomes (for continuous random variables the list would be infinite in length!). We will denote the k different values the random variable X can assume as $x_1, x_2, x_3, \ldots x_k$. For example, in the coin-toss example, where we were counting the number of heads in three tosses, we have $x_1 = 0$, $x_2 = 1$, $x_3 = 2$, and $x_4 = 3$, there being $k = 4$ different values assumed by the random variable X. Notice that the random variable is shown in uppercase while its outcomes are shown in lowercase. Also note that each x_i corresponds to one (or more) basic outcome in the sample space. Furthermore, each of the corresponding basic outcomes has an associated probability. Thus, we can sum the probabilities of the basic outcomes associated with each outcome of our random variable and, in so doing, assign a probability to each of the values assumed by the random variable.

Example

In our coin-toss example above, we have $X = 2$ (two heads came up in the three flips) associated with the basic outcomes {HHT, HTH, THH}. Thus, the probability of getting two heads is given by $P(X = 2) = P(X = \text{HHT} \cup X = \text{HTH} \cup X = \text{THH}) = P(\text{HHT}) + P(\text{HTH}) + P(\text{THH})$, since the outcomes are mutually exclusive. Independence implies this equals $P(\text{H})P(\text{H})P(\text{T}) + P(\text{H})P(\text{T})P(\text{H}) + P(\text{T})P(\text{H})P(\text{H})$. Then, assuming $P(\text{H}) = P(\text{T}) = 1/2$, this equals 3/8. Thus, $P(X = 2) = 3/8$.

Note: Sometimes we will write $P(X = x_i)$ as simply $P(x_i)$. For example, we might write $P(X = 1)$ as $P(1)$. This simply saves on notation.

3.3.2   Discrete Probability Distribution

We have now seen how to work out the probability for any given outcome of our random variable simply by calculating the probabilities of the basic outcomes in the sample space associated with that value of the random variable.

The *probability distribution* for a discrete random variable X is a list of all of the different values X can assume along with the probability that X assumes each of those values. Thus, a probability distribution simply shows how the probabilities are "distributed" across the different values X can assume.

Note: The probability distribution for a discrete random variable is often called the *probability function* and is denoted by $f(x_i) = P(X = x_i)$.

Example

For our coin-toss example above, X assumes the values 0,1,2, or 3. It is straightforward to calculate (as we did above for $X = 2$) the probability that $X = 0$, $X = 1$, $X = 2$, or $X = 3$. Doing the calculations (try it!) yields $P(X = 0) = 1/8$, $P(X = 1) = 3/8$, $P(X = 2) = 3/8$, and $P(X = 3) = 1/8$. The probability distribution for X then can be depicted using a graph or a table. Sometimes the distribution also can be expressed using a formula. The distribution of X is shown in Table 3.1.

Table 3.1 Probability Distribution for Number of Heads in Three Tosses of a Fair Die

X = number of heads in three tosses		Probability
0	$\left(\frac{1}{2}\right)\left(\frac{1}{2}\right)\left(\frac{1}{2}\right)$	1/8
1	$\left(\frac{1}{2}\right)^3 + \left(\frac{1}{2}\right)^3 + \left(\frac{1}{2}\right)^3$	3/8
2		3/8
3		1/8

(handwritten annotations: "Multiple combinations", "multiply bk they are independent", "(for elements)")

3.3.3 Properties of Discrete Probability Distributions

Discrete probability distributions must satisfy certain basic properties:

1. $0 \le P(X = x_i) \le 1$

2. $\sum_{i=1}^{k} P(X = x_i) = 1$

Notice the similarity between these properties and those specified for probabilities in Chapter 2. Since the probability associated with the outcome of a random variable is derived from the probabilities of the underlying basic outcomes, these similarities should not be surprising. Again, the assigned probabilities must be between 0 and 1, and if we sum over all possible values assumed by the random variable the sum must equal 1 (see Table 3.1).

3.3.4 Cumulative Probability Distributions

A *cumulative probability distribution* provides the probability that $X \le x_i$ for each of the values x_i assumed by the random variable X. That is, it shows the probability of seeing the outcome x_i or smaller for each of the k values associated with X.

Example

In our coin-toss example above, the probability of getting two or fewer heads on three flips is given by $P(X \le 2) = P(X = 0 \cup X = 1 \cup X = 2) = P(0) + P(1) + P(2) = 1/8 + 3/8 + 3/8 = 7/8$. Similarly, $P(X \le 0) = 1/8$, $P(X \le 1) = 4/8$, and $P(X \le 3) = 1$.

From Table 3.1, we find the cumulative probability for each x_i by summing the probabilities up to, and including, that x_i. We depict the cumulative probability distribution for X using a table or a graph. Table 3.2 shows the cumulative probability distribution for the coin-toss example.

Table 3.2   Cumulative Probability Distribution
for Number of Heads in Three Tosses of a Fair Die

X = Number of heads in three tosses	Probability
0	1/8
1	4/8
2	7/8
3	1

increasing to 1

APPLICATION 3.1   *Where Have All the Girls Gone?*

Traditionally, the human reproduction process has slightly favored the birth of boys over girls. Standard population estimates indicate that roughly 107 boys are born for every 100 girls born, or alternatively, boys comprise about 51.6% of all births. Interestingly, this birth ratio results in a roughly equal ratio of men and women of reproductive age because boys are slightly more likely to die as children. Therefore, more male births would be consistent with views of evolutionary biology; if it is best to have an equal number of men and women of reproductive age, then this requires a disproportionate share of male births.

Recently, in some populations the balance has tipped further to favor the birth of boys by an even greater margin. For instance, the sex ratio at birth in China in 1993 was 114.1 male births to every 100 female births; boys comprised 53.3% of all births. Other Southeast Asian countries, and particularly Korea, also have experienced similar changes in the sex ratio at birth.

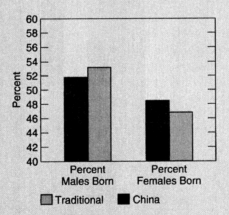

Evidence indicates that strong gender preferences explain the prevalence of male births in China. For instance, among those women who have already had two female births but no male births, the probability that the next birth is male is 69.2%. Ultrasound exams, which can determine the sex of a fetus, followed by selective abortions is considered to be a primary determinant of this. Before the introduction of this relatively recent technology, such selection was not possible.

SOURCE: Gu, Baochang and Krishna Roy, "Sex Ratio at Birth in China, with Reference to Other Areas in East Asia: What We Know," *Asia-Pacific Population Journal,* Vol. 10, No. 3 (September 1995), pp. 17–42.

APPLICATION 3.2 | *Saving a Little Extra for the Stretch Run*

One would think that after running 25 or so miles, "ordinary" marathon runners would not have sufficient energy to exert one last push to improve their time. But apparently this is not so. Beating the 4-hour barrier appears to be an important goal for many runners.

Below we have plotted the distribution of race times for the first 15,000 finishers from the 1999 New York City marathon. To do so, we have taken a distribution that is continuous in nature and calculated the percentage of runners finishing within 5-minute intervals. The winner of the marathon completed the course in 2 hours and 9 minutes, but only the elite runners finish anywhere close to that time; fewer than 50 finished in under 2½ hours. Among the first 15,000 finishers, the probability of finishing within a 5-minute interval increases virtually continuously until exactly the 4-hour mark. Just beyond that point, there is a noticeable dip in the fraction of runners finishing with those times. In fact, for faster times the 3-hour mark is the only other break from the trend toward higher fractions of runners finishing in longer time intervals up to that point. Clearly, that last push is enough for some runners to meet their personal goals.

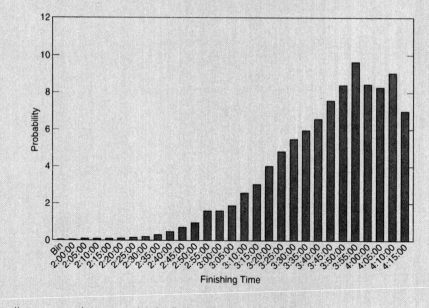

SOURCE: http://www.nycmarathon.msn.com/results_final.asp, September 19, 2000.

3.3.5 Properties of Discrete Cumulative Probability Distributions

1. $0 \leq P(X \leq x_i) \leq 1$. This implies that the cumulative probability never falls as x_i increases. For example, the probability that X is less than 10 will always be at least as large as the probability that X is less than 9.

2. $P(X \leq \max x_i) = 1$. That is, the probability X is at or below the largest value assumed by X is 1.

3. $P(X = x_i) = P(X \le x_i) - P(X \le x_{i-1})$. This is easily seen by rewriting this expression as: $P(X \le x_i) = P(X \le x_{i-1}) + P(X = x_i)$. That is, the probability X is at or below a number is equal to the probability that X equals that number plus the probability X is below that number. Thus, the probability distribution for X can easily be calculated given knowledge of the cumulative probabilities.

Example

From the coin-toss example, $P(X = 2) = P(X \le 2) - P(X \le 1) = 7/8 - 4/8 = 3/8.$

3.4   PROBABILITY DISTRIBUTION FOR A CONTINUOUS RANDOM VARIABLE

3.4.1   Assigning Probabilities

So far we have considered situations where the random variable is discrete, taking on a limited number of values. Random variables are often treated as being continuous—having an unlimited number of possible outcomes. This immediately presents us with a problem. Clearly, some value of X must occur on any given trial, but the relative frequency with which we observe any given outcome x_i approaches zero as the number of trials increases. Because of this, when a random variable is continuous we speak of the probability of X assuming a value within some *interval*.

Example

Suppose we have a spinner on a dial with four equal sections and the dividing lines between sections are labeled from 0 to 100 in 25-unit increments (that is, 0, 25, 50, 75, and 100). Since the spinner can land on any of an infinite number of positions on the dial, the probability associated with any particular position is zero (e.g., $P(X = 0) = 0$). We can, however, calculate the probability X lies in any finite interval on the dial (e.g., $P(0 \le X \le 50) = 1/2$ or $P(0 \le X \le 25) = 1/4$).

3.4.2   Probability Density Function

When a random variable is continuous, we denote by $f(x)$ a function where the probability that X falls between two values equals the area under the graph of the function between those values. Mathematically, the area under the graph of $f(x)$ is simply the *integral* of $f(x)$ between the values u and v. Thus, we have

$$P(u \le X \le v) = \int_u^v f(x)dx.$$

We refer to $f(x)$ as the *probability density function* for the random variable X. We call the graph of the probability density function the *density curve*.

Example

In the spinner example above, we can write the probability density function as

$$f(x) = \frac{1}{100}.$$

Then, we could calculate

$$P(0 \le X \le 25) = \int_0^{25} \frac{1}{100} dx$$

which equals

$$\frac{x}{100}\bigg|_0^{25} = \frac{25}{100} - \frac{0}{100} = \frac{1}{4}$$

as we informally calculated above.

3.4.3   Properties of Continuous Probability Distributions

1. $P(u \le X \le v) = \int_u^v f(x)dx \ge 0$

   Again, probabilities are nonnegative numbers. This also implies that the density curve does not cross the horizontal axis. If it did there would be regions associated with negative areas and, hence, negative probabilities.

2. $P(-\infty \le X \le \infty) = \int_{-\infty}^{\infty} f(x)dx = 1$

   That is, the area under the density curve must equal 1. This is analogous to the property that if we sum the probabilities associated with all possible values for a discrete random variable, the sum must be 1. Simply think of an integral as a continuous sum.

3. The probability density function can be zero for certain intervals. This simply means the random variable X does not take on values in those intervals. While density functions are defined for all real numbers, we will often indicate the range for which there are positive probabilities.

3.4.4   Cumulative Probability Distributions

A function, F, which gives the probability that a random variable X will assume a value less than or equal to a specified number x, is known as the *cumulative density function* or *distribution function* for the random variable. Mathematically,

$$F(x) = P(X \le x) = \int_{-\infty}^{x} f(t)dt$$

Example

From the spinner example above we can calculate

$$F(x) = \int_0^x \frac{1}{100} dt = \frac{x}{100}$$

Then, for example,

$$P(X \le 60) = \frac{60}{100} = .6$$

Notice that we did the integration from 0 to x since $f(x) = 0$ for x $\le$ 0.

3.4.5 Properties of Distribution Functions

1. $F(-\infty) = 0$. That is, the probability of X assuming a value below negative infinity is zero.
2. $F(\infty) = 1$. That is, the probability of X assuming a value below positive infinity is zero.
3. $P(X \geq u) = 1 - F(u)$. That is, the probability that X assumes a value above u is 1 minus the probability that X assumes a value below u.
4. $P(u \leq X \leq v) = F(v) - F(u)$. Thus, the probability X is between u and v is the probability X is below u less the probability X is below v. This property is very useful for calculating probabilities, as we shall see in future chapters.
5. $\dfrac{dF(x)}{d(x)} = f(x)$.

That is, the derivative of the distribution function with respect to x gives you the density function. This is analogous to property 3 for discrete random variables.

3.5 PROBABILITY DISTRIBUTIONS AND EMPIRICAL FREQUENCY DISTRIBUTIONS

There are an unlimited number of different probability distributions just as there are an unlimited number of experimental situations that could be described. The form taken by a probability distribution (or probability density function) is determined by the set of assumptions (theory) guiding the specification of the possible outcomes and their associated probabilities. Different assumptions give rise to different probability distributions (or probability density functions). The assumptions can be thought of as forming an approximation to some real-world phenomenon and, as such, collectively define a *probability model*. A variety of discrete and continuous probability distributions have been developed for different environments. We will consider some of the most popular distributions below. Ultimately, the probability model is used as a description of the chance process giving rise to observed data. For example, consider our discrete coin-toss example. We derived the probability distribution shown in Table 3.1 by assuming the tosses of the coin to be independent with equal probability of a head or a tail. We then defined our random variable as being the number of heads in three tosses and derived the probability distribution. All of this was done without ever tossing a coin. Suppose we actually conducted the experiment five times and recorded the number of heads in three tosses (i.e., the data). The results are found in Table 3.3.

Table 3.3

Trial number	Our result	X = number of heads
1	HTH	2
2	HHH	3
3	TTH	1
4	HHT	2
5	HTH	2

Now, with this data in hand we can form an *empirical frequency distribution*. This distribution is not based on any assumptions about the chance experiment, but is simply a tabulation of what we actually got when we conducted the experiment ourselves. Thus, empirically we never saw the outcome of 0 heads; we saw the outcome of 1 head 1 time in 5 trials and the outcome of 2 heads 3 times in 5 trials. Finally, we saw the outcome of 3 heads 1 time in 5 trials. How does this compare with what we would have expected based on our model assumptions of independence and a fair coin? We show in Table 3.4 both the empirical distribution (what we observed) and the probability distribution associated with our probability model.

Table 3.4

X = number of heads in three tosses	Probability (based on assumptions)	Empirical frequency (what we saw)
0	1/8	0
1	3/8	1/5
2	3/8	3/5
3	1/8	1/5

Now, the first thing you probably notice is that the probabilities based on our simple model are not the same as the results obtained when we actually did the experiment. That is, the "probabilities" differ from the "empirical frequencies." Why would this happen? The discrepancy can come from two sources. First, the deviation could simply be due to *chance*. We must recognize that the results we obtained were particular to that experiment. If we conducted another five trials we would likely get a different empirical frequency distribution. Indeed, many different empirical frequency distributions are consistent with our assumptions of independence and a fair coin. For example, it is really not terribly surprising to get 2 heads in 3 tosses 3 times in 5 trials. Indeed, we could (but won't) calculate just how likely it is for such differences to exist when the probability model is what we have assumed it to be. To do such a calculation we would have to specify some measure of the discrepancy (i.e., the difference, or squared difference, or absolute different, etc.) between the predictions based on our model and what we actually observe, along with the probability of observing the discrepancy when the model is correct. This calculation is too difficult to consider here, but will be discussed later in the book. Second, the deviation could arise because our model's assumptions could be wrong. That is, we could have the wrong model. Perhaps the coin is not fair. Perhaps the tosses are not independent. Perhaps coins land on their edge. Clearly it is important to distinguish between the two sources of the discrepancy. It would seem reasonable to conclude that the larger the discrepancy between the model and the data the more likely it is that the model is wrong and that the discrepancy is not simply due to chance.

Ultimately, the usefulness of a probability model lies in its ability to shed light on some real-world phenomenon by providing a succinct description of the process generating observed data. We will conclude this chapter by briefly considering several discrete and continuous distributions widely used by researchers.

3.6   SOME POPULAR DISCRETE DISTRIBUTIONS

To conclude this chapter we briefly consider a few popular probability distributions associated with probability models that have proven useful in many applied settings. Our treatment is brief as we will consider many of these distributions in more detail in later chapters.

3.6.1   The Bernoulli Distribution

Consider an experiment where there are only two possible outcomes. Such an experiment can describe any situation involving a strict dichotomy such as heads or tails, yes or no, on or off, win or lose, success or failure, and so on. For simplicity we will refer to the outcome as a success or a failure. Thus, $S = \{\text{success, failure}\}$. Let the random variable X be defined such that $X(\text{success}) = 1$ and $X(\text{failure}) = 0$. Thus, the qualitative outcomes "success" or "failure" are assigned the numerical values 0 or 1. Denoting the probability of a success by p we have $P(X = 1) = p$. This implies that $P(X = 0) = 1 - p$. An experiment satisfying these assumptions is called a *Bernoulli random trial* and the resulting random variable X is called a *Bernoulli random variable*. Formally, the probability function for a Bernoulli random variable is given by

$$f(x) = p^x (1 - p)^{1-x} \text{ for } x = 0,1$$

Notice that $P(X = 1) = f(1) = p^1(1 - p)^{1-1} = p$ and $P(X = 0) = f(0) = p^0(1 - p)^{1-0} = 1 - p$. The parameter p characterizes this distribution. Once we know p we can completely specify the two outcomes and their associated probabilities.

3.6.2   The Binomial Distribution

Repeating the Bernoulli random trial N times and summing the outcomes gives us a *binomial random variable*. That is,

$$B = \sum_{i=1}^{N} X_i$$

is a binomial random variable where the outcomes for the N Bernoulli random trials are denoted as $x_1, x_2, \ldots, x_N$. For example, we might toss a coin 5 times, recording heads as "1" and tails as "0". Summing the outcomes gives us the number of heads. A particular outcome might be $\{1,1,0,0,1\}$, or 3 heads in 5 trials. Now, assume the trials are independent so that the outcome of a given trial has no effect on other trials. Also assume that the probability of a success does not change between trials. Then, the probability function for the binomial random variable tells us the probability of seeing a given number of successes (i.e., "1's") in N trials and is formally given by

$$P(B = a) = \binom{N}{a} p^a (1 - p)^{N-a}$$

where:

$P(B = a)$ is the probability of "a" successes

N = number of trials

$p = P(X = 1)$, i.e., the probability of a success on any given trial

As for the Bernoulli distribution, it is the parameter that characterizes this distribution.

$$\binom{N}{a} = \frac{N!}{a!(N-a)!} \text{ and } a! = a(a-1)(a-2)\ldots(2)(1) \text{ and } 0! = 1 .$$

This is called the *binomial coefficient*. It shows the number of different ways there are to have "a" successes in N trials. We will explain this in more detail after considering an example. The exact shape of the binomial distribution depends on N and p. For large N the distribution looks much like a normal distribution (see below).

Example

Suppose a family is planning on having three children. What is the probability of having 0, 1, 2, or 3 girls? We will solve this using the binomial formula. Let G be the number of girls. Denote $x = 1$ if a given baby is a girl and let p be the probability of having a girl. We will assume that p equals .5. We are told there will be three trials (i.e., $N = 3$). Using the formula, we have:

$$P(G = 0) = \binom{3}{0}.5^0(1-5)^{3-0} = .125$$

$$P(G = 1) = \binom{3}{1}.5^1(1-.5)^{3-1} = .375$$

$$P(G = 2) = \binom{3}{2}.5^2(1-.5)^{3-2} = .375$$

$$P(G = 3) = \binom{3}{3}.5^3(1-.5)^{3-3} = .125$$

Thus, the probability of having no girls in a family of three (i.e., 3 "trials") is .125. The probability of having one girl in three trials is .375, and so forth. Let's look at the calculation of $P(G = 2)$ more carefully. There are three different outcomes giving rise to two girls in a family of three. They are {girl ∩ girl ∩ boy}, {girl ∩ boy ∩ girl}, and {boy ∩ girl ∩ girl}. It is simple to calculate the probability of each of these outcomes. For example, assuming independence, we have $P(\text{girl} \cap \text{girl} \cap \text{boy}) = P(\text{girl})P(\text{girl})P(\text{boy}) = (.5)(.5)(.5) = .125$. The probability is the same for the two other outcomes. Then, since $P(G = 2) = P(\{\text{girl} \cap \text{girl} \cap \text{boy}\} \cup \{\text{girl} \cap \text{boy} \cap \text{girl}\} \cup \{\text{boy} \cap \text{girl} \cap \text{girl}\}$, and, given that each of these outcomes is mutually exclusive and the trials independent, we have: $P(G = 2) = P(\text{girl})P(\text{girl})P(\text{boy}) + P(\text{girl})P(\text{boy})P(\text{girl}) + P(\text{boy})P(\text{girl})P(\text{girl})$. Assuming $P(\text{girl}) = .5$ we have $P(G = 2) = .125 + .125 + .125 = 3 \times .125 = .375$, exactly as calculated using the formula. Notice how the multiple 3 (i.e., "3" × .125) captures the three different ways of having two girls in three trials. The binomial coefficient provides this number for us directly. Hopefully you will agree that it is much easier to do calculations of this sort using the binomial formula! Indeed the calculation gets progressively more difficult as the number of trials increases.

Finally, if we combine the different values assumed by our random variable G and the associated probabilities we have the probability distribution as shown in Table 3.5.

Table 3.5

G = number of girls	$f(G)$
0	.125
1	.375
2	.375
3	.125

Notice that this distribution is the same as the probability distribution for the number of heads in three tosses of a fair coin. The two problems are mathematically identical. Again, we might consider whether this probability model is a good summary of reality. It assumes that boys and girls are equally likely, and that gender of the children is statistically independent (i.e., the gender of the "next" child is unaffected by the gender of previous children). We might test the model by comparing its predictions with actual gender composition of families with three children.

3.6.3 Discrete Uniform Distribution

Suppose we have N possible outcomes, each equally likely. The probability function is

$$f(x) = \frac{1}{N} \text{ for } x = 1, 2, \ldots, N$$

Example

Suppose we randomly select one person from a *population* of N persons. Then, the probability of any given person being selected is $1/N$.

3.7 SOME POPULAR CONTINUOUS DISTRIBUTIONS

3.7.1 The Normal Distribution

The normal distribution has a symmetric and bell-shaped density curve. It is in many ways the "classic" distribution. We will study its properties and demonstrate its importance in detail in later chapters. Its density function is given by

$$f(x) = \frac{1}{\sqrt{2\pi\sigma_X^2}} e^{-\frac{1}{2}\left(\frac{x-\mu_X}{\sigma_X}\right)^2} \text{ where } e = 2.718281828\ldots$$

The normal distribution is characterized by the parameters μ_X and σ_X, known as the mean and standard deviation respectively, which also will be discussed at length in later chapters.

To high school students looking forward to going to college, standardized tests typically represent an anxiety-ridden experience. Even after taking the exam and obtaining a score, understanding what the numbers mean for students who have had little formal experience with statistical analysis can be difficult. Yet knowledge of these tools provides considerable insight into the meaning of the reported numbers.

Consider, for instance, the Scholastic Aptitude Test (SAT). Students' answers are graded and a "raw score" is calculated that is a function of the total number of correct and incorrect answers provided. The raw score is converted into a "scaled score" that is reported to students. The scaled score has a normal distribution with a mean equal to 500 and a standard deviation equal to 110. These three pieces of information (that scores are distributed normally and the values of the mean and standard deviation) are sufficient to fully characterize this distribution. In fact, the probability that a score falls within a 10-point interval can be theoretically calculated and compared to the actual distribution reported by the College Board, which administers the SAT. The chart below shows that despite rounding error in the reported observed distribution, the two track each other quite closely. As subsequent chapters will address, these pieces of information are sufficient to allow one to determine the fraction of students with scores above a certain level, between two scores, and the like.

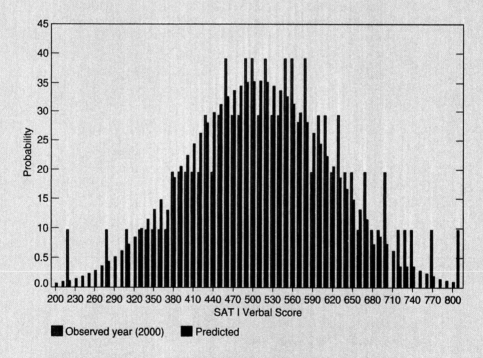

SOURCE: "2000 SAT I Test Performance." Copyright © 2000 by collegeboard.com, Inc. Reproduced with permission. All rights reserved. www.collegeboard.com. And authors' calculations.

APPLICATION 3.4 *Is Welfare Truly Addictive?*

The welfare system in the United States provides cash payments to (mostly) single mothers with children who earn little or nothing. Because these payments provide income support for individuals who may not work, some have claimed that recipients will become dependent on the system, receiving support for long periods of time rather than getting a job. Arguments supporting or refuting this proposition refer to the same data regarding the length of welfare spells, but appear to be contradictory. Those who claim that welfare is addictive point to the fact that some people on welfare have collected benefits for a substantial length of time. Those who argue against this highlight the fact that most welfare spells are short.

How can both of these facts be accurate? It turns out that if the length of welfare spells follows an exponential distribution, then most spells will be short even though some last for quite some time. Consider the figure below, which represents the observed distribution of completed welfare spells between 1979 and 1995 from one nationally representative sample of young people. The first thing that one notices is a reporting bias in that individuals tend to round off the length of their welfare spell to years rather than months. Beyond that, most spells are observed to be rather short; over half are completed in a year or less. On the other hand, 7% last longer than 5 years (60 months), indicating some recipients collect benefits for a very long period of time.

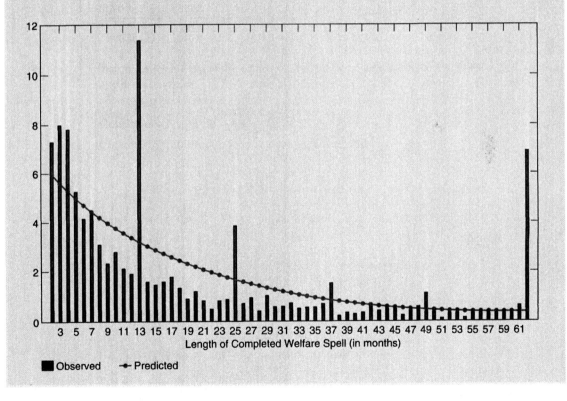

The figure also shows that the general pattern of the observed spell-length distribution can be approximated by the exponential distribution. We have calculated a predicted distribution of spell lengths assuming an exponential distribution where the parameter, λ, is equal to 0.6. Aside from the bunching at 12-month intervals caused by reporting bias, the exponential distribution fairly closely mimics the pattern of the observed distribution and may serve as a useful summary of these data.

SOURCE: Authors' calculations from the National Longitudinal Survey of Youth.

3.7.2 The Exponential Distribution

The density function for an exponential distribution is given by

$$f(x) = \lambda e^{-\lambda x} \text{ for } \lambda > 0 \text{ and } x > 0$$

For any value of λ, if one graphed the density curve it would be observed that the area below the curve falls as X increases. This property makes the exponential distribution useful for analyzing problems associated with the time before a certain event takes place (a duration). For example, it might be appropriate for considering the probability that a period of unemployment or welfare receipt lasts for x periods. It might also be used to characterize the probability that a piece of machinery operates for a period of time x before failing. The parameter λ determines the shape of this distribution.

3.7.3 The Uniform Distribution

The continuous analogue of the discrete uniform distribution is the uniform distribution. The density function is given by

$$f(x) = \frac{1}{b - a}$$

where x can assume any value on the interval $[a,b]$. An example of this distribution is provided by the spinner example considered earlier in the chapter.

3.8 PROBLEMS

1. Are the following proper probability density functions?

    a. $f(x) = \dfrac{x^2}{30}$ for $x = 0,1,2,3,4$

    b. $f(x) = \dfrac{2(1 - x)}{3}$ for $-1 \leq x \leq 2$

2. Let X be a discrete random variable with probability function

$$f(x) = cx^3 \text{ for } x = 1,2,3,4$$
$$= 0 \quad \text{otherwise}$$

    a. What must c be in order for $f(x)$ to be a proper probability function?

b. What is the probability that $1 \le X \le 2$?

3. Suppose X is a continuous random variable having the probability density function (p.d.f.)

$$f(x) = cx^3 \text{ for } 1 \le x \le 3$$
$$= 0 \quad \text{otherwise}$$

a. What must c be in order for $f(x)$ to be a proper p.d.f.?

b. What is the probability that $1 \le X \le 2$?

4. Suppose X is a continuous random variable having the probability density function (p.d.f.)

$$f(x) = x, \quad 0 \le x \le 1$$
$$= 2 - x, \ 1 \le x \le 2$$
$$= 0 \quad \text{elsewhere}$$

a. Graph the probability density function.

b. Graph the cumulative probability distribution.

c. Calculate $P(.5 \le X \le 1.5)$.

5. The probability density function for the random variable X is given by

$$f(x) = 6x(1 - x) \text{ for } 0 \le x \le 1$$
$$= 0 \text{ elsewhere}$$

a. Find $P(X \le 1/2)$.

b. Find the cumulative distribution function.

c. Calculate $P(X \le 1/2)$ using the distribution function.

6. Suppose the probability density function for the random variable x is given by

$$f(x) = \frac{1}{8}x \text{ for } 0 \le x \le 4$$
$$= 0 \quad \text{otherwise}$$

a. Find the value of m such that $P(X \le m) = .5$

b. Find the value of m such that $P(X \ge m) = .25$

7. Suppose 5% of drivers do not have proper insurance. Of 30 randomly selected drivers, what is the probability that no more than 1 will lack proper insurance?

8. Suppose X is a binomial random variable with $p = .5$. Graph the probability distribution for $n = 2,5,10,20$. What effect does an increase in n have on the shape of the distribution?

Chapter 4

Mathematics of Expectations

4.1 INTRODUCTION

In the previous chapter we considered the probability distribution for a random variable X. A probability distribution is a very detailed description of a random variable. In the case of a discrete random variable it shows all of the different values X can assume along with the associated probabilities. For many purposes the probability distribution provides too much detail and it is desirable to summarize the information contained in the distribution. In this chapter we consider two important types of summary measures: measures of central tendency and measures of dispersion.

4.2 SUMMARIZING A DISTRIBUTION

Consider the two density curves depicted in Figure 4.1. What are the essential differences between these density curves?

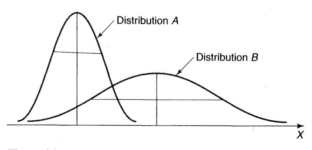

Figure 4.1

Typically, two basic differences are highlighted. First, the two distributions are "centered" at different values. That is, they have different "typical values." Second, the two distributions differ in how "spread out" they are. Thus, we might summarize a probability distribution by distilling it into two numbers: one capturing its "typical value" or "central tendency" and another capturing the "spread" or "dispersion" of the distribution. These summary measures capture certain important features of the distribution but will, in so doing, sacrifice detail. We will start by discussing different measures of central tendency.

4.3   MEASURES OF CENTRAL TENDENCY

Three different summary measures are typically used to capture the "typical" value or "central tendency" of a distribution. They are the *mean (expected value)*, the *median*, and the *mode*.

4.3.1   Mean or Expected Value

The *mean* (or *expected value*) of a random variable X is denoted by $E(X)$ or μ_X and given by:

1. $E(X) = \sum_{\text{all } X} x_i P(x_i)$ if X is a discrete random variable.

2. $E(X) = \int_{-\infty}^{\infty} xf(x)\,dx$ if X is a continuous random variable.

Notice that we sum (or integrate) over all values assumed by the random variable. Also notice that in the discrete case, if X has a uniform distribution (i.e., all N outcomes are equally likely: $P(x_i) = 1/N$ for all i), the mean simplifies to

$$E(X) = \frac{1}{N} \sum_{\text{all } X} x_i$$

Discrete Example

X	0	1	2	3	4
$P(X)$	.2	.2	.1	.3	.2

$E(X) = 0(.2) + 1(2) + 2(.1) + 3(.3) + 4(.2) = 2.1$. Notice that the expected value does not have to be any of the actual values assumed by the random variable X.

Continuous Example

Suppose we have a continuous random variable with density function:

$$f(x) = \frac{1}{100} \text{ for } 0 \leq X \leq 100$$

Then,

$$E(X) = \int_{-\infty}^{\infty} xf(x)dx = \int_{0}^{100} x\frac{1}{100} = \frac{x^2}{200}\Big|_{0}^{100} = 50$$

The mean is simply a weighted average of the different x's with the associated probabilities being the weights. Indeed, you can think of the mean as the center of gravity for the

---

APPLICATION 4.1   *Where Is the Best Place to Place Your Bets?*

The growing prevalence of casinos, Internet gambling, and state lotteries in the United States indicates that gambling has become much more common recently. These outlets offer a variety of ways to place bets hoping to hit the jackpot. But if the goal is to maximize the expected return on an investment, some are better bets than others.

Some games provide expected payout rates that are fixed. For instance, roulette offers the gambler several ways to bet on a ball that has an equal probability of falling into one of 38 slots, numbered 1 to 36 plus a zero and a double zero. Payouts are made as if there were only 36 slots even if the odds of winning are based on 38. Suppose, for instance, you bet $1 that the ball lands in an odd-numbered slot, which happens 18/38 = 47.4% of the time. If you win you get $2 (your original bet plus another dollar). Therefore, the expected payout from this bet is 2 × 0.0474 = 0.947. In other words, you could expect to get back about 95 cents on the $1 bet. Other games provide a variable rate of return. For instance, slot machines contain computer chips and the payout rate can be programmed; different machines typically provide different payout rates. Minimum payout rates are often legislated; Colorado requires that slots pay out at least 80%, making the expected value of a $1 bet no less than 80 cents. Despite the variability across machines, you can be assured that virtually all of them provide an expected payout of less than $1! State lotteries provide the worst expected return by far. States typically pay out only about half of the proceeds of the lottery, making the expected value of a $1 bet only equal to about 50 cents.

By nature, all games of chance will provide an expected payout lower than the amount bet because that is how the gambling operation makes money. On the other hand, if you want to find a more profitable way to "gamble," the stock market may provide a better outlet. Even though some stocks rise and fall over the course of time, over the long run stocks have provided roughly a 10% annual rate of return. Therefore, if you gambled on a stock, you may win or lose but the expected payout from a $1 investment would be $1.10 after one year. So if you want to gamble, you would be better off becoming a day trader!

---

distribution. The probabilities can be thought of as weights set on each seat of a teeter-totter (or seesaw). The mean gives the position where we must place the fulcrum for the distribution to be in balance. If the weights were equal, the teeter-totter would be balanced with the fulcrum right in the middle.

4.3.2   Properties of Expected Values

1. For any random variable X and any constants a and b: $E(a + bX) = a + bE(X)$. This property implies:
   a. The expected value of a constant is the constant itself (i.e., $E(a) = a$), and
   b. The expected value of a constant times a random variable is the constant times the expected value of the random variable (i.e., $E(bX) = bE(X)$).

2. For any function $g(X)$:

a. $E(g(X)) = \sum_{\text{all } X} g(x_i)P(x_i)$ if X is a discrete random variable.

b. $E(g(X)) = \int_{-\infty}^{\infty} g(x)f(x)dx$ if X is a continuous random variable.

Notice that the first property is a special case of the second property where $g(X) = a + bX$. In general, $E(g(X)) \neq g(E(X))$. That is, the expected value of a function of X is not the function evaluated at the expected value of X. For instance, consider the function $g(X) = X^2$:

$$E(X^2) = \sum_{\text{all } X} x_i^2 P(x_i) \neq \left[\sum_{\text{all } X} x_i P(x_i) \right]^2 = [E(X)]^2$$

In other words, the mean of the square of a variable is not equal to the square of its mean. The same generally holds for any function of a random variable. It is easy to forget this and make erroneous calculations.

3. $E(X^r)$ is called the rth moment of X about the origin. Thus, the mean is sometimes referred to as the first moment of the random variable X.

4. $E(X - \mu_X)^r$ is called the rth moment of X about its mean.

Discrete Example

Continuing with the discrete example above, suppose we define two new random variables. Let the random variable Y be a linear function of the random variable X. In particular, suppose $Y = 2 + 2X$. Also, let the random variable Z be a nonlinear function of X. In particular, suppose $Z = X^2$ (i.e., $Z = g(X)$ and $g(X) = X^2$):

X	0	1	2	3	4
$Y = 2 + 2X$	2	4	6	8	10
$Z = X^2$	0	1	4	9	16
$P(X)$	.2	.2	.1	.3	.2

Then, $E(Y) = 2(.2) + 4(.2) + 6(.1) + 8(.3) + 10(.2) = 6.2$, which is equal to $2 + 2E(X) = 2 + 2(2.1) = 6.2$. $E(Z) = 0(.2) + 1(.2) + 4(.1) + 9(.3) + 16(.2) = 8.1$. As shown earlier, notice that this does not equal the square of the expected value of X, that is, $E(X)^2 \neq E(X^2)$, since, in this example, $2.1^2 \neq 8.1$. Also note that $E(Z)$ can be called the second moment of X about the origin.

Continuous Example

Continuing with the continuous example above with

$$f(x) = \frac{1}{100} \text{ for } 0 \le X \le 100$$

suppose we define $Y = X^2$ (i.e., $Y = g(X)$ and $g(X) = X^2$). Then,

$$E(Y) = E(X^2) = \int_{-\infty}^{\infty} x^2 f(x)dx = \int_{0}^{100} x^2 \frac{1}{100} = \left. \frac{x^3}{300} \right|_0^{100} = 3333.3$$

4.3.3 Median

If the number m satisfies the two conditions

$$P(X < m) \leq \frac{1}{2} \text{ and } P(X > m) \leq \frac{1}{2}$$

then m is the median of the distribution of X. Thus, m is simply the middle of the distribution—the number for which half of the values assumed by X are larger and half are smaller.

Discrete Example

In our discrete example above, the median of X is between 2 and 3. By convention we define it to be 2.5.

Continuous Example

A simple way to calculate the median for a continuous distribution is to first derive the cumulative distribution function, $F(X)$, and then note that the median m satisfies $F(m) = .5$. Thus, for our continuous example:

$$F(x) = \int_0^x \frac{1}{100} \, dx = \frac{x}{100}$$

Then, $F(m) = .5$, implying $\dfrac{m}{100} = .5$ or $m = 50$.

4.3.4 Mode

The mode is simply the value of X associated with the largest probability (or probability density). Thus, it is the most likely outcome. Graphically, it is the value of X associated with the peak of the probability distribution (or density curve).

4.3.5 Mean, Median, or Mode: Which One?

In choosing whether to rely on the mean, median, or mode, certain factors should be kept in mind:

1. The mean is unique. That is, for any distribution there is only one mean.
2. The median and mode need not be unique, with several (perhaps infinite) different medians or modes being possible for a given distribution.
3. The mean is more affected by "unusual" outcomes (sometimes called "outliers") than is the median or mode.
4. Another way of selecting between the mean, median, and mode can be based on their utility in making predictions. Suppose your observations are being drawn from some probability distribution characterized by a probability function or probability density function $f(x)$. You are asked for your best prediction as to what the value of the next draw will be. Call your predicted value $\hat{\theta}$. What value

of $\hat{\theta}$ would you choose? Clearly your choice will depend on the criteria you select. Consider three criteria used in econometrics:

a. Choose $\hat{\theta}$ to minimize the mean squared error in prediction, that is, choose $\hat{\theta}$ to
   minimize

$$E\left[(X - \hat{\theta})^2\right]$$

One could show that the solution to this problem is to choose $\hat{\theta} = E(X)$ (i.e.,
guess the mean).

b. Choose $\hat{\theta}$ to minimize the mean absolute error in prediction, $E|X - \hat{\theta}|$. It can be
   shown that the solution to this problem is to choose $\hat{\theta} = median(X)$.

c. Choose $\hat{\theta}$ to maximize the probability the mean error in prediction is zero (i.e.,
   choose $\hat{\theta}$ to maximize $prob(X - \hat{\theta} = 0)$. Here the best choice is $\hat{\theta} = mode(X)$.

While all of these approaches are employed at different times, the mean is by far the most
popular. We will show some of the virtues of the mean later in the book.

4.4   MEASURES OF DISPERSION

A variety of different measures have been proposed to measure the extent to which a distribution
is spread out. We will consider the *range*, the *variance*, and the *standard deviation*.

4.4.1   Range

The *range* of a random variable X is simply the difference between the smallest and
largest possible values for the random variable. That is: range $= Max(X) - Min(X)$. The
principal weakness of the range as a measure of dispersion is that it uses only two values
associated with the random variable. As such, it will be very sensitive to what those values happen to be. Distributions that are almost identical can have very different ranges
simply because one distribution has a larger maximum value or a smaller minimum value
(either of which could be very unlikely to occur). Therefore, the range can provide a misleading summary of the characteristics of the distribution.

4.4.2   Variance

Obviously, a random variable does not always assume its "typical" value, however measured. That is, the random variable varies in the values it assumes. One might ask how
much the random variable *typically* (somehow measured) deviates from its *typical* value
(e.g., its mean). This would provide a measure of the dispersion of the random variable.
The variance (and standard deviation) builds on this notion of dispersion.

The variance of a random variable X is denoted by var(X) or σ^2_X and is given by:

1. var$(X) = \sum_{all\ X} (x_i - E(X))^2 P(x_i)$ if X is a discrete random variable.

2. $\text{var}(X) = \displaystyle\int_{-\infty}^{\infty} (x - E(X))^2 f(x)dx$ if X is a continuous random variable.

Example

Suppose X has the following probability distribution:

X	0	1	2	3	4
$P(X)$	.2	.2	.1	.3	.2

The mean, $E(X)$, of this distribution is 2.1. Thus,

$$\text{var}(X) = \sum_{\text{all } X} (x_i - E(X))^2 P(x_i) = (0 - 2.1)^2 (.2) + (1 - 2.1)^2(.2) +$$

$$(2 - 2.1)^2(.1) + (3 - 2.1)^2(.3) + (4 - 2.1)^2(.2) = 2.09$$

Thus, the variance is the mean squared deviation of X from its mean. Or, if you prefer, it is the average (squared) deviation of X from its average. Now, you might wonder why we square the differences. Why not simply measure the dispersion as the average deviation from the average? The simple answer to this is that the average deviation of X from its average is always zero. Values above the average cancel out values below the average. To see this, note that:

$$\sum_{\text{all } X} (x_i - E(X))P(x_i) = \sum_{\text{all } X} x_i P(x_i) - \sum_{\text{all } X} E(X)P(x_i) = E(X) - E(X)\sum_{\text{all } X} P(x_i) =$$

$$E(X) - E(X) = 0$$

since

$$\sum_{\text{all } X} P(x_i) = 1$$

Given this, we need to do something to eliminate the canceling. Squaring the deviations is the approach associated with the variance. Other approaches are certainly possible. For example, if you took the absolute value of the deviations you would have a different measure of dispersion, one called the mean absolute deviation. As we will see later, there are several good reasons for selecting the variance as a general measure of dispersion.

4.4.3 Standard Deviation

One basic problem with the variance as a measure of dispersion is that it tells us the average *squared* deviation of X from its average. Thus, if X is measured in dollars, the variance tells us the dispersion in squared dollars. A simple remedy to this problem is to put the variance into the same units as the random variable X. This is done by taking the square root of the variance, and the resulting measure of dispersion is called the *standard deviation*. Thus, the *standard deviation* of the random variable X is denoted by σ_X and is given by $\sigma_X = \sqrt{\text{var}(X)}$. Intuitively, we can think of the standard deviation as the typical deviation of X from its average value.

Example

For the last example given above for the variance, $\sigma_X = \sqrt{\text{var}(X)} = \sqrt{2.09} \cong 1.45$. Roughly speaking, this seems reasonable if you look at the distribution. The mean is around 2. Fifty percent of the time we are approximately 1 unit away from the mean, 40% of the time we are 2 units away from the mean, and 10% of the time we are almost the same as the mean. Thus, an "eyeball" estimate of the *typical* deviation from the mean would seem to be consistent with the result of 1.45 supplied by the standard deviation.

4.4.4   Properties of the Variance and Standard Deviation

1. $\text{var}(X) = E[(X - E(X))^2]$. This follows simply from the definition of an expected value. Notice that the variance is the second moment of X around the mean.

2. $\text{var}(X) = E[X^2] - E[X]^2$. That is, the variance of X is the mean of X^2 minus the square of the mean. This formula is particularly helpful for calculating the variance of a continuous random variable.

Proof. $\text{var}(X) = E[((X - E(X))^2] = E[X^2 - 2XE(X) + E(X)^2]$

$\qquad = E(X^2) - 2E(X)E(X) + E(X)^2$

$\qquad = E(X^2) - E(X)^2$

3. $\text{var}(a) = 0$ if a is a constant. That is, constants don't vary! Clearly, the standard deviation is also zero in this case.

4. If $Y = a + bX$, then $\text{var}(Y) = b^2\text{var}(X)$. Notice that this is b squared times the variance of X. We will use this property many times in upcoming chapters.

Proof. $E[((a + bX) - E(a + bX))^2] = E[((a + bX) - a - bE(X))^2]$

$\qquad\qquad = E[(b(X - E(X)))^2]$

$\qquad\qquad = b^2 E[(X - e(X))^2]$

$\qquad\qquad = b^2 \text{var}(X)$

5. If $Y = a + bX$, then the standard deviation of X is equal to $|b|\sigma_X$. This follows from property 4.

6. The variances of nonlinear functions of X are given by:

   a. $\text{var } g[(X)] = \sum_{\text{all } X} (g(x_i) - E(g(X)))^2 P(x_i)$ if X is a discrete random variable.

   b. $\text{var } g[(X)] = \int_{-\infty}^{\infty} (g(x) - E(g(X)))^2 f(x)dx$ if X is a continuous random variable.

APPLICATION 4.2   *The Risk from Russian Roulette*

In roulette, not all bets are created equal. As we discussed in the box on page 46, roulette is a game where a ball spins around a wheel and has an equal chance of falling into one of 38 slots, numbered 1 to 36 plus a 0 and 00. Half the nonzero numbers are red, half are black; the zeros are green. Several types of bets are available, including betting that the ball will land on red or black, odd or even, betting whether the ball lands in 1–12, 13–24, or 25–36, or betting on an exact number. The probability of winning and the payoff if you win on a $1 bet, along with the expected value of that bet are as follows:

Type of bet	Payoff	Probability of winning	Expected payoff
odd/even or red/black	$2	18/38 = 0.474	$(18/38) \times 2 + (20/38) \times 0 = 36/38 = \$0.95$
1–12, 13–24, or 25–36	$3	12/38 = .316	$(12/38) \times 3 + (26/38) \times 0 = 36/38 = \$0.95$
exact number	$36	1/38 = .026	$(1/38) \times 36 + (37/38) \times 0 = 36/38 = \$0.95$

Each type of bet has exactly the same expected value.

But, interestingly, each type of bet does not have the same variance. To see this, recall that we can rewrite the formula for variance as $E(X^2) - [E(X)]^2$. Based on this, the variance of the payoff from each bet can be calculated as: $\text{Var(payoff)} = E(\text{payoff}^2) - [E(\text{payoff})]^2$, where $[E(\text{payoff})]^2 = (36/38)^2 = 0.90$ for all three types of bets based on the calculations reported earlier:

Type of bet	Payoff^2	$E(\text{payoff}^2)$	Var(payoff)
odd/even or red/black	$4	$(18/38) \times 4 + (20/38) \times 0 = 1.89$	0.99
1–12, 13–24, or 25–36	$9	$(12/38) \times 9 + (26/38) \times 0 = 2.84$	1.94
exact number	$1,296	$(1/38) \times 1,296 + (37/38) \times 0 = 34.11$	33.21

Therefore, betting on an exact number is much riskier than either of the other two types of bets, but it does not provide any additional benefit in terms of a higher expected payoff.

Another interesting feature of the game of roulette is that the wheel used in the United States is not the same as the one used in Europe. Importantly, in Europe there is only one zero, not two. Therefore, the odds of winning are based on 37 possible outcomes rather than 38, even though the payoffs are identical. So if you must gamble and want to maximize your return with a minimum level of risk, go to Europe!

4.5 CHEBYSHEV'S INEQUALITY

When we know the probability distribution for a random variable we have a very complete description of that random variable. It is relatively straightforward to calculate any probabilities of interest to us. In the last section we saw how we can take all of the information embedded in a probability distribution and distill it into two numbers: a measure of central tendency and a measure of dispersion. An interesting question arises: Is it possible to say anything about the probability of events occurring given *only* knowledge of the summary measures? That is, suppose we were told the mean and variance (or standard deviation) of a random variable. Using this information *alone*, could we do calculations such as $P(a \leq X \leq b)$? Surprisingly, the answer is yes and the specific result is provided by *Chebyshev's inequality*.

Chebyshev's Inequality

$$P(\mu_X - k\sigma_X \geq X \geq \mu_X + k\sigma_X) \leq \frac{1}{k^2}$$

That is, the probability of the random variable X assuming a value within k (any given number) standard deviations of its mean is at most $1/k^2$. We can write this expression equivalently as

$$P(|X - \mu_X| \geq k\sigma_X) \leq \frac{1}{k^2}$$

This result is very general. It does not make any assumptions about the shape of the (unknown) probability distribution. For example, there are no assumptions regarding the symmetry of the underlying distribution. The result is depicted in Figure 4.2.

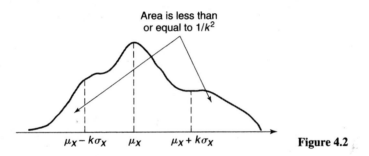

Area is less than
or equal to $1/k^2$

$\mu_X - k\sigma_X$ μ_X $\mu_X + k\sigma_X$

Figure 4.2

To prove Chebyshev's inequality we first make use of the *Markov inequality*.

Markov Inequality

Suppose X is a random variable such that $P(X \geq 0) = 1$ (i.e., X is always positive). Then, for any number $t > 0$:

$$P(X \geq t) \leq \frac{E(X)}{t}$$

Proof of Markov Inequality. The proof proceeds by first breaking up the sum in the first line so that we sum first over $x_i < t$ and then over $x_i \geq t$. That is,

$$\sum_{\text{all } X} x_i P(x_i) = \sum_{x_i < t} x_i P(x_i) + \sum_{x_i \geq t} x_i P(x_i)$$

Then, since the first term in this sum

$$\sum_{x_i < t} x_i P(x_i) \geq 0$$

we know that

$$\sum_{\text{all } X} x_i P(x_i) \geq \sum_{x_i \geq t} x_i P(x_i)$$

Furthermore, since we are summing over $x_i \geq t$ it must be that

$$\sum_{x_i \geq t} x_i P(x_i) \geq \sum_{x_i \geq t} tP(x_i)$$

Finally, it must be noticed that

$$\sum_{x_i \geq t} tP(x_i) = t \sum_{x_i \geq t} P(x_i) = tP(X \geq t)$$

Thus, we have $E(X) \geq tP(X \geq t)$, which yields the desired inequality.

Proof of Chebyshev's Inequality. The Chebyshev inequality can be proven easily given a judicious application of the Markov inequality. Let $Y = (X - \mu_X)^2$ and $t = k^2 \sigma^2_X$, noticing that $E(Y) = \sigma^2_X$. Then, applying the Markov inequality to Y we have

$$P(Y \geq t) \leq \frac{E(Y)}{t}$$

or (substituting the defined terms in)

$$P[(X - \mu_X)^2 \geq k^2 \sigma^2_X] \leq \frac{\sigma^2_X}{k^2 \sigma^2_X} = \frac{1}{k^2}$$

which is equivalent to $P[|X - \mu_X| \geq k\sigma_X] \leq \frac{1}{k^2}$.

Example

Consider the number of students arriving at a local restaurant each day for lunch. Suppose the mean number is 72 and the standard deviation is 8. Then, Chebyshev's inequality shows that for, say, $k = 3$, the probability is at most $(1/k^2)$ that the number of students arriving will be outside of the range $(\mu_X - k\sigma_X \geq X \geq \mu_X + k\sigma_X)$. Thus, there is only a 1/9 chance that the number of students arriving will be outside the range $(72 - 3(8) \geq X \geq 72 + 3(8))$ (i.e., above 96 or below 48).

4.6 PROBLEMS

1. You are organizing an outdoor concert and believe attendance will depend on the weather. You believe the following possibilities are appropriate:

Weather	Probability	Attendance
Terrible weather	.2	500
Mediocre weather	.6	1000
Great weather	.2	2000

  a. What is the expected attendance?

  b. Suppose each ticket costs $5 and the fixed costs (tents, band, etc.) are $2,000. What are the expected profits? Graph the probability distribution for profits.

  c. What is the most you could pay for the fixed costs and still have an 80% chance of making a profit on the event?

2. Overheard at the local pub: "Any Williams student who decides to transfer to Amherst will cause the average IQ score to rise at both schools." Is this possible? How?

3. A gamble is said to be fair if each player has the same expected outcome. Suppose we play a game in which the first of two players receives $50 each time the roll of a balanced die comes up with a 1 or 6. Player 2 wins if the die shows a 2, 3, 4, or 5. For the game to be fair, how much must player 2 receive if she wins?

4. The probability density function for the random variable X is given by

$$f(x) = 6x(1 - x) \text{ for } 0 \le x \le 1$$
$$= 0 \text{ elsewhere}$$

a. Find $E(X)$.

b. Find the median of X.

c. Find var(X).

5. Consider the following density function for the random variable X:

$$f(x) = \frac{\theta^2}{2} x \text{ for } 0 \le x \le c$$
$$= 0 \text{ otherwise}$$

a. Find the value of c for which $f(x)$ is a proper probability density function. Draw a graph of this distribution.

b. Find the mean and variance of X.

c. Calculate the probability that $\frac{1}{2\theta} \ge X \ge \frac{3}{4\theta}$.

d. Use Chebyshev's inequality to calculate an upper bound on the probability that $\frac{5}{6\theta} \ge X \ge \frac{11}{6\theta}$.

6. A random variable has a mean of 2 and a variance of 3. Find the expected value for the random variable $Y = 2x^2 + 5x + 4$.

7. Consider the number of people arriving at the Student Center for coffee between 10 A.M. and 11 A.M. on a given day. For this random variable X, it is known that $E(X) = 100$ and var$(X) = 10$.

a. Give an upper bound on the probability that the number of people is outside the range [75,125].

b. Give the range for X for which the probability is at most 1/100 that the number of people who show up is outside that range.

8. A car manufacturer is considering how many safety devices to install on a new car. The devices function independently and each one works with probability .9. Furthermore, they are connected "in parallel" so that if any one of the devices installed works the car will be safe. However, if they all fail the car will explode just as it is driven off the dealer's lot! The ensuing lawsuit (initiated by the estate for the unfortunate customer) will cost the manufacturer $1,000,000 every time this occurs. On the other hand, each safety device costs $100 to install. The car itself (without safety devices) costs $5,000 to build.

Assume that the manufacturer will sell N (a given) cars at $10,000 each no matter how many safety devices are installed and that the firm wants to maximize the expectation of its profits.

a. How many safety devices will be installed in each car?

b. Given the answer to part (a), what will be the expectation and variance of their profits?

c. If $N = 20$, what is the probability that the firm will have at least one fatality arising from their choice of the number of safety devices installed?

d. The existence of the deliberations is leaked to *Hard Copy* and their next show claims "Auto Firm Puts Value on Human Life." Did the firm put a value on human life, and, if so, is this in and of itself worthy of condemnation?

Chapter 5

Multivariate Distributions

5.1   INTRODUCTION

In the previous two chapters we considered the probability distribution for a single random variable. We then learned how to use various measures (e.g., mean and variance) to summarize the information in the distribution. We have, however, limited ourselves to looking at a single random variable (e.g., X). Thus, we have been considering *univariate* distributions. Often in economics we are interested in relationships existing between several random variables. That is, we are often interested in *multivariate* distributions. In this chapter we extend our analyses to include two random variables (i.e., *bivariate* or *joint* distributions). This is a straightforward extension of the previous two chapters but, importantly, with two random variables being considered we have the additional scope of looking at *relationships* between the two variables. The results developed for the bivariate case are easily extended beyond the bivariate situation. We will start with the case where both of the random variables are discrete.

5.2   DISCRETE BIVARIATE DISTRIBUTIONS

5.2.1   Joint Probability Function

Suppose we have two discrete random variables, X and Y, which each take on a finite set of values. We assume X takes on the values $\{x_1, x_2, x_3, \ldots, x_N\}$ and Y takes on the values

$\{y_1, y_2, y_3, \ldots, y_n\}$. Then, there will also be a finite set of pairs $\{x,y\}$ that X and Y may *jointly* assume.

Example

Suppose we flip a coin three times and record the number of heads. We will define the random variable X to equal the number of heads on the last (third) flip, and the random variable Y to equal the total number of heads in three flips. Then, $S = \{$HHH, HHT, HTH, HTT, THH, THT, TTH, TTT$\}$, and the random variable X takes on the values $\{0,1\}$ while the random variable Y takes on the values $\{0,1,2,3\}$. There are 8 possible different joint outcomes:

$$(X = 0, Y = 0), (X = 0, Y = 1), (X = 0, Y = 2), (X = 0, Y = 3),$$
$$(X = 1, Y = 0), (X = 1, Y = 1), (X = 1, Y = 2), (X = 1, Y = 3)$$

If we attach a probability to each of the different joint outcomes, we have a *discrete bivariate probability distribution* or, more formally, a *joint probability function*.

The *joint probability function* (or discrete joint density function) of two discrete random variables X and Y is the function $f(x,y)$ such that, for any point (x,y) in the X-Y plane, $f(x,y) = P(X = x \text{ and } Y = y)$. Thus, $f(x,y)$ gives us the probability our random variables X and Y assume the *joint* outcome (x,y). Recall that in the univariate case, we could represent the probability function with a table, a graph, and sometimes by an explicit formula (e.g., the binomial distribution). The same is true for the joint probability function. In this case the table is a matrix and the graph of the distribution would be three dimensional.

Example

Continuing with the above example, consider the outcome $(X = 0, Y = 0)$. This joint outcome occurs in one of the eight outcomes in the sample space (i.e., TTT). Thus, $P(X = 0 \text{ and } Y = 0) = 1/8$. Similarly, the joint outcome $(X = 0, Y = 1)$ occurs in two of the eight basic outcomes (i.e., HTT, THT). Thus, $P(X = 0 \text{ and } Y = 1) = 1/4$. Proceeding in a similar fashion we can calculate the probability associated with each joint outcome. It is helpful to depict this information in a table (matrix) as shown in Table 5.1.

Table 5.1

		Y			
		0	1	2	3
X	0	1/8	1/4	1/8	0
	1	0	1/8	1/4	1/8

Notice that we indicate the different values X can assume in the left column of the table (e.g., 0,1) and the different values Y can assume in the top row of the table (e.g., 0,1,2,3). The entries within the cells of the matrix are the probabilities associated with the different joint outcomes of X and Y (e.g., $P(X = 1 \text{ and } Y = 2) = 1/4$).

5.2.2   Properties of Joint Probability Function

The required properties of the joint bivariate distribution are analogous to the properties required of univariate distributions.

1. $f(x,y) = P(X = x \text{ and } Y = y) \geq 0$ for all (x,y) pairs. That is, the probabilities assigned to the joint outcomes are nonnegative.

2. $\displaystyle\sum_{\text{all } x} \sum_{\text{all } y} f\, 1x,y2 = 1$

That is, if we sum the probabilities associated with all possible joint outcomes the sum must equal 1. Notice that the cell entries in Table 5.1 sum to 1.

5.2.3   Cumulative Joint Probability Function

A function $F(x,y)$ that gives the probability that the random variable X is less than a given value x_i and the random variable Y is jointly less than a given value y_j:

$$F(x,y) = P(X \leq x \text{ and } Y \leq y)$$

$$= \sum_{s \leq x} \sum_{t \leq y} f(s,t)$$

is known as the *joint distribution function* or the *cumulative joint probability function*. Notice the similarity of the joint distribution function and the cumulative probability distribution for a univariate distribution. Note also that the calculation simply involves summing all the probabilities associated with outcomes satisfying $X \leq x$ and $Y \leq y$.

Examples

1. Continuing with the coin-toss example above, we could calculate the probability of X being less than or equal to 0 and Y (jointly) being less than or equal to 2. This would simply be the sum of the probabilities satisfying both of these conditions (i.e., $X \leq 0$ and $Y \leq 2$). Thus, $F(0,2) = P(X \leq 0 \text{ and } Y \leq 2) = 1/8 + 1/4 + 1/8 + 0 = 1/2$.

2. $F(1,3) = P(X \leq 1 \text{ and } Y \leq 3) = 1$. This must be the case as it covers all possible outcomes for X and Y.

5.2.4   Bivariate and Univariate Distributions

Sometimes, when given the bivariate distribution for two random variables X and Y, we would like to move back to the univariate distributions for X and Y. We call these the *marginal distributions* for X and Y. The *marginal distributions* for X and Y are, respectively, given by

$$g(x) = P(X = x) = \sum_{\text{all } y} f(x,y)$$

$$h(y) = P(Y = y) = \sum_{\text{all } x} f(x,y)$$

Example

Consider the matrix in Table 5.1 To calculate the probability that $X = 1$ we could simply sum all of the joint outcomes in which $X = 1$ (i.e., we sum over all values of Y while fixing X at 1):

$$g(1) = P(X = 1) = P(X = 1 \text{ and } Y = 0) + P(X = 1 \text{ and } Y = 1) +$$
$$P(X = 1 \text{ and } Y = 2) + P(X = 1 \text{ and } Y = 3) = 0 + 1/8 + 1/4 + 1/8 = 1/2$$

Thus, we simply sum across the row for $X = 1$. If we did this for each possible value of X we would generate the univariate probability distribution for X. We call this the "marginal" distribution of X as it is contained in the margin of the table for the joint probability distribution. Similarly, to calculate the marginal distribution for Y we sum down the columns of the joint distribution. The marginal (univariate) distributions for X and Y are shown in the margins of Table 5.2.

Table 5.2

		Y				Marginal distribution of X:
		0	1	2	3	⇓
X	0	1/8	1/4	1/8	0	½
	1	0	1/8	1/4	1/8	½
Marginal distribution of Y ⇒		1/8	3/8	3/8	1/8	Sum = 1

5.2.5   Conditional Distributions

Often we are interested in the distribution of one random variable *conditional* upon a second random variable assuming a particular value. For example, we might want to consider the distribution of Y *given* X assumes a particular value. This is called the *probability distribution of Y conditional on X*, or, more simply, the conditional distribution of Y given X. The conditional distributions of Y and X, respectively, are given by

$$f^c(x|y) = P(X = x \,/\, Y = y) = f(x,y) \,/\, h(y)$$
$$f^c(y|x) = P(Y = y \,/\, X = x) = f(x,y) \,/\, g(x)$$

Notice that this is simply the definition of a conditional probability developed in Chapter 1 where the calculation is done for each value of X (or Y) given the value of Y (or X).

Example

To find the conditional distribution of Y given that $X = 0$, notice from Table 5.2 that $f(0,0) = \frac{1}{8}$, $f(0,1) = \frac{1}{4}$, $f(0,2) = \frac{1}{8}$, and $f(0,3) = 0$ and that $g(0) = \frac{1}{2}$ (where $g(x)$ is the marginal distribution of X). Therefore, the conditional distribution of Y given $X = 0$, $f^c(y|0)$ is given in Table 5.3.

Table 5.3

Y			
0	1	2	3
¼	½	¼	0

5.3 CONTINUOUS BIVARIATE DISTRIBUTIONS

5.3.1 Joint Density Function

We denote by $f(x,y)$ a function with the property that $P(a \leq X \leq b$ and $c \leq Y \leq d) =$

$$\int_a^b \int_c^d f(x,y)dydx$$

This function is called a *bivariate (or joint) probability density function* for the random variables X and Y.

The joint density function is analogous to the density function for single random variables. To find the probability of X being between c and d and Y (jointly) being between a and b we simply integrate the density function over that range. Again, the area under the graph of the joint density function (the *density curve*) gives the probability that X and Y assume values in the given intervals (i.e., the probability of X being between a and b and Y between c and d). An infinite number of different bivariate distributions exist, with the shape of the density curve depending on the functional form taken by $f(x,y)$.

5.3.2 Properties of Joint Density Function

1. $P(a \leq X \leq b$ and $c \leq Y \leq d) = \int_a^b \int_c^d f(x,y)dydx \geq 0.$

Again, probabilities must be nonnegative.

2. $P(-\infty \leq X \leq \infty$ and $-\infty \leq Y \leq \infty) = \int_{-\infty}^{\infty} \int_{-\infty}^{\infty} f(x,y)dydx = 1.$

This asserts our typical requirement that the area under the entire density curve must total 1. This is analogous to our requirement that summing the probabilities associated with all possible outcomes must total 1.

3. The definition of a joint density function easily extends to handle the case where there is more than one random variable. For example,

$$P(a \leq X \leq b \text{ and } c \leq Y \leq d \text{ and } e \leq Z \leq f) = \int_a^b \int_c^d \int_e^f f(x,y,z)dzdydx.$$

Here we must specify the *trivariate density function* $f(x,y,z)$. Although extensions to more random variables are straightforward, we obviously lose the ability to represent these density functions graphically past the bivariate case.

Continuous Bivariate Distributions:

(1) Bivariate Roof Distribution

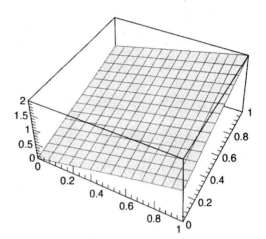

(2) Bivariate Normal Distribution

5.3.3   Cumulative Joint Density Function

A function $F(x,y)$ that gives the probability that the random variable X is less than a given value x and the random variable Y is jointly less than a given value y:

$$F(x,y) = P(X \leq x \text{ and } Y \leq y) = P(-\infty \leq X \leq x \text{ and } -\infty \leq Y \leq y)$$

$$= \int_{-\infty}^{x} \int_{-\infty}^{y} f(s,t)\,dt\,ds$$

is known as the *cumulative joint density function* or the *cumulative joint distribution function*.

5.3.4 Properties of Cumulative Joint Density Function

1. $F(-\infty,-\infty) = 0$. That is, the probability that X is less than negative infinity and Y is less than negative infinity is 0.

2. $F(\infty,\infty) = 1$. That is, the probability that X is less than infinity and Y is less than infinity is 1.

3. $\dfrac{\partial^2 F(x,y)}{\partial x dy} = f(x,y)$

   That is, we can generate the joint density function by taking the second (cross) derivative of the cumulative density function.

4. $P(a \leq X \leq b$ and $c \leq Y \leq d) = F(b,d) - mF(a,d) - F(b,c) + F(a,c)$. You can use a diagram to convince yourself of this property.

5.3.5 Bivariate and Univariate Distributions

When given the joint density function for two random variables X and Y we can calculate the *marginal density functions* for X and Y using the fact that

$$g(x) = \int_{-\infty}^{\infty} f(x,y)dy$$

$$h(y) = \int_{-\infty}^{\infty} f(x,y)dx$$

This is analogous to the calculation done in the discrete case. In the discrete case we calculated the marginal distribution of X by summing over Y. Similarly, in the continuous case we calculate the marginal distribution of X by integrating over all values of Y.

5.4 INDEPENDENCE

The concept of independence introduced in Chapter 2 naturally extends to the case of independent random variables. Recall that two events were said to be independent if knowledge that one event occurred had no effect on the probability of the second event occurring. In that case, $P(A \cap B) = P(A)P(B)$. Similarly, two random variables are independent if and only if $f(x,y) = g(x)h(y)$ (i.e., if the joint probability (or density) function can be written as the product of the two marginal probability (or density) functions). More generally, N random variables $\{X_1,X_2,X_3,\ldots,X_N\}$ are independent if and only if $f(x_1,x_2,x_3, \ldots,x_N) = f_{X_1}(x_1)f_{X_2}(x_2)\ldots f_{X_N}(x_N)$.

5.5 (MORE) MATHEMATICS OF EXPECTATIONS

If you want to calculate the mean or variance of the random variables X and Y from their joint distribution, you can proceed in one of two ways. First, you could simply calculate the marginal distribution of X and Y from the joint distribution (as described above) and then directly apply the mean and variance formulas given in Chapter 4. Alternatively (and equivalently), you can apply the formulas below directly using the joint probability (or density) function.

APPLICATION 5.1   *One Thumb, Two Thumbs, Drumming on a Drum*

With all the competition for ways to spend your entertainment dollars, deciding which movie to go to is an important decision. In fact, moviegoers often refer to critics' reviews before making their choice and, for several years, the Siskel and Ebert television show provided a popular source. These two reviewers would discuss the merits of a film before each rendered his ultimate judgment: thumbs up or thumbs down.

But how much information really is present in a rating of two thumbs up? Each reviewer's judgment may be viewed as a separate variable, so that random variation across reviews for each movie is bound to lead to some with two thumbs up. If the reviews were statistically independent, then the fact that a particular movie received two thumbs up would provide no information about its quality—rather, the outcome simply occurred by chance.

To assess this question, one study compiled 160 reviews by Roger Ebert and the late Gene Siskel over an 18-month period; the results are shown in the following table.

		Ebert's rating			
		Pro	Mixed	Con	Siskel's marginal distribution
Siskel's rating	Pro	64	9	10	83 (52%)
	Mixed	11	13	8	32 (20%)
	Con	13	8	24	45 (28%)
	Ebert's marginal distribution	88 (55%)	30 (19%)	42 (26%)	160

The marginal distributions tell us, for instance, that both Siskel and Ebert gave a thumbs up to 52% and 55% of movies, respectively. If their judgments were statistically independent, we should observe 0.52*0.55 = 28.6% of all movies to receive two thumbs up. Instead, we observe 64/160 = 40% of movies do so. More sophisticated statistical tests provide further support that their evaluations are not statistically independent. Therefore, one reviewer's likelihood of providing a favorable rating is positively related to that of the other reviewer. This either indicates that movies getting two thumbs up really are good movies or that Siskel and Ebert both have similar bad taste!

5.5.1 Discrete Random Variables

$$E(X) = \sum_{\text{all } x} \sum_{\text{all } y} xf(x,y) \qquad \text{var}(X) = \sum_{\text{all } x} \sum_{\text{all } y} (x - E(X))^2 f(x,y)$$

$$E(Y) = \sum_{\text{all } x} \sum_{\text{all } y} yf(x,y) \qquad \text{var}(Y) = \sum_{\text{all } x} \sum_{\text{all } y} (y - E(Y))^2 f(x,y)$$

Proof of E(X). $\displaystyle E(X) = \sum_{\text{all } x} \sum_{\text{all } y} xf(x,y) = \sum_{\text{all } x} \left[\sum_{\text{all } y} xf(x,y) \right] = \sum_{\text{all } x} xf(x)$

The final equality holds because x is a constant when we sum over all y and can be pulled outside of the summation. Then we use the relationship between the joint and marginal distributions, which indicates that

$$\sum_{\text{all } y} f(x,y) = f(x).$$

5.5.2 Continuous Random Variables

$$E(X) = \int_{-\infty}^{\infty} \int_{-\infty}^{\infty} xf(x,y)dydx \quad \text{var}(X) = \int_{-\infty}^{\infty} \int_{-\infty}^{\infty} (x - E(X))^2 f(x,y)dydx$$

$$E(Y) = \int_{-\infty}^{\infty} \int_{-\infty}^{\infty} yf(x,y)dydx \quad \text{var}(Y) = \int_{-\infty}^{\infty} \int_{-\infty}^{\infty} (y - E(Y))^2 f(x,y)dydx$$

Proof of E(X).

$$E(X) = \int_{-\infty}^{\infty} \int_{-\infty}^{\infty} xf(x,y)dydx = \int_{-\infty}^{\infty} x \left[\int_{-\infty}^{\infty} f(x,y)dy \right] dx = \int_{-\infty}^{\infty} xf(x)dx$$

The reasoning behind the last equality is analogous to that described earlier for the discrete case, but using the properties of integrals rather than sums.

5.6 EXPECTATIONS OF FUNCTIONS OF SEVERAL RANDOM VARIABLES

1. If $X_1, X_2, X_3, \ldots, X_N$ are N random variables, then $E(X_1 + X_2 + X_3 + \ldots + X_N) = E(X_1) + E(X_2) + E(X_3) + \ldots E(X_N)$, or, using summation notation,

$$E\left(\sum_{i=1}^{N} X_i \right) = \sum_{i=1}^{N} E(X_i)$$

That is, *the expected value of a sum is the sum of the expected values*. This property holds whether or not the random variables are independent.

2. Property 1 can be extended as follows when the random variables are multiplied by some number:

$$E\left(\sum_{i=1}^{N} a_i X_i\right) = \sum_{i=1}^{N} a_i E(X_i)$$

3. Suppose X and Y are two random variables with $f(x,y)$ being the joint density function. Then, if $g(x,y)$ is some function of X and Y:

   a. $E(g(X,Y)) = \sum_{\text{all } x} \sum_{\text{all } y} g(x,y) f(x,y)$ if X and Y are discrete.

   b. $E(g(X,Y)) = \int_{-\infty}^{\infty} \int_{-\infty}^{\infty} g(x,y) f(x,y) dy dx$ if X and Y are continuous.

4. If X and Y are two random variables and X and Y are independent, then $E(XY) = E(X)E(Y)$. Notice that this result holds *only* when X and Y are independent.

Proof.

$$E(XY) = \int_{-\infty}^{\infty} \int_{-\infty}^{\infty} xy f(x,y) dy dx = \int_{-\infty}^{\infty} \int_{-\infty}^{\infty} xy g(x) h(y) dy dx$$

since X and Y are independent

$$= \int_{-\infty}^{\infty} xg(x) dx \int_{-\infty}^{\infty} yh(y) dy$$
$$= E(X)E(Y)$$

5. If $X_1, X_2, X_3, \ldots, X_N$ are N independent random variables, then $\text{var}(X_1 + X_2 + X_3 + \ldots + X_N) = \text{var}(X_1) + \text{var}(X_2) + \text{var}(X_3) + \ldots \text{var}(X_N)$, or, using summation notation,

$$\text{var}\left(\sum_{i=1}^{N} X_i\right) = \sum_{i=1}^{N} \text{var}(X_i)$$

That is, *the variance of a sum is the sum of the individual variances*. Notice that this relation *only* holds when the random variables are independent.

Proof.   Let $N = 2$ and $Y = X_1 + X_2$. Then,

$$\text{var}(Y) = E(Y^2) - E(Y)^2 \text{ as always}$$

$$= E[(X_1 + X_2)^2] - (E(X_1 + X_2))^2$$
$$= E(X_1^2) + 2E(X_1 X_2) + E(X_2^2) - E(X_1)^2 - 2E(X_1)E(X_2) - E(X_2)^2$$
$$= E(X_1^2) + 2E(X_1)E(X_2) + E(X_2^2) - E(X_1)^2 - 2E(X_1)E(X_2) - E(X_2)^2$$
$$= E(X_1^2) - E(X_1^2) + E(X_2^2) - E(X_2)^2$$
$$= \text{var}(X_1) + \text{var}(X_2)$$

Notice that on line 4 of this proof we used the fact that X_1 and X_2 are independent and wrote $E(X_1 X_2)$ as $E(X_1)E(X_2)$. Thus, property 5 depends on X_1 and X_2 being independent.

5.7 CONDITIONAL EXPECTATIONS

Often we are interested in the expected value (mean) of one random variable given the value of another random variable. For example, we might want to know the mean level of earnings for those individuals who have graduated from college or the mean level of earnings for high school graduates. Knowledge of these two statistics would allow us to answer an additional question that has received considerable attention: How much more does a college graduate earn relative to a high school graduate? This question is answered by taking the difference between the mean level of earnings among college graduates and the mean level of earnings among high school graduates.

More generally, we could ask, How does the mean level of earnings change with the completed level of educational attainment? This amounts to a change in conditional expectations associated with a change in the conditioning variables. It is the fundamental question addressed by regression analysis, which we begin to discuss in Chapter 9 and throughout the remainder of the book.

Formally, conditional expectations are given by:

$$E(Y|x) = \sum_{\text{all } y} y f(y|x) = \sum_{\text{all } y} y \frac{f(x,y)}{g(x)} \qquad \text{if } Y \text{ is discrete and,}$$

$$E(Y|x) = \int_{-\infty}^{\infty} y f(y|x) dy = \int_{-\infty}^{\infty} y \frac{f(x,y)}{h(x)} dy \text{ if } Y \text{ is continuous.}$$

5.8 MEASURES OF ASSOCIATION: COVARIANCE AND CORRELATION

When summarizing the characteristics of a single random variable we developed various measures of central tendency and dispersion. When dealing with two (or more) random variables we can also develop measures of *association* between the various random variables. That is, we can measure the extent to which the variables "covary" or move together. Consider the four graphs depicted in Figure 5.1.

In panel 1 the random variables X and Y exhibit a *positive* linear relationship to one another. That is, when X increases in magnitude Y typically also increases in magnitude. In panel 2 we see a *negative* linear relationship between X and Y. That is, when X gets larger Y tends to get smaller. In panel 3 there appears to be little relation between the two random variables, while in panel 4 there is a nonlinear relationship between the two variables. Now, in designing a measure of association we would like to take the intuitive notion of positive, negative, or zero relation between two random variables and turn it into a number. We might also like the magnitude of the assigned number to indicate the *degree* of relation between the two variables. We will consider two measures of association: the *covariance* and the *correlation*.

5.8.1 Covariance

The *covariance* between two random variables X and Y is denoted by cov(X,Y) and is given by

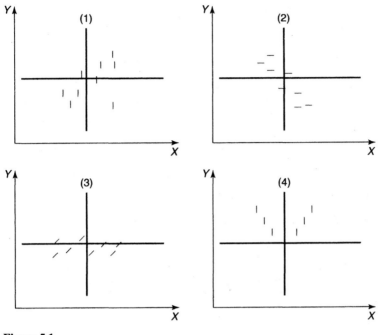

Figure 5.1

$$\text{cov}(X,Y) = E[(X - E(X))(Y - E(Y))]$$

The sign $(+, -, 0)$ of the covariance indicates whether the random variables are positively, negatively, or not related. For instance, when X is above (below) its mean, if Y is also typically above (below) its mean, then the two variables are positively related and the covariance, according to this formula, is positive. The magnitude of the covariance depends on the units used in measuring X and Y. As such, it provides a measure of the direction of association, but caution must be used in using it as a measure of the strength of that association.

5.8.2   Properties of Covariance

1. From the definition of an expected value we have:

   a. $\text{cov}(X,Y) = \displaystyle\sum_{\text{all } x} \sum_{\text{all } y} (X - E(X))(Y - E(Y))f(x,y)$ if X and Y are discrete.

   b. $\text{cov}(X,Y) = \displaystyle\int_{-\infty}^{\infty} \int_{-\infty}^{\infty} (X - E(X))(Y - E(Y))f(x,y)dydx$ if X and Y are continuous.

2. $\text{cov}(X,Y) = E(XY) - E(X)E(Y)$.

Proof.
$$\begin{aligned}
\text{cov}(X,Y) &= E[(X - E(X))(Y - E(Y))] \\
&= E[XY - E(X)Y - YE(X) + E(X)E(Y)] \\
&= E(XY) - E(X)E(Y) - E(Y)E(X) + E(X)E(Y) \\
&= E(XY) - E(X)E(Y)
\end{aligned}$$

3. If X and Y are independent, then $\text{cov}(X,Y) = 0$.

Proof.   When X and Y are independent, $E(X,Y) = E(X)E(Y)$, and thus from property 2 we have $\text{cov}(X,Y) = E(XY) - E(X)E(Y) = E(X)E(Y) - E(X)E(Y) = 0$.

It is important to realize that while independence implies zero covariance the converse is not true. That is, zero covariance does not imply independence. Indeed, in panel 4 of Figure 5.1 there is a strong nonlinear relationship between X and Y but there is a low covariance. This is because the covariance is a measure of the *linear association* between two random variables.

4. If $Y = X$, then $\text{cov}(X,X) = E[(X - E(X))(X - E(X))] = \text{var}(X)$. Thus, the covariance of a random variable with itself is its variance.

5. If X and Y are two random variables then:
   a. $\text{var}(X + Y) = \text{var}(X) + \text{var}(Y) + 2\,\text{cov}(X,Y)$
   b. $\text{var}(X - Y) = \text{var}(X) + \text{var}(Y) - 2\,\text{cov}(X,Y)$

Proof of 5a.

$$\begin{aligned}
\text{var}(X + Y) &= E[((X + Y) - E(X + Y))^2] \\
&= E[((X - E(X)) + (Y - E(Y)))^2] \\
&= E[(X - E(X))^2 + (Y - E(Y))^2 + 2(X - E(X))(Y - E(Y))] \\
&= \text{var}(X) + \text{var}(Y) + 2\,\text{cov}(X,Y)
\end{aligned}$$

Property 5b is proved similarly.

5.8.3   Correlation

The *correlation* between two random variables X and Y is denoted by $corr(X,Y)$ or by ρ_{XY} and is given by

$$\begin{aligned}
corr(X,Y) &= E\left[\left(\frac{X - E(X)}{\sigma_X}\right)\left(\frac{Y - E(Y)}{\sigma_Y}\right)\right] \\
&= \frac{\text{cov}(X,Y)}{\sigma_X \sigma_Y}
\end{aligned}$$

The correlation measure of association has an advantage over the covariance in that it is unit free and provides a measure of the *degree* of linear association between the two random variables that is not influenced by the units used to measure the variables.

APPLICATION 5.2   *The Long and Variable Road*

Predicting economic fluctuations is hard enough, but introducing government policies to counteract negative shocks may be even harder. In fact, Milton Friedman argued decades ago that such monetary policy interventions should not even be attempted. Through much of his career, he argued that such attempts may cause more harm than good.

To consider this argument, consider two random variables, X and Y, that represent the level of economic activity as measured by GDP that would result in the absence of government intervention (X) and the impact on economic activity brought about by monetary policy (Y). The resulting level of GDP would be the sum, $X + Y$. Monetary policy would be designed to expand the economy (an "easy money" policy) during economic contractions, and slow the growth of the economy during expansionary periods. Then the mean level of economic activity, $E(X + Y)$, would be more constant than if the economy was allowed to operate without intervention.

The criticism that Friedman made of this approach is that it is the variance of GDP that determines swings in the economy and that monetary "stabilization" policy may, in fact, be destabilizing. The basis of his argument relies on the simple properties of variance and covariance, particularly the property that

$$\text{var}(X + Y) = \text{var}(X) + \text{var}(Y) + 2 \times \text{cov}(X, Y)$$

If the economy operated without intervention, the variance in economic activity would be $\text{var}(X)$. Therefore, the policy reduces cyclical fluctuations only if $\text{var}(Y) + 2 \times \text{cov}(X,Y) < 0$.

This is insufficient to make Friedman's point, because the goal of monetary policy is precisely to offset changes that would occur in economic growth without intervention. In other words, it is the intention of the policy for $\text{cov}(X,Y) < 0$. The problem, Friedman argued, is that this term is relatively small because changes in monetary policy affect economic activity only with a "long and variable lag." By the time the impact is felt, economic conditions may have already changed, weakening the intended negative relationship between X and Y. Therefore, monetary interventions designed to help reduce economic fluctuations, Friedman claimed, may actually be contributing to greater volatility. That is one way to win a Nobel prize!

SOURCE: Friedman, Milton. *Essays in Positive Economics*. Chicago: University of Chicago Press, 1953.

5.8.4   Properties of Correlation

1. The correlation between two variables is bounded by –1 and 1: $-1 \leq \rho_{XY} \leq 1$.

Proof.   To prove property 1 we use the *Schwarz inequality*, which states that for two random variables U and V, $E(UV)^2 \leq E(U^2)E(V^2)$. If we let $U = X - \mu_X$ and $Y = Y - \mu_Y$, then we have $E((X - \mu_X)(Y - \mu_Y))^2 \leq E((X - \mu_X)^2)E((Y - \mu_Y)^2)$, which (dividing both sides by the right-hand-side expression) implies

$$\rho_{XY}^2 = E\left[\left(\frac{X - E(X)}{\sigma_X}\right)\left(\frac{Y - E(Y)}{\sigma_Y}\right)\right]^2 \leq 1$$

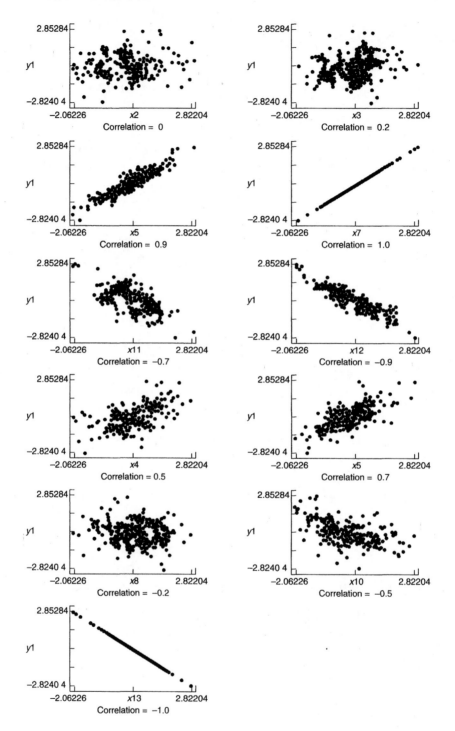

Thus, $-1 \le \rho_{XY} \le 1$.

2. $|\rho_{XY}| = 1$ if and only if $Y = a + bX$. Thus, the correlation between two variables will equal 1 in absolute value only if there is a perfect linear relationship between the two variables.

3. Correlation does not imply causality. Two variables may move together but not be causally related (e.g., shirt size and strength are probably positively related, but buying a larger shirt will probably not make you stronger!).

5.9 PROBLEMS

1. Consider the following joint probability distribution for the discrete random variables X and Y:

		Y		
		10	20	30
X	10	.2	.1	.1
	20	.3	.2	.1

a. What are the marginal distributions for Y and X?

b. Calculate $E(X)$ and $E(Y)$.

c. Are X and Y independent?

2. As you walk into your econometrics exam, a friend bets you $10 that she will outscore you on the exam. Let X be a random variable denoting your winnings. X can take on the values 10, -10, or 0 (you tie on the exam). You know that the distribution function for X, $P(X)$ depends on whether she studied for the exam or not. Let $Y = 0$ if she studied and $Y = 1$ if she did not. Consider the following joint distribution table:

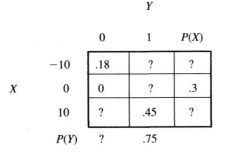

	0	1	P(X)
-10	.18	?	?
0	0	?	.3
10	?	.45	?
P(Y)	?	.75	

a. Fill in the missing elements in the table.

b. Compute $E[X]$ and $E[Y]$. Should you take the bet? Why?

3. Let the random variable X be distributed with $E[X] = 2$ and $\text{var}(X) = 4$. Let Y be distributed with $E[Y] = 1$ and $\text{var}(Y) = 2$. Find:

a. $E[3X + 2Y]$.

b. $\text{Var}[X - Y]$ assuming X and Y are independent.

c. $\text{Var}[3X + 2Y]$ assuming X and Y are independent.

If the covariance between X and Y is 3, how would your answers to parts (a), (b), and (c) change?

4. Let X, Y, and Z be random variables. Show $\text{Cov}(X + Y, Z) = \text{Cov}(X, Z) + \text{Cov}(Y, Z)$.

5. For any random variables X and Y and constants a, b, c, and d, show that $\text{Cov}(aX + b, cY + d) = ac\text{Cov}(X, Y)$.

6. Suppose a person's score on a mathematics aptitude test X is a number between 0 and 1. Similarly, his score on an English aptitude test Y is also a number between 0 and 1. Suppose the joint distribution of X and Y is given as follows:

$$f(x,y) = \frac{2}{5}[2X + 3Y] \text{ for } 0 \le x \le 1 \text{ and } 0 \le y \le 1$$

   a. Show $f(x,y)$ s a proper joint probability density function.
   b. Find $P(x \le .5 \text{ and } y \le .5)$.
   c. Find the marginal distribution for the random variable X.
   d. Find the mean of X.
   e. What is the probability that $y \le .5$ given that $x \le .5$?
   f. Are X and Y independent? Explain.

7. The conditional expectation of a random variable X given another random variable Y is defined as

$$E[X|Y] = \int_{-\infty}^{\infty} xg(x|y)dx$$

   where

$$g(x|y) = \frac{f(x,y)}{f(y)}$$

   where $f(x,y)$ is the joint distribution of X and Y and $f(y)$ is the marginal distribution of Y.

   Suppose $f(x,y) = 2x$ for $0 \le x \le 1$ and $0 \le y \le 1$.
   a. Find the means of X and Y.
   b. Find the variances of X and Y.
   c. Find the covariance between X and Y.
   d. Find the conditional mean of X given Y.

8. Consider the following record on the free-throw performance of Larry Bird (Boston Celtics Basketball) during the 1980–81 and 1981–82 seasons. It is sometimes claimed that players get "hot hands." That is, they are more likely to make the second throw if they make the first throw than if they miss the first throw. Does the evidence support the idea that Bird had hot hands?

		Second shot:		
		Hit	Miss	Total
First shot:	Hit	251	34	285
	Miss	48	5	53
	Total	299	39	338

9. Is it true that correlation implies causality and vice versa? Explain using an example.

Chapter 6

Sampling and Sampling Distributions

6.1 INTRODUCTION

The first five chapters of this book have introduced the basics of probability theory. As noted in the first chapter, probability theory forms the logical foundation of statistical inference. Often the motivation behind applied research is to use sample data to learn more about some population of interest. It is to this important topic that we now turn. We start by defining some key concepts.

6.2 POPULATIONS

A *population* or *universe* is the set of all things (people, firms, etc.) under consideration.

Examples

1. The incomes of all the people in the United States
2. The grade point averages for all of the students in your class

3. The voting preferences for all voters in the United States

4. The heights of all students at Princeton

The critical characteristic of populations is that they contain *all* of the elements of inter-est. Populations can be finite or infinite in size. We might be interested in learning the mean or standard deviation of a population.

6.3 SAMPLES

A *sample* is a subset of the population selected for analysis.

Examples

1. The incomes for 10,000 people selected at random from the United States

2. The grade point averages for 5 randomly selected students in your class

3. The set of voting preferences for 500 voters canvassed in a local shopping mall

4. The set of heights for the members of the Princeton basketball team

The way in which we select our sample is very important. A variety of methods are avail-able but the key thing to keep in mind is that we typically take a sample from a population to learn more about the population. Thus, we want our sample to be representative of the population at large. In essence, the sample should be a replica—in miniature—of the pop-ulation. Clearly, selecting only members of the Princeton basketball team will produce a sample so biased as to limit our ability to characterize heights at Princeton. A poor sample selection can make it very difficult to learn much about the population. Knowing whether a sample is representative of a population is difficult since it is probably our limited knowledge of the population that is leading us to sample in the first place. This suggests we must develop an approach to gathering our sample that safeguards against possible biases. One common approach to gathering a useful sample is called *simple random sam-pling*.

6.3.1 Simple Random Samples

A *simple random sample* is a sample where (1) each element of the population has an equal chance of being chosen and (2) the selection of one element has no effect on the probability of another element being selected. Thus, the observations are equally likely and are statistically independent. Since the sample observations are drawn from the same population, we say they are *identically distributed*. Taking all of the characteristics of simple random sampling together, we sometimes say the observations are *independent, identically distributed (i.i.d.)*. We assume simple random sampling throughout this book.

Example

To learn more about the heights of students at Princeton we randomly select names from the student phone book and ask the selected individuals their height. Notice that each ele-ment in the population (comprised of *all* students at Princeton) has an equal chance of se-lection (assuming everyone is listed in the phone book). Notice also that the observations

---

APPLICATION 6.1   *How Were They Supposed to Know?*

The authors of the U.S. Constitution included language indicating that a complete count, or census, of the population be conducted every 10 years for the purposes of apportionment (i.e., dividing up congressional representatives across the states). In a modern society with roughly 275 million people, obtaining an accurate count is no simple task. In fact, for the year 2000 Census, the Census Bureau proposed using statistical sampling techniques to reduce the cost of obtaining the count. The Supreme Court decided, however, that the use of sampling is not allowed by the Constitution for the purposes of apportionment and that a complete count needs to be conducted.

The way that the census has traditionally been conducted is that an initial mailing is sent out to all residences in the United States with a form indicating the number of individuals living in the household (along with other information). Unfortunately, not all households return their forms and the Census Bureau employs people to go door-to-door attempting to count these people. With over one-third of households neglecting to return their form in 1990 (source: www.census.gov/dmd/www/mailresp.html), this procedure is very costly. Moreover, if the residents of these houses are difficult to locate or refuse to respond, they may not be counted at all, resulting in a Census undercount. Estimates from the 1990 Census indicate that the undercount amounted to almost 2% of the population.

Alternatively, the Census Bureau had proposed using sampling to obtain counts from those households that do not return their forms. The Census had planned to sample the nonrespondents so that 90% of the total number of households were counted by mail-in response or door-to-door visits. The use of sampling would greatly reduce the cost of the census since the last households to count are the hardest to contact, requiring the greatest number of additional visits, and therefore, the highest cost. To improve upon the precision of the estimate, the Census Bureau had then planned to use an approach where an independent enumeration was conducted in some areas and compared to the census count. The extent to which individuals appeared in the new count, but not in the census, provides an indication of the magnitude of the undercount (see the discussion of the "capture/recapture" method in Chapter 7). This estimate of the undercount would be added to that estimated through mail-in responses and the door-to-door visits. The Supreme Court decision invalidated the sampling plan, but this approach to address the undercount will still be utilized. Regarding sampling, it appears that cost lost to the dictates of a 200-year-old document.

SOURCE: Wright, Tommy and Howard Hogan, "Census 2000: Evolution of the Revised Plan," *Chance*, Vol. 12, No. 4 (Fall 1999), pp. 11–19.

are statistically independent. The probability of drawing any particular name is not affected by the names previously drawn.

6.3.2   Why Sample?

If we gather samples to learn more about populations, why not simply survey the entire population? The answer to this question is obvious if the population is infinite in size, but what if it is finite? One important reason is cost. A sample can provide useful information about a population at a much lower cost than a complete census. Samples can also be generated much more quickly, allowing the information to be more timely. Later in the book

| APPLICATION 6.2 | *Without the CPS, It Would Be Anybody's Guess* |

On the first Friday of every month, you can turn on the evening news and learn what the unemployment rate was for the preceding month. That number is an invaluable gauge of the strength of the economy and of great interest to the Federal Reserve Board (among others), which uses this information along with other indicators in determining monetary policy. The stock market also anxiously awaits its release; if its value is different from what had been forecast, the market is certain to react strongly.

But where does the unemployment rate (and many other labor market indicators) come from? It turns out the primary source of labor market data in the United States is a household survey that is conducted monthly, called the Current Population Survey (CPS). It has been conducted each month for more than 50 years and it now samples about 50,000 households. Sophisticated sampling strategies are employed so that nationally representative estimates can be derived along with estimates representative for individual states. The survey collects considerable data on labor market activity (like wages, hours worked, occupation, and industry), along with the demographic characteristics (like age, sex, race, marital status, and educational attainment) of respondents. Supplements are often included in particular surveys to provide additional information on the lives of the respondents. In particular, the primary source of income data in the United States comes from a supplement administered every March in which respondents are asked to report their income in the preceding year. Estimates of the poverty rate, among other things, come from this survey.

To estimate the unemployment rate itself, the responses to a series of questions are analyzed. First, based on individuals' answers, they are classified as employed, unemployed (defined as being on temporary layoff or looking for work), or "out of the labor force," where the labor force is defined as those employed or unemployed. The unemployment rate is just the percentage of individuals in the labor force that are classified as unemployed. This figure is released on the first Friday of every month at 8:30 A.M. Eastern time and can be obtained at http://www.bls.gov/news.release/empsit.nr0.htm.

we will consider how to decide how large a sample to select. The desired size for a sample will be linked to the degree of precision with which we will want to infer characteristics of the population.

6.4   POPULATIONS, PROBABILITY DISTRIBUTIONS, AND DATA

We can think of a sample from a population as being a set of random variables. Many different samples might be selected from a population and we don't know the outcome until we actually draw the sample.

Suppose we select a simple random sample of size n (with replacement) from a population of size N. The sample can be denoted as $X_1, X_2, X_3, \ldots, X_n$, where X_i is a random variable denoting the outcome of the ith observation in the sample. You might think of X_i as simply being a label for the outcome of the ith observation selected in the sample. The probability distribution for the random variable X_i would be given by the frequency distribution for the population. Indeed, the frequencies of the different outcomes in the population give the probabilities associated with each random variable X_i under simple random

---

APPLICATION 6.3   *How Does the Boss Get Paid When His Songs Get Played?*

When radio stations play a song, they are required to pay royalties to those who wrote and performed it. Yet there are hundreds of radio stations playing dozens of songs each day, so in theory, thousands of individual payments would be required each day and millions each year. How are they supposed to keep track of who owes what to whom?

The solution involves two important components. First, radio stations do not pay individual per-formers, but rather pay a single licensing fee to an organization that represents the artists, the Ameri-can Society of Composers, Authors, and Publishers (ASCAP). Once the license is obtained, the radio station can play any song by any artist that is a member of ASCAP. This solves the radio station's problem, but still leaves ASCAP with the task of figuring out how to distribute the proceeds to its members.

Therefore, the second part of the solution involves a program in which ASCAP uses statistical sampling techniques to determine the volume of songs played by their member artists. When a radio station signs a licensing agreement with ASCAP, it also agrees to provide lists of songs it plays. Sam-ples of these lists are chosen to determine how often works of an individual artist are performed, and they are paid according to that. So even one-hit wonders can expect their fair share of the licensing revenue!

SOURCE: Finkelstein, Michael O. and Bruce Levin. *Statistics for Lawyers.* New York: Springer-Verlag, 1990.

---

sampling. Thus, if the population can be characterized by a normal distribution with mean 10 and variance 5, then each random variable X_i will also be normal with mean 10 and variance 5. We will write the actual outcomes for a particular sample as $x_1, x_2, x_3, \ldots, x_n$. The particular outcomes will comprise our data and can be thought of as realizations of the set of random variables. You might also notice that the joint density function for our sample $f(x_1, x_2, x_3, \ldots, x_n)$ can be written as $f(x_1)f(x_2)\ldots f(x_n)$, given the assumption of simple random sampling. We will use this result later.

It is critical to notice that the sample actually gathered is only one of many possible samples that could have been selected. Since we are using simple random sampling, it is "chance" that determines the sample we ultimately obtain. To see this more clearly con-sider the following "thought experiment." Think of your school class as comprising the population. A simple random sample of 5 people are taken as a sample and asked their GPAs. Given the above discussion, we denote any sample of size 5 from the population as X_1, X_2, X_3, X_4, X_5, where X_1 is a random variable denoting the GPA reported by the first person selected in a given sample, and so on. Again, X_1 is a random variable since we are selecting the person at random and won't know the outcome until we actually gather the sample. We now conduct a sample and get some data: $x_1 = 3.0, x_2 = 2.8, x_3 = 3.9, x_4 = 1.5, x_5 = 4.0$. Thus, our random variable X_1 takes on ("realizes") the value 3.0, our random variable X_2 takes on the value 2.8, and so forth. Now, if we conducted another sample of 5 people we might get the observations $x_1 = 2.0, x_2 = 4.0, x_3 = 3.2, x_4 = 3.7, x_5 = 2.2$. That is, the 5 (possibly different) people sampled report different GPAs and so our random variables assume different values. Again, the idea is very simple: There are many possible samples a researcher might gather with a sample of size *n* from a population. The notation developed above is used to build on this fact.

6.5 SAMPLE STATISTICS

Now, suppose $X_1, X_2, X_3, \ldots, X_n$ form a simple random sample of size *n* from a population characterized by some unknown parameter θ. For example, suppose θ is the mean (expected value) of the population (i.e., $\theta = \mu_X$). We want to use our sample data to form an *estimate* of the population parameter. Another way of saying this is that we want to *infer* the population characteristic (e.g., mean) from the sample data. To do so, we form a *sam-*

APPLICATION 6.4   *It's Only Money*

The distribution of household income in the United States provides a perfect example of the differences between the mean, median, and mode. As displayed in the figure below with nationally representative data for 1998, the distribution of household income is skewed; fewer and fewer households fall in higher and higher income categories. The most common range is between $10,000 and $20,000, so this would be the mode based on these categories (there is no mode when income is measured as a continuous variable because the probability of observing any particular value is so small). The exact median is $38,885. Because the distribution is not symmetric, the mean and the median are quite different. In particular, because of the relatively small fraction of very-high-income households, the mean is driven up above the median. It is estimated to be $51,855.

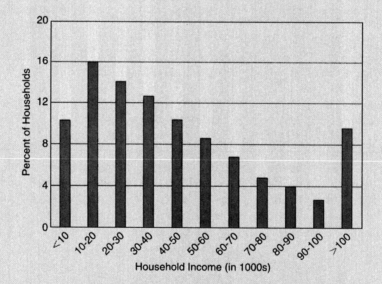

SOURCE: U.S. Census Bureau, Current Population Reports, P60-206. *Money Income in the United States: 1998.* Washington, DC: U.S. Government Printing Office, 1999.

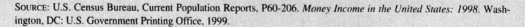

ple statistic. A sample statistic is a real-valued function $T = r(X_1, X_2, X_3, \ldots, X_n)$ of the random variables $X_1, X_2, X_3, \ldots, X_n$. That is, it is a formula showing how to combine the sample data to form a *(point) estimate* of the population parameter. As such, it is called an *estimator*. Once we have gathered our data and $X_1, X_2, X_3, \ldots, X_n$ have taken on the particular numerical values $x_1, x_2, x_3, \ldots, x_n$, we can plug these values into the function T and generate an *estimate* of the unknown population parameter θ.

Example

Suppose we want to use the sample data to estimate the population mean μ_X. A reasonable candidate would be to use the *sample mean*

$$\overline{X} = \frac{1}{n} \sum_{i=1}^{n} X_i$$

to estimate the population mean. Here the sample statistic is the sample mean and the unknown population parameter is μ_X. If we gathered a simple random sample of size $n = 5$ and got data $x_1 = 3.0$, $x_2 = 2.8$, $x_3 = 3.9$, $x_4 = 1.5$, $x_5 = 4.0$ and applied our estimator we would have

$$\overline{X} = \frac{1}{5}(3.0 + 2.8 + 3.9 + 1.5 + 4.0) = 3.04$$

Thus, our estimate of the population mean based on our sample would be 3.04. We call this a *point estimate* as the estimate is a single number rather than a range of numbers.

6.6 SAMPLING DISTRIBUTIONS

Since the sample statistic T is a function of $X_1, X_2, X_3, \ldots, X_n$ and since $X_1, X_2, X_3, \ldots, X_n$ are random variables, it follows that T is also a random variable. That is, the value of T will vary from sample to sample since the values assumed by $X_1, X_2, X_3, \ldots, X_n$ will vary from sample to sample. Thus, the value our sample mean (for example) takes on *depends on the actual sample selected*. For each different possible sample we could generate a value of T. Thus, just as many different samples can be drawn from a population, many different sample means can also be formed. This idea is very important because it suggests that *sample statistics have probability distributions showing the different possible values the sample statistic can assume, along with the associated probability*. The probability distribution for a sample statistic is called a *sampling distribution*.

Example

Consider the following thought experiment. We want to estimate the average height of students at Williams College. To do so, we take a sample of 50 students each day for 30 days. Thus, each day we get a sample statistic—namely, the sample mean. At the end of the month we have 30 sample means: $\overline{X}_1, \overline{X}_2, \overline{X}_3, \ldots, \overline{X}_{30}$. We could graph the different means we got along with the frequency with which we got them, thus forming a frequency distribution of means. To extend this thought experiment further, we could conceive of having a computer (robot?) select *all possible samples of size 50* from the population of heights at Williams College, calculating the mean for each sample, and tabulating the frequency with which the different means arose. Then, we would have a virtually continuous probability distribution for the sample means.

6.7 THE NORMAL PROBABILITY DISTRIBUTION

As we will see subsequently, the normal probability distribution is very useful in describing the distribution of some important sample statistics, particularly the sample mean. Before describing this relationship, we first turn our attention to a detailed description of this distribution.

The normal distribution is symmetric, continuous, and bell shaped. Mathematically, it is given by the probability density function:

$$f(X) = \frac{1}{\sqrt{2\Pi\sigma_X^2}} e^{-\frac{1}{2}\left(\frac{X-\mu_X}{\sigma_X}\right)^2} \text{ where } e = 2.718281828\ldots$$

6.7.1 Properties of the Normal Distribution

1. If a random variable X is distributed normally with mean μ_X and variance σ_X^2 we write $X \sim N(\mu_X, \sigma_X^2)$. Note: This suggests writing the Central Limit Theorem as $\bar{X} \sim N(\mu_X, \sigma_{\bar{X}}^2)$ where

$$\sigma_{\bar{X}}^2 = \frac{\sigma_X^2}{n}.$$

2. The normal distribution is completely characterized by two parameters: the mean μ_X and variance σ_X^2. That is, once we know μ_X and σ_X^2 we can draw a unique density curve for $f(X)$. In general, there is a different normal density curve for each (μ_X, σ_X^2) pair. Changing μ_X changes the mean (center) of the distribution, while changing σ_X^2 changes the spread in the distribution.

3. The normal distribution is symmetric with .5 probability on each side of the mean. Also, the mean = median = mode for the normal distribution.

4. Any linear function of a normal random variable is distributed normally. That is, if $X \sim N(\mu_X, \sigma_X^2)$, and $Y = a + bX$ (and so, $E(Y) = a + b\mu_X$ and $var(Y) = b^2\sigma_X^2$), then $Y = a + bX \sim N(a + b\mu_X, b^2\sigma_X^2)$. Notice with the special case where

$$a = -\frac{\mu_X}{\sigma_X}$$

and

$$b = \frac{1}{\sigma_X}$$

we have

$$\frac{X - \mu_X}{\sigma_X} \sim N(0,1).$$

Proof of Special Case.

$$E\left(\frac{X - \mu_X}{\sigma_X}\right) = \frac{E(X - \mu_X)}{\sigma_X} = \frac{E(X) - \mu_X}{\sigma_X} = \frac{\mu_X - \mu_X}{\sigma_X} = 0$$

Similarly,

$$var\left(\frac{X - \mu_X}{\sigma_X}\right) = \frac{1}{\sigma_X^2} var(X - \mu_X) = \frac{1}{\sigma_X^2}\left(var(X) + var(\mu_X) - 2\,cov(X, \mu_X)\right) = \frac{1}{\sigma_X^2} var(X) = \frac{\sigma_X^2}{\sigma_X^2} = 1$$

since $var(\mu_X) = 0$ and $cov(X, \mu_X) = 0$.

5. Any linear combination of normal random variables is distributed normally. For example, if $X_1 \sim N(\mu_{X_1}, \sigma_{X_1}^2)$ and $X_2 \sim N(\mu_{X_2}, \sigma_{X_2}^2)$, then $X_1 + X_2 \sim N(\mu_{X_1} + \mu_{X_2}, \sigma_{X_1}^2 + \sigma_{X_1}^2 + 2\text{cov}(X_1, X_2))$. Notice that the variance of the sum of random variables is equal to the sum of the variances plus two times the covariance (as shown in Chapter 5). This result underlies the statement above that $\overline{X}$ is distributed normally even when n is not large if the population (and, hence, each X_i) is normal.

6.7.2   Standard Normal Random Variables

As is the case for all continuous distributions, we can find the $P(a \leq X \leq b)$ by calculating the area under the density curve. Here we run into two problems. First, it is not possible to integrate the normal density function as it yields no closed-form solution. That is, it is not possible to simply integrate the normal density function between a and b and get the desired probability. For this reason, the areas for certain values of a and b can be tabulated in Table B.1 at the end of the book. However, it has already been pointed out that there is a different density curve for every combination of μ_X and σ_X^2. This creates a problem as we would need an infinite number of tables—one for each possible mean and variance. The solution to this dilemma is provided by property 4 (above) of the normal distribution. The special case of property 4 showed that any normal random variable can be transformed into a normal random variable with a mean of 0 and a variance (and standard deviation) of 1 by subtracting the mean of that random variable and dividing by the standard deviation of that random variable. We call such a transformed random variable a *standardized normal random variable* and denote it by Z. Since any normal random variable can be transformed into a standardized random variable in this way we only need a table of probabilities associated with a standardized normal random variable.

Examples

1. Suppose $X \sim N(\mu_X, \sigma_X^2)$. Then, $Z = \dfrac{X - \mu_X}{\sigma_X} \sim N(0,1)$.

2. From the central limit theorem we have $\overline{X} \sim N\left(\mu_X, \dfrac{\sigma_X^2}{n}\right)$. Then,

$$Z = \frac{\overline{X} - \mu_X}{\sqrt{\dfrac{\sigma_X^2}{n}}} = \frac{\overline{X} - \mu_X}{\dfrac{\sigma_X}{\sqrt{n}}} \sim N(0,1)$$

Notice how in each case we subtract the mean and standard deviation associated with the random variable being standardized. Thus, standardization is a *procedure* that can be applied to any normally distributed random variable.

6.7.3   Finding Probabilities for a Standard Normal Random Variable

The standard normal distribution has probability density function

$$f(Z) = \frac{1}{\sqrt{2\Pi}} e^{-\frac{1}{2}z^2}$$

(notice that this is the same as the probability density function for a normal random variable with mean 0 and variance 1) and distribution function

$$F(z) = P(Z \le z) = \int_{-\infty}^{z} \frac{1}{\sqrt{2\Pi}} e^{-\frac{1}{2}t^2} dt.$$

The distribution function tells us the probability that a standard normal random variable Z is less than or equal to some number z. Some rules covered in Chapter 4 are useful in employing the distribution function. To review, notice that:

1. $P(a \le Z \le b) = F(b) - F(a)$.
2. $P(Z \ge b) = 1 - F(b)$.
3. Since $f(Z)$ is symmetric, $P(Z \ge a) = P(Z \le -a)$.

Given the standard normal distribution function, we might answer two types of questions:

1. If you are given z, what is $P(Z \le z)$?
2. What value of z is associated with a given probability?

Notice that in the first question you are given z and asked to find the associated probability. In the second question you are given a probability and asked to find the associated z.

The probabilities associated with a standard normal distribution are presented in Table B.1 where the table contains different values of z and the associated probability. Here are some examples showing how to use the table.

Examples

It is highly advisable when working out probabilities of this sort to draw a quick graph of the density curve for Z and shade in the area you are interested in finding. This makes remembering the rules much easier.

1. $P(Z \le 0) = .5$ This makes sense since 0 is the center of a standard normal distribution.
2. $P(0 \le Z \le 1.96) = F(1.96) - F(0) = .975 - .5 = .475$.
3. $P(Z \ge 1.96) = 1 - F(1.96) = 1 - .975 = .025$.
4. Suppose $X \sim N(1,9)$. What is the $P(X \le 4)$?

Notice that the distribution of X is centered at its mean of 1 and has a variance of 9. The first step in doing this calculation is to standardize X by subtracting the mean and dividing by the standard deviation. That is,

$$P(X \le 4) = P\left(Z \le \frac{4 - 1}{\sqrt{9}}\right) = P(Z \le -1) = F(1) = .8413 =$$

Thus, there is a 84.13 percent chance of seeing a value of X at or below 4 when it has a mean of 1 and a variance of 9.

6.7.4   Some Standard Normal Probabilities Worth Remembering

1. $P(-1.645 \le Z \le 1.645) = .90$
2. $P(-1.960 \le Z \le 1.960) = .95$
3. $P(-2.576 \le Z \le 2.576) = .99$

Notice that we can write $P(-1.960 \leq Z \leq 1.960)$ as

$$P\left(-1.960 \leq \frac{X - \mu_X}{\sigma_X} \leq 1.960 \right) = .95$$

Rearranging this yields $P(\mu_X - 1.960\sigma_X \leq X \leq \mu_X + 1.960\sigma_X) = .95$. In words, this states that the probability of X being within 1.96 standard deviations of its mean is .95. Alternatively, the probability of X being more than 1.96 standard deviations from its mean is less than or equal to $1 - .95 = .05$. Similarly, the probability X is within 2.576 standard deviations of its mean is .99.

6.8   THE DISTRIBUTION OF THE SAMPLE MEAN: $\bar{X}$

With the groundwork so far laid, we can develop the sampling distribution for a sample mean. As noted above, the sample mean is denoted by $\bar{X}$ and is given by

$$\bar{X} = \frac{1}{n} \sum_{i=1}^{n} X_i$$

Notice the similarity between the definition of the sample mean and the population mean for a finite population. The population mean is given by

$$\mu_X = \sum_{\text{all } X} x_i P(x_i)$$

If each outcome x_i in the population were equally likely (i.e., $P(x_i) = 1/N$), this would simplify to

$$\mu_X = \frac{1}{N} \sum_{i=1}^{N} x_i$$

where N is the number of elements in the population. Thus, the sample mean is analogous to the population mean except that the sample mean is a random variable, dependent upon the specific sample drawn, whereas the population mean is a constant.

As noted above, the sample mean is a random variable since the value it assumes will depend on the sample chosen. As such, it has an expected value (mean) and variance. Let's calculate these.

$$E(\bar{X}) = E\left(\frac{1}{n} \sum_{i=1}^{n} X_i \right)$$

(a)
$$= \frac{1}{n} \sum_{i=1}^{n} E(X_i)$$

$$= \frac{1}{n} \sum_{i=1}^{n} \mu_X = \frac{n\mu_X}{n} = \mu_X$$

Thus, the expected value of $\bar{X}$ is μ_X. That is, the sampling distribution of $\bar{X}$ is centered at the population mean. Notice the last line in the derivation has $E(X_i) = \mu_X$ for all of the n observations. This is because x_i is simply the label for the ith observation. As noted above, the distribution of each X_i is the same as the population distribution and, therefore, has the same expected value, and so on. Alternatively, if we repeatedly drew a "first" observation from a population, it would have a mean of μ_X. Similarly, it would have a variance of σ^2_X. The same logic holds for all of the x_i's.

$$\text{var}(\overline{X}) = \text{var}\left(\frac{1}{n} \sum_{i=1}^{n} X_i\right)$$

$$(b) \quad = \frac{1}{n^2} \sum_{i=1}^{n} \text{var}(X_i)$$

$$= \frac{1}{n^2} \sum_{i=1}^{n} \sigma^2_X = \frac{n\sigma^2_X}{n^2} = \frac{\sigma^2_X}{n}$$

Thus the variance of the sample mean is simply the population variance of the random variable X (which is probably unknown to us) divided by the sample size n.

Now, to add some intuition to the above derivations, reconsider the thought experiment we introduced above where we had a computer calculate the probability distribution for the sample mean of heights at Williams using $n = 50$. Derivations (a) and (b) above claim that this distribution would be centered at the true mean and would have a variance equal to the population variance for heights at Williams divided by 50. Now, the only piece of information missing concerns the exact shape of the distribution of means. We know the mean will be μ_X and the variance will be

$$\frac{\sigma^2_X}{n}$$

but exactly what will the distribution look like? That is, what probability distribution will $\overline{X}$ follow? This question illustrates a central occupation in statistical analyses. Much of statistical inference centers on discovering the distribution followed by random variables or functions of random variables. Here, the sample mean is the function of random variables whose distribution we want to discover. The answer is provided by one of the most important ("central") theorems in statistics: the *Central Limit Theorem*.

6.8.1 The Central Limit Theorem

Central Limit Theorem. If $X_1, X_2, X_3, \ldots$, constitute a simple random sample from a population with mean μ_X and variance σ^2_X, then the random variable

$$\frac{\overline{X} - \mu_X}{\sqrt{\dfrac{\sigma^2_X}{n}}}$$

has an *approximately normal distribution* with mean 0 and variance 1. The approximation improves as n increases.

We may state the theorem a little more roughly but more succinctly as *sample means are approximately normal*, meaning that the sampling distribution of $\overline{X}$ follows a normal distribution when n is large (usually $n > 30$ is sufficient). Notice that this result holds regardless of the form of the population distribution. If the sample is small, this result will still hold if the population we are sampling from is itself normal.

APPLICATION 6.5   *Dewey Beats Truman?*

A critical element in public opinion polls is that the sample be representative of the population as a whole. Otherwise, estimates from the sample may provide misleading indicators of the population's sentiment. The classic example of this was the 1948 Presidential election when the news media declared Dewey the winner on the basis of a telephone poll where phone numbers were drawn randomly. Unfortunately, in 1948 not everyone had phones, and since having a phone was correlated with income, the survey results were not representative of the population and led to the infamous gaffe.

Modern survey techniques tend to avoid such problems, but are still at risk of providing incorrect inferences if respondents systematically do not vote in the manner they report. We can examine this proposition using the results of 13 public opinion polls conducted the week before the 2000 Presidential election. The proportion of survey respondents who report that they will vote for George W. Bush represents a sample mean of a random variable that has the binomial distribution. The results of the public opinion polls, therefore, reflect 13 sample means. By the Central Limit Theorem, that sample mean is distributed approximately normally with mean equal to the true population mean, which is known from the actual election result. The polls would be considered biased if their mean were not close to the actual election result. In the 13 sets of poll results we identified, the mean percentage of decided voters who indicated they would vote for George W. Bush was 48.6%. In the actual election, 48% cast their ballots for him.

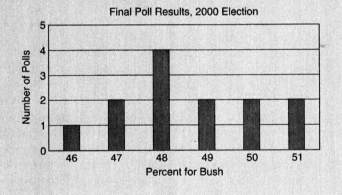

Often we will express the Central Limit Theorem simply as:

$$\overline{X} \sim N\left(\mu_X, \frac{\sigma_X^2}{n}\right)$$

In words, we read this as: "$\overline{X}$ is distributed (asymptotically) approximately normal with mean μ_X and variance $\dfrac{\sigma_X^2}{n}$."

6.9   PROBABILITY STATEMENTS ABOUT $\overline{X}$

The Central Limit Theorem tells us that

$$\overline{X} \sim N\left(\mu_X, \frac{\sigma_X^2}{n}\right)$$

As we have seen, we can standardize this random variable by subtracting its mean and dividing by its standard deviation. That is:

$$Z = \frac{\overline{X} - \mu_X}{\sqrt{\dfrac{\sigma_X^2}{n}}} = \frac{\overline{X} - \mu_X}{\dfrac{\sigma_X}{\sqrt{n}}} \sim N(0,1)$$

Thus,

$$P(a \leq \overline{X} \leq b) = P\left(\frac{a - \mu_X}{\sigma_X} \leq \frac{\overline{X} - \mu_X}{\sigma_X} \leq \frac{b - \mu_X}{\sigma_X}\right)$$

where all we did was subtract μ_X and divide by σ_X from each of $a, \overline{X}, b$. Now, notice that the newly transformed random variable

$$\frac{\overline{X} - \mu_X}{\sigma_X}$$

follows the standard normal probability distributions. Since we typically label such a variable by Z, we have:

$$P(a \leq \overline{X} \leq b) = P\left(\frac{a - \mu_X}{\sigma_X} \leq Z \leq \frac{b - \mu_X}{\sigma_X}\right)$$

Example

Suppose $\overline{X} \sim N(10,25)$. Find $P(\overline{X} \leq 5)$. To solve this, simply standardize $\overline{X}$ and look up the probabilities for the then-standardized normal random variable in Table B.1. That is:

$$P(\overline{X} \leq 5) = P\left(\frac{\overline{X} - \mu_X}{\dfrac{\sigma_X}{\sqrt{n}}} \leq \frac{5 - 10}{\sqrt{25}}\right) = P\left(Z \leq \frac{5 - 10}{5}\right) = P(Z \leq -1) = 1 - P(Z \leq 1)$$

$$1 - .8413 = .1587$$

6.10   THE CHI-SQUARED AND T DISTRIBUTIONS

Thus far we have derived the sampling distribution for the sample mean. We can similarly derive the sampling distribution for the *sample variance*. Just as the sample mean is defined analogously to the population mean, the sample variance is defined analogously to the population variance. Recall that the population variance is given by

$$\sigma_X^2 = \sum_{\text{all } X} (x_i - E(X))^2 \, P(x_i)$$

for a discrete random variable. If each outcome x_i in the population were equally likely (i.e., $P(x_i) = 1/N$), this would simplify to

$$\sigma_X^2 = \frac{1}{N} \sum_{\text{all } X} (x_i - E(X))^2$$

The *sample variance* is denoted by S_X^2 and is given by

$$S_X^2 = \frac{1}{n-1} \sum_{i=1}^{n} (x_i - \overline{X})^2$$

Notice the similarity between the definition of the sample variance and the population variance. The only notable difference that makes the analogue less than perfect is that we divide by the size of the population for the (population) variance and divide by the sample size *minus 1* for the sample variance. We will show in the next chapter that dividing by $n-1$ rather than by n has certain advantages.

Now, let's consider again the thought experiment involving sampling the heights of students at Williams College. In the thought experiment we repeatedly draw samples of 50 students and calculate the mean of the sample yielding a set of means: $\overline{X}_1, \overline{X}_2, \overline{X}_3, \ldots,$ $\overline{X}_{1000}, \ldots$. We have already seen that the means follow a normal distribution centered at the true mean μ_X with variance $\frac{\sigma_X^2}{n}$.

We could likewise calculate for each of our samples the sample variance S_X^2 yielding $(S_X^2)_1, (S_X^2)_2, (S_X^2)_3 \ldots (S_X^2)_{1000}$. Thus, the sample variance is also a random variable having a probability distribution. What distribution does it follow? To answer this we need to introduce a new probability distribution: the *chi-squared distribution*.

6.10.1   The Chi-Squared Distribution

Let $Z_1, Z_2, Z_3, \ldots, Z_n$ be n independent random variables each with a standard normal distribution. Then

$$\sum_{i=1}^{n} Z_i^2 \sim \chi_n^2$$

where χ_n^2 denotes the chi-squared distribution. Thus, if we square and sum n standard normal random variables we create a new random variable which follows a new distribution—the chi-squared distribution. The chi-squared distribution's exact shape depends on n (known in this context as its *degrees of freedom*). Now, it can be shown that

$$\frac{(n-1)S_X^2}{\sigma_X^2} \sim \chi_{n-1}^2$$

Thus the random variable formed by dividing $n-1$ times the sample statistic S_X^2 (a random variable) by the population variance follows a chi-squared distribution. While the full proof of this proposition is difficult, you might note that

$$\sum_{i=1}^{n} \left(\frac{X - \mu_X}{\sigma_X} \right)^2 = \sum_{i=1}^{n} Z_i^2 \sim \chi_n^2$$

Then, we have

$$\sum_{i=1}^{n}\left(\frac{X-\overline{X}}{\sigma_X}\right)^2 = \frac{(n-1)S_X^2}{\sigma_X^2} \sim \chi_{n-1}^2$$

Thus, replacing μ_X with $\overline{X}$ simply reduces the degrees of freedom for the chi-squared distribution to $n-1$. For the time being, we simply need to know the chi-squared distribution to develop another useful distribution—the t distribution. Later we will see how we can use the fact that

$$\frac{(n-1)S_X^2}{\sigma_X^2} \sim \chi_{n-1}^2$$

to make inferences about the population variance using information provided by a sample.

6.10.2   The *t* Distribution

Consider two independent random variables A and B. Suppose that A follows a normal distribution with a mean of 0 and a variance of 1. That is, $A \sim N(0,1)$. Suppose B follows a chi-squared distribution with v degrees of freedom. That is, $B \sim \chi_v^2$. Then, if we form a new random variable

$$\frac{A}{\sqrt{\dfrac{B}{v}}}$$

this random variable follows the t distribution with v degrees of freedom. That is,

$$\frac{A}{\sqrt{\dfrac{B}{v}}} \sim t_v$$

The graph of the t distribution is nearly identical to that of the approximately normal distribution. Both are symmetric and bell shaped. The main difference is that (for $N \leq 120$) the t distribution has more probability in the tails of the distribution. For $N > 120$ the t and standard normal distributions are virtually identical.

To see why the t distribution is useful to us, remember that we have been using the fact that

$$Z = \frac{\overline{X} - \mu_X}{\dfrac{\sigma_X}{\sqrt{n}}} \sim N(0,1)$$

Usually, however, we would not know the population standard deviation σ_X. Suppose we took the logical leap of faith and used the sample standard deviation s_X in its place. That is, we form the random variable

$$\frac{\overline{X} - \mu_X}{\frac{s_X}{\sqrt{n}}}.$$

Unfortunately, this new random variable is not standard normal but rather follows the
t distribution with $n - 1$ degrees of freedom. To see this notice that

$$\frac{\overline{X} - \mu_X}{\frac{s_X}{\sqrt{n}}} = \frac{\left.\begin{array}{c}\dfrac{\overline{X} - \mu_X}{\frac{\sigma_X}{\sqrt{n}}}\end{array}\right\} \text{which is distributed } N(0,1)}{\sqrt{\dfrac{(n-1)s^2}{(n-1)\sigma_X^2}}\Bigg\} \text{ which is distributed } \sqrt{\dfrac{\chi_{n-1}^2}{n-1}}}$$

With the random variable

$$\frac{\overline{X} - \mu_X}{\frac{s_X}{\sqrt{n}}}$$

written in this way, we can see that it is expressed in the form

$$\frac{A}{\sqrt{\dfrac{B}{n-1}}} \sim t_{n-1}$$

as above. Thus, the bottom line of the result is that the random variable

$$\frac{\overline{X} - \mu_X}{\frac{s_X}{\sqrt{N}}}$$

follows a t distribution with $N - 1$ degrees of freedom. This result will prove to be quite
useful.

6.11   PROBLEMS

1. Suppose we have observations on the variable weight (in pounds) for 10 people:

   100, 120, 210, 175, 155, 110, 160, 185, 200, 220

   a. Calculate the sample mean and sample standard deviation.
   b. Suppose the scales underreport weight by 10 pounds. What is the mean and standard deviation of the correct weight in pounds?
   c. What is the mean and standard deviation of weight in kilograms? Note: 1 kilogram equals 2.2046 pounds.

2. How many different samples of 2 observations can be drawn from a population of size 4?

3. What does it mean to say that $\overline{X}$ is a random variable? Relate this to your answer in Problem 2.

4. Suppose heights in a population are normally distributed with a mean of 68″ and variance 25″. What is the probability that a randomly selected individual will have a height between 58″ and 78″?

5. In one law school class the entering students averaged 700 on the LSAT test with a standard deviation of 40. Assuming the distribution of test scores was normal, what fraction of the class scored above 750?

6. Calculate $P(6 \le X \le 8)$ and $P(6 \le \overline{X} \le 8)$ if X is normally distributed with a mean of 7 and variance 25 and the sample size is 100. Explain intuitively why the probabilities differ.

7. Suppose X is a normally distributed random variable with mean $\mu = 200$ and standard deviation $\sigma = 20$.

   a. Sketch the probability density function of X. On the same graph, sketch the probability density function of the sample mean $\overline{X}$ from a sample of 16 observations.

   b. Calculate $P(180 \le X \le 220)$.

   c. Calculate $P(160 \le X \le 240)$.

   d. Calculate $P(195 \le X \le 205)$ for $n = 4, 10, 20, 50, 100$. Graph the calculated probabilities against n on a graph.

   e. Calculate $P(195 \le X \le 205)$ for $\sigma = 2, 4, 12, 16, 20, 30$. Graph the calculated probabilities against σ on a graph.

   f. Suppose we wanted to conduct a survey. It is desired that we produce an interval estimate of the mean that is ± 5 from μ with 99% confidence. Assume a value of $\sigma = 15$. How big should your sample be?

8. How often would the sample mean deviate from the population mean by more than:

   a. One standard deviation?

   b. Two standard deviations?

   c. Three standard deviations?

9. You are throwing a party and fill a bowl with 63 ounces of punch. Suppose the expected size of each cup of punch is 2 ounces and the standard deviation of the size of a cup of punch is ½ ounce and each cup is poured independently. You want to know the probability that the bowl will not be empty after 36 cups have been poured.

   a. Use Chebyshev's inequality to calculate an upper limit of this probability.

   b. You are not satisfied with knowing an upper limit and would like a closer approximation of the probability that the bowl will not be empty. What distribution does the Central Limit Theorem suggest would approximate the probability distribution of the number of ounces needed for 36 cups? Use this distribution to calculate the probability the bowl will not be empty.

Chapter 7

Estimation

7.1 INTRODUCTION

At several points in previous chapters, we have seen examples of population distributions that can be characterized by one or more parameters. For instance, a normal distribution can be characterized by its mean, μ_X, and variance, σ_X^2. The binomial distribution is characterized by the parameter p. The exponential distribution is completely specified by the parameter λ. Statistical analysis uses sample data to learn about some unknown characteristic of the population by estimating the parameters of a distribution. In the previous chapter, specifically, we discussed using the sample mean, $\bar{X}$, and the sample variance, s_X^2, to estimate the population mean μ_X and variance σ_X^2, respectively. In this chapter, we provide a more general analytical framework for estimating population parameters.

7.2 POINT ESTIMATION

An *estimator* is a random variable used to estimate a characteristic ("parameter") or relationship in the population. It is a mathematical function that provides a rule for combining the available data to provide an estimate of the unknown population parameter. This rule is written down before we actually gather a sample. An actual numerical value obtained from an estimator is called an *estimate*. When a single number is presented as an estimate of the population characteristic or relationship, it is known as a *point estimate*. When a range of numbers is provided, it is known as an *interval estimate*. In this chapter we will focus on point estimators. For a given population characteristic there are a virtually unlimited number of potential estimators. Thus, a key problem of estimation is choosing a "good" estimator. If we are given two estimators, we would like to be able to compare them based on some sort of criterion and choose the better of the two.

Example

Suppose a population has an unknown true mean of μ_X. Given a sample $X_1, X_2, X_3, \ldots, X_n$ from this population we could estimate μ_X using the sample mean

$$\bar{X} = \frac{1}{n} \sum_{i=1}^{n} X_i$$

Alternatively, we could take the average of the largest and smallest values observed in the sample:

$$\frac{X_{min} + X_{max}}{2}$$

Which of these two proposed estimators is better? Why?

Typically the properties used to judge between estimators are classified as *finite sample* and *asymptotic* properties. Finite sample properties are those that we can appeal to regardless of the size of the sample used in generating our estimates. Unfortunately, sometimes it is not possible to calculate the finite sample properties, which forces us to consider properties that hold only when the sample size is large. Such properties are called asymptotic properties.

APPLICATION 7.1   *How Do They Count Spotted Owls, Anyway?*

In a variety of circumstances, we need to know the size of a population that inherently cannot be counted. Examples include wildlife, the homeless, and the number of people uncounted by the U.S. Census, among others. In instances like these, one particular statistical methodology, called the capture-recapture method, provides the means to estimate the size of such populations.

Using spotted owls as an example, the approach would proceed as follows. Researchers would go out and capture a number, n_1, of spotted owls, tag them with markers indicating that they were captured, and then release them. A short time later a new set of owls, n_2, would be captured and the number that were marked from the first round, m_2, would be counted. Assuming that no migration, births, or deaths had occurred over the interval and that each owl had an equal probability of getting captured each time, one can estimate the population of owls to be

$$\hat{N} = \frac{n_1 \cdot n_2}{m_2}$$

The reason for this is that after the initial capture, the actual probability that an owl was marked is $p = n_1/N$, where N is the true, unknown population size. If the assumptions stated earlier hold, then the probability that a recaptured owl was tagged would equal p, so one estimate of p is m_2/n_2. In other words, m_2/n_2 provides an estimate of n_1/N, but since n_1 is known, $n_1 n_2/m_2$ provides an estimate of N.

Source: Manly, Bryan F. J. and Lyman L. McDonald, "Sampling Wildlife Populations," *Chance*, Vol. 9, No. 2 (Spring 1996), pp. 9–19.

7.3   FINITE SAMPLE PROPERTIES

For generality we will refer to the unknown population parameter as θ and the proposed estimator as $\hat{\theta}$. In econometrics, ^ (a "hat") is often used to indicate that a particular random variable is an estimator. Any proposed estimator will combine the sample information in some way to provide an estimate of the population characteristic. That is, $\hat{\theta} = T(X_1, X_2, X_3, \ldots, X_n)$, where T is some function of the data.

Example

For example, $\theta = \mu_X$ is estimated using the estimator

$$\hat{\theta} = \frac{1}{n} \sum_{i=1}^{n} X_i$$

Several properties would seem to be desirable in an estimator, but a critical requirement would seem to be that the estimator produces estimates close to the true (unknown) population parameter.

7.3.1   Unbiasedness

An estimator is said to be *unbiased* if the expected value of the estimator is equal to the true population parameter being estimated. More formally, an estimator is unbiased if $E(\hat{\theta}) = \theta$. The difference between the expected value and the true value is known as the *bias* of the estimator: $Bias = E(\hat{\theta}) - \theta$. To say an estimator is unbiased is simply to say that the sampling distribution of the estimator is centered at the true population parameter. That is, if you repeatedly drew samples from the population and used your estimator to estimate the population parameter, the estimates you generate would, on average, be correct. Of course, your estimates could sometimes be too high and sometimes too low, but on average you would be correct.

Examples

1. Suppose we have a random sample $X_1, X_2, X_3, \ldots, X_n$ from a population with a mean of μ_X. Since each observation is independently drawn from this population, we know that $X_i \sim N(\mu_X, \sigma^2_X)$. Now, consider two proposed estimators:

$$\hat{\theta}_1 = \frac{X_1 + X_2}{2}$$

and

$$\hat{\theta}_2 = \frac{X_1 + 2X_2}{3}.$$

To see if these estimators are unbiased we must take their expected value and see if it is equal to the population parameter—in this case μ_X. Notice that

$$E(\hat{\theta}_1) = E\left(\frac{X_1 + X_2}{2}\right) = \frac{E(X_1) + E(X_2)}{2} = \frac{\mu_X + \mu_X}{2} = \mu_X$$

Thus, the first estimator is unbiased. Similarly, it is easily seen that $E(\hat{\theta}_2) = \mu_X$ and so the second estimator is also unbiased. Thus, if we drew repeated samples of size n from the population and, for each sample, generated estimates using the two estimators $\hat{\theta}_1$ and $\hat{\theta}_2$, the average of the many estimates calculated would equal the population mean μ_X. This indicates the important fact that there are often a virtually unlimited number of unbiased estimators—some doubtless better than others. Thus, we will need to have additional criteria that define "good" estimators to select from a set of unbiased estimators.

2. In the previous chapter we defined the sample estimator of the population variance as

$$s_X^2 = \frac{1}{n-1} \sum_{i=1}^{n} (X_i - \overline{X})^2.$$

We simply asserted that dividing by $n-1$ was desirable. The reason we divide by $n-1$ instead of n is that it produces an unbiased estimator of the population variance. To see this we will show that the alternative estimator

$$s_n^2 = \frac{1}{n} \sum_{i=1}^{n} (X_i - \overline{X})^2$$

is biased.

Proof.
$$E(s_n^2) = E\left(\frac{1}{n} \sum_{i=1}^{n} (X_i - \overline{X})^2 \right)$$

$$= \frac{1}{n} E\left(\sum_{i=1}^{n} (X_i - \overline{X})^2 \right) = \frac{1}{n} E\left(\sum_{i=1}^{n} X_i^2 - \sum_{i=1}^{n} \overline{X}^2 \right)$$

$$= E(X^2) - E(\overline{X}^2)$$

From here, recall from Chapter 4 that $\text{var}(X) = E(X^2) - E(X)^2$. Applying this to both terms and recognizing that

$$\text{var}(\overline{X}) = \frac{\text{var}(X)}{n}$$

yields

$$= \{\text{var}(X) + E(X)^2\} - \left\{ \frac{\text{var}(X)}{n} + E(X)^2 \right\}$$

$$= \frac{n-1}{n} \text{var}(X)$$

Notice that the bias associated with this estimator, equal to

$$\frac{n-1}{n}$$

becomes smaller as n gets larger. Also notice that the estimator we proposed earlier,

$$E(s_X^2) = E\left(\frac{n}{n-1} s_n^2\right) = \text{var}(X)$$

is unbiased.

7.3.2 Efficiency

If two estimators are both unbiased, having their sampling distribution centered at the true population value, then we know they are both going to give the correct result on average. They may, however, have sampling distributions with very different variances. Thus, we might choose the estimator whose estimates will be more closely concentrated around the population value. More generally, we say that one estimator is more *efficient* than another if it has a smaller sampling variance. If $\text{var}(\hat{\theta}_1) < \text{var}(\hat{\theta}_2)$, then $\hat{\theta}_1$ estimates θ more efficiently than $\hat{\theta}_2$.

Example

Consider our estimators

$$\hat{\theta}_1 = \frac{X_1 + X_2}{2}$$

and

$$\hat{\theta}_2 = \frac{X_1 + 2X_2}{3}$$

from above. To see which is more efficient, we must calculate their variances. We see that

$$\text{var}(\hat{\theta}_1) = \text{var}\left(\frac{X_1 + X_2}{2}\right) = \frac{1}{4}\left(\text{var}(X_1) + \text{var}(X_2)\right) = \frac{1}{4}\left(\sigma_X^2 + \sigma_X^2\right) = \frac{\sigma_X^2}{2}$$

Similarly,

$$\text{var}(\hat{\theta}_2) = \text{var}\left(\frac{X_1 + 2X_2}{3}\right) = \frac{1}{9}\left(\text{var}(X_1) + 4\,\text{var}(X_2)\right)\frac{1}{9}\left(\sigma_X^2 + 4\sigma_X^2\right) = \frac{5\sigma_X^2}{9}$$

Thus, $\text{var}(\hat{\theta}_1) < \text{var}(\hat{\theta}_2)$, so $\hat{\theta}_1$ is a more efficient estimator of θ than $\hat{\theta}_2$.

Remember that in practice we might know that the sampling distribution for a particular estimator follows a certain probability distribution (e.g., normal) and is centered at the true population parameter, but *we do not know the actual value of the parameter.* While conceptually we can draw repeated samples, in practice we often draw only one sample. Thus, we will likely only observe one estimate drawn from this distribution. We won't know for sure if that estimate is dead on target or is off in one of the tails of the sampling distribution—though we do know it is more likely to be near the center than out in the tails. The smaller the sampling variance is for the estimator, however, the more likely it is that we are close to our target. That is, the odds are higher of coming up with an estimate close to the population parameter.

7.3.3 Mean Squared Error

The lesson of the above discussion on efficiency and bias is that when picking between two unbiased estimators it makes sense to choose the one with the smaller sampling variance. Doing so increases the odds we will generate estimates close to the true population value. If, however, we are confronted with two estimators, one that is unbiased (desirable) but has a large sampling variance (undesirable) and one that is biased (undesirable) but has a small sampling variance (desirable), which should we choose? The unbiased estimator will, on average, give us the correct answer. There is, however, a significant chance that any given estimate will deviate considerably from the population parameter. The biased estimator with the smaller variance will, on average, gives us the wrong answer but might tend to provide estimates closer to the true value. This seems to imply a possible tradeoff of sorts between bias and efficiency. There is no hard-and-fast way to choose in this context, but a reasonable approach entails thinking about what costs are associated with mistakes of different sizes. That is, we must think about the sorts of decisions we are going to try to answer using our point estimate. Perhaps small errors don't present a problem, but large errors do. In this case it might make sense to choose the biased estimator with the smaller variance. Perhaps estimates that are too high incur large costs while estimates that are too low do not. In this case you might pick the estimator with the smaller likelihood of generating estimates that are too high.

We can formalize some of these ideas by defining a *loss function* that shows explicitly the loss (costs) associated with deviations between θ and $\hat{\theta}$. Formally, let $L(\hat{\theta}, \theta)$ be a function measuring the loss we incur when the true population parameter is θ and we estimate it to be $\hat{\theta}$. The most commonly used loss function is the *mean squared error (MSE)* loss function, where $MSE = E(\theta - \hat{\theta})^2$. Thus, the loss is assumed to be the expectation of the square of the deviation between the truth and the estimate. This loss function implicitly assumes that positive and negative errors are equivalent. Also, it assumes the larger the error the larger the loss. It can be shown that we can decompose the mean squared error such that $MSE = \text{var}(\hat{\theta}) + Bias^2$. Thus, it has the virtue of encompassing both the properties of efficiency and bias. Notice, however, that for two unbiased estimators the MSE criterion simply amounts to choosing the more efficient estimator.

Example

It can be shown that while the sample estimator

$$s_X^2 = \frac{1}{n-1} \sum_{i=1}^{n} (X_i - \bar{X})^2$$

is an unbiased estimator of the population variance, it has a higher MSE than the biased estimator

$$s_n^2 = \frac{1}{n} \sum_{i=1}^{n} (X_i - \bar{X})^2$$

7.4   ASYMPTOTIC PROPERTIES

Finite sample properties relate to an estimator's sampling distribution. They do not depend in any way on the sample size. If an estimator is unbiased, it is unbiased regardless of the size of the sample drawn. Thus, the relative merits (e.g., bias, efficiency) of two estimators can be compared without reference to the number of observations used in generating estimates. Sometimes, however, it is next to impossible (or is impossible) to find an estimator possessing these properties in a finite sample. The sampling distribution of the estimator may change as the sample size changes. For this reason, econometricians often consider the sampling distribution associated with the competing estimators when the sample size is large. This sampling distribution is referred to as the *limiting* or *asymptotic* distribution. While we may not be able to say much about the properties of an estimator in a small sample, it is often possible to characterize the sampling distribution of the estimators for very large samples. Therefore, properties of this sort are called large sample or *asymptotic* properties. They can be shown to hold only for very large samples. For example, the bias of an estimator may depend on the size of the sample used. If the bias associated with such an estimator approaches zero as the sample size grows large, then we say the estimator is *asymptotically unbiased*. Intuitively, we can conceptualize a series of estimators arrayed based on the size of the sample used to construct the estimator, $\{T_1(X_1), T_2(X_1, X_2), T_3(X_1, X_2, X_3), \ldots, T_n(X_1, X_2, X_3, \ldots, X_n)\}$, where T_k is the estimator based on a sample of size k. Each estimator in this series can have its own sampling distribution. An estimator is asymptotically unbiased if the expected value of T_k gets closer and closer to the population parameter as k approaches infinity. More formally, an estimator $\hat{\theta}_n$ is said to be *asymptotically unbiased* if

$$\lim_{n \to \infty} E(\hat{\theta}_n) = \theta$$

That is, as n grows large the expectation of the estimator $\hat{\theta}_n$ converges to the true value θ.

Another desirable asymptotic property of an estimator is called *consistency*. An estimator is said to be *consistent* if

$$\lim_{n \to \infty} P(|\hat{\theta}_n - \theta| > \varepsilon) = 0$$

That is, the probability that $\hat{\theta}$ deviates from the population parameter, θ, by more than some arbitrarily small value ε approaches zero as the sample size approaches infinity. When $\hat{\theta}$ converges in probability to θ we can express it more simply as $p \lim \hat{\theta}_n = \theta$, where $p \lim$ indicates the *probability limit*. Graphically, this is illustrated by the fact that the sampling distribution of $\hat{\theta}$ collapses to the population parameter θ as the sample size approaches infinity. Finally, an estimator is referred to as *asymptotically efficient* if it converges to the population parameter more quickly than any other estimator.

7.5   METHODS OF FINDING ESTIMATORS

Now that we have specified some characteristics of good estimators, we turn to the problem of actually finding good estimators. We will develop three approaches to finding estimators: the *method of moments*, the *method of maximum likelihood*, and the *method of least squares*.

7.5.1 Method of Moments

The method of moments (MOM) is a relatively simple estimation procedure that allows us to find consistent estimators for the population parameters. The method seeks to equate the moments (mean, variance, etc., as defined in Chapter 4) implied by a statistical model of the population distribution with the actual moments observed in the sample. Thus, it treats the sample as if it were a representation—in miniature—of the population and assumes that the relations holding in the population will also hold in the sample. For example, suppose the population distribution is characterized as having a density function $f(x|\theta)$, where θ is the unknown population parameter we are interested in estimating. Notice that we write the distribution as being conditional upon θ since the actual shape of the distribution will depend on what value θ assumes. Then, we know that

$$E[X] = \int_{-\infty}^{\infty} xf(x|\theta)dx$$

This, in turn, will be a function of θ (we'll show this with an example shortly). Thus, $E[X] = g(\theta)$ with the population moment $E[X]$ depending on the unknown parameter θ. Inverting this, we have $\theta = g^{-1}(E[X])$. Replacing the unknown population moment $E[X]$ with its sample counterpart $\bar{X}$ yields our estimator: $\hat{\theta} = g^{-1}(\bar{X})$. Notice that we could have started with the sample variance, found $\text{var}(X) = h(\theta)$, and proceeded in a similar fashion. Thus, the method of moments doesn't necessarily yield a unique estimator. In practice, this is useful since the different estimators should yield similar results if the assumptions made concerning the population distribution are correct.

MOM estimators are often referred to as *analog estimators* as they proceed, in a sense, by analogy. The frequency distribution of the data is treated as if it were the population and estimators are derived accordingly. For example, if the population moment we are interested in is the population mean, we estimate it with the sample mean. We would use the sample maximum to estimate the population maximum. We would use the sample correlation to estimate the correlation in the population. As such, the MOM provides estimators that are typically quite intuitive. Such estimators are generally consistent in random sampling.

Example

Suppose we believe the population distribution follows a uniform distribution with unknown parameter θ. That is,

$$f(X) = \frac{1}{\theta} \text{ for } 0 \le X \le \theta$$
$$= 0 \text{ otherwise}$$

You gather a random sample $X_1, X_2, X_3, \ldots, X_n$ and the problem facing you is how to use this sample information to form an estimate of the unknown population parameter θ. Using the method of moments, we first find the expected value of the population distribution,

$$E(X) = \int_0^{\theta} x \frac{1}{\theta} dx = \frac{\theta}{2}$$

for example, $E(X) = g(X)$ where $g(X) = \dfrac{\theta}{2}$.

Thus, $\theta = 2E(X)$ (i.e., $\theta = g^{-1}(E(X))$). This is the relationship that holds in the population. Using the sample mean in place of the population expected value yields a method of moments estimator: $\hat{\theta} = 2\overline{X}$. For practice, try finding another MOM estimator implied by the population variance for this distribution.

7.5.2 Method of Maximum Likelihood

The method of maximum likelihood draws on the simple notion that the data we observe are more likely to be associated with some distributions than with others. Typically, we start by assuming our data is drawn from some population distribution (e.g., normal) with unknown parameter(s) θ. We then select our estimate of θ so as to maximize the likelihood of seeing the sample we actually saw. For example, suppose we assume our data is drawn from a normal distribution. We don't, however, know the population mean and variance for the distribution. This is illustrated in Figure 7.1.

On the horizontal axis we show the actual data drawn in the sample. It should be clear that these data are more likely to arise if the population distribution is as characterized by the distribution on the left. In practice, rather than comparing just two normal distributions we could try out all possible normal distributions and find which one is most likely to give rise to the data we observed. This would be the maximum likelihood estimator(s) (MLEs) of the population parameter(s). More formally, we can think of observing a random sample $X_1, X_2, X_3, \ldots, X_n$ drawn from a distribution $f(X|\theta)$ with unknown parameter(s) θ. The likelihood of seeing the sample we saw is the joint density $f(x_1, x_2, x_3, \ldots, x_n|\theta)$, which, if the observations are independent, can be written as $f(x_1|\theta)\,f(x_2|\theta)\ldots f(x_n|\theta)$. This is known as the *likelihood function*. We then choose θ so as to maximize the probablility of seeing the sample we saw—that is, the value of θ that maximizes the likelihood function. The solution to this problem $\hat{\theta}$ is called the maximum likelihood estimator of θ. In practice we often maximize the logarithm of the likelihood function. This often greatly simplifies the mechanics of the maximization problem. Thus, if $L(\theta) = f(x_1|\theta)f(x_2|\theta)\ldots f(x_n|\theta)$ is the likelihood function, we maximize $L(\theta) = \ln f(x_1|\theta) + \ln f(x_2|\theta) \ldots \ln f(x_n|\theta)$ with respect to θ.

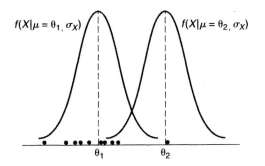

Figure 7.1 Maximum likelihood estimation.

Example

Suppose our data can be characterized as independent Bernoulli trials (defined in Chapter 3) with $P(X = 1) = \theta$ and $P(X = 0) = 1 - \theta$. We can write this using the density function $f(x_i|\theta) = \theta^{x_i}(1 - \theta)^{1-x_i}$. For a random sample $X_1, X_2, X_3, \ldots, X_n$ the joint density function would be

$$L(\theta) = f(x_1|\theta) f(x_2|\theta) \ldots f(x_n|\theta)$$
$$= \theta^{x_1} (1 - \theta)^{1-x_1} \theta^{x_2} (1 - \theta)^{1-x_2} \ldots \theta^{x_n} (1 - \theta)^{1-x_n}$$
$$= \prod_{i=1}^{n} \theta^{x_i} (1 - \theta)^{1-x_i}$$

where

$$\prod_{i=1}^{n} a_i = a_1 a_2 \ldots a_n$$

is the *product operator*.

Taking logarithms we have:

$$\ln L(\theta) = x_1 \ln \theta + (1 - x_1) \ln(1 - \theta) + x_2 \ln \theta + (1 - x_2) \ln(1 - \theta) + \ldots +$$
$$x_n \ln \theta + (1 - x_n) \ln(1 - \theta)$$
$$= \sum_{i=1}^{n} [x_i \ln \theta + (1 - x_i) \ln(1 - \theta)]$$

Maximizing the log of the likelihood function with respect to θ yields:

$$\frac{\partial \ln L(\theta)}{\partial \theta} = \sum_{i=1}^{n} x_i \frac{1}{\theta} - (1 - x_i) \frac{1}{1 - \theta} = 0$$

$$\Rightarrow (1 - \theta) \sum_{i=1}^{n} x_i = \theta \sum_{i=1}^{n} (1 - x_i)$$

The MLE $\hat{\theta}$ is the value of θ achieving this maximum. It is

$$\hat{\theta} = \frac{1}{n} \sum_{i=1}^{n} x_i$$

or the mean! Thus, the sample fraction of "successes" (i.e., $x_i = 1$) is the best estimate of the population $P(x_i = 1)$. This is pretty much what we might have expected—the population proportion is estimated by the sample proportion. More complex problems are not quite so transparent. We will see some examples of this later in the book.

The maximum likelihood estimator has several desirable properties. First, if the MLE is unbiased, then it is the most efficient unbiased estimator possible. Clearly this is a desirable property, since if we can show the estimator is unbiased we know it is the best. We need not search and compare it against other unbiased estimators. Second, almost all MLEs are consistent. Finally, most MLEs follow a normal distribution when the sample size is large (i.e., they are *asymptotically normal*).

7.5.3 Method of Least Squares

The method of least squares (MLS), while not as generally applicable as the previous two estimation methods, is extremely useful for generating estimates in certain situations. In

APPLICATION 7.2   *Who Knew?*

The capture-recapture method used to estimate difficult-to-count populations that we described in the preceding box actually can be derived as both a maximum likelihood estimator (MLE) and method of moments (MOM) estimator. To see this, first note that the process of marking, say, spotted owls generates a Bernoulli random variable, since with some probability p an individual owl will be marked and with probability $(1 - p)$ it will not. The Bernoulli distribution takes the form $P(x) = p^x(1 - p)^{1-x}$ for $x = 0, 1$. If n_1 owls are marked out of an (unknown) population of N owls, then this distribution can be restated as:

x_i	$P(x_i)$
1 (marked)	$p = n_1/N$
0 (not marked)	$1 - p = 1 - n_1/N$

Now, consider the recaptured sample of size n_2 that we want to use to estimate the proportion of marked owls in the entire population, p. As we saw earlier in this chapter, the maximum likelihood estimator of p is simply the sample proportion

$$\hat{p} = \frac{\sum_{i=1}^{n} x_i}{n_2}$$

Since

$$\sum_{i=1}^{n} x_i$$

is the number of marked owls in the sample, m_2, we have

$$\hat{p} = \frac{m_2}{n_2}$$

From the Bernoulli distribution above, if we knew p, we would also know N since $N = n_1/p$. However, if we substitute in the MLE for p, we would have an MLE for N;

$$\hat{N}_{\text{MLE}} = \frac{n_1}{\hat{p}} = \frac{n_1 \cdot n_2}{m_1}$$

which is the formula we described in the preceding box.

Similarly, we could derive the same estimator using a method of moments approach. In this case we have $E(X) = p$. Using the sample mean from the recaptured sample in place of the population mean we have.

$$\overline{X} = \frac{\sum_{i=1}^{n} x_i}{n_2} = \frac{m_2}{n_2} = \hat{p}.$$

From the property of the Bernoulli distribution that $N = n_1/p$ and substituting the MOM estimator, p for $\hat{p}$, yields the MOM estimator for N of

$$\hat{N}_{\text{MOM}} = \frac{n_1}{\hat{p}} = \frac{n_1 \cdot n_2}{m_1}$$

So, both the MLE and the MOM estimators give us the same estimator in the context of the capture-recapture approach.

particular, it is widely used when estimating parameters for linear models—a topic we will be much concerned with in future chapters.

For example, suppose we have a random sample, $Y_1, Y_2, Y_3, \ldots Y_n$, drawn from a population with mean μ_Y and var$(Y) = \sigma_Y^2$. We want to use our sample data to form an estimate $\hat{\mu}_Y$ of the population mean. First, notice that we can express each sample observation using a simple linear model: $Y_i = \mu_Y + \varepsilon_i$ where $E(\varepsilon_i) = 0$ and var$(\varepsilon_i) = \sigma_Y^2$. Next, notice that any sample observation, y_i, provides an unbiased estimator of the population mean since $E(Y_i) = \mu_Y$. After gathering the sample observations, the error associated with each of the n possible estimates is $e_i = y_i - \mu_Y$; $i = 1 \ldots n$. The MLS selects the single best estimator by minimizing the sum of the squared errors for the whole sample. That is, the least squares estimator $\hat{\mu}_Y$ is found by choosing the $\hat{\mu}_Y$ that minimizes the sum of squared errors

$$\sum_{i=1}^{n} e_i^2 = \sum_{i=1}^{n} (y_i - \mu_Y)^2$$

—hence its name "least squares." Defining the *sum of squared errors* as *SSE* and taking the derivative with respect to μ_Y, we have:

$$\frac{dSSE}{d\mu_Y} = \frac{d \sum_{i=1}^{n} (y_i - \mu_Y)^2}{d\mu_Y} = -2 \sum_{i=1}^{n} (y_i - \hat{\mu}_Y) = 0$$

$$\Rightarrow \sum_{i=1}^{n} y_i = n\hat{\mu}_Y$$

$$\Rightarrow \hat{\mu}_Y = \frac{\sum_{i=1}^{n} y_i}{n}$$

That is, the sample mean is the least squares estimator in this example. While we might have guessed the outcome in this simple context, we will see in future chapters how useful the method of least squares is in more complicated situations.

7.6 PROBLEMS

1. Consider the following probability density function for the random variable x:

$$f(x_i) = \theta e^{-\theta x_i}; \, x_i > 0$$

   a. Suppose a random sample of 5 observations on x yields data: 1, .8, 1.3, 1.6, 2. What is the maximum likelihood estimate for θ?

   b. Find the maximum likelihood estimator (MLE) for θ.

   c. Is the MLE always the best choice for an estimator?

   d. Outline how you would find a method of moments (MOM) estimator.

2. Suppose $f(x) = (\alpha + 1)x^{\alpha}$ for $0 \leq x \leq 1$.

   a. Find a MOM estimator for α.

   b. Suppose a random sample of 5 observations on x yields data: 1, 4, 2, 7, 3. What is the MOM estimate for α?

3. What is the MLE for the mean of a normal distribution whose variance is known to be 2?

4. Suppose X is distributed uniformly with

$$f(x) = \frac{1}{b}; \ 0 \leq x \leq b.$$

   a. Find a MOM estimator for b.

   b. Find an MLE for b.

5. Show that $MSE = \text{var}(\hat{\theta}) + Bias^2$.

6. "Unbiased estimators are always preferred to biased estimators." Comment.

7. Which of the following estimators for the mean of a distribution is more efficient:

   (a) $\dfrac{4x_1 + 12x_2 + 3x_3}{19}$ or (b) $\dfrac{x_1 + x_2 + x_3}{3}$?

8. You see a random sample of size n from a population which is described as $Y_i = \beta + \varepsilon_i$ with $P(\varepsilon_i = 1) = P(\varepsilon_i = -1) = 1/2$.

   a. Show that

$$\bar{Y} = \frac{1}{n}\sum_{i=1}^{n} Y_i$$

   is an unbiased estimator of β.

   b. Suppose that you know that $\beta = 0$ or $\beta = 2$, but you don't know which. Consider the following estimator:

$$\hat{\beta} = 0 \text{ if any } Y_i = -1$$
$$\hat{\beta} = 2 \text{ if any } Y_i = 3, \text{ and}$$
$$\hat{\beta} = \bar{Y} \text{ otherwise}$$

Is $\hat{\beta}$ a better estimator than $\bar{Y}$? Why or why not?

Chapter 8

Interval Estimation
and Hypothesis Testing

8.1 INTRODUCTION

In the previous chapter we discussed the problem of generating a single numerical (point) estimate of an unknown population parameter. In this chapter we consider the problem of providing a numerical range within which we have some degree of certainty the true population parameter lies. In addition, we consider a method for deciding whether certain statements (or hypotheses) about the value of a population parameter are plausible in light of the sample data.

8.2 INTERVAL ESTIMATION

8.2.1 Interval Estimation of the Population Mean

Basic Idea and Notation

An *interval estimate* of the population mean μ_X consists of two bounds within which we expect μ_X to reside. That is, $LB \leq \mu_X \leq UB$, where LB and UB are the lower and upper bounds, respectively. The probability that μ_X lies within the provided interval estimate is called the *confidence coefficient* and is denoted by $1 - \alpha$. We call α the *significance level*. For a specified α we refer to the interval $LB \leq \mu_X \leq UB$ as a $100(1 - \alpha)\%$ *confidence interval*.

Example

Suppose $\alpha = .05$. Then, $1 - \alpha = .95$ or 95%. We can derive an interval within which 95 times out of 100 the true population mean μ_X will reside, $P(LB \leq \mu_X \leq UB) = 1 - \alpha = .95$.

Derivation of Confidence Interval for Population Mean

We want to construct an interval such that $P(LB \leq \mu_X \leq UB) = 1 - \alpha$. That is, we want to be $100(1 - \alpha)\%$ confident that the population mean lies between the two bounds. Now, from our earlier discussion of the sampling distribution of the sample mean, we know that if either (1) the sample size is large or (2) the population is normal then

$$\overline{X} \sim N\left(\mu_X, \frac{\sigma_X^2}{n}\right)$$

Furthermore, if we standardize we have

$$Z = \frac{\overline{X} - \mu_X}{\frac{\sigma_X}{\sqrt{n}}} \sim N(0,1)$$

Define $z_{1-\alpha/2}$ to be the value of Z for which $F(z_{1-\alpha/2}) = 1 - \alpha/2$, where F is the distribution function for the standard normal distribution. Thus, $z_{1-\alpha/2}$ is the value of Z with $1 - \alpha/2$ probability to its left. Since the standard normal distribution is symmetric, the probability of being above a particular value is equal to the probability of being below the negative of that value. In other words, $z_{\alpha/2} = -z_{1-\alpha/2}$. This is most easily seen with a diagram (see the figure below).

Example

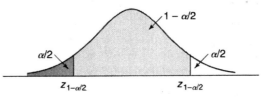

If we choose α to be .05, then $1 - \alpha/2 = .975$. Then, the value of Z with .975 probability to its left is 1.96. Thus, $z_{.975} = 1.96$ (see Table B.1), so that the probability of Z being below the number 1.96 is 97.5%. Notice that the probability of Z being below 1.96 is .975. Thus, the probability of Z being above 1.96 is $1 - .975 = .025$. Similarly, the probability of Z being below -1.96 is .025.

Now, continuing with the derivation, since

$$Z = \frac{\overline{X} - \mu_X}{\frac{\sigma_X}{\sqrt{n}}} \sim N(0,1)$$

we have the observation that

$$P(-z_{1-\alpha/2} \leq Z \leq z_{1-\alpha/2}) = 1 - \alpha$$

$$\Rightarrow P\left(-z_{1-\alpha/2} \leq \frac{\overline{X} - \mu_X}{\dfrac{\sigma_X}{\sqrt{n}}} \leq z_{1-\alpha/2}\right) = 1 - \alpha$$

Rearranging this expression by solving in terms of μ_X yields

$$P\left(\overline{X} - z_{1-\alpha/2}\frac{\sigma_X}{\sqrt{n}} \leq \mu_X \leq \overline{X} + z_{1-\alpha/2}\frac{\sigma_X}{\sqrt{n}}\right) = 1 - \alpha$$

which is our $100(1 - \alpha)\%$ confidence interval for the population mean. Thus, we are $100(1 - \alpha)\%$ that μ_X lies in the given interval. Equivalently, we can say with $100(1 - \alpha)\%$ confidence that the population mean μ_X is between the sample mean plus or minus $z_{1-\alpha/2}$ standard deviations of the sample mean.

Example

A 95% confidence interval around the sample mean may be expressed as

$$P\left(\overline{X} - 1.96\frac{\sigma_X}{\sqrt{n}} \leq \mu_X \leq \overline{X} + 1.96\frac{\sigma_X}{\sqrt{n}}\right) = 0.95$$

In other words, 95% of the time the true mean of the distribution will lie almost 2 (actually 1.96) standard deviations above or below the sample mean.

Interpreting the Confidence Interval

To precisely interpret the meaning of the $100(1 - \alpha)\%$ confidence interval consider the following thought experiment. Suppose we repeatedly draw a large number of samples of size n from a population that has a mean of μ_X. For each sample we generate the lower and upper bounds

$$\left(\overline{X} - z_{1-\alpha/2}\frac{\sigma_X}{\sqrt{n}}, \overline{X} + z_{1-\alpha/2}\frac{\sigma_X}{\sqrt{n}}\right)$$

The frequentist interpretation of this confidence interval indicates that the true population mean μ_X will lie within the calculated bounds in $100(1 - \alpha)\%$ of the samples.

Example

Suppose we repeatedly drew samples from a distribution with true population mean μ_X. For each of these samples, suppose we estimated the sample mean and constructed 95% confidence intervals around the sample mean. In 95% of these samples, the calculated confidence interval around the sample mean would include the true population mean.

One-Sided Confidence Intervals: Upper Bound

Forming a one-sided confidence interval is a straightforward extension of the two-sided confidence interval we just described. For example, suppose we wanted an upper bound only. Then, since

$$P(-\infty \leq Z \leq z_{1-\alpha}) = 1 - \alpha$$

$$\Rightarrow P\left(-\infty \leq \frac{\overline{X} - \mu_X}{\frac{\sigma_X}{\sqrt{n}}} \leq z_{1-\alpha}\right) = 1 - \alpha$$

we can solve for μ_X, yielding

$$P\left(-\infty \leq \mu_X \leq \overline{X} + z_{1-\alpha}\frac{\sigma_X}{\sqrt{n}}\right) = 1 - \alpha$$

Thus, we are $100(1 - \alpha)\%$ confident that μ_X is below the upper bound

$$\overline{X} + z_{1-\alpha}\frac{\sigma_X}{\sqrt{n}}$$

One-Sided Confidence Intervals: Lower Bound

To form a lower bound we note that

$$P(-z_{1-\alpha} \leq Z \leq \infty) = 1 - \alpha$$

$$\Rightarrow P\left(-z_{1-\alpha} \leq \frac{\overline{X} - \mu_X}{\frac{\sigma_X}{\sqrt{n}}} \leq \infty\right) = 1 - \alpha$$

Solving this for μ_X yields the lower-bound interval

$$P\left(\overline{X} - z_{1-\alpha}\frac{\sigma_X}{\sqrt{n}} \leq \mu_X \leq \infty\right) = 1 - \alpha$$

Examples

A 95% confidence interval for a population mean with only an upper bound is

$$P\left(-\infty \leq \mu_X \leq \overline{X} + 1.645\frac{\sigma_X}{\sqrt{n}}\right) = .95$$

Similarly, a 95% confidence interval for a population mean with only a lower bound is

$$P\left(\overline{X} - 1.645\frac{\sigma_X}{\sqrt{n}} \leq \mu_X \leq \infty\right) = .95$$

In other words, 95% of the time, the true sample mean is below the level set by 1.645 standard deviations above the mean and 95% of the time it is above the level indicated by 1.645 standard deviations below the mean.

One Minor Complication

The above derivation of the confidence interval for the population mean rested on the initial fact that (for large n, or X's normal)

$$\overline{X} \sim N\left(\mu_X, \frac{\sigma_X^2}{n}\right)$$

which, in turn, implied that

$$Z = \frac{\overline{X} - \mu_X}{\dfrac{\sigma}{\sqrt{n}}} \sim N(0,1)$$

The derivation did no more than exploit this observation. Often, however, we don't know the population standard deviation σ_X^2 and must estimate it with s_X^2. Then, as we have seen, if the population is normal but n is small,

$$\frac{\overline{X} - \mu_X}{\dfrac{s_X}{\sqrt{n}}} \sim t_{n-1}$$

The derivation then flows exactly as before:

$$P\left(- t_{n-1,1-\alpha/2} \leq \frac{\overline{X} - \mu_X}{\dfrac{s_X}{\sqrt{n}}} \leq t_{n-1,1-\alpha/2}\right) = 1 - \alpha$$

Solving this in terms of μ_X yields

$$P\left(\overline{X} - t_{n-1,1-\alpha/2} \frac{s_X}{\sqrt{n}} \leq \mu_X \leq \overline{X} + t_{n-1,1-\alpha/2} \frac{s_X}{\sqrt{n}}\right) = 1 - \alpha$$

In practice, if $n \geq 120$ $t_{n-1,1-\alpha/2} = Z_{1-\alpha/2}$ (see Table B.2 to calculate probabilities for the t distribution) and so you can use either the t or Z distributions. If, however, the sample is small and we don't know the population is normal, then we must use the t distribution.

Summary: Confidence Interval for the Population Mean

The appropriate confidence for the population mean for a given set of assumptions is summarized in Table 8.1.

Table 8.1

Assumption	$100(1 - \alpha)\%$ Confidence interval (two-sided)
n large and σ_X^2 known, or population normal and σ_X^2 known.	$P\left(\overline{X} - z_{1-\alpha/2}\, \dfrac{\sigma_X}{\sqrt{n}} \leq \mu_X \leq \overline{X} + z_{1-\alpha/2}\, \dfrac{\sigma_X}{\sqrt{n}} \right) = 1 - \alpha$
n large and σ_X^2 unknown	$P\left(\overline{X} - z_{1-\alpha/2}\, \dfrac{s_X}{\sqrt{n}} \leq \mu_X \leq \overline{X} + z_{1-\alpha/2}\, \dfrac{s_X}{\sqrt{n}} \right) = 1 - \alpha$
n small, population normal, and σ_X^2 unknown	$P\left(\overline{X} - t_{n-1,1-\alpha/2}\, \dfrac{s_X}{\sqrt{n}} \leq \mu_X \leq \overline{X} + t_{n-1,1-\alpha/2}\, \dfrac{s_X}{\sqrt{n}} \right) = 1 - \alpha$

8.2.2 Interval Estimation of Difference Between Means

Suppose we want to form a confidence interval for the difference in the means of two independent random variables X and Y. Then, if

$$\overline{X} \sim N\left(\mu_X, \frac{\sigma_X^2}{n_X} \right)$$

and

$$\overline{Y} \sim N\left(\mu_Y, \frac{\sigma_y^2}{n_Y} \right)$$

and X and Y are independent then the difference

$$\overline{X} - \overline{Y} \sim N\left(\mu_X - \mu_Y, \frac{\sigma_X^2}{n_X} + \frac{\sigma_y^2}{n_Y} \right)$$

Then, the appropriate confidence interval is given by

$$P\left(\overline{X} - \overline{Y} - \sqrt{\frac{\sigma_X^2}{n_X} + \frac{\sigma_Y^2}{n_Y}}\, z_{1-\alpha/2} \leq \mu_X - \mu_y \leq \overline{X} - \overline{Y} + \sqrt{\frac{\sigma_X^2}{n_X} + \frac{\sigma_Y^2}{n_Y}}\, z_{1-\alpha/2} \right) = 1 - \alpha$$

8.2.3 Interval Estimation of a Population Proportion

Suppose we have a simple random sample $X_1, X_2, X_3, \ldots, X_n$ where each X_i takes on the value 0 or 1 with probabilities $1 - \pi$ and π, respectively. Recall from the properties of Bernoulli trials and the binomial distribution, $E(X_i) = \pi$ and $\mathrm{var}(X_i) = \pi(1 - \pi)$. The sample proportion is given by

$$\hat{\pi} = \frac{1}{n} \sum_{i=1}^{n} x_i$$

You can easily show that $E(\hat{\pi}) = \pi$ (i.e., the sample proportion is an unbiased estimator of the population proportion). You can also show

$$\mathrm{var}(\hat{\pi}) = \frac{\pi(1 - \pi)}{n}$$

Then, for large n, the sample proportion is approximately normally distributed so that

$$\hat{\pi} \sim N\left(\pi, \frac{\pi(1 - \pi)}{n}\right)$$

We can then derive confidence intervals just as we did for the sample mean. That is,

$$P\left(\hat{\pi} - z_{1-\alpha/2}\sqrt{\frac{\hat{\pi}(1 - \hat{\pi})}{n}} \leq \pi \leq \hat{\pi} + z_{1-\alpha/2}\sqrt{\frac{\hat{\pi}(1 - \hat{\pi})}{n}}\right) = 1 - \alpha$$

where we use the sample proportion in forming the variance of $\hat{\pi}$.

Example

Suppose we gather a sample of 1000 voters and it shows 55% support for the Republican party. What is the 95% confidence interval for Republican support in the population?

$$P\left(\hat{\pi} - z_{1-\alpha/2}\sqrt{\frac{\hat{\pi}(1 - \hat{\pi})}{n}} \leq \pi \leq \hat{\pi} + z_{1-\alpha/2}\sqrt{\frac{\hat{\pi}(1 - \hat{\pi})}{n}}\right) = 1 - \alpha$$

which in this case suggests we are 95% sure Republican support is between

$$.55 \pm 1.96\sqrt{\frac{.55 \times .45}{1000}}$$

or between about 52% and 58%.

8.2.4   Interval Estimation of the Population Variance

From Chapter 6 on sampling distributions we know that

$$\frac{(n - 1)s_X^2}{\sigma_X^2} \sim \chi_{n-1}^2$$

Thus, proceeding in a fashion similar to our derivation of the confidence interval for a mean we have

$$P\left(\chi_{\alpha/2,n-1}^2 \leq \frac{(n - 1)s_X^2}{\sigma_X^2} \leq \chi_{1-\alpha/2,n-1}^2\right) = 1 - \alpha$$

where $\chi_{\alpha/2,n-1}^2$ is defined analogously to $Z_{\alpha/2}$. Solving this expression in terms of σ_X^2 yields the $100(1 - \alpha)\%$ confidence interval for the population variance:

$$P\left(\frac{(n - 1)s_X^2}{\chi_{1-\alpha/2,n-1}^2} \leq \sigma_X^2 \leq \frac{(n - 1)s_X^2}{\chi_{\alpha/2,n-1}^2}\right) = 1 - \alpha$$

Again, notice that the logic of the derivation is similar to what we did above. Once we know the distribution of the sample statistic, we solve the implied relation in terms of the population parameter in which we are interested.

APPLICATION 8.1   *How Can 1200 People Decide an Election?*

Public opinion polls in the months preceding a Presidential election are ubiquitous and their results play a critical roll in determining campaign strategy, fund-raising, and ultimately, in predicting its outcome. But these polls are almost universally conducted based on the responses of roughly 1200 randomly selected individuals even though the voting-age population of the United States is around 200 million. When poll results are released, the percentage of respondents favoring a particular candidate is generally reported along with a confidence interval of typically ± 4% around this estimate. Where does this confidence interval come from? Why are there always 1200 people in the sample?

The answers lie in the statistical properties of the poll. One can think of an individual's response in favor of a particular candidate as a random variable that follows the binomial distribution since it results from a series of Bernoulli trials (i.e., each survey respondent's vote for or against the candidate). The binomial distribution is centered on its true mean and has variance $p \cdot (1 - p)/n$ (where p is the fraction favoring a particular candidate and n is the sample size of the survey). Moreover, it can be approximated by the standard normal distribution. Therefore, the 95% confidence interval around the poll's estimate, $\hat{p}$ of p, is given by

$$- 1.96 \cdot \sqrt{\hat{p} \cdot (1 - \hat{p})/n} < \hat{p} - p < 1.96 \cdot \sqrt{\hat{p} \cdot (1 - \hat{p})/n}$$

where the true population variance is estimated using data from the sample. These surveys typically restrict the sample to those who report they are likely to vote in the election; generally slightly more than half do so. Therefore, in a poll with 1200 eligible voters, 600 or so will be likely voters. With values of $\hat{p}$ around 0.5, as one would expect in a Presidential election, this indicates that the true value of p will fall within ±4% of the estimated value.

Alternatively, one could ask how large the survey's sample needs to be to obtain a confidence interval of this magnitude. This can be determined by squaring either the lower or upper bound, equating it to 0.04, and solving for n:

$$n = \left(1.96^2 \Big/ .04^2 \right) \cdot \hat{p} \cdot (1 - \hat{p})$$

Again, if $\hat{p}$ is around 0.5, then $n = 600$. Assuming that only half of the eligible voters will report that they are likely to vote indicates that the survey size needs to be doubled to 1200 respondents to obtain the desired sample.

8.2.5 Overview

Notice that we proceeded in a similar fashion for each of the confidence intervals we considered above. First, we recognize that we are interested in some population parameter. Second, we select a sample statistic to estimate the population parameter. Third, we derive (or, more likely, someone has already derived) the sampling distribution for the sample statistic. Fourth, we select what we regard to be an appropriate significance level. Fifth, we indicate bounds within which our sample statistic will reside with the desired level of confidence. Finally, we solve this relation in terms of the unknown population parameter. The resulting interval is the confidence interval for the population parameter.

8.3 HYPOTHESIS TESTS ON THE POPULATION MEAN

Suppose we are interested in testing a hypothesis concerning the population mean. A variety of hypotheses might concern us. We might want to test whether $\mu_X = a$, $\mu_X \neq a$, $\mu_X > a$, or $\mu_X < a$ for any number a that is of interest. For example, someone claims that the average height at Williams College is 5 feet 10 inches. A commonsense approach to evaluating such an assertion might proceed as follows. First we would gather a sample of data on heights from Williams College, being careful that the sample was gathered in such a way that we could trust its being representative of the population of all students at the college. Next, we would select some estimator for the population mean. As we have seen, the sample mean is a reasonable choice. Then, if the sample mean was "close" to the claimed average of 5 feet 10 inches we might conclude that the claim seems "plausible." That is, the data are consistent with the hypothesis. If, on the other hand, the estimated mean was quite different from the claimed average height, we might decide that the claim appears "implausible." That is, the sample estimate is somewhat "surprising" in light of the hypothesis. So, the approach essentially says, "I'll assume the alleged hypothesis is true. Then I'll see whether the sample evidence deviates from the alleged hypothesis by so much that it is implausible that the hypothesis is true." Notice that we can never *prove* the alleged hypothesis to be true. It is always possible that a different sample would invalidate it. The evidence may, however, be so at odds with the hypothesis that we are compelled to reject its validity.

This commonsense approach describes the basic approach to hypothesis testing. Formalizing this approach requires us to be more specific about what we mean by "close," "plausible," "implausible," or "surprising."

8.3.1 Null and Alternative Hypotheses

To formalize the basic approach to hypothesis testing we first explicitly define the *null* and *alternative* hypotheses. The null hypothesis is denoted by H_0 and the alternative hypothesis as H_1. The null hypothesis *always* specifies a specific value for the population parameter (e.g., $H_0:\mu_X = a$). The alternative can take one of three forms: $H_1:\mu_X \neq a$, $H_1:\mu_X > a$, or $H_1:\mu_X < a$. These alternative hypothesis are referred to as two-sided, one-sided (upper-tail), and one-sided (lower-tail), respectively.

8.3.2 Test Statistic and Critical Region

Next we choose an estimator for the population parameter of interest—in this case the population mean. The sample mean $\overline{X}$ is a reasonable choice. In the context of hypothesis testing this estimator is referred to as a *test statistic*. Then, to facilitate our test, we want to specify a *decision rule* that tells us whether to accept or reject the null hypothesis for any given value of the test statistic. The set of values for which we will accept the null hypothesis is called the *acceptance region*. The set of values for which we will reject the null hypothesis is called the *rejection region*. For example, suppose the null and alternative hypotheses are

$$H_0:\mu_X = a$$
$$H_1:\mu_X \neq a$$

APPLICATION 8.2   *What's Wrong with This Picture?*

How is vote fraud detected? In one recent election in Philadelphia, the court partially relied on statistical reasoning in reaching its decision. At issue was a special election for a vacant state senate seat in which the vote from absentee ballots was far different than that recorded in voting machines. The loser claimed that the absentee ballots had been improperly obtained and processed and wanted the result of the election overturned.

Specifically, on election day, only 49.3% of those using voting machines pulled the lever of the Democratic candidate, but that candidate won because he received 79.0% of the vote from those using absentee ballots. As the figure below demonstrates, a 29.7 point differential in the percentage voting for the Democrat is quite unusual on the basis of past elections. Traditionally, the absentee vote is slightly more likely to go in favor of the Republican compared to the machine vote. Moreover, a 29.7 point differential in favor of the Democrat is far greater than anything that had been observed in the past.

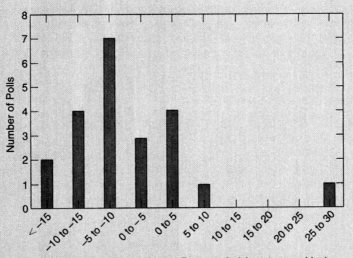

Difference in Percent Voting Democratic (absentee–machine)

Nevertheless, this evidence is not necessarily conclusive of any impropriety in the election result because this outcome still could have occurred simply by chance. One would be more likely to determine that it was due to fraud if this probability were quite low. Based on the 22 elections before and including this one, the standard deviation for the difference in percentage voting Democratic between the two methods is 10.5. Under the null hypothesis that there is no difference, the *t*-statistic for this test would equal 2.83. With 21 degrees of freedom, the critical value at the 5% level is 2.08, so we would reject the null hypothesis at this level of significance. That's bad news for the Democrat, which is what the judge decided!

SOURCE: Authors' unpublished tabulations.

If the value of our test statistic $\bar{X}$ is sufficiently far from a, we would reject the null hypothesis. We define "sufficiently far" as a value of $\bar{X}$ that is in the rejection region. We will discuss how you go about setting up the rejection region shortly.

8.3.3 Type I and Type II Errors

In deciding between the two hypotheses we, the fallible researchers, can make one of two possible errors. First, we can reject the null hypothesis when, in fact, the null is true. This is called a *Type I* error. On the other hand, we might fail to reject the null when, in fact, it is false. This is a *Type II* error.

Example

Suppose that the height of students at Williams College is distributed normally with mean equal to 5'10" and a variance of 16 inches. Suppose further that we drew a random sample of 16 students and estimated the sample mean. We want to test the claim (which we will assume is correct) that the mean height of students at Williams College is 5'10". Based on the available information, a 95% confidence interval of the sample mean would span from 5'9" to 5'11". If, in the particular sample of students we drew, the mean height was 6', we would reject the null hypothesis. We would obtain a sample mean outside of the confidence interval 5% of the time and this draw would represent one of those times. It provides an example of Type I error. Alternatively, suppose that the true mean was 6'. Our test of the null hypothesis that the true mean is 5'10" proceeds as above, still yielding a confidence interval of 5'9" to 5'11". But some fraction of the time we would obtain a sample with a mean height within this confidence interval (of, say, 5'10½") and we would not reject the null hypothesis even though it is false. This is an example of Type II error.

A fundamental problem we face is that there is a tradeoff between Type I and Type II errors. Reducing the odds of committing one type of error will increase the odds of committing the other. If, for example, we decide that we will not reject H_0 unless the sample mean is more than 100 standard deviations from the hypothesized value (pretty "far" indeed) then we will almost never reject the null hypothesis. In this case our huge acceptance region creates a relatively high risk of committing a Type II error. On the other hand, if we are easily "surprised" then perhaps we'd reject the null if our sample mean was more than, say, 0.5 standard deviations from the hypothesized mean. In this case our large rejection region (or, equivalently, our small acceptance region) will create a relatively high chance of committing a Type I error. So, if we are quick to reject the null we will be more apt to commit a Type I error, but if we are quick to accept the null we will be more apt to commit a Type II error; hence, the tradeoff.

Example

Continuing the height example from above, suppose that we would reject a null hypothesis only if the observed value was more than 5 standard deviations away from the sample mean. Using this very strict standard, if our null hypothesis was 5'10", the acceptance region would span from 5'5" to 6'3" and would be virtually impossible to reject.

In the traditional approach to hypothesis testing (referred to as Neyman–Pearson Theory) we focus on Type I errors. That is, we decide how large a Type I error we can live with and, given the selected likelihood of committing a Type I error, we select a test statistic that minimizes the probability of committing a Type II error. If the rejection region minimizes the chances of committing a Type II error *given* the size of the selected Type I error, we say the rejection region is the *best* or the *most powerful*. That is, it is the region that will maximize our ability to detect the alternative hypothesis for a given Type I error probability.

8.3.4   Statistical Decision Rule for the Population Mean (Two-Sided Alternative)

Now, let's look into the mechanics of doing hypothesis testing. Suppose we want to test the following two-sided hypothesis:

$$H_0 : \mu_X = a$$
$$H_1 : \mu_X \neq a$$

This test is referred to as "two-sided" because we will tend to reject the null hypothesis if the sample mean is *either* larger or smaller than *a*. That is, a sample mean that is far enough away on *either side* of *a* will lead us to reject the null.

Recall that, in deriving the confidence interval for the population mean we made use of the fact that

$$P\left(-z_{1-\alpha/2} \leq \frac{\overline{X} - \mu_X}{\dfrac{\sigma_X}{\sqrt{n}}} \leq z_{1-\alpha/2} \right) = 1 - \alpha$$

We then solved this expression for μ_X to form the desired confidence interval. Suppose we solve the expression instead for $\overline{X}$. This would give us the following result:

$$P\left(\mu_X - z_{1-\alpha/2}\frac{\sigma_X}{\sqrt{n}} \leq \overline{X} \leq \mu_X + z_{1-\alpha/2}\frac{\sigma_X}{\sqrt{n}} \right) = 1 - \alpha$$

Now, when doing hypothesis testing we assume the null is true and see how surprising the data is in light of this assumption. Thus, we assume $\mu_X = a$. Given this, our interval becomes

$$P\left(a - z_{1-\alpha/2}\frac{\sigma_X}{\sqrt{n}} \leq \overline{X} \leq a + z_{1-\alpha/2}\frac{\sigma_X}{\sqrt{n}} \right) = 1 - \alpha$$

This interval captures the basic fact that *if the null is true*, then $100(1 - \alpha)\%$ of the time our sample mean $\overline{X}$, generated from a simple random sample, will reside within the given bounds

$$\left(a \pm z_{1-\alpha/2}\frac{\sigma_X}{\sqrt{n}} \right)$$

Thus, *if our sample mean is outside of these bounds we would reject the null.* To see this more clearly, suppose our sample mean was outside of the bounds. This *could* occur when the null is true, but would only be expected to occur at most $100\alpha\%$ of the time. (e.g., if α was .05 we would only see a value of $\overline{X}$ outside the bounds 5% of the time if the null hypothesis was true). We might conclude that "the null very well *might* be true, but the sample mean I observed is such that I would only see it at most 5% of the time if this was the case. I consider such a rare result to be so *surprising* that I choose to reject the null in favor of the more plausible alternative hypothesis."

Notice that we can write our decision rule slightly differently. We would reject the null if

$$\left| \frac{\overline{X} - a}{\frac{\sigma_X}{\sqrt{n}}} \right| \leq z_{1-\alpha/2}$$

This simply says that we reject the null if the deviation between our sample mean and the value hypothesized by the null, *a*, is more than $z_{1-\alpha/2}$ standard deviations. Again, this follows from the fact that deviations this large will only occur by chance $100\alpha\%$ of the time when the null is true.

8.3.5 *P*-Values

The essence of the approach to hypothesis testing described above is to reject the null hypothesis if the sample evidence is very unlikely were the null hypothesis true. Often we define "very unlikely" using the significance level of 5%—though the selection of this value is up to the researcher. Alternatively, we could calculate exactly how often we would expect to see a sample statistic as large as the one we saw *if the null was true*. That is, rather than asking whether the sample result is rare enough (i.e., has probability less than the significance level), we could calculate exactly how rare the result actually is. This value is called the *p-value*. Thus, if the *p*-value was 0.001 we would know that the odds of seeing a sample mean as far from the hypothesized value as we did would be at most one in a thousand if the null was true. Since this is quite unlikely, we would tend to reject the null in favor of the alternative hypothesis. More generally, we would reject the null whenever the *p*-value was less than the desired significance level. Thus, the *p*-value gives us the smallest significance level at which we could reject the null hypothesis.

8.3.6 Statistical Decision Rule for the Population Mean (One-Sided Alternatives)

Testing a one-sided (upper-tail) hypothesis proceeds similarly. Suppose our hypotheses are now

$$H_0 : \mu_X = a$$
$$H_1 : \mu_X > a$$

Values of $\overline{X}$ that are much larger than *a* would lead us to favor the alternative hypothesis H_1. Thus, if $\overline{X}$ is "large enough" (i.e., enough greater than *a* to be unlikely to have arisen by chance if the null was true), we would conclude H_1. More formally, we would conclude H_1 when

| APPLICATION 8.3 | *If the Price Is High, Women Need Not Apply* |

A large component of the wage paid to wait staff at restaurants comes in the form of tips, so it pays to work at a restaurant where the price of a meal is more expensive. If men are more likely to be employed at higher-priced restaurants, this would lead to a wage differential between male and female food servers. If men and women are equally qualified, this differential would reflect discrimination.

One research study provided an intriguing examination of the restaurant industry by employing actors to test whether men and women had different rates of success in obtaining employment at higher- and lower-priced restaurants. Male and female college students were each provided with equivalent fake resumes indicating that he or she had experience at restaurants across the price spectrum. In this approach, one could simply compare men's and women's likelihood of success in obtaining an interview and being offered a job at restaurants in different price ranges. Of course, an important complication is that differences may exist just on the basis of random variation and we would need to test whether any difference is statistically significant.

The results of the study provide clear evidence that differences by sex exist in the rate of obtaining interviews and offers. Men are five times more likely than women (0.48 compared to 0.09) to receive a job offer at a high-priced restaurant and women are four times more likely than men (0.38 compared to 0.10) to receive an offer at a low-priced restaurant. Moreover, these differences have a *p*-value of 0.01, indicating that we would observe a difference this large just due to random variation only 1% of the time. The very low rate of such an occurrence would probably lead us to conclude that men and women are treated differently by restaurants in the hiring process.

	High-price restaurants			Low-price restaurants		
	Male	Female	*P*-value of difference	Male	Female	*P*-value of difference
p(interview)	0.61	0.26	0.04	0.19	0.38	0.18
p(offer)	0.48	0.09	0.01	0.10	0.38	0.01

SOURCE: Neumark, David, Roy J. Bank, and Kyle D. Van Nort, "Sex Discrimination in Restaurant Hiring: An Audit Study." *Quarterly Journal of Economics*, Vol. 111, No. 3 (August 1996), pp. 915–941.

$$\frac{\overline{X} - a}{\frac{\sigma_X}{\sqrt{n}}} \geq z_{1-\alpha}$$

This simply says that we conclude H_1 when the sample mean deviates from the hypothesized value a by more than $z_{1-\alpha}$ standard deviations. Deviations of this magnitude would occur at most $100\alpha\%$ of the time if the null was true. Since such outcomes are quite rare, this evidence would lead us to reject the null in favor of the more plausible alternative hypothesis.

To test a one-sided (lower-tail) hypothesis we proceed similarly. In this case our hypotheses are given by

$$H_0 : \mu_X = a$$
$$H_1 : \mu_X < a$$

In this case, values of $\overline{X}$ that are much smaller than a would lead us to favor the alternative hypothsis H_1. Thus, if $\overline{X}$ is "small enough" (i.e., enough smaller than a to be unlikely to have arrisen by chance if the null was true), we would conclude H_1. More formally, we would conclude H_1 when

$$\frac{\overline{X} - a}{\dfrac{\sigma_X}{\sqrt{n}}} < -z_{1-\alpha}$$

This simply says that we conclude H_1 when the sample mean falls below the hypothesized value a by more than $z_{1-\alpha}$ standard deviations. Deviations of this magnitude would occur at most $100\alpha\%$ of the time if the null was true. Again, since such outcomes are quite rare, this evidence would lead us to reject the null in favor of the more plausible alternative hypothesis.

Finally, notice that we could form p-values (in this case, one-tailed) to test these hypotheses as well.

8.4 PROBLEMS

1. "If the significance level used in a hypothesis test is 10%, then there is a 10% chance that you will accept the null hypothesis when the null hypothesis is false." True, False, or Uncertain? Explain.

2. When we say we are "95% confident" that the true mean is within the interval $\overline{X} + z_{1-\alpha/2} S_{\overline{x}}$, what *exactly* do we mean?

3. A random variable X is known to be distributed either $N(1,3)$ or $N(2,3)$. The null hypothesis is that the mean is equal to 1. The alternative hypothesis is that the mean is 2.

   a. With a sample of 10 draws from the distribution, what is the cutoff for a test with probability of Type I error of at most .01?

   b. What is the probability of a Type II error?

   c. Repeat parts (a) and (b) using a sample size of 100 draws. What does this tell you about keeping the probability of a Type I error constant as the sample size becomes larger?

4. Polygraphs used in criminal investigations typically measure such things as respiration, blood pressure, pulse rate, muscle movement, and galvanic skin response. In principle, the magnitudes of these responses when asked a question ("Do you really love econometrics?") indicate whether you are lying or telling the truth. The procedure, of course, is not infallible. Several experienced polygraphy experts were given a set of 40 records—20 from innocent suspects and 20 from guilty suspects. The subjects had been asked 11 questions on the basis of which each examiner was to make an overall judgment: "Guilty" or "Innocent."

		Suspects' true status	
		Innocent	Guilty
Examiner's Decision	Innocent	131	15
	Guilty	9	125

a. What would be the numerical value of the Type I and Type II errors in this context?

b. In a judicial setting, do we typically think of Type I or Type II errors as carrying equal weight?

5. Suppose the Gap is considering putting a factory outlet store on Main Street and they hire you to conduct some required research. You implement a survey and ask 225 students how much they believe they would spend at the store each year. The student responses have a mean of $200 and a standard deviation of $150. Given this information, answer the following questions:

a. What is the 95% confidence interval for (true) mean per-student expenditure?

b. Form a lower bound for the (true) mean per-student expenditure. Use a 99% confidence interval.

c. Use a decision rule to test the hypothesis that the (true) mean per-student expenditure is less than $225. Use a 1% significance level.

d. Suppose you somehow knew that the true mean per-student expenditure was $215. What (approximately) is the probability that you would see a sample mean of $200 or lower if this was the case?

6. *Consumer Reports* has hired you to study gas mileage obtained by the new Federico Fellini Fuel-Efficient Ferrari. Specifically, you are asked to test the manufacturer's claim that, on average, the car travels 30 miles per gallon.

To conduct the test, you fill the tank of the test car 10 times, and you record the car's mileage per gallon on each tank. The results of the ten trials are 29.0, 29.5, 28.8, 28.7, 31.0, 26.0, 28.0, 30.5, 30.2, 28.3. Suppose you have good reason to believe that miles per gallon on each tank of gas is an independent normal variable with a standard deviation of 3.

a. If the manufacturer's claim is true, what is the probability of a sample mean less than or equal to the one you observed?

b. After you turn in your report, you regret not having been able to make more confident statements about the validity of the manufacturer's claim. You decide that, in future tests of other cars, if the sample mean is at least 1 mile per gallon less than the manufacturer's claim, you would like to reject the claim. How many tankfuls must you sample in a future test to make the probability less than 0.05 that you reject a claim when in fact it is true? Continue to assume that miles per gallon on a tank of gas is independently, normally distributed with a standard deviation of 3.

7. Suppose you have been hired by a consulting company to gauge support for a proposal to reform the Social Security system. You conduct a survey, and the people interviewed respond either yes (I do support the proposed reforms) or no (I do not support the proposed reforms). You code "yes" as 1 and "no" as 0 in your data. After randomly surveying 1000 people you have assembled the following information:

$$\sum_{i=1}^{1000} X_i = 450$$

where $X_i = 1$ if the person responded "yes"

$\quad X_i = 0$ if the person responded "no"

a. Calculate a 90% confidence interval for the population proportion responding "yes."

b. You are 95% sure the population proportion lies above what percentage?

8. The decision whether to publish papers submitted to scholarly journals is typically based on the opinions solicited by the editor of the journal from knowledgeable referees. An article in the *American Economic Review* reported the results of an experiment in which a randomly assigned fraction of the referees of papers submitted for publication were not told of the identity

of the author (the "Blind" sample). The goal was to determine whether there was any bias caused by the referee's knowledge of who the author of the paper was. The following table contains some of the results of the experiment:

Acceptance rates
(estimated standard errors in parentheses)

Blind sample	Nonblind sample	
10.6%	14.1%	All papers
(1.1)	(1.4)	
10.0%	11.2%	Female authors
(3.0)	(3.5)	
11.0%	15.0%	Male authors
(1.2)	(1.5)	

a. Why is it important to assign papers to blind (as opposed to nonblind) referees randomly? What test can you propose for the success of randomization?

b. Test the null hypothesis that it makes no difference in acceptance rates whether papers are assigned to blind or nonblind referees.

c. Calculate the *p*-value associated with part (b).

d. Test the null hypothesis that it makes no difference in acceptance rates whether papers are assigned to blind or nonblind referees for male and female authors separately.

e. Do these data imply that there is discrimination against female authors?

9. Suppose we wanted to conduct a survey. It is desired that we produce an interval estimate of the population mean that is ± 5 from the true population mean with 99% confidence. Based on a historical planning value of 15 for σ, how big should your sample be? Derive the result and show your work.

10. A negative income tax experiment was conducted in Seattle and Denver to see if a guaranteed annual income would cause people to work less. The experiment contained two sample groups. The "experimental group" was guaranteed a minimum income; the "control group" was not. One way to investigate the work-incentive effects of the guaranteed-income program is to compare the annual earnings (not counting the subsidy) of the two groups. The average earnings of the sample families are given in the table below, with the number in parenthesis representing the standard deviation of earnings within each group in each period (before and during the experiment).

	Experimental families	Control families
Before experiment:	6889	7384
	(3146)	(3276)
During experiment:	7604	8541
	(3696)	(3749)
Number of families:	1095	939

a. Using a 5% significance level, test whether the mean earnings of the experimental group differed from the mean earnings of the control group in the period before the experiment began. What does this suggest about the way families were assigned into each group?

b. One estimator of the program's effect on earnings is the difference in average earnings between the experimental and control families during the experiment. Using a 5% significance level, test whether this estimated difference is significantly different from zero. Would you want to use a one-tailed or two-tailed test? What is the probability that a sample difference as large as (or larger than) this one would occur if the true difference were zero?

c. Why is the above estimator of the program's effect likely to be biased? Suggest and compute an alternative estimator of the effect of the income guarantee on family earnings, and again test whether the program has zero average effect. (Use the fact that the sample covariance between earnings before and during the experiment is 6,771,923 for the experimental families and 6,757,797 for the control families.)

11. You are operating an experimental training program and will take post-program earnings as a measure of benefits. Suppose posttraining mean earnings for a randomly assigned control group of size n_2 is $\bar{X}_2$, while pre-training mean earnings is $\bar{X}_1$.

a. Show that

$$\text{var}(\bar{X}_1 - \bar{X}_2) = \frac{\sigma_2}{\rho(1 - \rho)n}$$

where σ^2 is the variance of earnings (assumed unchanged by the program) and

$$\rho = \frac{n_1}{n} \text{ and } n = n_1 + n_2$$

b. Suppose it costs a dollars to collect data on a participant (whether treatment or control) and b dollars to put someone through the program. You have a total budget of R dollars for the experiment. Show that if b = 0 you should assign 50% of the sample to the program to minimize the sampling variance (i.e., $\text{var}(\bar{X}_1 - \bar{X}_2)$).

c. Derive the formula for ρ that minimizes the variance of the treatment effect as a function of the cost parameters a and b, subject to the budget constraint that $R \geq n_1(a + b) + n_2a$. Graph the optimal ρ as a function of

$$\frac{a}{b}$$

Chapter 9

Simple Linear Regression

9.1   INTRODUCTION

Most economic theory centers on establishing a relationship between two or more variables. For example, we might want to learn the income elasticity of demand, the sensitivity of investment to the interest rate, the impact of education on earnings, the impact the overall stock market has on the price of a particular stock, or the relationship between inflation and unemployment. In many ways, such an investigation will resemble work we have done in previous chapters. For instance, there will be a relationship between education and earnings in some population we are interested in. We will summarize that relationship into some key unknown parameters. This is analogous to summarizing a probability distribution using the expected value. We will then draw a sample from the population and estimate the unknown parameters. We might then form confidence intervals or conduct hypothesis tests.

We will begin this chapter by discussing how we might express the relationship between two variables using a linear function. Then, we will lay out the statistical model underlying regression analysis. We will then turn to the problem of estimating the key parameters in this model (i.e., the slope and intercept of the line) using the method of least squares, the method of moments, and the method of maximum likelihood.

9.2   RELATING TWO VARIABLES

Economic theory is typically directed toward establishing a relationship between two or more economic variables. *Regression analysis* provides a set of tools for estimating these relations.

122

Examples

1. The Law of Demand asserts that increases in the price of heating fuel will, other things equal, lead to a reduction in the the amount of heating fuel consumed. It does not, however, tell us by how much quantity will fall. Regression analysis can help measure this relationship.

2. The Phillips Curve relates unemployment and inflation and suggests there may be a tradeoff between the two: Lower unemployment relates to higher inflation. Regression analysis can help to measure the terms of this tradeoff.

3. The Capital Asset Pricing Model asserts that the rate of return on a particular security is a function of the rate of return on the overall securities market. Different stocks will, however, be more or less influenced by movements in the overall market. Regression analysis can help quantify this link and provide a measure of a stock's responsiveness to aggregate shocks.

4. Regression analysis can be applied in many different areas. It is certainly not limited to standard economic problems. For example, regression analysis has been used to measure the impact rainfall has on wine quality. It has also been used to relate a baseball team's revenue to the batting average of its players. The applicability is limited only by your imagination.

The term *regression* stems back to a classic paper written by Sir Francis Galton (1822–1911). Galton believed that the height of a child is a function of the height of the child's parents. He believed that a child whose parents were taller than average would also tend to be taller than average—though by a lesser amount than were the child's parents. He termed this idea "regression toward mediocrity in hereditary stature." The term regression thus related (in Galton's work) to the tendency for familial heights to revert (*regress*) over time to the average. The usage of the term has broadened considerably over time. It is now seen as a general technique used in establishing the relationship between two or more variables.

In regression analysis, we thus seek to explain one variable with one or more other variables. We will refer to the variable we are seeking to explain as the *dependent variable* and denote it by Y. We are seeking to *explain* the dependent variable using one or more other variables called, appropriately, *explanatory variables*. In the case of *simple regression* we are seeking to explain our dependent variable with *one* explanatory variable. In *multiple regression* we seek to explain our dependent variable using more than one explanatory variable. In this chapter we will focus on simple regression and will denote our explanatory variable by X.

Now, following in Galton's tradition, suppose we are interested in learning the relationship between the heights of fathers and sons. In this case the dependent variable is the child's height and the explanatory variable is the parent's height (both in inches). Data on 730 father-and-son pairs, taken from the *National Longitudinal Survey of Youth*, looks like the following:

Observation	Son's height (Y)	Father's height (X)
1	66	70
2	67	71
3	63	66
4	72	70
.	.	.
etc.	etc.	etc.
.	.	.
730	68	63

We can plot these data in a *scatter diagram* as shown below.

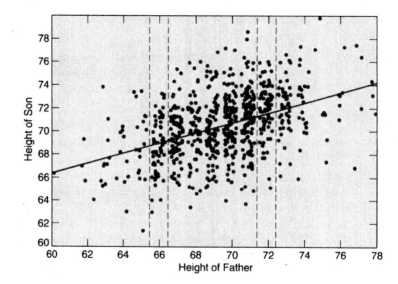

It seems clear from the scatter diagram that there is a relationship between these two variables. Taller fathers tend, on average, to have taller sons. Notice that fathers around five feet six inches (66 inches) have sons who are, on average, about 69 inches tall while fathers who are 72 inches tall have sons that are, on average, about 71 inches tall. We might summarize this relationship between father's height and son's height by drawing a line through our observations. This line would provide the y-intercept and slope that represent its parameters and act in much the same way as the sample mean and variance parameters summarize the characteristics of a frequency distribution. The line (shown in the diagram) expresses the son's height as a linear function of the father's height.

Drawing such a line raises several questions. First, what does such a line mean? That is, how do we interpret its defining slope and intercept? Second, how do we find the equation of the line? Perhaps we could just let people draw the line of their choice using a ruler. But, such a procedure would seem risky and there would seem to be benefits to explicitly defining what a good line is and laying out a systematic approach to finding it.

Finally, we might recognize that the line we drew would be affected by the sample we happened to select. As usual, different samples yield different estimates. So, we would have to think about the relationship between the line derived from a sample and the line in the population. This distinction would lead us back to familiar issues concerning hypothesis testing and confidence intervals. To help us in answering these questions we will now lay out an explicit probability model that could generate the type of data we have been studying.

9.3   THE LINEAR REGRESSION MODEL

So far, we have postulated that the dependent variable, Y, is a function of the explanatory variable X. More formally

$$Y_i = f(X_i)$$

where i indexes the observations.

Notice, however, in our scatter plot graph above that for any given value of X there might be *several different* values of Y. For example, we certainly wouldn't expect everyone whose father is 66 inches to be the same height. After all, a variety of other things (the mother's height, nutrition, etc.) also affect the child's height. Formally, we can say that the relationship between Y and X is *not deterministic*. That is, the value of Y is not completely determined by the value assumed by X. We can incorporate this observation into our model by the addition of an *error term* or *residual*. Thus, our model—which now provides a *statistical relationship*—becomes $Y_i = f(X_i) + \varepsilon_i$, where ε_i (Greek *epsilon*), the error term, is a random variable.

In this case, for any given level of X there are a variety of different possible values of Y depending on the value assumed by ε. That is, there is a *distribution* of values of Y for any level of X. Suppose further that Y is a *linear* function of X. This yields the first maintained assumption in our statistical model:

$$Y_i = \beta_0 + \beta_1 X_i + \varepsilon_i \tag{A1}$$

Assumption (A1) says that our dependent variable is a linear function of our explanatory variable plus an error term that is a random variable. Notice that since Y is a linear function of ε and, since ε is a random variable, Y is also a random variable. The error term represents the deviation between the actual value of Y_i and the value predicted by the model (i.e., $\beta_0 + \beta_1 X_i$). Observations that are above the regression line would have positive errors, while observations below the regression line would have negative errors. The intercept (β_0) and slope (β_1) are the unknown population parameters we are interested in. In that sense, they are analogous to the population mean, or proportion, and so on that we have studied in earlier chapters.

To complete this model we need to make some assumptions about the random variable error term. For starters, we will assume that the mean error is zero. That is:

$$E(\varepsilon_i) = 0 \tag{A2}$$

This assumption asserts that in the population the average error is zero. That is, errors above and below the regression line for any value of X tend to balance out. The error term plays an important part in the model and can arise from a variety of sources. First, human behavior may simply not be deterministic. It may be inherently unpredictable. Second, we leave a large number of potential explanatory variables out of the model. The error term can capture their collective effect on the dependent variable (i.e., it is what we left out). Third, we might have measured our dependent variable imperfectly. This measurement error would be incorporated into the error term. We will investigate the importance of these sources of the error term in more detail later.

APPLICATION 9.1   *Wine Appreciation*

Although most people probably consider wine to be a consumption good, perhaps it makes sense to think about some fine wines as an investment. Here's why. Consider French Bordeaux wines. These wines generally are not consumed until they are several years old because they are rather astringent when they are "young," but lose their astringency with age. That means that the wines must be stored for quite some time before they are consumed and their owners must be compensated or else they would be unwilling to lay out the funds to purchase them (or vintners would be unwilling to expend resources to grow them). These funds have an opportunity cost in that they could be invested in some other investment vehicle and reap some rate of return if they were not used to purchase wine.

How much does the price of wine appreciate as it ages? One study collected data from thousands of wine auctions on prices of red Bordeaux wines from the 1952 to 1980 vintages. A simple scatter plot of the log of the vintage price and the age of the vintage clearly shows that wine prices increase with age.

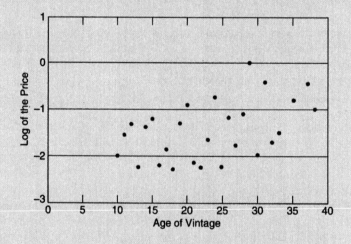

An OLS regression line fitted through these points indicates that wine prices appreciate at 3.5% per year (after adjusting for inflation). This is comparable to the real rate of return on other secure investments, like U.S. Treasury bills.

SOURCE: Ashenfelter, Orley, David Ashmore, and Robert Lalonde, "Bordeaux Wine Vintage Quality and the Weather," *Chance*, Vol. 8, No. 4 (Fall 1995), pp. 7–14. Reprinted with permission from *Chance*. Copyright © 1995 by the American Statistical Association. All rights reserved.

Assumptions (A1) and (A2) together imply that

$$E(Y_i) = \beta_0 + \beta_1 X_i$$

This is often called the *population regression function*. That is, it defines the regression line in the population. The parameter β_0 (said, *"Beta zero,"* or *"Beta naught"*) is the population intercept. The parameter β_1 (said, *"Beta one"*) is the population slope and measures the change in Y from a unit change in X. Thus, our model asserts that the expected value of the variable Y varies linearly with X.

Now, from a practical point of view, we probably don't know all of the observations in the population. Thus, we will typically need to estimate the slope and intercept using sample data. To develop confidence intervals and do hypothesis tests on the population slope and intercept parameters we will need to make some additional assumptions about the error term.

$$\text{var}(\varepsilon_i) = \sigma_\varepsilon^2 \text{ for all } i \tag{A3}$$

$$\Rightarrow \text{Cov}(\varepsilon_i, \varepsilon_j) = 0 \text{ for all } i \neq j \tag{A4}$$

$$\Rightarrow \text{Cov}(\varepsilon_i, \varepsilon_j) = 0 \text{ for all } i \neq j$$

We have seen that the value of the dependent variable for each observation is being determined by the value of a linear function of X plus a random error term. Assumption (A3) says that the errors are drawn from a distribution with a constant variance. That is, the variance associated with the error for one observation is the same as for another. Thus, the errors are drawn from a common distribution with mean zero and variance σ_ε^2.

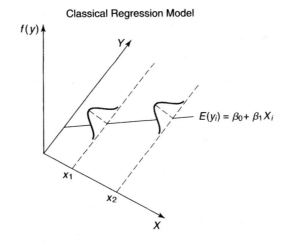

Classical Regression Model

Assumption (A4) says that the error for one observation is not influenced by the error for another observation. One implication of assumption (A4) is that the errors are uncorrelated. Assumptions (A3) and (A4) together imply that the observations are independent and identically distributed. Failure of (A3) is usually called *heteroskedasticity* while failure of (A4) is usually called *serial correlation of the errors*. In future chapters, we will discuss the intuition behind these assumptions and the consequences if they are violated.

$$\text{Cov}(X_i, \varepsilon_i) = 0 \text{ for all } i \tag{A5}$$

Assumption (A5) says that the error term is uncorrelated with the explanatory variable. In an experimental setting, this assumption is defended through the device of *random assignment*. That is, we would assign different people different levels of X (called a *treatment* in that context) with the assignment of the different levels being done randomly. This being the case, there would be no association between X and any other things affecting the dependent variable as captured by the error term. But this assumption may be maintained even without random assignment. Indeed, this is fortunate because random assignment is often difficult in economics. For example, suppose we are trying to learn the effect of schooling on wages. Random assignment would require us to randomly assign different levels of schooling to different people—quite a difficult task!

Finally, we sometimes assume that the error term follows a normal distribution. That is, in addition to having a mean of zero and a constant variance the error is distributed normally:

$$\varepsilon_i \sim N(0, \sigma_\varepsilon^2) \tag{A6}$$

Notice that this implies that $Y_i \sim N(\beta_0 + \beta_1 X_i, \sigma_\varepsilon^2)$.

9.4   ESTIMATION (THREE WAYS)

Given the above assumptions, how exactly should we go about finding the slope and the intercept for this line? Given a sample, we might do it by eye—fitting the line that looks best to us. Unfortunately, different people will draw different lines and it would be nice to have a formal method for finding the line that would consistently provide us with the best line possible. What would a "best possible line" look like? Intuitively, it would seem to have to be a line that *fit* the data well. That is, the distance of the line from the observations should be as small as possible. If we call the estimated intercept of the line $\hat{\beta}_0$ and the estimated slope $\hat{\beta}_1$, then the fitted line is given by the linear equation

$$\hat{Y}_i = \hat{\beta}_0 + \hat{\beta}_1 X_i$$

where i indexes the different observations. Then, the deviation of the observation from the line would be given by $e_i = Y_i - \hat{Y}_i$, where e_i denotes the *estimated error* or *residual*.

Thus, e_i measures the deviation of the estimated regression line from the data for the ith observation. That is, $\hat{Y}_i = \hat{\beta}_0 + \hat{\beta}_1 X_i + e_i$. Graphically it looks like this:

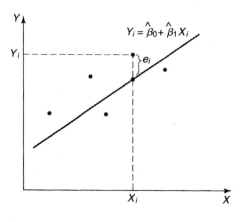

Note that ε_i is unknown to us and is estimated by e_i.

Within this framework, this chapter will present three different estimation approaches (ordinary least squares or OLS, method of moments, and maximum likelihood) to find the best-fitting line. Each of these approaches was discussed more generally in Chapter 7. Luckily, for our particular purpose of estimating regression lines, they all provide exactly the same answer for the best way to calculate the slope and y-intercept of the line.

9.4.1   Ordinary Least Squares

Broadly speaking, the OLS approach is designed to minimize the magnitude of the estimated residuals. To do this, a variety of different specific goals are possible. For example, we might choose our line based on one of the following three possible criteria:

1. Pick $\hat{\beta}_0$ and $\hat{\beta}_1$ to minimize the sum of the errors. That is, select $\hat{\beta}_0$ and $\hat{\beta}_1$ to minimize

$$S = \sum_{i=1}^{n} e_i = \sum_{i=1}^{n} (Y_i - \hat{Y}_i)$$

2. Pick $\hat{\beta}_0$ and $\hat{\beta}_1$ to minimize the sum of the *absolute* errors. That is, select $\hat{\beta}_0$ and $\hat{\beta}_1$ to minimize

$$S = \sum_{i=1}^{n} |e_i| = \sum_{i=1}^{n} |Y_i - \hat{Y}_i|$$

3. Pick $\hat{\beta}_0$ and $\hat{\beta}_1$ to minimize the sum of the *squared* errors from the line. That is, select $\hat{\beta}_0$ and $\hat{\beta}_1$ to minimize

$$S = \sum_{i=1}^{n} e_i^2 = \sum_{i=1}^{n} (Y_i - \hat{Y}_i)^2$$

The problem with the first criterion is that large negative errors are desirable. Lines far from the scatter of observations would yield large negative values of S. The second criterion takes care of this problem by taking the absolute value of the deviations, while the third criterion takes care of the problem by squaring the errors. This criterion says we should select $\hat{\beta}_0$ and $\hat{\beta}_1$ to minimize the *sum of squared errors*. This criterion is usually called *ordinary least squares* (OLS) and is, by far, the most popular criterion used for fitting a line. We will discuss its many virtues in coming chapters.

The method of ordinary least squares requires that we select $\hat{\beta}_0$ and $\hat{\beta}_1$ to minimize

$$S = \sum_{i=1}^{n} e_i^2$$

$$= \sum_{i=1}^{n} (Y_i - \hat{Y}_i)^2$$

$$= \sum_{i=1}^{n} (Y_i - \hat{\beta}_0 - \hat{\beta}_1 X_i)^2$$

This is referred to as *ordinary least squares* because we are simply minimizing the sum of the squared errors. Other estimators might minimize a function (e.g., some weighted average) of the sum of squared errors and, so, would not be *ordinary*.

The problem of identifying the values of the parameters $\hat{\beta}_0$ and $\hat{\beta}_1$ that minimize the function S is a standard optimization problem in multivariable calculus. It is solved by taking first partial derivatives with respect to $\hat{\beta}_0$ and $\hat{\beta}_1$, setting them equal to zero, and solving the resulting system of two equations for $\hat{\beta}_0$ and $\hat{\beta}_1$ (second-order conditions need to be checked as well, but we do not present this below). The solution to this problem represents the formulas for the OLS estimators, $\hat{\beta}_0$ and $\hat{\beta}_1$. We present a formal derivation of these estimators here to demonstrate that the formulas used in an OLS regression do represent the solution to this minimization problem.

To begin, we take first partial derivatives and equate them to zero (i.e., the first-order conditions), making some simplifications along the way:

$$\frac{\partial S}{\partial \hat{\beta}_0} = \frac{\partial \sum_{i=1}^{n} (Y_i - \hat{\beta}_0 - \hat{\beta}_1 X_i)^2}{\partial \hat{\beta}_0}$$

$$= 2 \sum_{i=1}^{n} (Y_i - \hat{\beta}_0 - \hat{\beta}_1 X_i)(-1) = 0$$

$$\Rightarrow \sum_{i=1}^{n} (Y_i - \hat{\beta}_0 - \hat{\beta}_1 X_i) = 0$$

or, more simply (dividing both sides by n before the second step):

$$\sum_{i=1}^{n} Y_i = n\hat{\beta}_0 + \hat{\beta}_1 \sum_{i=1}^{n} X_i \tag{N1}$$

$$\Rightarrow \bar{Y} = \hat{\beta}_0 + \hat{\beta}_1 \bar{X}$$

and

$$\frac{\partial S}{\partial \hat{\beta}_1} = \frac{\partial \sum_{i=1}^{n} (Y_i - \hat{\beta}_0 - \hat{\beta}_1 X_i)^2}{\partial \hat{\beta}_0}$$

$$= 2 \sum_{i=1}^{n} (Y_i - \hat{\beta}_0 - \hat{\beta}_1 X_i)(-X_i) = 0$$

$$\Rightarrow \sum_{i=1}^{n} (Y_i - \hat{\beta}_0 - \hat{\beta}_1 X_i)(X_i) = 0$$

or, expanding the sum out:

$$\sum_{i=1}^{n} Y_i X_i = \hat{\beta}_0 \sum_{i=1}^{n} X_i + \hat{\beta}_1 \sum_{i=1}^{n} X_i^2 \tag{N2}$$

Equations (N1) and (N2) are known as the *normal equations*. Notice that there are two normal equations and two unknowns—namely, $\hat{\beta}_0$ and $\hat{\beta}_1$, so we can solve these two equations for those parameters and that will provide our OLS estimators. Equation (N1) suggests that an estimator for the intercept of the regression line is

$$\hat{\beta}_0 = \bar{Y} - \hat{\beta}_1 \bar{X} \tag{*1}$$

Notice also that the normal equation (N1) implies that the regression line passes through the point $(\bar{X}, \bar{Y})$. Multiplying equation (N1) by

$$\sum_{i=1}^{n} X_i$$

and subtracting n times equation (N2) and (after a little messy algebra) solving in terms of $\hat{\beta}_1$ yields an estimator for the slope of the regression line:

$$\hat{\beta}_1 = \frac{n \sum_{i=1}^{n} Y_i X_i - \sum_{i=1}^{n} Y_i \sum_{i=1}^{n} X_i}{n \sum_{i=1}^{n} X_i^2 - \left(\sum_{i=1}^{n} X_i \right)^2} \tag{*2}$$

This expression can be written in many ways, but two of the more useful versions are:

$$\hat{\beta}_1 = \frac{\sum_{i=1}^{n} (Y_i - \bar{Y})(X_i - \bar{X})}{\sum_{i=1}^{n} (X_i - \bar{X})^2} \tag{*2 cont.}$$

$$= \frac{\sum_{i=1}^{n} (Y_i - \bar{Y}) X_i}{\sum_{i=1}^{n} (X_i - \bar{X})^2}$$

where the second equality follows from the fact that:

$$\sum_{i=1}^{n} (Y_i - \bar{Y})(X_i - \bar{X})$$

$$= \sum_{i=1}^{n} (Y_i - \bar{Y}) X_i - \sum_{i=1}^{n} (Y_i - \bar{Y}) \bar{X}$$

$$= \sum_{i=1}^{n} (Y_i - \bar{Y}) X_i - \bar{X} \sum_{i=1}^{n} (Y_i - \bar{Y})$$

$$= \sum_{i=1}^{n} (Y_i - \bar{Y}) X_i$$

Similarly, using the same logic, we could write this expression as

$$\sum_{i=1}^{n} (X_i - \bar{X}) Y_i.$$

We will use this trick in various proofs that follow.

APPLICATION 9.2   *If You've Got the Data, You Can Get the Beta*

The concept of "beta" holds an important place in financial economics. It identifies the relationship between an individual stock's return and that of the market as a whole. For instance, if in response to a 10% increase (decrease) in the value of the overall market, an individual stock rises (falls) by more than 10%, then the value of beta would be greater than 1. In other words, higher values of beta correspond to greater risk.

How does one estimate a stock's beta? It turns out that it can be estimated using a simple linear regression with time series data on stock market performance overall and for an individual stock. The regression equation takes the form

$$(r_{it} - r_{ft}) = \alpha + \beta(r_{mt} - r_{ft}) + \varepsilon_{it}$$

where r represents the rate of return for an individual stock (i), the market as a whole (m), and a risk-free investment (f), such as short-term treasury bills, and t indexes time. Examples of firms' betas include:

Firm	Beta
Philip Morris	0.4
General Motors	1.0
Microsoft	1.7
Amazon.com	2.7

SOURCE: Authors' calculations.

Notice also that

$$\hat{\beta}_1 = \frac{\sum_{i=1}^{n}(Y_i - \overline{Y})(X_i - \overline{X})}{\sum_{i=1}^{n}(X_i - \overline{X})^2} = \frac{\sum_{i=1}^{n}\left(\frac{Y_i - \overline{Y}}{n}\right)\left(\frac{X_i - \overline{X}}{n}\right)}{\sum_{i=1}^{n}\left(\frac{X_i - \overline{X}}{n}\right)^2}$$

which is the ratio of the estimated covariance between Y and X and the estimated variance of X.

Thus, equations (*1) and (*2) in their various forms provide estimators for the slope and intercept of the population regression line in much the same way that $\overline{X}$ was used to estimate μ_X or $\hat{\pi}$ was used to estimate π, the population proportion. Notice that no other estimators will make the sum of squared errors smaller than the *ordinary least squares estimator*.

9.4.2   Method of Moments

As described in Chapter 7, the method of moments seeks to equate the moments (i.e., mean, variance, etc.) implied by a statistical model of the population distribution with the actual moments observed in the sample. For the present purposes, we can use this approach to derive estimators for $\hat{\beta}_0$ and $\hat{\beta}_1$.

First, notice that certain restrictions are implied in the population. For the population regression equation $Y_i = \beta_0 + \beta_1 X_i + \varepsilon_i$ we have:

$$E(\varepsilon) = 0 \text{ from assumption (A2), and} \qquad (R1)$$

$$Cov(X_i \varepsilon_j) = 0 \; \forall_{i,j} \text{ from assumption (A5)} \qquad (R2)$$

Another way to write (R2) is evident by using the formula for covariance:

$$Cov(X_i, \varepsilon_i) = E[(X - \overline{X})(\varepsilon - \overline{\varepsilon})]$$

Using the fact that ε has zero mean, R2 simplifies to: $E(X_i \varepsilon_i) = 0 \; \forall_i$.

The analoguous restrictions for the sample regression equation $\hat{Y}_i = \hat{\beta}_0 + \hat{\beta}_1 X_i + e_i$ would be:

$$\sum_{i=1}^{n} \frac{e_i}{n} = 0 \qquad (R1')$$

$$\Rightarrow \sum_{i=1}^{n} e_i = 0$$

and

$$\sum_{i=1}^{n} X_i e_i = 0 \qquad (R2')$$

Restriction (R1') implies

$$\sum_{i=1}^{n} e_i = 0$$

$$\Rightarrow \sum_{i=1}^{n} Y_i = \sum_{i=1}^{n} \hat{b}_0 + \hat{b}_0 \sum_{i=1}^{n} X_i + \underbrace{\sum_{i=1}^{n} e_i}_{=0}$$

$$\Rightarrow \sum_{i=1}^{n} Y_i = n\hat{b}_0 + \hat{b}_0 \sum_{i=1}^{n} X_i$$

which is identical to the first *normal equation* we derived using ordinary least squares.

Restriction (R2') implies

$$\sum_{i=1}^{n} Y_i X_i = \hat{b}_0 \sum_{i=1}^{n} X_i + \hat{b}_1 \sum_{i=1}^{n} X_i^2 + \underbrace{\sum_{i=1}^{n} e_i X_i}_{=0}$$

$$\Rightarrow \sum_{i=1}^{n} Y_i X_i = \hat{b}_0 \sum_{i=1}^{n} X_i + \hat{b}_1 \sum_{i=1}^{n} X_i^2$$

which is identical to the second *normal equation*. Thus, the *method of moments* (MOM) estimators would yield the same estimators as *least squares*! Notice from restriction (R1') the mean of the sample residuals will be zero. This is a result of the way in which we construct the estimator and is most clearly seen from the MOM derivation.

9.4.3 Maximum Likelihood

Recall from Chapter 7 that the method of maximum likelihood is designed to maximize the probability of observing the sample we actually see. Here, there exists a probability distribution for the residuals in the regression model and we are trying to choose a line with the parameters $\hat{\beta}_0$ and $\hat{\beta}_1$ that maximize the likelihood of observing the individual observations present in our particular sample.

To implement this approach, we rely on Assumption (A6), which indicates that $\varepsilon_i \sim N(0, \sigma_\varepsilon^2)$. Notice that it implies $Y_i \sim N(\hat{\beta}_0 + \hat{\beta}_1 X_i, \sigma_\varepsilon^2)$. Based on this, the probability of observing an individual observation, y^i, is given by the particular functional form of the normal distribution:

$$f(y_i) = \frac{1}{\sqrt{2\pi\sigma_\varepsilon^2}} e\left\{-\frac{1}{2}\frac{\left(Y_i - \beta_0 - \beta_1 X_i\right)^2}{\sigma_\varepsilon^2}\right\}$$

The likelihood function establishes the probability of observing all of the n observations in our sample: $L(\beta_0, \beta_1, \sigma_\varepsilon^2) = f(y_1, y_2, y_3, \ldots, y_n)$. Assuming the observations are independent and identically distributed (as per our assumptions), we would have $L(\beta_0, \beta_1, \sigma_\varepsilon^2) = f(y_1)f(y_2)f(y_3)\ldots f(y_n)$, where each of $f(y_i)$ has the form indicated earlier. Therefore, the likelihood function takes the form

$$L(\beta_0, \beta_1, \sigma_\varepsilon^2) = f(y_1)f(y_2)f(y_3)\ldots f(y_n)$$

$$= \frac{1}{\sqrt{2\pi\sigma_\varepsilon^2}} e\left\{-\frac{1}{2}\frac{\left(Y_i - \beta_0 - \beta_1 X_i\right)^2}{\sigma_\varepsilon^2}\right\} \frac{1}{\sqrt{2\pi\sigma_\varepsilon^2}} e\left\{-\frac{1}{2}\frac{\left(Y_2 - \beta_0 - \beta_1 X_2\right)^2}{\sigma_\varepsilon^2}\right\} \ldots \frac{1}{\sqrt{2\pi\sigma_\varepsilon^2}} e\left\{-\frac{1}{2}\frac{\left(Y_n - \beta_0 - \beta_1 X_n\right)^2}{\sigma_\varepsilon^2}\right\}$$

$$= \left(\frac{1}{\sqrt{2\pi\sigma_\varepsilon^2}}\right)^n e\left\{-\frac{1}{2\sigma_\varepsilon^2}\sum_{i=1}^{n}(Y_i - \beta_0 - \beta_1 X_i)^2\right\}$$

Taking logs yields

$$\ln L(\beta_0, \beta_1, \sigma_\varepsilon^2) = n\ln\left(\frac{1}{\sqrt{2\pi\sigma_\varepsilon^2}}\right) - \frac{1}{2\sigma_\varepsilon^2}\sum_{i=1}^{n}(Y_i - \beta_0 - \beta_1 X_i)^2$$

We would take the derivative of the log likelihood function with respect to β_0, β_1 to find the maximum likelihood estimators. But, notice that when taking these derivatives we will simply minimize

$$\sum_{i=1}^{n}(Y_i - \beta_0 - \beta_1 X_i)^2$$

which is the same as doing *ordinary least squares!* For example:

$$\frac{\partial \ln L(\beta_0,\beta_1,\sigma_\varepsilon^2)}{\partial \beta_0} = \frac{\partial \dfrac{1}{2\sigma_\varepsilon} \sum_{i=1}^{n} (Y_i - \beta_0 - \beta_1 X_i)^2}{\partial \beta_0} = 0$$

$$\Rightarrow \frac{\partial \sum_{i=1}^{n} (Y_i - \beta_0 - B_1 X_i)^2}{\partial \beta_0} = 0$$

Thus, both the method of maximum likelihood (assuming the errors are normal) and the method of moments yield the same estimators as ordinary least squares. That is, they all lead to the estimators given in (*1) and (*2).

9.5 INTERPRETATION OF THE REGRESSION SLOPE COEFFICIENT

The regression model specifies $Y_i = \beta_0 + \beta_1 X_i + \varepsilon_i$. Given that $E(\varepsilon) = 0$, we have the population regression equation: $E(Y_i) = \beta_0 + \beta_1 X_i$. Notice that the derivative

$$\frac{dE(Y_i)}{dX_j} = \beta_1$$

This tells us that increasing the explanatory variable, X, by one unit results in the mean value of the dependent variable changing by β_1 units. In short, it tells us the effect X has on Y.

9.5.1 Units of Measurement and Regression Coefficients

The magnitude of the regression coefficients will depend on the units used to measure the dependent and explanatory variables. Consider, for example, the simple regression model: $Y_i = \beta_0 + \beta_1 X_i + \varepsilon_i$. Suppose now that the explanatory variable is scaled such that it is 100 times larger (e.g., $X_i^* = 100 X_i$). For example, perhaps we measure X in cents rather than dollars.

Example

Consider a model relating savings and income. We might measure income in dollars or in cents, for example:

$$Savings_i = \hat{\beta}_0 + \hat{\beta}_1 X_i \quad \text{where } X \text{ is income measured in dollars, or}$$

$$Savings_i = \hat{\beta}_0^* + \hat{\beta}_1^* X_i^*$$
$$= \hat{\beta}_0^* + \hat{\beta}_1^* 100 X_i$$

where X_i^* is income measured in cents

Notice that $X_i = 100 X_i^*$.

In this case, the OLS estimate of β_1^* would be 1/100 the size of the OLS estimate of $\hat{\beta}_1$.

Proof. $\hat{\beta}_1^* = \dfrac{\sum\limits_{i=1}^{n}(Y_i - \overline{Y})(X_i^* - \overline{X}^*)}{\sum\limits_{i=1}^{n}(X_i^* - \overline{X}^*)^2}$

$= \dfrac{\sum\limits_{i=1}^{n}(Y_i - \overline{Y})(100X_i - 100\overline{X})}{\sum\limits_{i=1}^{n}(100X_i - 100\overline{X})^2}$

$= \dfrac{\sum\limits_{i=1}^{n}100(Y_i - \overline{Y})(X_i - \overline{X})}{\sum\limits_{i=1}^{n}100^2(X_i - \overline{X})^2}$

$= \dfrac{\hat{\beta}_1}{100}$

This result is quite intuitive. Recall that $\hat{\beta}_1^*$ tells us the impact a penny increase in income has on savings, while $\hat{\beta}_1$ tells us the impact a dollar increase in income has on savings. If the relationship between income and savings is linear (as assumed) we would expect the impact of the penny increase in income to be 1/100 the impact of a dollar (or 100-penny) increase in income.

It is easy to show that, should we multiply *both* the dependent and explanatory variables by the same amount, the slope is unaffected (though the intercept will be 100 times larger). Similarly, multiplying the dependent variable alone by some amount will cause the slope to increase by that amount.

9.5.2   Models Including Logarithms

Economists often measure variables in logarithms. For example, consider the *log-linear* model $\ln Y_i = \beta_0 + \beta_1 X_i + \varepsilon_i$. Recall that

$$\frac{d \ln Y}{dY} = \frac{1}{Y}$$

$$\Rightarrow d \ln Y = \frac{dY}{Y}$$

This suggests that the change in the natural logarithm of Y is equal to the proportional change in Y. Now, notice that, for our simple regression model:

$$\frac{d \ln Y}{dX} = \beta_1$$

$$\Rightarrow \beta_1 = \frac{\dfrac{dY}{Y}}{dX}$$

Thus, β_1 is the *proportionate* change in Y arising from a *unit* change in X.

APPLICATION 9.3   *It's More than Just the Parties*

A college education turns out to be a very valuable investment. To estimate the return to a college investment, we can run a regression of the level of a worker's wage on his or her years of education. Wages are typically measured in logs so that we can interpret the result as indicating the percentage increase brought about by an additional year of education. We use data from a 1991 nationally representative sample of men and women who usually work full time to estimate this model. The results indicate that each additional year of schooling is worth an additional 8.4% in wages; four years of college would increase wages by 38%. For the median full-time worker, who earns about $550 per week in 2000, a wage increase of that magnitude would amount to about $210 per week. Over, say, a 30-year worklife, that amounts to about $170,000 in present discounted value terms at a 5% real rate of return. That tops the cost of even the most expensive colleges and makes state-supported schools a great deal!

Some have argued, however, that this estimated relationship may not adequately represent a "causal" impact on wages, in that workers who obtained more education may have attributes that would have led them to have higher earnings even without the additional schooling. Yet subsequent research (some of which is described in subsequent boxes) has largely ruled out this alternative interpretation, indicating that the estimates obtained from this simple regression model are, if anything, perhaps a little low.

SOURCE: Author's calculations from the 1991 *Current Population Survey Outgoing Rotation Group* file.

Now, suppose we consider the *log-log* model $\ln Y_i = \beta_0 + \beta_1 \ln X_i + \varepsilon_i$. Now, both Y and X are measured in logarithms. Then,

$$\frac{d \ln Y}{d \ln X} = \beta_1$$

$$\Rightarrow \beta_1 = \frac{\dfrac{dY}{Y}}{\dfrac{dX}{X}}$$

Here, β_1 is the *proportionate* change in Y arising from a *proportionate* change in X. Or, alternatively, it is the percentage change in Y arising from a 1% change in X. This measures the *elasticity of Y with respect of X,* a quantity often used in economic analysis.

Finally, it is easy to show for the *linear-log model* $Y_i = \beta_0 + \beta_1 \ln X_i + \varepsilon_i$ that β_1 is the unit change in Y arising from a *proportionate* change in X.

9.6   PROBLEMS

1.   Suppose $Y_i = \beta_0 + \beta_1 X_i + \varepsilon_i$ and the error term satisfies the assumptions outlined in the chapter. For a sample of 500 observations it is found that:

$$\sum_{i=1}^{500} X_i = 3000, \ \sum_{i=1}^{500} Y_i = 1400, \ \sum_{i=1}^{500} X_i Y_i = 18{,}000,$$

$$\sum_{i=1}^{500} X_i^2 = 66{,}000, \sum_{i=1}^{500} Y_i^2 = 7200$$

Find the ordinary least squares estimates of β_0, β_1.

2. In "An Economic Theory of Suicide," published in the *Journal of Political Economy,* Jan./Feb. 1974, Hamermesh and Soss state, "When unemployment rises, individuals' expectations of future incomes (and utilities) are revised downward. Holding real income of the employed constant, an increased number of people will believe future prospects to have dimished and will commit suicide." As a crude test of their hypothesis, we can estimate the equation $s_t = a + bU_t + \varepsilon_t$, where s_t is the number of suicides per 100,000 population in year t, U_t is the unemployment rate in year t, and ε_t is a random error term satisfying the usual assumptions. The relevant data are:

t	s_t	U_t
1968	10.7	3.6
1969	11.1	3.5
1970	11.5	4.9
1971	11.7	5.9
1972	12.0	5.6
1973	12.0	4.9
1974	12.1	5.6
1975	12.7	8.5
1976	12.5	7.7
1977	13.3	7.0
1978	12.5	6.0

a. Construct a scatter diagram with suicide rates on the vertical axis and the unemployment rate on the horizontal axis.

b. Compute the ordinary least squares estimate of the parameters β_0 and β_1 by hand. Check your results using statistical software.

c. How would these coefficients change if suicide rates were reported per 1000 population?

d. Calculate the predicted suicide rates for each year. Calculate the estimated error for each year.

e. What is the average estimated error? Why?

f. The unemployment rate was 5.8 in 1979. Based on your estimates, what suicide rate would you have expected that year?

3. The Capital Asset Pricing Model postulates a relationship between the returns to a particular stock and the return on the market. Go to the Internet and obtain monthly stock price data for Microsoft, GE, IBM, Procter & Gamble, and the S&P 500:

a. Calculate the slope coefficient from a regression of the firms' return data on the S&P 500— that is, the "beta" for each company. (See Application Box 9.2.)

b. Which firm's stock is the most sensitive to changes in the market?

c. Would you expect the "beta" for a firm to be stable (i.e., unchanging over time)? Why or why not?

4. The Phillips Curve is one of the most famous empirical relationships in macroeconomics. It describes a negative relationship between the unemployment rate and the rate of inflation. The dataset for this problem contains three variables; year, unemployment rate (U_t), and $Infl$ = inflation rate for the years 1954 through 1989. It can be found in http://www.wiley.com/college/ashenfelter.

a. For the period 1954–1967, estimate the model

$$U_t = a + bInfl_t + \varepsilon_t$$

b. What is the meaning of the slope and intercept terms in this model?

c. Estimate the model for the full sample period. What are the estimated slope and intercept coefficients now?

d. Graph the data using a scatterplot. Can you see why the coefficients change so much?

e. What assumptions of the regression model are unlikely to be satisfied by these data?

Chapter 10

Inferences in Simple Linear Regression

10.1 INTRODUCTION

10.2 SAMPLING DISTRIBUTION OF $\hat{\beta}_0$ AND $\hat{\beta}_1$ BASED ON SIMULATION

10.3 SAMPLING DISTRIBUTION OF $\hat{\beta}_0$ AND $\hat{\beta}_1$ BASED ON THEORY

10.4 CONFIDENCE INTERVALS

10.5 HYPOTHESIS TESTING

10.6 GOODNESS OF FIT (R^2)

10.7 THE GAUSS–MARKOV THEOREM

10.8 PROBLEMS

10.1 INTRODUCTION

In the previous chapter we derived estimators for the slope and intercept of the population regression line. In this chapter we will investigate the sampling distribution for these estimators. We will then show how confidence intervals and hypothesis tests are conducted in a fashion completely analogous to the approach we used in considering means and proportions. We will then develop a measure of how well our line is fitting the data. Finally, we will demonstrate the Gauss–Markov theorem—a powerful theorem that provides a justification for using the *ordinary least squares* estimators.

10.2 SAMPLING DISTRIBUTION OF $\hat{\beta}_0$ AND $\hat{\beta}_1$ BASED ON SIMULATION

Suppose we are interested in measuring the relationship, if any, between grades and hours studied. Also, suppose we are in the extraordinary position of having the data for the entire population of relevance to us. Remember, we usually have access to only a sample from the population. Suppose the population is comprised of the 150 students enrolled in an econometrics class. We have data on both their midterm exam grades and the number of hours they studied for the exam. The scatterplot of the population along with the population regression line are shown below.

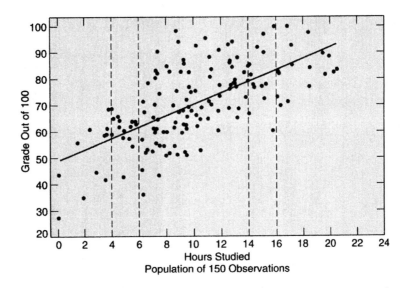

Population of 150 Observations

Notice that, in the population, higher grades seem to be associated with longer study hours. For example, students who study between 4 and 6 hours received, on average, a grade of about 60. Students studying between 14 and 16 hours received, on average, a grade of about 80. Formalizing this relation, the equation for the population regression line is given by $E(Grades) = 50 + 2\ Hours$. Thus, in the population, the mean grade for students who studied zero hours was 50 points. Each additional hour studied increased grades by 2 points. Notice that we would predict that someone studying 10 hours would receive a grade of $50 + 2(10) = 70$ points.

Now, suppose we were in our more typical situation of not knowing the slope and intercept in the population. Indeed, our research goal is to learn about the population slope and intercept by way of using sample data. Suppose we gather from our population a random sample of 20 students and plot the scatter diagram for the sample, as shown below.

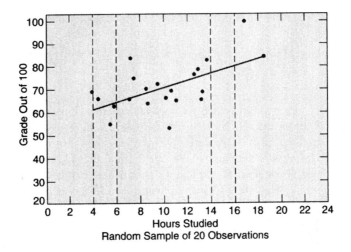

Random Sample of 20 Observations

This sample regression line has an intercept of 55 and a slope of 1.5. Thus, while the *true* (or, population) regression line has intercept and slope $\beta_0 = 50$, $\beta_1 = 2$, with just our sample of 20 we have produced intercept and slope estimates of $\hat{\beta}_0 = 55$, $\hat{\beta}_1 = 1.5$. Now, as when we studied the sampling distribution of sample means, we have the basic observation that different samples yield different estimates. Consider four more samples in the graph below.

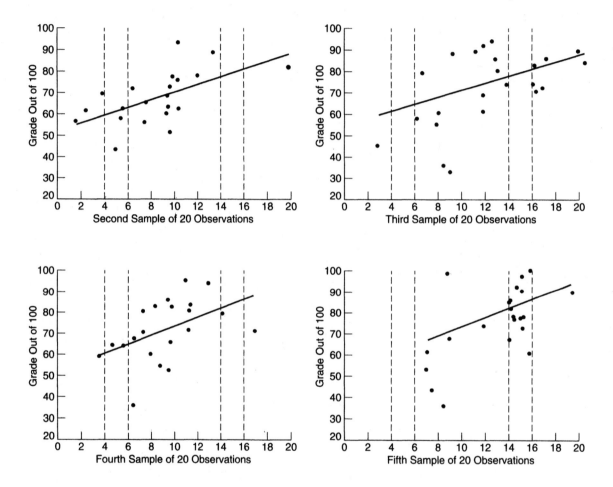

Each sample yields a somewhat different slope and intercept. For example, the slopes from the second, third, fourth, and fifth samples were 1.8, 1.6, 2.1, 2.5. Now, suppose we let the computer calculate *all* of the slope estimates that are possible from a sample of size 20 from our population. We might graph the distribution of the possible values and use this distribution in conducting confidence intervals and hypothesis tests. In the graph below we plot a histogram showing the distribution of slopes arising from 10,000 different samples of size 20 from our population. This graph will give us an idea of the different possible slopes, and their associated probability of occurrence, that can be estimated from a sample of size 20 from our population of 150.

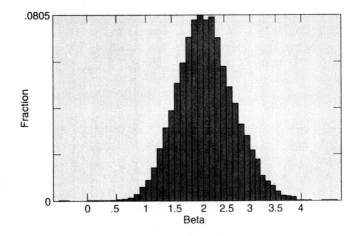

A few critical features of the above histogram deserve comment. First, the histogram is centered roughly at the population slope of 2 and has a standard deviation of about .55. Second, the histogram is approximately normally distributed. Notice that it is possible, though unlikely, to gather samples that yield slope estimates of under .5 and above 4. In a sense, such samples are just plain bad luck.

Now, based on the simulation exercise conducted above, we might be willing to make the following statements. First, the estimated slope and intercepts are random variables. That is, the value they take on is dependent on the random sample we happen to gather. Second, the mean of the different estimates is equal to the population value. That is, the mean of the different slope estimates that we can gather from a sample of a given size is equal to the population slope. Third, the distribution of the estimators is approximately normal. We will now derive some of these results more formally.

10.3 SAMPLING DISTRIBUTION OF $\hat{\beta}_0$ AND $\hat{\beta}_1$ BASED ON THEORY

In the previous chapter we used the methods of ordinary least squares, moments, and maximum likelihood to derive estimators for the population slope and intercept. For now we will focus on the slope and derive some of its properties.

10.3.1 The Linearity of the OLS Estimators

A linear estimator is one that satisfies the condition that it is a linear combination of the dependent variable (i.e., $\hat{\beta}_1 = w_1 Y_1 + w_2 Y_2 + \ldots + w_n Y_n$). The estimator for the population slope is given by

$$\hat{\beta}_1 = \frac{\sum_{i=1}^{n}(Y_i - \bar{Y})(X_i - \bar{X})}{\sum_{i=1}^{n}(X_i - \bar{X})^2}$$

We will refer to this as the ordinary least squares (OLS) estimator. What we want to show is that the OLS estimator is a linear estimator. This property will be important later in this chapter when we describe the advantages of OLS.

To accomplish this, recall from Chapter 9 that we can write the OLS estimator as

$$\hat{\beta}_1 = \frac{\sum_{i=1}^{n}(X_i - \overline{X})Y_i}{\sum_{i=1}^{n}(X_i - \overline{X})^2}$$

Now, to simplify the notation, define $X_i - \overline{X} = x_i$. Thus, we may write the estimator as

$$\hat{\beta}_1 = \frac{\sum_{i=1}^{n} x_i Y_i}{\sum_{i=1}^{n} x_i^2} = \sum_{i=1}^{n}\left(\frac{x_i}{\sum_{i=1}^{n} x_i^2}\right)Y_i = \sum_{i=1}^{n} w_i Y_i$$

which is of the desired form. Therefore, the OLS estimator is a linear estimator.

10.3.2 The Unbiasedness of the OLS Estimators

Recall that an unbiased estimator is one whose mean value is equal to the true value. In the present context, OLS is unbiased if we can show that $E(\hat{\beta}_1) = \beta_1$. To see this, consider the expected value of this estimator:

$$E(\hat{\beta}_1) = E\left(\frac{\sum_{i=1}^{n}(Y_i - \overline{Y})(X_i - \overline{X})}{\sum_{i=1}^{n}(X_i - \overline{X})^2}\right)$$

Notice that $Y_i - \overline{Y} = (\beta_0 + \beta_1 X_i + \varepsilon_i) - (\beta_0 + \beta_1\overline{X}) = \beta_1(X_i - \overline{X}) + \varepsilon_i$, so:

$$E(\hat{\beta}_1) = E\left(\frac{\sum_{i=1}^{n}\beta_1(X_i - \overline{X})^2 + (X_i - \overline{X})\varepsilon_i}{\sum_{i=1}^{n}(X_i - \overline{X})^2}\right) = \beta_1 + E\left(\frac{\sum_{i=1}^{n}(X_i - \overline{X})\varepsilon_i}{\sum_{i=1}^{n}(X_i - \overline{X})^2}\right)$$

Therefore, OLS is unbiased if this second expression equals zero. If we treat the explanatory variable X as if it was a constant—set, in effect, by the researcher—then this expression equals zero because of assumption (A2) in Chapter 9, which states that $E(\varepsilon_i) = 0$. Alternatively, as is often more plausible, X is itself a random variable. Even then, it is still possible to show that $E(\hat{\beta}_1) = \beta_1$ so long as the covariance between X and ε is zero, which we have maintained in assumption (A5) in Chapter 9.

So, we have demonstrated that ordinary least squares produces an unbiased estimator for the population slope. A similar derivation can be used to show the intercept is also unbiased given the model's assumptions. This derivation serves to show what we learned from the simulation exercise conducted above. Namely, the sampling distribution of the OLS estimators is centered at the population values.

10.3.3   The Variance of the OLS Estimators

The variance of the OLS slope estimator describes the dispersion in the distribution of OLS estimates around its mean (which we just proved is equal to the true value). From the definition of variance,

$$\text{var}(\hat{\beta}_1) = E[(\hat{\beta}_1 - E(\hat{\beta}_1))^2] = E[(\hat{\beta}_1 - \beta_1)^2]$$

where the last equality follows from our proof that OLS is unbiased. Note also from that proof that

$$\hat{\beta}_1 - \beta_1 = \frac{\sum_{i=1}^{n}(X_i - \bar{X})\varepsilon_i}{\sum_{i=1}^{n}(X_i - \bar{X})^2}$$

which means that

$$\text{var}(\hat{\beta}_1) = \frac{\sum_{i=1}^{n}(x_i - \bar{x})^2\text{var}(\varepsilon_i)}{\sum_{i=1}^{n}(X_i - \bar{X})^4} = \frac{\sigma_\varepsilon^2}{\sum_{i=1}^{n}(X_i - \bar{X})^2} = \frac{\sigma_y^2}{\sum_{i=1}^{n}(X_i - \bar{X})^2}$$

if we assume that the variance of ε_i is constant and equal to σ_ε^2 and the last equality comes from the property described in Chapter 9 that $\text{var}(\varepsilon_i) = \text{var}(Y_i)$. (Note: We will typically denote the variances of $\hat{\beta}_0$ and $\hat{\beta}_1$ as $\sigma_{\hat{\beta}_0}^2$ and $\sigma_{\hat{\beta}_1}^2$, respectively.) Thus, $\text{var}(\hat{\beta}_1)$ is smaller if the variance of Y is smaller. The smaller the variance of Y the less likely we are to observe extreme samples—simply because extreme samples are less likely to occur. Second, if we divided the denominator

$$\sum_{i=1}^{n}(X_i - \bar{X})^2$$

by $n - 1$ it would be equal to the sample variance of X. Thus, the smaller the variance of the explanatory variable the larger the variance of the sampling distribution of $\hat{\beta}_1$. Concerning the sample size, suppose that instead of taking a random sample of 20 observations we took a random sample of 2 observations. It should be clear that more extreme slope estimates can arise in this situation. Indeed, in our example of the effect of hours studied and grades, we might even get lines that sloped downward. Remember, the sample line would be determined by whatever 2 observations we happened to gather. With 20 observations such extreme results are less likely.

10.3.4   The Normality of the OLS Estimators

Since

$$\hat{\beta}_1 = \sum_{i=1}^{n} w_i Y_i$$

is a linear function of Y and since under assumption (A6) $Y_i \sim N(\hat{\beta}_0 + \hat{\beta}_1 X_i, \sigma_\varepsilon^2)$, we know that $\hat{\beta}_1 \sim N(\cdot)$. That is, $\hat{\beta}_1$ is a linear function of normally distributed random variables and is, therefore, normally distributed. Given that we have shown that the mean of $\hat{\beta}_1$ is β_1 and the variance of $\hat{\beta}_1$ is

$$\frac{\sigma_Y^2}{\sum_{i=1}^{n}(x_i - \overline{X})^2}$$

this tells us that

$$\hat{\beta}_1 \sim N\left(\beta_1, \frac{\sigma_Y^2}{\sum_{i=1}^{n}(X_i - \overline{X})^2}\right)$$

Similarly, it can be shown that

$$\hat{\beta}_0 \sim N\left(\beta_0, \frac{\sigma_Y^2 \sum_{i=1}^{n} X_i^2}{n \sum_{i=1}^{n}(X_i - \overline{X})^2}\right)$$

10.4   CONFIDENCE INTERVALS

We will focus on deriving confidence intervals for the population slope. We can standardize $\hat{\beta}_1 \sim N(\beta_1, \sigma_{\hat{\beta}_1}^2)$ by subtracting the mean and dividing by the standard deviation. This gives us

$$\frac{\hat{\beta}_1 - \beta_1}{\sigma_{\hat{\beta}_1}} \sim N(0,1)$$

Following the same procedure as used in Chapter 8, define $z_{(1-\alpha/2)}$ to be the value of Z for which $F(z_{1-\alpha/2}) = 1 - \alpha/2$, where F is the distribution function for the standard normal distribution. Then, it follows that

$$P(-z_{1-\alpha/2} \leq Z \leq z_{1-\alpha/2}) = 1 - \alpha$$

$$\Rightarrow P\left(-z_{1-\alpha/2} \leq \frac{\hat{\beta}_1 - \beta_1}{\sigma_{\hat{\beta}_1}} \leq z_{1-\alpha/2}\right) = 1 - \alpha$$

$$\Rightarrow P(\beta_1 - z_{1-\alpha/2}\sigma_{\hat{\beta}_1} \leq \hat{\beta}_1 \leq \beta_1 + z_{1-\alpha/2}\sigma_{\hat{\beta}_1}) = 1 - \alpha$$

which is the $100(1 - \alpha)\%$ confidence interval for $\hat{\beta}_1$.

We will typically have to estimate $\sigma_{\hat{\beta}_1}$ because we usually don't know the population variance σ_Y^2. An unbiased estimator of σ_Y^2 is given by

$$s_Y^2 = \frac{\sum_{i=1}^{n} e_i^2}{n - 2}$$

We can then proceed in deriving a similar confidence interval, though now we use the *t distribution* in place of the standard normal distribution. That is, our confidence interval is $P(\hat{\beta}_1 - t_{(n-2,1-\alpha/2)}s_{\hat{\beta}_1} \le \beta_1 \le \hat{\beta}_1 + t_{(n-2,1-\alpha/2)}s_{\hat{\beta}_1}) = 1 - \alpha$ where

$$s_{\hat{\beta}_1}^2 = \frac{s_Y^2}{\sum_{i=1}^{n} (X_i - \overline{X})^2}$$

and

$$s_{\hat{\beta}_1} = \sqrt{s_{\hat{\beta}_1}^2}$$

Forming one-tailed confidence intervals is done analogously to the approach used for means in Chapter 8.

10.5   HYPOTHESIS TESTING

Hypothesis tests are also conducted analogously to how we tested hypotheses concerning population means or proportions. Suppose, for example, someone alleges the population slope equals a. Suppose the alternative hypothesis is that β_1 does not equal a. More formally, we have the following null and alternative hypothesis:

$$H_0: \beta_1 = a$$
$$H_1: \beta_1 \ne a$$

Intuitively, we would be unable to reject the null hypothesis if the sample slope $\hat{\beta}_1$ was "close" to a. The farther it was from a the more plausible the alternative hypothesis would be. To formalize this, we can form the Z-statistic:

$$Z = \left| \frac{\hat{\beta}_1 - a}{\sigma_{\hat{\beta}_1}} \right|$$

This statistic literally tells us the number of standard deviations our sample slope is from the slope hypothesized under the null. The larger this number, the more plausible the alternative hypothesis. Recall that we would expect to observe a sample slope, $\hat{\beta}_1$, that deviates from the true slope, β_1, by more than 1.96 standard deviations, at most 5% of the time. Thus, if we use a significance level of 5%, we would decide in favor of the alternative hypothesis when

$$|Z| = \left| \frac{\hat{\beta}_1 - a}{\sigma_{\hat{\beta}_1}} \right| > 1.96$$

More generally, we would decide in favor of the alternative when

$$|Z| = \left| \frac{\hat{\beta}_1 - a}{\sigma_{\hat{\beta}_1}} \right| > z_{1-\alpha/2}$$

where α is the desired significance level. Similar to our earlier discussion regarding confidence intervals, if we have to use the sample to estimate the standard deviation of the slope, $s_{\hat{\beta}}$, we use the t distribution rather than the normal distribution to determine our critical values.

To test one-sided alternatives we proceed in a fashion analogous to that used when testing hypotheses for means and proportions. For example, to test the one-sided (upper tail) hypothesis

$$H_0 : \beta_1 = a$$
$$H_1 : \beta_1 > a$$

we would decide in favor of the alternative when

$$\frac{\hat{\beta}_1}{\sigma_{\hat{\beta}_1}} - a > z_{1-\alpha}$$

An alternative approach would calculate p-values rather than comparing a z- or t-statistic to the relevant critical values. As described in Chapter 8, this approach would start with the z- or t-statistics just defined and calculate the probability of observing the value of $\hat{\beta}_1$ or larger that we observed in the sample assuming the null hypothesis is true. In other words, with the z-statistic we would use the relationship

$$|Z| = \left| \frac{\hat{\beta}_1 - a}{\sigma_{\hat{\beta}_1}} \right| = z_{1-\alpha/2}$$

to estimate the value of α. Once we have computed this probability, our statistical inference would simply rely on an assessment regarding whether that probability was sufficiently small to reject the null hypothesis.

10.6 GOODNESS OF FIT (R^2)

Intuitively, it would seem that some lines are a good fit of the data while other lines are not such a good fit. Consider the two scatter plots below.

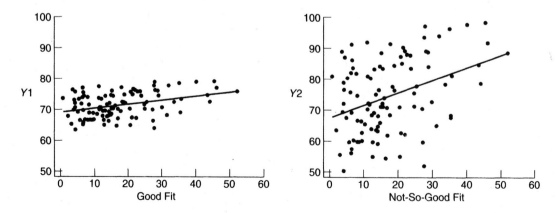

APPLICATION 10.1   *Learning the Lingo*

Interpreting the results of hypothesis tests requires learning a new language that may make the grammar confusing, but is required to be statistically accurate. Perhaps most important, it brings a whole new meaning to the word "significant," restricting its use to very particular circumstances. One must also ignore all rules regarding the use of double negatives.

Consider, for instance, the box, "Wine Appreciation," presented in Chapter 9 in which we described a regression of the log of the wine's price on its age and obtained a coefficient of 0.035. We said that this means that every additional year that a wine ages, its value increases by 3.5% (see section 9.5.2 regarding the interpretation of regression results in which the dependent variable is in logs). But this does not mean that wine prices definitely appreciate at 3.5% per year, just that 3.5% is the best estimate. That estimate comes with an associated standard error, which is 0.017. Based on this information, we can conduct a hypothesis test where we establish a null hypothesis that the slope is zero. Then the t-statistic would be 0.035/0.017 = 2.06. If we are conducting a two-sided hypothesis test (which is customary unless there is a specific reason to do otherwise) at the 5% significance level, the critical values for the t-distribution with 30 observations would be 2.04, so we would reject the null hypothesis. We would then say that the slope estimate is statistically significant at the 5% level. Notice that the word "significant" has a very specific statistical definition and does not mean "big." It means that the estimate is far enough from zero that we are willing to conclude that the "true" slope coefficient is, in fact, not zero.

Alternatively, suppose that we had decided to conduct a stronger test where we wanted to impose a 1% level of significance. The critical values for this test would be 2.75 with 30 observations. Here we say that we cannot reject the null hypothesis that the slope is zero. We can never accept the null hypothesis, which is what the rules of grammar may lead us to try to do, because we do not know if it is really true. All we can say is that we are not quite "certain enough" that it is false to reject it.

The line on the graph on the left seems to fit the data quite well, while the line on the graph on the right seems a rather poor fit. The intuition behind this assessment seems to be that the data are more scattered around the line on the right than on the left. We can formalize this basic intuition into a summary measure of the goodness of fit for a regression line. This measure is called the R^2, or "R-squared."

Intuitively, we start with the basic idea that our dependent variable varies across observations. Our model purports to explain part of this variation. For example, different people received different grades on their econometrics midterm examination. That is, the grades vary. We explain part of the variation in grades by noting that different people studied for different durations. We might ask: What fraction of the variation in grades can be explained by hours studied? The R^2 for a regression provides the answer. It tells us the fraction of the variation in the dependent variable that is explained by the explanatory variable. Clearly, the R^2 must be less than or equal to zero (i.e., none of the variation in Y can be explained by X) and at most 1 (i.e., all of the variation in Y can be explained by X).

To help in constructing the R^2 measure, consider the following decomposition.

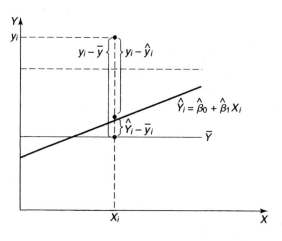

Here, we note first that our observation, Y_i, deviates from the average $\overline{Y}$. This deviation is equal to $Y_i - \overline{Y}$. Now, think of the observation as being for a particular person. Why isn't their value of Y equal to the average? There are two basic reasons. First, their value for X may differ from the average. In this case, they have a value of X higher than the average. That explains part of the difference. Indeed, this part of the difference is precisely what the regression line captures. That is, given their value of X we would predict their value of Y to be $\hat{Y}_i$. Thus, the deviation $\hat{Y}_i - \overline{Y}$ is that part of the total deviation of Y from the mean that is attributable to X. The remaining difference is contained in the error term in the regression (i.e., $Y_i - \hat{Y}_i$). In sum, we can decompose the deviation of each observation from the mean into two components:

$$(Y_i - \overline{Y}) = (\hat{Y}_i - \overline{Y}) + (Y_i - \hat{Y}_i)$$

It is possible to show that we can square and sum these deviations as follows:

$$\underbrace{\sum_{i=1}^{n}(Y_i - \overline{Y})^2}_{\substack{\text{Total sum} \\ \text{of squares} \\ \text{(TSS)}}} = \underbrace{\sum_{i=1}^{n}(\hat{Y}_i - \overline{Y})^2}_{\substack{\text{Explained sum} \\ \text{of squares} \\ \text{(ESS)}}} + \underbrace{\sum_{i=1}^{n}(Y_i - \hat{Y}_i)^2}_{\substack{\text{Unexplained sum} \\ \text{of squares} \\ \text{(USS)}}}$$

The goodness-of-fit measure, R^2, is then simply the ratio of the explained to the total variation. Or, equivalently, it is 1 minus the ratio of the unexplained to the total variation. That is,

$$R^2 = \frac{\sum_{i=1}^{n}(\hat{Y}_i - \overline{Y})^2}{\sum_{i=1}^{n}(Y_i - \overline{Y})^2} = 1 - \frac{\sum_{i=1}^{n}(Y_i - \hat{Y})^2}{\sum_{i=1}^{n}(Y_i - \overline{Y})^2}$$

or equivalently

$$R^2 = \frac{ESS}{TSS} = 1 - \frac{USS}{TSS}$$

Notice that ordinary least squares maximizes the value of R^2. This follows simply from the fact that OLS minimizes the sum of squared residuals, which is simply the unexplained variation.

An important point to recognize in evaluating regression results in light of the estimated R^2 is that one should not place too much importance on obtaining a high value. It is true that if all else is equal, a model that has a higher R^2 does explain a higher fraction of the variance or, alternatively, that the model has more explanatory power. However, the R^2 can be influenced by factors such as the nature of the data in a way that indicates one should not use it as the sole judge of the quality of the econometric model.

For instance, one regression model may use individual data on hours studied on a test score. Differences in individual abilities are certainly a large factor in explaining the variation in test scores. Since our simple model does not take that into account, one would expect the R^2 from this regression to be rather low. Alternatively, one could estimate an analogous model where observations represent the mean level of study time and the mean exam grade across dorms on campus. One would expect the variation in average student

---

APPLICATION 10.2   *Is It Hip to Be Square?*

Students are sometimes prone to compare the relative strength of regression models by the size of the R^2. The R^2 does measure the share of the variation in the dependent variable that can be explained by the independent variables in the model and, all else equal, explaining more of the variation is certainly valuable. But that does not mean that a model with a higher R^2 is necessarily better than a model with a lower R^2.

Consider, for example, the box in Chapter 9 that described regression results from a model where the dependent variable was the log of a full-time worker's weekly wage and the independent variable was his or her years of education. The data used to estimate that model came from a very large cross-sectional data set of individuals across the United States. The R^2 from that model was 0.18, indicating that differences in education can explain 18% of the variation in workers' wages. Suppose that, rather than using the data on individuals, those data were used to construct state averages and we estimated an alternative model where we regress the log of mean state wages on the mean level of education across the 50 states and the District of Columbia. The R^2 from that regression is 0.40, indicating that 40% of the variation in cross-state wages can be explained by differences in average levels of education.

Is the second model *better* than the first because the R^2 is higher even though the underlying data are identical? Probably not. By taking averages within states, we have eliminated a lot of the individual-specific variation that makes people different and cannot possibly be captured by a regression model.

SOURCE: Author's calculations from the 1991 Current Population Survey Outgoing Rotation Group file.

ability across dorms to be relatively low. On the other hand, in some dorms activities may have taken place that hindered residents' study time (a party or a pulled fire alarm?) and affected their performance on the exam. In this example, the R^2 would be relatively high because study time would reflect a large share of the differences in average test scores across dorms after differences in ability across students have been averaged out. But both examples are estimating the same underlying relationship. Therefore, one should use caution in judging the quality of a regression model on the basis of the R^2.

10.7   THE GAUSS–MARKOV THEOREM

As we have seen, our regression model is comprised of the following assumptions:

$$Y_i = \beta_0 + \beta_1 X_i + \varepsilon_i \tag{A1}$$
$$E(\varepsilon) = 0 \tag{A2}$$
$$\text{var}(\varepsilon_i) = \sigma_\varepsilon^2 \text{ for all } i \tag{A3}$$
$$\varepsilon_i \text{ and } \varepsilon_j \text{ are independent} \tag{A4}$$
$$\Rightarrow \text{Cov}(\varepsilon_i, \varepsilon_j) = 0 \ \forall_{i \neq j}$$
$$\text{Cov}(X, \varepsilon) = 0 \tag{A5}$$
$$\varepsilon_i \sim N(0, \sigma_\varepsilon^2) \tag{A6}$$

The *Gauss–Markov theorem* states that *if* assumptions (A1) – (A5) hold true ((A6) is not required), then among the class of linear unbiased estimators, ordinary least squares is the best. Here we use the word "best" in the sense that it is the most efficient (have the smallest sampling variance). In short, OLS is the *best linear unbiased estimator,* or *OLS is B. L. U. E.* Assumptions (A2) and (A5) are necessary for OLS to be unbiased. Assumptions (A3) and (A4) are required for OLS to be efficient.

This theorem provides a powerful justification for using OLS. We have already shown that, given certain assumptions, the OLS estimators are unbiased and normally distributed. The Gauss–Markov theorem states that, given we restrict ourselves to linear, unbiased estimators, OLS is the best. No other estimator in this class will be more efficient.

The proof of this theorem is somewhat more difficult than other proofs we have considered and may be omitted if desired. We will do the proof for the slope estimator.

Proof (Gauss–Markov Theorem). First, the Gauss–Markov theorem restricts us to the class of linear estimators. Thus, the estimator of β_1 must take the form

$$\hat{\beta}_1 = \sum_{i=1}^{n} w_i Y_i$$

Second, the theorem requires the estimator to be unbiased. This implies

$$E(\hat{\beta}_1) = \sum_{i=1}^{n} w_i E(Y_i)$$
$$= \sum_{i=1}^{n} w_i (\beta_0 + \beta_1 X_i)$$
$$= \beta_0 \sum_{i=1}^{n} w_i + \beta_1 \sum_{i=1}^{n} w_i X_i$$

$$= \beta_1$$

$$\Leftrightarrow \sum_{i=1}^{n} w_i = 0 \text{ and} \tag{GM1}$$

$$\sum_{i=1}^{n} w_i X_i = 1 \tag{GM2}$$

Equations (GM1) and (GM2) imply restrictions that are necessary for the estimator to be unbiased. Now, the variance of $\hat{\beta}_1$ is equal to

$$\text{var}(\hat{\beta}_1) = \text{var}\left(\sum_{i=1}^{n} w_i Y_i \right)$$

$$= \sum_{i=1}^{n} w_i^2 \, \text{var}(Y_i)$$

$$= \sigma_Y^2 \sum_{i=1}^{n} w_i^2$$

Our goal is to find the most efficient estimator. Therefore, we will select w_i to make the variance of $\hat{\beta}_1$ as small as possible, given the restrictions imposed by equations (GM1) and (GM2).

To conduct this constrained minimization problem, we first set up the Lagrangian

$$\mathsf{L} = \sum_{i=1}^{n} w_i^2 - \lambda_1 \sum_{i=1}^{n} w_i - \lambda_2 \left(\sum_{i=1}^{n} w_i x_i - 1 \right)$$

where we define $x_i = X_i - \overline{X}$ to simplify the notation. Recall:

$$\sum_{i=1}^{n} X_i - \overline{X} = 0$$

Taking the partial derivatives of the Lagrangian yields

$$\frac{\partial \mathsf{L}}{\partial w_i} = 2w_i - \lambda_1 - \lambda_2 x_i = 0 \; \forall_i \tag{GM3}$$

$$\frac{\partial \mathsf{L}}{\partial \lambda_1} = \sum_{i=1}^{n} w_i = 0 \tag{GM4}$$

$$\frac{\partial \mathsf{L}}{\partial \lambda_2} = \sum_{i=1}^{n} w_i x_i - 1 = 0 \tag{GM5}$$

We must solve these three equations for w_i.

Equation (GM3) implies

$$w_i = \frac{\lambda_1}{2} + \frac{\lambda_2}{2} x_i \; \forall_i \tag{GM6}$$

Substituting (GM6) into (GM4) yields

$$\sum_{i=1}^{n} \frac{\lambda_1}{2} + \frac{\lambda_2}{2} x_i = 0 \tag{GM7}$$

$$\Rightarrow \frac{n\lambda_1}{2} + \frac{\lambda_2}{2} \underbrace{\sum_{i=1}^{n} x_i}_{= 0} = 0$$

$$\Rightarrow \frac{n\lambda_1}{2} = 0 \Rightarrow \lambda_1 = 0$$

To solve for λ_2 substitute (GM6) into (GM5):

$$\sum_{i=1}^{n} w_i x_i - 1 = 0$$

$$\Rightarrow \sum_{i=1}^{n} \left(\frac{\lambda_1}{2} + \frac{\lambda_2}{2} x_i \right) x_i = 1 \qquad \text{(GM8)}$$

$$\Rightarrow \sum_{i=1}^{n} \frac{\lambda_2}{2} x_i^2 = 1$$

$$\Rightarrow \lambda_2 = \frac{2}{\sum_{i=1}^{n} x_i^2}$$

Finally, substituting (GM7) and (GM8) into equation (GM6) yields

$$w_i = \frac{x_i}{\sum_{i=1}^{n} x_i^2} \; \forall_i \qquad \text{(GM9)}$$

which implies that

$$\hat{\beta}_1 = \sum_{i=1}^{n} \left(\frac{x_i}{\sum_{i=1}^{n} x_i^2} \right) Y_i \qquad \text{(GM10)}$$

which is the OLS estimator. Thus, among the class of linear, unbiased estimators, OLS has the smallest sampling variance.

10.8 PROBLEMS

1. Suppose you have the following data on 11 students' combined SAT scores (X) and their cumulative grade point average at graduation (Y):

Y	X
3.63	1490
2.37	1300
3.33	1510
3.32	1420
3.27	1490
2.37	1180
3.61	1550

3.23	1460
2.59	1300
3.30	1450
3.21	1550

    a. Calculate the following: n, $\overline{X}$, $\overline{Y}$, $\Sigma(X_i - \overline{X})(Y_i - \overline{Y})$, $\Sigma(X_i - \overline{X})^2$, $\hat{\beta}_0$, $\hat{\beta}_1$.

    b. Calculate $\hat{Y}_i$ and e_i for each observation.

    c. Calculate R^2.

2. There are very few empirical laws in economics. One such law that seems to hold most of the time is *Engel's law*. Engel's law simply states that the share of the household budget devoted to food should decline as income rises. Consider the following sample of 10 households.

i	Food share (w_i)	Log income (ln I_i)
1	0.54	9.2
2	0.67	8.9
3	0.36	9.4
4	0.55	9.2
5	0.61	8.8
6	0.39	9.4
7	0.47	9.2
8	0.29	9.5
9	0.62	9.0
10	0.52	9.1

If P_F is the price of a unit of food, and Q_{Fi} is the number of units of food purchased by household i, then the food share of household i is given by $w_i = P_F Q_{Fi} / I_i$.

    A simple specification of the "Engel curve" is given by

$$w_i = \beta_0 + \beta_1 (\ln I_i) + \varepsilon_i$$

where ε_i is i.i.d. $N(0,\sigma^2)$.

    a. Showing your work, compute the ordinary least squares estimates of β_0 and β_1, as well as the standard error associated with $\hat{\beta}_1$.

    b. How would you specify the "null hypothesis" if you wanted to test the validity of Engel's law? Using this null hypothesis, test whether Engel's law appears to hold using a 95% confidence test. (That is, can you conclude that food share falls as the log of income rises?)

    c. Compute the R^2 for the regression. What does this R^2 suggest about using the log income variable to predict household food share?

3. Suppose that you estimated a regression model of the form $Y_i = \beta_0 + \beta_1 X_i + \epsilon_i$ using OLS and that you obtained an estimated value of the slope coefficient, $\hat{\beta}_1$. Now suppose that you used OLS to estimate the model, $X_i = \gamma + \delta Y_i + u_i$. Is it true in general that $\hat{\delta} = 1/\hat{\beta}_1$? In your answer, use the formulas for the slope coefficients, $\hat{\beta}_1$ and $\hat{\delta}$, to determine if this relationship still holds.

4. Having become disgruntled with the vagaries of the stock market, you decide to start a wine cellar and invest in a more liquid asset. You consider adding a California Cabernet Sauvignon to your collection. But, before writing the check you decide to do some research to determine what the return from holding this wine is. To answer this question, you realize that wine increases in value as it ages. The critical question is: By how much? That is, what is the return to holding wine as an investment?

To answer this question, you realize that the price of a wine of vintage (year of production) $T-1$ (denote this P_{T-1}) must be greater than the price of the less-aged vintage T by $r\%$. r is called the "real return to holding wine." We may express this by

$$P_T = P_{T-1}(1-r) \tag{1}$$

Furthermore, since $P_T = P_{T-1}(1-r)^1 = P_{T-2}(1-r)^2 = P_{T-3}(1-r)^3 \ldots$, we can write (1) as:

$$P_T = P_{T-V}(1-r)^V \tag{2}$$

where P_{T-V} is the price of the wine of vintage period $T-V$.

Notice that this analysis assumes that the quality of the wine of different vintages is the same. This may be false. Suppose that the difference in quality between wines of age T and $T-V$ is given by a disturbance term u_T, which depends on the weather, the wine maker, and so on (and which is not correlated across time). Taken together, these assumption imply that

$$P_T = P_{T-V}(1-r)^V * u_T \tag{3}$$

Taking the natural logarithm of both sides of (3) we have

$$\ln P_T = \ln P_{T-V} + V\ln(1-r) + \ln u_T \tag{4}$$

and using the fact that for small r, $\ln(1-r)$ is approximately equal to $-r$, yields.

$$\ln P_T = \ln P_{T-V} - rV + \ln u_T \tag{5}$$

which is a simple linear regression model of the form

$$\ln P_T = \beta_0 + \beta_1 V + u'_T \tag{6}$$

where the dependent variable, $\ln P_T$, is the natural logarithm of the auction price for wine of vintage T. The coefficient β_1 is an estimate of $-r$ (minus 1 times), the return to holding wine.

Consider the following data from the year 1987 on the average auction price for Beaulieu Vineyards Private Reserve Cabernet Sauvignon. Prices are in U.S. dollars per case.

Vintage year	Vintage "V" (age in 1987)	Auction price (in 1987) ("Price")
1960	−27	607
1962	−25	720
1963	−24	425
1964	−23	813
1966	−21	817
1967	−20	475
1968	−19	1,111
1969	−18	436
1970	−17	894
1971	−16	270
1973	−14	338
1974	−13	587
1975	−12	250
1976	−11	360
1978	−9	350

The vintage year is the year the wine was produced. The "vintage" is the age of the wine in 1987. We define vintage 1987 to be vintage zero; hence vintage year 1960 is vintage −27, etc. Finally, the third column contains the auction price data for wine of this vintage.

a. Plot the natural logarithm of the auction price in 1987 against the vintage year (from 1960 up).

b. What is an "eyeball" estimate of r, the return to holding wine (i.e., estimate the slope of the line)?

c. Calculate the ordinary least squares estimate of r. Note: The dependent variable is not "Price" but rather the *natural log* of the auction price in 1987, i.e., ln("Price"). The independent variable is "Vintage." Remember that the slope estimates minus 1 times the return.

d. What is the 95% confidence interval for the return to holding wine?

e. What are the ln(auction prices) *predicted* for each vintage (i.e., the predicted values from the regression)? What are the prediction *errors?* What is the average of these errors?

f. Complete this sentence: "Good" vintages are those with (positive/negative) errors and "Bad" vintages are those with (positive/negative) errors. Which are the top 3 vintages by this criteria?

g. Calculate and interpret the R^2 for the model.

Chapter **11**

Multiple Regression

11.1   INTRODUCTION

Up to this point, we have specified our dependent variable, Y, to be a function of a single explanatory variable, X. In this chapter we extend the model by allowing Y to be a function of more than one explanatory variable.

Such an extension is imperative if we are to apply econometric techniques to address most interesting real-world problems. For instance, in Chapter 9 we indicated that econometrics allows us to estimate the income elasticity of demand, the sensitivity of investment to the interest rate, and the impact of education on earnings. But demand for a product is a function of income and prices, the level of investment depends on economic conditions as well as the interest rate, and earnings is a function of other personal characteristics beyond the level of education. In this chapter, we will develop techniques that will allow us to identify the impact of a change in one explanatory variable on the dependent variable, assuming all of the other explanatory variables are held constant.

11.2   THE MULTIPLE REGRESSION MODEL

The *simple regression model* helped us to measure the relationship between a *dependent* variable, Y, and a single *explanatory* variable, X. It is relatively simple to extend this model to allow the dependent variable to be a function of *several* explanatory variables. This is accomplished by using a *multiple regression model*.

The multiple regression model is comprised of the following seven assumptions.

$$Y_i = \beta_0 + \beta_1 X_{1i} + \beta_2 X_{2i} + \beta_3 X_{3i} + \ldots + \beta_k X_{ki} + \varepsilon_i \tag{A1}$$

$$E(\varepsilon_i) = 0 \text{ for all } i \qquad\qquad\text{(A2)}$$

$$\text{var}(\varepsilon_i) = \sigma_\varepsilon^2 \text{ for all } i \qquad\qquad\text{(A3)}$$

$$\varepsilon_i \text{ and } \varepsilon_j \text{ are independent} \qquad\qquad\text{(A4)}$$

$$\Rightarrow \text{Cov}(\varepsilon_i, \varepsilon_j) = 0 \; x_{ji \neq j}$$

$$\text{Cov}(X_j, \varepsilon) = 0 \; x_{jj} \qquad\qquad\text{(A5)}$$

$$\varepsilon_i \sim N(0, \sigma_\varepsilon^2) \qquad\qquad\text{(A6)}$$

No explanatory variable is an exact linear function of other explanatory variables   (A7)

These assumptions are very similar to those invoked in the simple regression model. Assumption (A1) indicates that the dependent variable Y is a linear function of the explanatory variables $X_1, X_2, X_3, \ldots, X_k$. As in the case of simple regression, the relationship is not deterministic. That is, even if all of the X's were the same for two observations we would not expect the dependent variable to take on the same value. The inclusion of the error term builds this into the model. Also, as in the case of the simple regression model, the errors are assumed to have mean zero (A2), and constant variance (A3), and to be uncorrelated across observations (A4). Assumption (A5) asserts that the error term is not correlated with any of the explanatory variables. Assumption (A6) assumes the errors are drawn from a normal distribution. We will discuss assumption (A7) a little later.

Note that how reasonable these assumptions are varies in practice. When the assumptions are true we can show that the ordinary least squares estimators of $\beta_0, \beta_1, \beta_2, \beta_3, \ldots, \beta_k$ are the best linear unbiased estimators (i.e., BLUE). This need not be the case, however, when the assumptions fail. Many of the methods developed in econometrics have arisen precisely to deal with challenges that arise when the assumptions fail. Indeed, we will spend much time in future chapters investigating the consequences should they prove false.

11.3   INTERPRETATION OF THE REGRESSION COEFFICIENTS

The multiple regression model specifies $Y_i = \beta_0 + \beta_1 X_{1i} + \beta_2 X_{2i} + \beta_3 X_{3i} + \ldots + \beta_k X_{ki} + \varepsilon_i$. Given that $E(\varepsilon) = 0$, we have the population regression equation $E(Y_i) = \beta_0 + \beta_1 X_{1i} + \beta_2 X_{2i} + \beta_3 X_{3i} + \ldots + \beta_k X_{ki}$. Notice that the partial derivative

$$\frac{\partial E(Y_i)}{\partial X_j} = \beta_j$$

This tells us that increasing the explanatory variable, X_j, by one unit results in the mean value of the dependent variable changing by β_j units, *other things equal*. That is, if we hold all of the other explanatory variables constant and increase X_j by one unit, then the mean level of Y will change by β_j units. This interpretation corresponds to the economist's notion of *ceteris paribus*; it tells us the effect of X on Y, holding *other things equal (or constant)*. It is precisely this ability to make ceteris paribus comparisons in estimating the relationship between one variable and another that is the value of econometric analysis.

11.4 ESTIMATION (THREE WAYS)

Estimators for the unknown parameters $\beta_0, \beta_1, \beta_2, \ldots, \beta_k$ can be derived using the method of ordinary least squares, the method of moments, and the method of maximum likelihood. We will briefly sketch the derivation for each approach. As in the case of the simple regression model, the three approaches give rise to the same estimators.

11.4.1 Ordinary Least Squares

The method of ordinary least squares requires that we select $\hat{\beta}_0, \hat{\beta}_1, \hat{\beta}_2, \ldots, \hat{\beta}_k$ to minimize:

$$S = \sum_{i=1}^{n} e_i^2$$

$$= \sum_{i=1}^{n} (Y_i - \hat{Y}_i)^2$$

$$= \sum_{i=1}^{n} (Y_i - \hat{\beta}_0 - \hat{\beta}_1 X_{1i} - \hat{\beta}_2 X_{2i} - \hat{\beta}_3 X_{3i} \ldots - \hat{\beta}_k X_{ki})^2$$

Setting the partial derivatives

$$\frac{\partial S}{\partial \hat{\beta}_0} = 0, \frac{\partial S}{\partial \hat{\beta}_1} = 0, \ldots, \frac{\partial S}{\partial \hat{\beta}_k} = 0$$

supplies us with $k + 1$ normal equations. As in the case of simple regression, we could solve these normal equations in terms of the $k + 1$ unknown parameters $\hat{\beta}_0, \hat{\beta}_1, \hat{\beta}_2, \ldots, \hat{\beta}_k$. You should note that the estimator for, say, $\hat{\beta}_1$ is not the same as that derived for the simple regression model. Indeed, the functional form will be considerably more complicated. Its complete presentation largely requires the use of linear algebra, which is beyond the scope of this book, so we do not present it here. We present an example of the form of $\hat{\beta}_1$ in the simple regression model compared with a model with two explanatory variables in section 11.4.4.

11.4.2 Method of Moments

Using the method of moments, we recognize certain restrictions in the population that are implied in the multiple regression model. There are the following $k + 1$ restrictions:

$$(R_1) \sum_{i=1}^{n} e_i = 0$$

$$(R_2) \sum_{i=1}^{n} X_{1i} e_i = 0$$

$$(R_3) \sum_{i=1}^{n} X_{2i} e_i = 0$$

$$(R_4) \sum_{i=1}^{n} X_{3i}e_i = 0$$

$$\vdots$$

$$(R_{k+1}) \sum_{i=1}^{n} X_{ki}e_i = 0$$

Again, there are $k + 1$ restrictions that could be solved for the $k + 1$ unknown parameters. It can easily be shown that the equations implied by these restrictions give rise to the same $k + 1$ normal equations as those derived using ordinary least squares.

11.4.3   Maximum Likelihood

Suppose assumption (A6) holds. Then, $Y_i \sim N(\beta_0 + \beta_1 X_{1i} + \beta_2 X_{2i} + \beta_3 X_{3i} + \ldots + \beta_k X_{ki}, \sigma_\varepsilon^2)$. We observe a sample of n observations $y_1, y_2, y_3, \ldots, y_n$, which would have a likelihood function $L(\beta_0, \beta_1, \sigma_\varepsilon^2) = f(y_1, y_2, y_3, \ldots, y_n)$. Assuming the observations are independent and identically distributed (as per our assumptions) yields $L(\beta_0, \beta_1, \sigma_\varepsilon^2) = f(y_1) f(y_2) f(y_3) \ldots f(y_n)$. Since $Y_i \sim N(\beta_0 + \beta_1 X_{1i} + \beta_2 X_{2i} + \beta_3 X_{3i} + \ldots + \beta_k X_{ki}, \sigma_\varepsilon^2)$ implies

$$f(y_i) = \frac{1}{\sqrt{2\pi\sigma_\varepsilon^2}} e\left\{ -\frac{1}{2} \left(\frac{Y_i - \beta_0 - \beta_1 X_{1i} - \beta_2 X_{2i} - \beta_3 X_{3i} - \ldots - \beta_k X_{ki}}{\sigma_\varepsilon^2} \right)^2 \right\}$$

then,

$$L(\beta_0, \beta_1, \sigma_\varepsilon^2) = f(y_1) f(y_2) f(y_3) \ldots f(y_n)$$

$$= \frac{1}{\sqrt{2\pi\sigma_\varepsilon^2}} e\left\{ -\frac{1}{2} \left(\frac{Y_1 - \beta_0 - \beta_1 X_{11} - \beta_2 X_{21} - \beta_3 X_{31} - \ldots - \beta_k X_{k1}}{\sigma_\varepsilon^2} \right)^2 \right\} \cdot \frac{1}{\sqrt{2\pi\sigma_\varepsilon^2}} e\left\{ -\frac{1}{2} \left(\frac{Y_2 - \beta_0 - \beta_1 X_{12} - \beta_2 X_{22} - \beta_3 X_{32} - \ldots - \beta_k X_{k2}}{\sigma_\varepsilon^2} \right)^2 \right\} \cdot$$

$$\ldots \cdot \frac{1}{\sqrt{2\pi\sigma_\varepsilon^2}} e\left\{ -\frac{1}{2} \left(\frac{Y_n - \beta_0 - \beta_1 X_{1n} - \beta_2 X_{2n} - \beta_3 X_{3n} - \ldots - \beta_k X_{kn}}{\sigma_\varepsilon^2} \right)^2 \right\}$$

$$= \left(\frac{1}{\sqrt{2\pi\sigma_\varepsilon^2}} \right)^n e\left\{ \frac{-1}{2\sigma_\varepsilon^2} \left(\sum_{i=1}^{n} Y_i - \beta_0 - \beta_1 X_{1i} - \beta_2 X_{2i} - \beta_3 X_{3i} - \ldots - \beta_k X_{ki} \right)^2 \right\}$$

Taking logs yields

$$\ln L(\beta_0, \beta_1, \sigma_\varepsilon^2) = n \ln\left(\frac{1}{\sqrt{2\pi\sigma_\varepsilon^2}} \right) - \frac{1}{2\sigma_\varepsilon^2} \sum_{i=1}^{n} (Y_i - \beta_0 - \beta_1 X_{1i} - \beta_2 X_{2i} - \beta_3 X_{3i} - \ldots - \beta_k X_{ki})^2$$

We would take the derivative of the log likelihood function with respect to β_0, β_1 to find the MLE estimators. But, notice that when taking these derivatives we will simply minimize

$$\sum_{i=1}^{n} (Y_i - \beta_0 - \beta_1 X_{1i} - \beta_2 X_{2i} - \beta_3 X_{3i} - \ldots - \beta_k X_{ki})^2$$

which is the same as doing ordinary least squares.

11.4.4   Example: The Simple and Two-Variable Regression Models

In the simple regression model $Y_i = \beta_0 + \beta_1 X_i + \varepsilon_i$ the OLS estimators were shown to be $\hat{\beta}_0 = \bar{Y} - \hat{\beta}_1 \bar{X}$, and

$$\hat{\beta}_1 = \frac{\sum_{i=1}^{n}(Y_i - \bar{Y})(X_i - \bar{X})}{\sum_{i=1}^{n}(X_i - \bar{X})^2}$$

The OLS estimators in the two-variable regression model $Y_i = \beta_0 + \beta_1 X_{1i} + \beta_2 X_{2i} + \varepsilon_i$ are considerably more complicated to derive, but can be shown to be $\hat{\beta}_0 = \bar{Y} - \hat{\beta}_1 \bar{X}_1 - \hat{\beta}_2 \bar{X}_2$, and

$$\hat{\beta}_1 = \frac{\left(\sum_{i=1}^{n}(X_{1i} - \bar{X}_1)(Y_i - \bar{Y})\right)\left(\sum_{i=1}^{n}(X_{2i} - \bar{X}_2)^2\right)}{\left(\sum_{i=1}^{n}(X_{1i} - \bar{X}_1)^2\right)\left(\sum_{i=1}^{n}(X_{2i} - \bar{X}_2)^2\right)}$$
$$\frac{-\left(\sum_{i=1}^{n}(X_{2i} - \bar{X}_2)(Y_i - \bar{Y})\right)\left(\sum_{i=1}^{n}(X_{1i} - \bar{X}_1)(X_{2i} - \bar{X}_2)\right)}{-\left(\sum_{i=1}^{n}(X_{1i} - \bar{X}_1)(X_{2i} - \bar{X}_2)\right)^2}$$

$$\hat{\beta}_2 = \frac{\left(\sum_{i=1}^{n}(X_{2i} - \bar{X}_2)(Y_i - \bar{Y})\right)\left(\sum_{i=1}^{n}(X_{1i} - \bar{X}_1)^2\right)}{\left(\sum_{i=1}^{n}(X_{1i} - \bar{X}_1)^2\right)\left(\sum_{i=1}^{n}(X_{2i} - \bar{X}_2)^2\right)}$$
$$\frac{-\left(\sum_{i=1}^{n}(X_{1i} - \bar{X}_1)(Y_i - \bar{Y})\right)\left(\sum_{i=1}^{n}(X_{1i} - \bar{X}_1)(X_{2i} - \bar{X}_2)\right)}{-\left(\sum_{i=1}^{n}(X_{1i} - \bar{X}_1)(X_{2i} - \bar{X}_2)\right)^2}$$

If you moved to a three-variable regression model, the formulas would become even longer. In reality, these formulas are derived and calculated using the rules of linear algebra. Fortunately, from a practical standpoint, the formulas will be programmed into a computer for our use and we will never have to do the calculations by hand!

11.5 R^2 REVISITED

In the case of multiple regression, the goodness-of-fit measure, R^2, tells us the proportion of the variation in the dependent variable, Y, that is explained by the explanatory variables $X_1, X_2, X_3, \ldots, X_k$ collectively. As such, R^2 will be between zero (i.e., the linear function of the X's explains none of the variation in Y) and 1 (i.e., the linear function of the X's explains all of the variation in Y). It should be clear that adding another explanatory variable cannot make the R^2 fall. That is, you cannot reduce the proportion of the variation explained when you have additional variables with which to do the explaining. The worst that can happen is that an additional "explanatory variable" has no explanatory power. In that case, adding the variable to the regression model will leave R^2 unchanged. The definition of R^2 is, as before:

$$R^2 = \frac{\sum_{i=1}^{n}(\hat{Y}_i - \bar{Y})^2}{\sum_{i=1}^{n}(Y_i - \bar{Y})^2} = 1 - \frac{\sum_{i=1}^{n}(Y_i - \hat{Y})^2}{\sum_{i=1}^{n}(Y_i - \hat{Y})^2}$$

or equivalently,

$$R^2 = \frac{ESS}{TSS} = 1 - \frac{USS}{TSS}$$

where ESS, USS, and TSS were defined in Chapter 10 to be the explained, unexplained, and total sum of squares. But in the multiple regression model, $\hat{Y}_i = \hat{\beta}_0 + \hat{\beta}_1 X_{1i} + \hat{\beta}_2 X_{2i} + \hat{\beta}_3 X_{3i} + \ldots + \hat{\beta}_k X_{ki}$.

Remember that ordinary least squares minimizes the sum of squared errors. In so doing it serves to maximize the value of R^2.

11.6   INFERENCE IN THE MULTIPLE REGRESSION MODEL

The starting point for creating confidence intervals and conducting tests of hypotheses is the recognition that different samples will yield different estimates for the population intercept and slope coefficients. As such, $\hat{\beta}_0, \hat{\beta}_1, \hat{\beta}_2, \ldots, \hat{\beta}_k$ are random variables and will have sampling distributions with standard errors. We will denote the standard errors for the estimated coefficients by $\sigma_{\hat{\beta}_0}^2, \sigma_{\hat{\beta}_1}^2, \sigma_{\hat{\beta}_2}^2, \ldots, \sigma_{\hat{\beta}_k}^2$. Since these variances will typically need to be estimated, we will denote their estimated values by $s_{\hat{\beta}_0}^2, s_{\hat{\beta}_1}^2, s_{\hat{\beta}_2}^2, \ldots, s_{\hat{\beta}_k}^2$.

11.6.1   Confidence Intervals

In the multiple regression model, assuming normality of the error term, each $\hat{\beta}_j \sim N(\beta_j, \sigma_{\hat{\beta}_j}^2)$. Standardizing, we have

$$\frac{\hat{\beta}_j - \beta_j}{\sigma_{\hat{\beta}_j}} \sim N(0,1)$$

Then, defining (as usual) $z_{1 - \alpha/2}$ to be the value of Z for which $F(z_{1 - \alpha/2}) = 1 - \alpha/2$, where F is the distribution function for the standard normal distribution it follows that

$$P(-z_{(1-\alpha/2)} \leq Z \leq z_{1-\alpha/2}) = 1 - \alpha$$

$$\Rightarrow P\left(-z_{1-\alpha/2} \leq \frac{\hat{\beta}_j - \beta_j}{\sigma_{\hat{\beta}_j}} \leq z_{1-\alpha/2}\right) = 1 - \alpha$$

$$\Rightarrow P(\hat{\beta}_j - z_{1-\alpha/2}\sigma_{\hat{\beta}_j} \leq \beta_j \leq \hat{\beta}_j + z_{1-\alpha/2}\sigma_{\hat{\beta}_j}) = 1 - \alpha$$

which is the $100(1 - \alpha)\%$ confidence interval for $\hat{\beta}_j$.

We will typically have to estimate $\hat{\sigma}_{\hat{\beta}_j}$ using an unbiased estimator we will denote by $s_{\hat{\beta}_j}$. We can then proceed in deriving a similar confidence interval, though now we use the t distribution in place of the standard normal distribution when n is small. Recall, when n is large $t_{n-1,1-\alpha/2} \approx Z_{1-\alpha/2}$. That is, our confidence interval is $P(\hat{\beta}_j - t_{(n-k-1-\alpha/2)}s_{\hat{\beta}_j} \le \beta_j \le \hat{\beta}_j + t_{(n-k-1-\alpha/2)}s_{\hat{\beta}_j}) = 1 - \alpha$, where the formula used to calculate $s_{\hat{\beta}_j}$ will generally be a fairly complicated function (programmed into the computer, in practice).

Forming one-tailed confidence intervals is done analogously to the approach used for means in Chapter 8. For example, to form an upper bound on the population slope parameter β_j we use the interval $P(-\infty \le \beta_j \le \hat{\beta}_j + t_{(n-k-1-\alpha)}s_{\hat{\beta}_j}) = 1 - \alpha$. To form a lower bound we use the interval $P(\beta_j - t_{(n-k-1-\alpha)}s_{\hat{\beta}_j} \le \beta_j \le \infty) = 1 - \alpha$.

11.6.2   Hypothesis Tests on a Single Coefficient

Hypothesis tests for individual coefficients are conducted using the same approach used for the simple regression model. Suppose we have the following null and alternative hypotheses:

$$H_0: \beta_j = a$$
$$H_1: \beta_j \ne a$$

The farther the sample estimate $\hat{\beta}_j$ is from a, the less plausible would be the null hypothesis. More formally, the statistic

$$\left| \frac{\hat{\beta}_j - a}{\sigma_{\hat{\beta}_j}} \right|$$

tells us the number of standard deviations our sample slope is from the slope hypothesized under the null. The larger this number, the less plausible is the null hypothesis. Recall that we would expect to observe a sample slope, $\hat{\beta}_j$, that deviates from the true slope, β_j, by more than 1.96 standard deviations at most 5% of the time. Thus, if we use a significance level of 5%, we would decide to reject the null hypothesis when

$$\left| \frac{\hat{\beta}_j - a}{\sigma_{\hat{\beta}_j}} \right| > 1.96$$

More generally, we would decide to reject the null hypothesis when

$$\left| \frac{\hat{\beta}_j - a}{\sigma_{\hat{\beta}_j}} \right| > z_{1-\alpha/z}$$

where α is the desired significance level. As when constructing confidence intervals, we use the t distribution with, in this case, $n - k$ degrees of freedom if we use $s^2_{\hat{\beta}_j}$ the estimated variance. That is, our decision rule would have us choose against the null hypothesis when

$$\left| \frac{\hat{\beta}_j - a}{s_{\hat{\beta}_j}} \right| > t_{(n-k-1-\alpha/2)}$$

To test the one-sided (upper tail) hypotheses

$$H_0: \beta_1 = a$$
$$H_1: \beta_1 > a$$

we would decide to reject the null hypothesis when

$$\left| \frac{\hat{\beta}_1 - a}{s_{\hat{\beta}_1}} \right| > t_{(n-k-1,\, 1-\alpha)}$$

11.6.3   The Rule of 2

Often we are interested in testing whether a particular explanatory variable has any impact (other things equal) on the dependent variable. Suppose, for example our model is $Y_i = \beta_0 + \beta_1 X_{1i} + \beta_2 X_{2i} + \beta_3 X_{3i} + \ldots + \beta_k X_{ki} + \varepsilon_i$, with all of the other usual assump-

---

APPLICATION 11.1   *It's a Tough Job, but Someone Has to Do It*

College admissions officers spend weeks poring over applicants' records determining whom to admit and whom to reject. Predicting who will succeed academically at the particular institution is an important component of that decision process; high school grades and SAT scores are important inputs in this process. But how well do these factors predict academic success in college? Do they predict success at all?

These questions can be answered by an appropriate econometric analysis and past research has done just that. For instance, one research paper uses data from the University of California at San Diego in which the author of the study has access to a wide range of information on the characteristics and high school preparation for over 5000 enrolled students over a three-year period. In one regression model, the impact of SAT scores and high school GPA are included as the only explanatory variables in a model of college GPA. The results are as follows:

	Coefficient	Standard error	T-statistic
Intercept	−0.2758	0.082	−3.38
High school GPA	0.5272	0.018	29.22
SAT math	0.0008	0.00008	9.90
SAT verbal	0.0009	0.00007	13.07

These results indicate that each of these factors is positively and statistically significantly related to academic performance in college. Importantly, the R^2 from this regression is only 0.28, indicating that these measures can explain only 28% of the variability in college GPA across students. In fact, in subsequent models that include a large array of additional explanatory variables, including demographic characteristics of the student's household and the characteristics of the high school the student attended, no more than 40% of this variation could be explained. Therefore, college admissions officers must be spending most of their time trying to uncover the less quantifiable factors that are linked to success. Econometrics can get you only part of the way there!

SOURCE: Betts, Julian and Darlene Morrell, "The Determinants of Undergraduate Grade Point Average," *Journal of Human Resources*, Vol. 34, No. 2 (Spring 1999), pp. 268–293.

APPLICATION 11.2 | *If the Sun Don't Shine, Don't Buy the Wine*

In Chapter 9, we described the relationship between wine prices and their vintage. But the scatter plot presented there clearly indicated that a wine's age does not perfectly predict its price; individual data points diverge significantly from the regression line. In fact, the R^2 from that regression is 0.21, indicating that vintage explains only 21% of the variation in wine prices. What else is related to a wine's price? Knowing these factors may help identify those wines that will be more valuable in the future long before wine tasters are capable of assessing whether a particular vintage is a good one.

The same study described earlier also hypothesized that the quality of a vintage, and hence its price, should be affected by weather conditions just prior to and during the growing season. The authors estimated a multiple regression model to test their hypothesis and the results are reported below (an intercept was included in their model, but not reported in the study). Results indicate that the average temperature during the growing season and the amount of rainfall during the growing season and in the preceding winter all have statistically significant effects on wine prices. Prices tend to be higher when the growing season is hot and dry and when rainfall was heavy in the preceding winter. The R^2 for this regression is 0.83, indicating that 83% of the variation in wine prices can be explained by the model.

	Coefficient	Standard error	T-statistic
Age of vintage	0.024	0.007	3.43
Average growing season temperature	0.616	0.095	6.48
Rainfall in August and September	−0.0039	0.0008	−4.88
Rainfall in the preceding winter	0.0012	0.0005	2.40

SOURCE: Ashenfelter, Orley, David Ashmore, and Robert Lalonde, "Bordeaux Wine Vintage Quality and the Weather," *Chance*, Vol. 8, No. 4 (Fall 1995), pp. 7–14.

---

tions holding. Now, to say, for example, that X_1 has an impact on Y is to say that $\beta_1 \neq 0$. After all, β_1 measures the effect of X_1 on Y, other things equal. More generally, this suggests we are often interested in testing the hypotheses

$$H_0: \beta_j = 0$$
$$H_1: \beta_j \neq 0$$

Testing this is done as described above. We form the test statistic

$$\left| \frac{\hat{\beta}_j - 0}{s_{\hat{\beta}_j}} \right|$$

(assuming we must estimate the standard error) and see if it exceeds the critical value $t_{(n-k, 1-\alpha/2)}$. Notice that the test statistic for this hypothesis simplifies to

$$\left| \frac{\hat{\beta}_j}{s_{\hat{\beta}_j}} \right|$$

which is the ratio of the estimated coefficient to the estimated standard error in absolute value. More intuitively, it tells us the number of standard deviations our estimated coefficient is from zero. If $n - k$ is greater than roughly 20 and our desired significance level is 5%, then the cutoff $t_{(n - k, 1 - \alpha/2)}$ is approximately equal to 2. This suggests the following rule of thumb: If the ratio of the estimated coefficient to its standard error exceeds 2 (in absolute value), we reject the null that the explanatory variable has no effect on the dependent variable. More simply, reject H_0 if

$$\left| \frac{\hat{\beta}_j}{s_{\hat{\beta}_j}} \right| > 2$$

11.7 PROBLEMS

1. A regression of cumulative GPA on math and verbal SAT scores from a large sample of students yields the following equation (the numbers in parentheses are the standard errors for the associated coefficient):

   GPA = .65 +   .0020V + .0015M; where V is verbal SAT and M is math SAT

   (.086)   (.0011) (.0011)

   a. How would you interpret the coefficients in this equation?
   b. Could you conclude that the coefficients are significantly different from zero? At what significance level could you reject the claim that verbal SAT has no impact on grades?
   c. What is the 99% confidence interval for the effect of math SAT on grades?
   d. Suppose we changed our data so that our verbal and math SAT scores were all divided by 100 (e.g., what had been a 1500 score in our data would now be coded as 15). How would this change the estimated equation?
   e. What grade would you predict for someone who scored 500 on both SAT tests? Why might this person's actual grade deviate from the grade predicted by the model?

2. A higher-education management consultant wanted to see whether a university computer help desk had sufficient resources to assist faculty with computer problems. The consultant randomly sampled 200 faculty, and found their waiting times on the phone had an average of 15 minutes and a standard deviation of 5 minutes. To determine the factors that influence waiting time, he estimated a multiple regression model finding:

   Wait = 45 − 1.2*Lines − 7*Staff

   (.8)   (3.2)

   where:

   The numbers in parentheses are the standard errors for the corresponding coefficient estimates

   Wait = waiting time in minutes

   Lines = the number of phone lines available

   Staff = the usual number of staff working at the help desk

   a. Interpret the coefficient estimates.
   b. You are 95% sure the average waiting time is between what lower and upper bound?

c. What is the probability we would see a regression estimate of the impact of number of phone lines on waiting time as large as the one we saw if this variable really had no effect on waiting times?

3. Suppose you are interested in estimating the impact of years of schooling and labor market experience on wages. To do so, you estimate an equation of the form $\ln(wages_i) = \beta_0 + \beta_1 S_i + \beta_2 E_i + \varepsilon_i$, where S is years of schooling and E is years of labor market experience. Using the data provided in http://www.wiley.com/college/ashenfelter.

   a. Estimate β_0, β_1, and β_2. Write out the estimated regression equation and interpret the coefficients.

   b. What fraction of the variance in log wages is explained by the two explanatory variables?

   c. Test the hypothesis that the coefficient on the return to education is greater than 10% percent using a 5% significance level.

   d. At what significance level can you reject the hypothesis that schooling has no impact on wages?

   e. At what significance level can you reject the hypothesis that the effect of schooling on wages does not equal 5%?

   f. (optional) Now, estimate the model $\ln(earnings_i) = \beta_0 + \beta_1 S_i + \beta_2 E_i + \beta_2 E_i^2 + \varepsilon_i$, where the variable E_i^2 is the square of the number of years of labor market experience. Why would you include a quadratic expression of this type in this model? At what number of years of experience is earnings maximized?

4. On March 4, 1990, the *New York Times* reported "Wine Equation Puts Some Noses Out of Joint." In this problem you will estimate an equation that predicts the quality of wine. Typically wine is rated long before it is ready to drink by having an "expert" taste the premature wine from the barrel. Their pronouncements on the quality of the wine help determine the wholesale price. Often it will take many years before the wine can be ranked with any precision. Professor Ashenfelter, however, has devised a regression model that predicts wine quality by incorporating as explanatory variables the weather that prevailed when the wine was grown. The belief that weather affects wine quality is widespread, but Ashenfelter offered an explicit equation to assess the quality of red wine from the Bordeaux region of France. The data you will use contains four variables: an index of auction prices for wine that has matured (measured in logs), the level of winter rain (October through March—measured in millimeters), average temperature during the growing season (April through September—measured in degrees celsius), and the level of harvest rain (August through September—measured in millimeters). These data are available in http://www.wiley.com/college/ashenfelter.

   a. Estimate the wine equation through the period 1987. Interpret the coefficients.

   b. What proportion of the variation in wine prices does the model explain?

   c. Explain how you would use this model to predict the quality of wines that are not yet mature.

5. The data found in http://www.wiley.com/college/ashenfelter contains information from the year-2000 Professional Golfers' Association tour. It includes the players' names, their average score, the average distance they drive the golfball, the number of greens they "hit in regulation" (i.e., the number of times their ball is on the green in 1 shot for a par three, 2 for a par four, and 3 for a par five), and the number of putts they take per greens hit in regulation.

   a. Estimate a model relating score to driving distance, greens in regulation, and putts. How do we interpret these results? Do any of the results look peculiar? Why? What might explain this fact?

b. If we view the error in this equation as "luck," which player is the luckiest? Which is the un-luckiest? Is it appropriate to think of the error as luck? Why or why not?

c. For Corey Pavin (winner of the 1995 U.S. Open) the statistics look like the following for 1995 and 2000:

	1995	2000
Average score	70.04	71.7
Rank on money list	4	156
Rank on scoring list	11	140
Driving distance	254.9	251.3
Greens in regulation	11.898	10.476
Putts per round	28.99	28.51

Using the scoring model, how would you explain Corey's fall from glory?

Chapter 12

Extending the Multiple Regression Model

12.1 INTRODUCTION

12.2 DUMMY EXPLANATORY VARIABLES

12.3 HYPOTHESIS TESTS ON SEVERAL REGRESSION COEFFICIENTS: F TESTS

12.4 PROBLEMS

12.1 INTRODUCTION

We would frequently like to include explanatory variables in our regression model that are *qualitative* in nature. For example, we might want to study the link between gender or race (both qualitative variables) and earnings (a quantitative variable). A *dummy variable* allows us to incorporate such qualitative variables into our regression model. In this chapter we will show how dummy variables can be used to allow the intercept in the regression model to differ across different groups (e.g., defined by race or gender) in the sample. We will also show how dummy variables can be used to allow the slope(s) in a regression model to vary across groups. We will then show other applications of dummy variables and end the chapter by showing how they can be used to do hypothesis tests on several coefficients jointly in the regression model (as compared to tests on a single variable as considered in the previous chapter).

12.2 DUMMY EXPLANATORY VARIABLES

Dummy variables (also called *qualitative* or *categorical* variables) allow us to incorporate qualitative variables into our regression model.

Example

1. A wide body of academic literature studies the impact of gender on earnings. Gender is a qualitative variable taking on the value "male" or "female." A dummy variable will convert gender into a quantitative variable, perhaps taking on the value 0 for men and 1 for women.

2. A researcher wants to include measures for the region of the country in which a person lives. She breaks the country down into two broad regions: "north" and "south." She then quantifies these variables by creating a dummy variable taking

on the value 0 if the person is from the north and 1 if the person is from the south. Notice that dummy variables are *mutually exclusive* and *exhaustive*. That is, it must be possible to assign each observation a single value for the dummy variable. In the above examples, at least at a point in time, a person is either male or female, and they live in either the north or the south.

12.2.1 Defining and Interpreting Dummy Variables

Dummy variables allow the *intercept* of the regression line to vary for different *groups* in the population.

Example

By *group,* we mean any variable that is qualitative in nature. It could be race, gender, union status, region of country, whether the country is at war, and so on. Consider the following regression equation comprised of one dummy explanatory variable:

$$Earnings_i = \beta_0 + \beta_1\ Gender_i + \varepsilon_i \tag{1}$$

where

$$Gender = \begin{cases} 1 \text{ if the observation is for a woman} \\ 0 \text{ if the observation is for a man} \end{cases}$$

This model relates earnings to gender and incorporates the qualitative variable *Gender* by turning it into a quantitative variable taking on the value 1 for women and 0 for men.

How do we interpret the coefficients in this simple model? If we take the expected value of the equation for women (i.e., *Gender* = 1) we have the following conditional expectation:

$$E(Earnings/Gender = 1) = \beta_0 + \beta_1 \tag{1a}$$

That is, the mean earnings for women are given by the sum of the coefficients β_0 and β_1.

Taking the expected value of the equation for men (i.e., *Gender* = 0) gives us:

$$E(Earnings/Gender = 0) = \beta_0 \tag{1b}$$

This tells us that the coefficient β_0 measures the mean earnings for men. Next, notice that subtracting (1b) from (1a) yields:

$$\underbrace{E(Earnings/Gender = 1)}_{\text{Mean female earnings}} - \underbrace{E(Earnings/Gender = 0)}_{\text{Mean male earnings}} = \beta_1 \tag{1c}$$

That is, the coefficient β_1 measures the difference in mean earnings between women and men.

Now, let's include another explanatory variable, *Education,* into the model. Figure 12.1 displays an example of a scatter plot of men's and women's wages in relation to their level of education, along with their predicted relationship. These data can be characterized by the following regression equation:

$$Earnings_i = \beta_0 + \beta_1 \, Gender_i + \beta_2 \, Education_i + \varepsilon_i \tag{2}$$

where

$$Gender = \begin{cases} 1 \text{ if the observation is for a woman} \\ 0 \text{ if the observation is for a man} \end{cases}$$

Then we have

$$E(Earnings/Gender = 1) = \underbrace{(\beta_0 + \beta_1)}_{\text{Intercept for women}} + \beta_2 \, Education \tag{2a}$$

$$E(Earnings/Gender = 0) = \underbrace{\beta_0}_{\text{Intercept for men}} + \beta_2 \, Education \tag{2b}$$

Notice that adding the dummy variable for gender allows the intercept to vary by gender. That is, the intercept of the regression line is β_0 for men and $\beta_0 + \beta_1$ for women. To interpret the dummy variable notice that

$$\underbrace{E(Earnings/Gender = 1)}_{\text{Mean female earnings controlling for education}} - \underbrace{E(Earnings/Gender = 0)}_{\text{Mean male earnings controlling for education}} = \beta_1 \tag{3}$$

That is, the coefficient β_1 measures the difference in mean earnings between women and men, *holding education constant*. That is, it is the impact of gender on earnings after controlling for education.

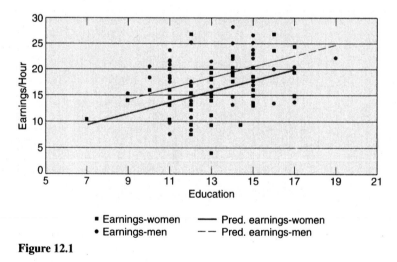

Figure 12.1

12.2.2   Interaction Variables

As we have seen, dummy variables allow the intercept of the regression line to vary between different groups as characterized by some qualitative variable. It is sometimes useful, how-

---

APPLICATION 12.1   *If the* t *Is Greater than Two, the Verdict May Go against You*

How do courts decide whether a firm is discriminating against, say, women in an employment discrimination case? It turns out that statistical evidence often plays an important role. In economics, we would say that discrimination exists if a group of workers is paid less than what they deserve based on their productivity. Statistically, we can implement this definition by determining whether women are paid the same as men once we hold constant differences in their productivity. In its simplest form, this may be implemented by estimating the regression model $\ln W_i = \beta_0 + \beta_1 \cdot X_i + \beta_2 \cdot F_i + \varepsilon_i$, where W represents wages, X represents productivity-related factors, F indicates whether the worker is female, and i indexes individuals at a particular firm. Discrimination would be said to exist if β_2 is negative and statistically significantly different from zero at, say, the 5% level (i.e., $|t| > 2$).

The key stumbling block to this approach, however, is determining what X variables to include in the model. To the extent that some productivity-related characteristics are not included, β_2 may be negative even if employers are not discriminating (this is called omitted variable bias and it is described in detail in Chapter 13). On the other hand, if variables are included that have nothing to do with productivity but are related to gender (height, for instance), some of the disadvantages women face may be captured by these variables, reducing the coefficient of β_2 and, therefore, reducing the appearance of discrimination.

Consider, for example, a wage discrimination case brought in the 1970s against the *New York Times*. The following regression results on the *level* (not log) of weekly wages were entered into the court record:

	In models that include:		
	(1)	(2)	(3)
			(2) plus past job experience,
	No other	Education and	awards, past promotions and merit
	explanatory variables	experience	pay raises, and marital status
Coefficient and standard error (in parentheses) on female dummy variable	−96.78 (9.35)	−77.14 (8.51)	−13.68 (11.04)

The first regression indicates that women made $97 per week (or 22%) less than men, on average. After controlling for education and experience, that differential drops to $77. Both these estimates are statistically significant. The differential becomes small and statistically insignificant after including variables like past pay raises and promotions. The defense would therefore argue that there is no discrimination. The plaintiff's lawyers would rebut that past pay and promotions reflect the same inequities and do not belong in the model. The outcome would depend on who makes a more convincing argument. That's why we have lawyers!

SOURCE: Finkelstein, Michael O. and Bruce Levin. *Statistics for Lawyers.* New York: Springer-Verlag, 1990; and unpublished documents.

ever, to allow the slope coefficient(s) to vary across the groups as well. This is accomplished by using an *interaction variable* (or *interaction term*). Consider again model (2):

$$Earnings_i = \beta_0 + \beta_1\, Gender_i + \beta_2\, Education_i + \varepsilon_i$$

As we have seen, the coefficient on *Gender* tells us the difference between female and male earnings, holding education constant. In this model β_1 measures the difference in earnings between women and men, holding education constant. The slope coefficient on education, β_2, measures the increment in earnings resulting from an additional year of schooling, that is,

$$\frac{\partial E\,(Earnings)}{\partial Education} = \beta_2$$

In this specification, this "return" to education is assumed to be equal for men and women. But it is possible that it differs by gender as represented in Figure 12.2. To allow for this possibility we include a new variable in the model that is the education variable *multiplied* by the gender variable. Such a variable is called an *interaction variable* or *interaction term*. It will capture any *interaction* between gender and the impact of education on earnings. The model is now:

$$Earnings_i = \beta_0 + \beta_1\, \underbrace{Gender_i}_{\text{Dummy variable}} + \beta_2\, Education_i + \beta_3\, \underbrace{Gender_i \times Education_i}_{\text{Interaction variable}} + \varepsilon_i \quad (3a)$$

Now, to see how the inclusion of an interaction term broadens the model, consider the following partial derivative:

$$\frac{\partial E\,(Earnings)}{\partial Education} = \beta_2 + \beta_3\, Gender \quad (3b)$$

$$= \begin{cases} \beta_2 \text{ for men (i.e., } Gender = 0) \\ \beta_2 + \beta_3 \text{ for women (i.e., } Gender = 1) \end{cases}$$

In model (3) the "return" to education *depends on gender*. For men, it is β_2 and for women it is $\beta_2 + \beta_3$. Therefore, β_3 represents the difference in the slope between men and women.

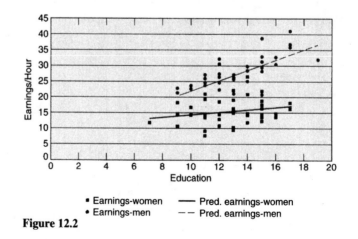

Figure 12.2

In summary, dummy variables allow the intercept to differ across groups, whereas interaction terms allow the slope to differ across groups. A model might contain *neither* dummy variables *nor* interaction terms (i.e., all groups have the same intercept and slopes), *both* dummy variables *and* interaction terms (i.e., intercept and slopes vary across groups), *only* dummy variables (i.e., only the intercept varies across groups), or *only interaction terms* (only the slopes vary across groups). In addition, you may *interact* a dummy variable with some, but not all, explanatory variables. In this case, only the interacted variables are allowed to have a different effect, by group, on the dependent variable. For example, consider the following model:

$$Y_i = \beta_0 + \beta_1 X_{1i} + \beta_2 X_{2i} + \beta_3 X_{1i} \times X_{3i} + \varepsilon_i \tag{4}$$

where

$$X_1 = \begin{cases} 1 \text{ if the observation is in group 1} \\ 0 \text{ if the observation is in group 2} \end{cases}$$

In model (4) X_1 is a dummy variable, while X_2 and X_3 are assumed to be continuous. Notice that the effect of X_1 on Y varies by group, that is,

$$\frac{\partial Y}{\partial X_1} = \beta_1 + \beta_3 X_3$$

For group 1, the effect of X_1 on Y is given by $\beta_1 + \beta_3$. For group 2, the effect of X_1 on Y is given by β_1. If we consider the effect of X_2 on Y we see that it equals β_2 and does not vary across groups, that is,

$$\frac{\partial Y}{\partial X_2} = \beta_2$$

12.2.3 Experimental versus Observational Studies

Dummy variables can be used to provide a nice summary of the key differences between *experimental* and *observational* studies. If we are trying to identify the effect of one variable (call it X) on another variable (call it Y), a nice place to begin would be with an experiment. We might randomly assign half of our sample into a group for which $X = 1$ (call it the *treatment* group) and the other half into a group for which $X = 0$ (call it the *control* group). For example, X might equal 1 if a person received a particular drug (i.e., a *treatment*). Or, using an example more linked to economic policy, X might equal 1 if a person participated in an experimental worker training program. The outcome of interest (Y) might then be the person's wage. To measure the effect of X (i.e., the training program) on Y (i.e., wages) we would simply compare the wages of the treatment group to the control group. The fact that people are randomly assigned to the groups would provide us a basis for believing that the two groups do not systematically differ in other ways (i.e., besides the treatment) that would be related to wages.

We might frame this description of an experiment using a simple dummy variable model. Consider the model:

$$Y_i = \beta_0 + \beta_1 X_i + \varepsilon_i$$

APPLICATION 12.2   *Maybe It's Something in the Brownies*

Auctions represent an important method by which goods and services are bought and sold in the economy. Beyond the sale of Van Gogh paintings and Jacqueline Kennedy's possessions, auctions are used to set the interest rate on U.S. Treasury bills and to set the purchase price for communications spectrum rights that are required for wireless technologies.

There are different ways that auctions can be run and, for the seller of these goods, finding out which way elicits the highest possible bid from potential buyers is serious business. Two of the mechanisms are Dutch auctions and first-price, sealed-bid auctions. In a Dutch auction, the price starts at a level so high that no one is willing to pay it and then the price continues to fall until one bidder claims the item and pays that price. First-price, sealed-bid auctions (used to sell U.S. Treasury bills) require bidders to submit bids privately, and at the stated deadline the sale is made to the highest bidder (which is the lowest offered interest rate in the case of Treasury bills). Economic models of auctions indicate that the two types of auctions should yield identical selling prices, but empirical tests of this prediction are quite difficult. Rarely is one able to identify the same good being sold in the two different types of auctions under identical conditions, and it is difficult to fully capture all of these differences in a regression framework.

One recent research paper, however, offers a clever experimental method to test this proposition, thanks to the growing popularity of the Internet and its tremendous advantage in cheaply and broadly disseminating information. The author of the paper purchased a large number of trading cards from a game called *Magic: The Gathering*. Trading cards for this game are routinely auctioned over the Internet using a variety of auction types. The paper reports the results of the auctions run for the same trading cards at the same time using the different auction strategies, setting up a perfect experimental framework. Results indicate that the Dutch auction elicited selling prices that were 30% higher. U.S. Treasury, take note!

SOURCE: Lucking-Reiley, David, "Using Field Experiments to Test Equivalence Between Auction Formats: Magic on the Internet," *American Economic Review*, Vol. 89, No. 5 (December 1999), pp. 1063–1081.

---

where

Y is the outcome variable of interest, and

$$X = \begin{cases} 1 \text{ for individuals in the treatment group} \\ 0 \text{ for individuals in the control group} \end{cases}$$

Notice that in this model the *treatment effect* is given by $\beta_1 = E(Y/Treatment) - E(Y/Control)$, which is the difference in the mean value of the outcome measure between the treatment and control groups. Notice further that our usual assumption that $cov(X,\varepsilon) = 0$ would be supported by the fact that people are randomly assigned to the treatment and control groups. That is, random assignment suggests that there is no reason to believe that the differences between the outcomes of the groups are systematically related to anything besides the treatment. This can be contrasted to *observational studies* in which we simply *observe* the earnings differences between people, some of whom received training and some of whom did not. In this case, our confidence that the groups are comparable might be reduced and we would strive to control for other possible differences that might affect the outcome. We will discuss this in more detail later.

12.2.4   Dummy Variables When There Are More than Two Groups

It is straightforward to extend our model to the case where the qualitative variable can take on *more than two* possible values. Consider a model relating the earnings of a child (Y) to the education of the child's parents. Here we assume the education of the parents is classified into four groups:

$$\text{Parents' education} = \begin{cases} \text{less than high school,} \\ \text{high school,} \\ \text{some college,} \\ \text{college graduate or higher} \end{cases}$$

We incorporate the parents' education into the model by creating *three* dummy variables. We create three dummy variables despite the fact that we have four categories because this approach will allow us to estimate one intercept for each group, as shown below. In general, if a qualitative variable assumes J outcomes, $J - 1$ dummy variables are included into the model. Equivalently, one category is always dropped. This is because knowing a person is not in one of the $J - 1$ categories tells us they must be in the Jth category. Hence, the Jth category is redundant. More technically, including J dummy variables would create perfect *multicollinearity*—a problem we will study in the next chapter.

Now, we can structure the above model as follows:

$$Y_i = \beta_0 + \beta_1 \, Educ_{1i} + \beta_2 \, Educ_{2i} + \beta_3 \, Educ_{3i} + \varepsilon_i$$

where

$$Educ_1 = \begin{cases} 1 \text{ if parents' education is less than high school} \\ 0 \text{ otherwise} \end{cases}$$

$$Educ_2 = \begin{cases} 1 \text{ if parents' education is exactly high school} \\ 0 \text{ otherwise} \end{cases}$$

$$Educ_3 = \begin{cases} 1 \text{ if parents' education is some college} \\ 0 \text{ otherwise} \end{cases}$$

Notice that we did not include a dummy variable indicating those parents with college education or higher. In effect, we left out:

$$Educ_4 = \begin{cases} 1 \text{ if parents' education is college graduate or higher} \\ 0 \text{ otherwise} \end{cases}$$

We might have left out any group—the choice is ours—but the interpretation of the regression coefficients is affected by the group left out. To see this, consider the following conditional expectations:

$$E(Y/Educ_1 = 1) = \beta_0 + \beta_1$$
$$E(Y/Educ_2 = 1) = \beta_0 + \beta_2$$
$$E(Y/Educ_3 = 1) = \beta_0 + \beta_3$$
$$E(Y/Educ_4 = 1) = \beta_0$$

The interpretation of these relationships is facilitated by Figure 12.3. Notice that the intercept measures the mean value of the dependent variable for the *excluded group* (i.e., $Educ_4$). Notice further that:

$$E(Y/Educ_1 = 1) - E(Y/Educ_4 = 1) = \beta_1$$
$$E(Y/Educ_2 = 1) - E(Y/Educ_4 = 1) = \beta_2$$
$$E(Y/Educ_3 = 1) - E(Y/Educ_4 = 1) = \beta_3$$

That is, the coefficients on the included dummy variables measure the impact of the corresponding explanatory variable *compared to the excluded category*. Thus, in our example, β_1 measures the difference in mean earnings between children whose parents had less than a high school education and those who had completed a college education (i.e., the excluded category). Similarly, β_3 measures the difference in mean earnings between children whose parents had some college education and those who had completed a college education. We might have excluded some other category. For example, had we excluded $Educ_1$ and included $Educ_4$, then the effects would be compared to those whose parents' education was less than high school. The results are always compared to the one category that is left out.

Finally, if additional explanatory variables were included in this model, we would simply change the interpretation given above by adding the phrase: *other things equal*.

12.3 HYPOTHESIS TESTS ON SEVERAL REGRESSION COEFFICIENTS: *F* TESTS

In the previous chapter we learned how to do hypothesis tests on individual regression coefficients. For example, if our model is specified as $Y_i = \beta_0 + \beta_1 X_{1i} + \beta_2 X_{2i} + \beta_3 X_{3i} + \varepsilon_i$, we could test whether $\beta_1 = 0$. We might also test whether $\beta_3 = 5$. In this section we will learn how to test more complicated hypotheses. For example, we might test whether both $\beta_1 = 0$ *and* $\beta_3 = 0$ or whether $\beta_1 = 0$ *and* $\beta_3 = 5$ jointly. Such tests are called *F tests*.

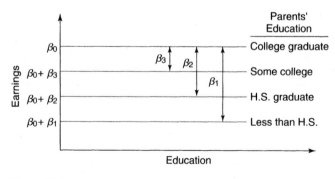

Figure 12.3

12.3.1   Joint Tests on Several Regression Coefficients

Continuing with this example, suppose we have a regression model given by

$$Y_i = \beta_0 + \beta_1 X_{1i} + \beta_2 X_{2i} + \beta_3 X_{3i} + \varepsilon_i$$

and we want to test whether both $\beta_1 = 0$ *and* $\beta_3 = 0$. To do so, we would specify the null and alternative hypotheses as follows:

$$H_0 : \beta_1 = 0 \text{ and } \beta_3 = 0$$
$$H_1 : \text{not } H_0$$

Notice that the alternative hypothesis, H_1, just indicates that the null hypothesis is false, without necessarily indicating why it is false. In particular, even if we knew for sure that the null hypothesis is not true, we would not necessarily know that both β_1 and β_3 are not equal to zero. It could be the case that just one of them was different from zero. This null hypothesis is very specific in indicating that *both* coefficients are equal to zero.

That said, we then form the regression that embodies the null hypothesis: $Y_i = \beta_0 + \beta_2 X_{2i} + \varepsilon_i$. This becomes the *restricted* regression. This regression is considered *restricted* in the sense that it *imposes* the null hypothesis under consideration on the model. This *restricted model* is the model *if* the null is true.

This model can be contrasted to an *unrestricted model* that does not impose the restrictions embodied in the null hypothesis. The unrestricted regression does not restrict the coefficients in any way and is given by the original model $Y_i = \beta_0 + \beta_1 X_{1i} + \beta_2 X_{2i} + \beta_3 X_{3i} + \varepsilon_i$.

The basic idea behind the test we seek to conduct is to see whether imposing the null hypothesis has much of an impact on how well the model fits the data. Suppose we estimated both models. If the null hypothesis is true, then both models should "fit" the data equally well. Of course, even if the null hypothesis were true, the unrestricted model would better capture random variation in the sample (in other words, β_1 and β_2 may not be exactly equal to zero in the sample) and would provide somewhat better fit. What we want to know is whether the unrestricted model provides sufficiently better fit that we are willing to reject the null hypothesis.

To implement a test of this nature, we can rely on the tools covered in Chapter 10 regarding measures of goodness of fit. In that chapter, we introduced the concepts of total, explained, and unexplained sums of squares and used them to derive a statistic, the R^2, that provides a summary measure of goodness of fit. In particular, recall from this discussion that the unexplained sum of squared residuals is defined to be

$$USS = \sum_{i=1}^{n} (Y_i - \hat{Y})^2$$

and the total sum of squared residuals is defined to be

$$TSS = \sum_{i=1}^{n} (Y_i - \bar{Y})^2, \text{ and } R^2 = 1 - \frac{USS}{TSS}$$

If the null hypothesis is true, then the *USS*, and hence the R^2, in both the restricted and unrestricted models would be the same. Again, they may differ somewhat in practice because the unrestricted model is better suited to explaining some of the random variation that exists in the data. Therefore, a relevant test statistic would compare the USS or the R^2 in both the restricted and unrestricted models and determine whether the difference is "big enough" to be statistically significant. In practice, the statistic we employ to accomplish this is

$$F = \frac{(USS_{\text{restricted}} - USS_{\text{unrestricted}})/m}{(USS_{\text{unrestricted}})/(n - k - 1)}$$

where:

$USS_{\text{unrestricted}}$ is the unexplained sum of squared residuals for the unrestricted regression

$USS_{\text{restricted}}$ is the unexplained sum of squared residuals for the restricted regression

m is the number of restrictions

$n - k - 1$ is the number of observations minus the number of explanatory variables

We can apply the relationship between USS and R^2 to convert the format of the F statistic to contain the R^2 itself. To do this, note that

$$USS_{\text{unrestricted}} = TSS*(1 - R^2_{\text{unrestricted}}) \text{ and } USS_{\text{restricted}} = TSS*(1 - R^2_{\text{restricted}})$$

When we substitute these expressions into our test statistic and simplify, the test statistic becomes

$$F = \frac{(R^2_{\text{unrestricted}} - R^2_{\text{restricted}})/m}{(1 - R^2_{\text{unrestricted}})/(n - k - 1)}$$

Importantly, the value of F will be close to zero when the null is true, because in this situation $R^2_{\text{restricted}} \approx R^2_{\text{unrestricted}}$. This suggests that values of F that are "far" from zero would provide evidence favoring the alternative hypothesis. To define "far" we need to know something of the sampling distribution of F. Fortunately, we know that F follows the F distribution with m, and $n - k - 1$ degrees of freedom. Therefore, we can compare F to $F^*_{m,n-k-1}$ (as reported in Table B.3) and reject the null hypothesis if $F > F^*_{m,n-k-1}$.

We can also test hypotheses regarding whether sets of coefficients take on specific values besides zero. For instance, suppose we want to test whether $\beta_1 = 0$ *and* $\beta_3 = 5$ jointly. To do so, we would specify the null and alternative hypotheses as follows:

$$H_0 : \beta_1 = 0 \text{ and } \beta_3 = 5$$
$$H_1 : \text{not } H_0$$

We then form the regression that embodies the null hypothesis: $Y_i = \beta_0 + \beta_2 X_{2i} + 5X_{3i} + \varepsilon_i$. Rewriting this gives us the *restricted* regression

$$(\textit{Restricted regression}): \underbrace{Y_i - 5 X_{3i}}_{Y_i^*} = \beta_0 + \beta_2 X_{2i} + \varepsilon_i$$

where you should notice that the dependent variable is $Y_i - 5X_{3i}$; call this Y_i^*. Thus, to estimate the restricted regression, we regress Y_i^* on X_{2i}. The unrestricted regression does not restrict the coefficients in any way and is given by the original model $Y_i = \beta_0 + \beta_1 X_{1i} +$

$\beta_2 X_{2i} + \beta_3 X_{3i} + \varepsilon_i$. We can then estimate the restricted and unrestricted regressions and apply the R^2 from each specification directly to the F test we described earlier.

In summary, implementing an F test involves four separate steps. First, run the unrestricted regression and calculate the resulting R^2. Second, run the restricted regression, again calculating the resulting R^2. Third, form the F statistic. Fourth, find the value of $F_{m,n-k-1}$ in Table B.3 that is large enough so that, say 5% (in general, use whatever significance level you think appropriate) of the probability lies to its right. Call this critical value $F^*_{m,n-k-1}$. Finally, if $F > F^*_{m,n-k-1}$ you would reject the null hypothesis. The logic is the same as usual. Values of $F > F^*_{m,n-k-1}$ will result at most 5% of the time when the null is true. This is regarded as a sufficiently low probability event that the evidence will be deemed to support the alternative hypothesis.

Example

In macroeconomics the aggregate output in an economy is sometimes specified as taking a *Cobb–Douglas* form. That is, $Q_t = A K_{t\,1}^{\beta} L_{t\,2}^{\beta}$, where L is labor, K is capital, Q is output, and A, β_1 and β_2 are parameters to be estimated. We can make this model look more like a linear regression model by taking the logarithm of both sides of the equation. That is, $\ln Q_t = \ln A + \beta_1 \ln K_t + \beta_2 \ln L_t$.

Taking logs changes the model from being multiplicative to one that is additive. Notice that this model is deterministic. For any given amounts of labor and capital the amount of output is perfectly predictable. We turn this into a statistical model by introducing an error term:

$$\ln Q_t = \ln A + \beta_1 \ln K_t + \beta_2 \ln L_t + \varepsilon_t$$

Notice that this is a *log-log* model. As such, the coefficients are interpreted as elasticities.

An important characteristic of a production function is whether it exhibits constant, increasing, or decreasing returns to scale. For example, a production function exhibits constant returns to scale if doubling inputs (K and L in this case) results in doubling the output. In the Cobb–Douglas framework, notice that constant returns to scale implies a *restriction* on the model:

$$\underbrace{2Q_t}_{\text{Double output}} = A \left(\underbrace{2K_t}_{\text{Double capital}} \right)^{\beta_1} \left(\underbrace{2L_t}_{\text{Double labor}} \right)^{\beta_2}$$

$$= 2^{(\beta_1 + \beta_2)} A K_t^{\beta_1} L_t^{\beta_2}$$

$$= 2^{(\beta_1, \beta_2)} Q_t$$

$$\Leftrightarrow \beta_1 + \beta_2 = 1$$

Thus, constant returns to scale implies that the sum of $\beta_1 + \beta_2$ equals 1.

To test for constant returns to scale we first establish our null and alternative hypotheses:

$$H_0 : \beta_1 + \beta_2 = 1$$
$$H_1 : \text{not } H_0$$

Then we set up a restricted and an unrestricted regression model. As always, the *unrestricted* model imposes no restrictions on the coefficients. Then, to form the restricted

---

APPLICATION 12.3 | *It's Only a Piece of Paper (or Is It?)*

As we discussed in Chapter 9, investments in additional years of education pay a handsome return. But do employers only care about the years spent in school or do they pay an additional premium for the receipt of a degree? This premium has been called the "sheepskin" effect and some evidence suggests it is substantial.

One study tested for sheepskin effects by taking advantage of a special national survey that asked respondents both about their years of education and their highest degree received. It turns out that only 91% of high school graduates and 78% of college graduates have been in school for 12 and 16 years, respectively. In both cases, some take longer and some finish early. Then the authors of the study estimated regression models where the dependent variable was the log hourly wage and the independent variables included measures of years of education along with a series of dummy variables indicating whether degrees at different levels had been received. Point estimates indicate, for instance, that among white men a high school degree holder earns 12% more than another individual with the same years of education, but no degree. Similarly, the recipient of a college diploma earns 25% more. These coefficients, along with those at some, but not all, other degree levels are statistically significant at the 5% level. For instance, the premium to obtaining a master's degree is not statistically significant.

To test the proposition that, in general, earning a degree matters, requires us to conduct an F test for the series of degree dummy variables. We want to test the proposition that *all* of the coefficients are collectively significantly different from zero. The R^2 from the unrestricted model (with the degree dummy variables) is 0.154 and the R^2 from the restricted model (without the degree dummy variables) is 0.147. The sample size is 8957, there are 8 degree dummy variables that we are testing, and the regression model includes 11 other variables. Substituting these values into the formula for an F test, we have:

$$F = \frac{(0.154 - 0.147)/8}{(1 - 0.154)/(8957 - 20)} = 9.24$$

With 8 and 8937 degrees of freedom, the critical value for this F test is 2.51 at the 1% level, so we can reject the null hypothesis that there are no sheepskin effects. So get that degree!

SOURCE: Jaeger, David A. and Marianne E. Page, "Degrees Matter: New Evidence on Sheepskin Effects in the Returns to Education," *Review of Economics and Statistics,* Vol. 78, No. 4 (November 1996), pp. 733–739.

---

regression we impose the restrictions imposed by the null hypothesis (notice, H_0 implies $\beta_2 = 1 - \beta_1$):

$$\ln Q_t = \ln A + \beta_1 \ln K_t + (1 - \beta_1) \ln L_t + \varepsilon_t$$

$$= \ln A + \beta_1 (\ln K_t - \ln L_t) + \ln L_t + \varepsilon_t$$

Manipulating this further by taking $\ln L_t$ to the left-hand side of the equation yields the restricted model:

$$(\textit{Restricted model}): \ln Q_t - \ln L_t = \ln A + \beta_1 (\ln K_t - \ln L_t) + \varepsilon_t$$

This can be estimated using ordinary least squares with the dependent variable being $\ln Q_t - \ln L_t$ and the explanatory variable being $\ln K_t - \ln L_t$.

We then proceed as before. First, run the regressions and calculate the R^2 for the restricted and unrestricted models. Then, form the ratio

$$F = \frac{(R^2_{\text{unrestricted}} - R^2_{\text{restricted}})/m}{(1 - R^2_{\text{unrestricted}})/(n - k - 1)} \sim F_{m,n-k-1}$$

Finally, if $F > F^*_{m,n-k-1}$ you would reject the null hypothesis.

12.3.2 Testing Whether All of the Regression Slope Coefficients Are Zero: *"The F Test"*

So far we have discussed the use of F tests to test hypotheses about a subset of coefficients. But one specific F test is so commonly reported on computer printouts of regression results that it is sometimes called "*The F* Test." It tests the hypothesis that *all* of the slope coefficients in a model are jointly zero (notice that it does not require the intercept to be zero). It is important to recognize that "*The F* Test" is not "The *Only F* Test". As we described in the preceding section, F tests can be used to test any hypotheses on subsets of coefficients jointly.

"*The F* Test" is really just a specific example of the more general form of F tests described earlier. Consider, for instance, the regression model:

$$Y_i = \beta_0 + \beta_1 X_{1i} + \beta_2 X_{2i} + \beta_3 X_{3i} + \varepsilon_i$$

Here we want to test whether all three coefficients are equal to zero. The null and alternative hypotheses may be defined as

$$H_0 : \beta_1 = 0, \beta_2 = 0, \text{ and } \beta_3 = 0$$
$$H_1 : \text{not } H_0$$

Again, the null hypothesis states that *none* of the variables in the model (excluding the intercept) is statistically significant.

Now, in the special case of "*The F* Test", when the null is true, our restricted model involves a regression of Y on a constant alone. We should not expect a constant to explain the variation in the dependent variable! As such, the R^2 for the restricted model would be zero. In addition, the number of restrictions would be equal to the number of parameters set to zero; namely k. Thus, for "*The F* Test*" the F statistic would simplify to

$$F = \frac{R^2_{\text{unrestricted}}/k}{(1 - R^2_{\text{unrestricted}})/(n - k - 1)} \sim F_{m,n-k-1}$$

With the exception that the test statistic, F, simplifies to this form, the approach to conducting "*The F* Test" is identical to that described earlier.

12.4 PROBLEMS

1. You have been hired by a New York (Long Island) real estate firm to assess the determinants of local house prices. You understand that house prices are determined by the interaction of supply and demand and opt to employ a "hedonic regression" framework. This framework specifies the price of a house to be a linear function of the various attributes of the house. Although the house is sold as a bundled commodity, you could estimate the contribution of various attributes in the determination of the final price. To assist this research, you conduct a survey of housing prices for five geographical locations in Nassau county. There are a total of 362 observations on 20 variables. Each variable contains data labels so you can understand how each one is coded. The original data may be found in http://www.wiley.com/college/ashenfelter. BASIC BUSINESS STATISTICS, 5/E. by Berenson/Levin ©. Reprinted by permission of Pearson Education, Inc., Upper Saddle River, NJ. The first step in using this data is to create dummy variables for certain qualitative variables.

   a. What fraction of the houses in the sample are located in each region? What fraction of the houses in the sample are of each style? (Hint: Consider the means of the dummy variables.)

   b. Run a regression of "value" on the other variables (except taxes, which is a function of value), using the dummy variables you created in part (a). As noted above, a regression of this type is called a "hedonic" regression. Which variables are significantly different from zero at the 5% level and which are not? Interpret your output, responding in particular to the following expert advice: "Location is everything!", "Extra baths mean big bucks!", "Forget swimming pools, they don't pay!"

   c. Explain how you could use this model to find "bargains" in the housing market.

2. This problem set considers some of the empirical issues involved in implementing a comparable worth policy (a policy that assigns equal wages to jobs that are judged to be "comparable").

   Economists typically do not think of the "worth" of a job independently from market forces, but the use of formal job evaluation methods has existed for some time. Hay Associates, a national compensation consulting company, has conducted job evaluations for a number of states. The company relates the wages for a given job to a number of "compensable" factors including skills, responsibility, effort, and working conditions. The trained job evaluators assign a specified number of points ("Hay Points") to each of the four job characteristics for each job. The scores are then added to get a total point score for the job.

   This problem set employs data from 116 job titles used by the state of New York for its employees in 1982. Workers with these job titles represent 1/3 of the state's employees. These data are found in http://www.wiley.com/college/ashenfelter.

   a. Define male-dominated jobs as those with fewer than 30% women and female-dominated jobs with greater than 70% women (this is the same approach Hay follows). Compute the mean percentage of women in both male- and female-dominated jobs.

   b. What is the mean wage in female-dominated and male-dominated jobs? Does the differential necessarily indicate discrimination? What is the mean score for the five compensable factors (skills, effort, responsibility, working conditions, and total points) for male-dominated and female-dominated jobs and how do they compare?

   c. Run a regression of wages on *skills, effort, responsibility,* and *working conditions.* Do the coefficients have the anticipated signs? Are they significantly different from zero? What fraction of the variance in wages do they explain?

   d. Run a regression of wages on *points.* What is the relationship between this regression and the regression in part (c)? What restriction on the regression in part (c) would yield this specification? How would you test this restriction? Conduct this test and report your results.

e. Now add another variable to the regression you ran in part (c). Define the variable such that it equals 1 if the job is female-dominated and zero otherwise. Interpret the coefficients from this regression. What is the importance of the coefficient on the new variable added to the regression? What does it seem to suggest?

3. Consider the following linear regression model:

$$Y_i = \alpha + \beta_1 X_{1i} + \beta_2 X_{2i} + \beta_3 X_{3i} + \beta_4 X_{4i} + \beta_5 X_{5i} + u_i$$

Explain exactly how you would test the following hypotheses:

a. $\beta_1 = 0$.

b. $\beta_1 = 0$ and $\beta_4 = \beta_5$.

c. $\beta_1 = 0$ and $\beta_3 = 2$ and $\beta_4 = \beta_5$.

Chapter 13

Specification Error, Multicollinearity, and Measurement Error

13.1   INTRODUCTION

We have seen that using ordinary least squares (OLS) to estimate the parameters of the multiple regression model produces estimators that are the best linear unbiased estimators (BLUE) when the assumptions underlying the model hold true. What happens when the assumptions do not hold true? Will OLS still produce unbiased estimates? Will they still be the best in the sense of having the smallest sampling variance? If not, what estimator is the best? Finally, how might we detect the existence of a violation of one of the assumptions underlying the multiple regression model in the first place?

In this chapter we consider the causes, consequences, and potential solutions to five potential violations of the assumptions underlying the regression model.

13.2   INCLUDING AN IRRELEVANT VARIABLE

In specifying our regression model we might include too many explanatory variables. That is, we might make the mistake of including a variable in the model that, in fact, doesn't belong. For example, suppose we (the fallible researcher) specify the following regression model

$$\text{(Our specification) } Y_i = \tilde{\beta}_0 + \tilde{\beta}_1 X_{1i} + \tilde{\beta}_2 X_{2i} + \tilde{\varepsilon}_i$$

when, in fact, the true model is

$$\text{(True specification) } Y_i = \beta_0 + \beta_1 X_{1i} + \varepsilon_i$$

Note that we use tildes (~) in our specification to distinguish the parameters between the two models. We also assume that the true residual, ε, satisfies all the usual assumptions.

In our specification we wrongly include X_2 as an explanatory variable. When we run the regression given by our specification (the one with one-too-many variables, i.e., X_2), we will generate the parameter estimates $\hat{\tilde{\beta}}_0, \hat{\tilde{\beta}}_1, \hat{\tilde{\beta}}_2$. What relation will these estimates bear to the true parameters β_0 and β_1? Will the estimate $\hat{\tilde{\beta}}_1$ really tell us the change in Y resulting from a unit change in X_1? In particular, will the estimates from the incorrectly specified model that we are using provide unbiased estimates of the true parameters? In other words, will $E(\hat{\tilde{\beta}}_1) = \beta_1$? Further, even if the estimates from the incorrectly specified model are, on average, correct, will they be efficient? That is, will their sampling distribution be the smallest possible?

Example

Suppose the price of a particular stock (e.g., IBM) on a particular day is determined by the level of the S&P 500 stock market index on that day. That is, $\text{Price}_{\text{IBM}_t} = \beta_0 + \beta_1 \text{S\&P500}_t + \varepsilon_t$. In this model, β_1 would tell us the change in IBM's price arising from a unit change in the S&P 500. Now, suppose we included in this model a new variable: the number of inches of rain that fell in Orillia, Ontario Canada. Thus, we estimate $\text{Price}_{\text{IBM}_t} = \tilde{\beta}_0 + \tilde{\beta}_1 \text{S\&P500}_t + \tilde{\beta}_2 \text{(Rainfall in Orillia)}_t + \varepsilon_t$. Would $E(\tilde{\beta}_1) = \beta_1$? That is, could we look at the coefficients from this misspecified model and interpret them with any confidence?

The short answer to the questions posed above is that the OLS estimates based on the equation containing too many explanatory variables will indeed be unbiased estimates of the true parameters. In addition, the standard errors associated with these estimates will also be unbiased, allowing us to form valid confidence intervals and hypothesis tests. That is the good news. The bad news is that the estimates are not efficient. Had we estimated the correct model we would have generated more precise estimates of the true parameters. Indeed, it can be shown that the larger the correlation between X_1 and X_2, the larger the cost of our error in terms of efficiency (if these variables were uncorrelated there would be no efficiency loss). So, in short, what we estimate is usable, but we could have done better by specifying the model correctly in the first place.

Proof (sketched).   We show here that including an extra variable does not result in bias. From our earlier notes on multiple regression we have seen that the OLS estimators for the model $Y_i = \tilde{\beta}_0 + \tilde{\beta}_1 X_{1i} + \tilde{\beta}_2 X_{2i} + \tilde{\varepsilon}_i$ can be written

$$\hat{\tilde{\beta}}_1 = \frac{\left(\sum_{i=1}^{n}(X_{1i} - \bar{X}_1)(Y_i)\right)\left(\sum_{i=1}^{n}(X_{2i} - \bar{X}_2)\right) - \left(\sum_{i=1}^{n}(X_{2i} - \bar{X}_2)(Y_i)\right)\left(\sum_{i=1}^{n}(X_{1i} - \bar{X}_1)(X_{2i} - \bar{X}_2)\right)}{\left(\sum_{i=1}^{n}(X_{1i} - \bar{X}_1)^2\right)\left(\sum_{i=1}^{n}(X_{2i} - \bar{X}_2)^2\right) - \left(\sum_{i=1}^{n}(X_{1i} - \bar{X}_1)(X_{2i} - \bar{X}_2)\right)^2}$$

Substituting in the true relation $Y_i = \beta_0 + \beta_1 X_{1i} + \varepsilon_i$ gives us

$$\hat{\hat{\beta}}_1 = \frac{\left(\sum_{i=1}^{n}(X_{1i} - \overline{X}_1)(\beta_0 + \beta_1 X_{1i} + \varepsilon_i)\right)\left(\sum_{i=1}^{n}(X_{2i} - \overline{X}_2)\right)}{\left(\sum_{i=1}^{n}(X_{1i} - \overline{X}_1)^2\right)\left(\sum_{i=1}^{n}(X_{2i} - \overline{X}_2)^2\right)}$$

$$\frac{-\left(\sum_{i=1}^{n}(X_{2i} - \overline{X}_2)(\beta_0 + \beta_1 X_{1i} + \varepsilon_i)\right)\left(\sum_{i=1}^{n}(X_{1i} - \overline{X}_1)(X_{2i} - \overline{X}_2)\right)}{-\left(\sum_{i=1}^{n}(X_{1i} - \overline{X}_1)(X_{2i} - \overline{X}_2)\right)^2}$$

Taking the expected value of this expression and noting that $E(X_1\varepsilon) = 0$ and $E(X_2\varepsilon) = 0$ (and doing a little algebra) you can show $E(\hat{\hat{\beta}}_1) = \beta_1$.

To help with the intuition of the result, note that in the population, the coefficient on the irrelevant variable would be zero. So, on average, when estimating β_1 with the wrongly specified model you would still get the right answer. On the other hand, when the irrelevant variable is correlated with the correct variable, its inclusion will cause the estimate of β_1 to move around (as we'll show below in Section 13.3). On average, it will have no effect, but if we were to do repeated sampling, the variation of $\hat{\hat{\beta}}_1$ would be larger because of the inclusion of the irrelevant variable. So, although we are correctly measuring the variation of $\hat{\hat{\beta}}_1$, the variation of $\hat{\beta}_1$ (from the correctly specified model) would be smaller.

13.3 EXCLUDING A RELEVANT VARIABLE (OMITTED VARIABLE BIAS)

The result above suggests that including too many variables, while certainly not desirable, might not be disastrous in terms of using the sample data to learn how X_1 affects Y. Excluding a relevant variable may have more worrisome consequences. Suppose now that the correct model is $Y_i = \beta_0 + \beta_1 X_{1i} + \beta_2 X_{2i} + \varepsilon_i$, but we erroneously estimate $Y_i = \tilde{\beta}_0 + \tilde{\beta}_1 X_{1i} + \tilde{\varepsilon}_i$. That is, we wrongly omit X_2 from the model. Can our OLS estimate $\tilde{\beta}_1$ of β_1 be used with any confidence? The answer depends on whether the variable we wrongly left out (i.e., X_2) is correlated with the variable included (i.e., X_1). To see this, remember we showed in Chapter 9 that we could write the formula for the slope coefficient in a simple regression model as

$$\hat{\tilde{\beta}}_1 = \frac{\sum_{i=1}^{n} Y_i(X_{1i} - \overline{X}_1)}{\sum_{i=1}^{n}(X_{1i} - \overline{X}_1)^2}$$

Substituting in the correct model, $Y_i = \beta_0 + \beta_1 X_{1i} + \beta_2 X_{2i} + \varepsilon_i$, and taking the expected value yields

$$E(\hat{\hat{\beta}}_1) = E\left(\frac{\sum_{i=1}^{n}(\beta_0 + \beta_1 X_{1i} + \beta_2 X_{2i} + \varepsilon_i)(X_{1i} - \overline{X}_1)}{\sum_{i=1}^{n}(X_{1i} - \overline{X}_1)^2}\right)$$

$$= \beta_0 \underbrace{\frac{\sum_{i=1}^{n}(X_{1i} - \overline{X}_1)}{\sum_{i=1}^{n}(X_{1i} - \overline{X}_1)^2}}_{=0} + \beta_1 \underbrace{\frac{\sum_{i=1}^{n}X_{1i}(X_{1i} - \overline{X}_1)}{\sum_{i=1}^{n}(X_{1i} - \overline{X}_1)^2}}_{=1} + \beta_2 \underbrace{\frac{\sum_{i=1}^{n}X_{2i}(X_{1i} - \overline{X}_1)}{\sum_{i=1}^{n}(X_{1i} - \overline{X}_1)^2}}_{\substack{\text{Slope coefficient of a}\\\text{regression of } X_2 \text{ on } X_1}} + \underbrace{\frac{E\left(\sum_{i=1}^{n}\varepsilon_i(X_{1i} - \overline{X}_1)\right)}{\sum_{i=1}^{n}(X_{1i} - \overline{X}_1)^2}}_{=0}$$

$$= \beta_1 + \beta_2 \frac{\sum_{i=1}^{n}X_{2i}(X_{1i} - \overline{X}_1)}{\sum_{i=1}^{n}(X_{1i} - \overline{X}_1)^2}$$

To simplify notation, note that in a simple model where the dependent variable was X_2 and the independent variable was X_1, we could write a regression equation of the form $X_{2i} = b_{12}X_{1i} + v_i$, where, for simplicity, we have assumed that the intercept equals zero and where the notation for the slope coefficient, b_{12}, indicates the impact of X_1 on X_2. In this specification, applying the same formula for a regression coefficient that we used just above, one can see that $E(\hat{\hat{\beta}}_1) = \beta_1 + \beta_2 b_{12}$. Thus $\hat{\hat{\beta}}_1$ will be a biased estimator of β_1 if $\beta_2 b_{12} \neq 0$. Notice that there is no bias if $b_{12} = 0$. In other words, if the omitted variable is unrelated to the included variable, an OLS regression of the misspecified model will still yield unbiased estimates of β_1. If b_{12} is nonzero, then the direction and magnitude of the bias will depend on β_2 and b_{12}. If β_2 and b_{12} are of the same sign, then their product will be positive and, on average, $\hat{\hat{\beta}}_1$ will be larger than β_1. If β_2 and b_{12} are of the opposite sign, then their product will be negative and, on average, $\hat{\hat{\beta}}_1$ will be smaller than β_1. The bias that results from omitting a relevant variable from our regression model is usually called "omitted variable bias."

To see this somewhat differently, suppose we substitute the relationship $X_{2i} = b_{12}X_{1i} + v_i$ into the correctly specified regression model that includes both X_1 and X_2. Then, the true model would become

$$\begin{aligned} Y_i &= \beta_0 + \beta_1 X_{1i} + \beta_2 X_{2i} + \varepsilon_i \\ &= \beta_0 + \beta_1 X_{1i} + \beta_2 b_{12} X_{1i} + \beta_2 v_i + \varepsilon_i \\ &= \beta_0 + (\beta_1 + \beta_2 b_{12})X_{1i} + \beta_2 v_i + \varepsilon_i \end{aligned}$$

So, when erroneously running a regression of Y on X_1 alone, the slope coefficient is not equal to the (ceteris paribus) effect of X_1 on Y, but is rather equal to the effect of X_1 on Y *plus* the effect of X_1 on X_2, which will, in turn, affect Y. In sum, if the variable we leave out is positively correlated with the variable we include and also has itself a positive effect on the dependent variable, then our misspecified model will produce an upward-biased estimator of the effect of X_1 on Y. In other words, estimates, on average, are overstated. In

---

APPLICATION 13.1   *More Bad News for Smokers?*

The health consequences of smoking are well known, but do smokers face any economic consequences? Smokers may receive lower levels of pay because they are less productive (if the act of smoking takes a worker away from his or her job); because they may be absent from work more often (due to their greater risk of respiratory infections); because it is more expensive to provide them with health insurance; or simply because firms discriminate against them.

Regression analysis can be employed to determine whether smokers receive lower wages based on their behavior. Consider a regression model of the form $\ln W_i = \beta_0 + \beta_1 \cdot X_i + \beta_2 \cdot S_i + \varepsilon_i$, where W represents wages, X represents productivity-related characteristics, S is a dummy variable indicating whether the worker smokes, and i indexes individuals at a particular firm. The coefficient, β_2, indicates the ceteris paribus difference in wages that smokers receive.

	Specification 1	Specification 2	Specification 3
Smoking Dummy variable	−0.176	−0.080	−0.069
	(0.021)	(0.021)	(0.019)
Education		0.070	0.045
		(0.004)	(0.005)
Other factors included	no	no	yes

Note: Standard errors in parentheses.

An important consideration in such an analysis, however, is the potential for omitted variable bias. The results of one study provide dramatic evidence of this. Using nationally representative data on workers in their late twenties and early thirties, the study found that a smoker earns 18% less than a nonsmoker before controlling for any other factors, as shown in the above table. Including just one variable, years of education, however, reduced this deficit to just 8%. Since smokers have more than a year less education than nonsmokers and education is such an important determinant of wages, omitting this single variable led to an estimated effect more than twice as great as when it was included. Interestingly, including aptitude test scores, family background characteristics, work experience, and a host of other variables reduced the estimated effect just slightly. This may mean that the bias resulting from other omitted variables may have been minimized since all of the likely culprits have already been included in the regression.

SOURCE: Levine, Phillip B., Tara A. Gustafson, and Ann D. Velenchik. "More Bad News for Smokers? The Effects of Cigarette Smoking on Wages," *Industrial and Labor Relations Review*, Vol. 50, No. 3 (April 1997), pp. 493–509.

effect, our included variable is capturing both its own effect and the effect of the excluded variable. You must keep in mind that the direction of the bias will depend on the sign of $\beta_2 b_{12}$. If either β_2 or b_{12} equal zero, then there would not be an omitted variable bias. That is, if the excluded variable does not affect the dependent variable (in which case you aren't misspecified in the first place), or the excluded variable is not correlated with the included variable(s), then there will be no omitted variable bias.

Example

Suppose we were trying to figure out the effect of smoking on cancer. We might have a group of smokers and a group of nonsmokers and observe their incidences of cancer. Suppose, however, that the nonsmokers were more apt to exercise and exercise reduces cancer. Then, the higher incidence of cancer among the smokers might be overstating the effect of smoking in that it may also be capturing the effect of reduced exercise. More formally, suppose the true model is $Cancer_i = \beta_0 + \beta_1 \, Smoking + \beta_2 \, Exercise_i + \varepsilon$ and $Exercise_i = b_{12} \, Smoking_i + v_i$. Then, in erroneously running our regression of cancer on smoking alone, we are estimating $Cancer_i = \beta_0 + (\beta_1 + \beta_2 b_{12}) \, Smoking_i + v_i + \varepsilon_i$. Thus our slope estimate would not be β_1 but would rather be $(\beta_1 + \beta_2 b_{12})$. This would overstate the effect of smoking on cancer if $\beta_2 < 0$ (i.e., exercise, other things equal, reduces the incidence of cancer) and $b_{12} < 0$ (i.e., smoking is negatively correlated with exercise). Notice that if it was claimed that estimates of the effect of smoking on cancer were biased upward for this reason we could include exercise as an explanatory variable in our model. If the claim is true, then the effect of smoking on cancer would fall when exercise is included in the model. If the coefficient does not fall, this would be evidence against the claim of "omitted variable bias." In reality, the omitted variable argument does not hold up too well in this example.

13.4   NONLINEARITIES

The linear regression model can easily handle many situations where the explanatory variable is thought to have a nonlinear effect on the dependent variable. For example, consider the following nonlinear relationship:

$$Y_i = \beta_0 + \beta_1 X_{1i} + \beta_1 X_{1i}^2 + \varepsilon_i.$$

Here the model, while being nonlinear in the variable X_1, is still linear in the parameters β_0, β_1, β_2. To estimate such a model we simply redefine the model as follows: Let $X_2 = X^2$. We then estimate the multiple regression model $Y_i = \beta_0 + \beta_1 X_{1i} + \beta_2 X_{2i} + \varepsilon_i$. Thus, nonlinear models can often be turned into linear models simply by redefining the variables in an appropriate way. This particular model is ideal for estimating a quadratic relationship between Y and X. It allows for the identification of a slope that may increase (decrease) at an increasing (decreasing) rate. In terms of calculus, the derivative of Y with respect to X_1 is equal to $\beta_1 + 2\beta_2 X_1$ and the second derivative is $2\beta_2$. Therefore, β_2 determines the rate of change of the slope, while the slope itself is determined by a function of both β_1 and β_2.

Another common way of transforming a nonlinear model into a model that can be handled by regression techniques is to use logarithms. Recall that the relationship between a variable and its natural logarithm is a nonlinear one. In particular, the natural log of a positive number is less than the number itself and that reduction is much greater for larger values. When, for instance, we estimate a model using logarithms to estimate elasticities, as described in Chapter 9, we are making a nonlinear transformation of the data. In that specific application, we made this transformation for ease of interpretation of the results.

As an additional example of logarithmic transformations, consider a Cobb–Douglas production function, which has the form $Q_i = A K_i^{\beta_1} L_i^{\beta_2} e^{\varepsilon_i}$. Taking the logarithm of the model gives us $\ln Q_i = \ln A + \beta_1 \ln K_i + \beta_2 \ln L_i + \varepsilon_i$. Then, redefining the variables such that $X_1 = \ln K$ and $X_2 = \ln L$, we have a standard multiple regression model: $\ln Q_i = \beta_0 +$

$\beta_1 X_{1i} + \beta_2 X_{2i} + \varepsilon_i$. Estimating this model gives us the parameters needed in our specification of the Cobb–Douglas production function.

APPLICATION 13.2 *Less Gold in the Golden Years*

How do wages change over a worker's lifetime? One can answer this question using perhaps one of the most common regressions estimated by economists, the *human capital earnings function.* It relates a worker's log wage to his or her education and level of labor market experience and experience squared. Because actual years of labor market experience are typically not observed, this variable is frequently proxied by something called "potential experience," which equals age minus years of education minus six (since children typically start first grade at age 6). Potential experience squared is included because the human capital model suggests that wages should grow rapidly when a worker is young, but the rate of growth should decline with age; the squared term is required to capture this nonlinearity. Because older workers have fewer years to reap the return on investments in their own productivity, they make fewer of them, slowing their wage growth. Moreover, at the end of a worker's career, the worker's wages may even fall as his or her skills depreciate faster than new investments are made.

We estimated the human capital earnings function using nationally representative data from a sample of almost 150,000 full-time workers in 1991:

	Coefficient	Standard error	T statistic
Intercept	0.766	0.007	109.1
Years of education	0.091	0.0005	197.8
Potential experience	0.033	0.0003	101.4
Potential experience squared	−0.00051	0.000007	−72.2

One cannot interpret the change in wages brought about by an additional year of work directly from these results because both experience and experience squared are included in the regression model. To see this, consider a simplification of the model where $Y_i = \beta_0 + \beta_1 X_i + \beta_2 X_i^2 + \varepsilon_i$. Here, $\partial y/\partial x = \beta_1 + 2\beta_2 \cdot X$, or, in the present context, a one-unit increase in years of potential experience increases wages by $.033 - .00102 \cdot X$. Therefore, real wages increase with a year of experience by 3.3% for a new labor market entrant, and by 2.3% for a 10-year veteran. Notice that after about 33 years an additional year of experience actually lowers real wages. For a college graduate who finishes school at age 22, this means that real wages peak around age 55.

SOURCE: Author's calculations from the 1991 Current Population Survey Outgoing Rotation Group file.

13.5 MULTICOLLINEARITY

One of the assumptions of the multiple regression model is that no exact linear relationship exists among the explanatory variables. For example, suppose we were interested in estimating the following model: $Y_i = \beta_0 + \beta_1 X_{1i} + \beta_1 X_{2i} + \varepsilon_i$, but it was the case that the two explanatory variables were perfectly correlated. That is, suppose $X_2 = \gamma X_1$. In this

APPLICATION 13.3 *Some Like It Cold*

Needless to say, running a marathon is hard work, and doing so in hot weather may drain the body of additional fluids, reducing runners' performance. Data from the New York City marathon not only confirm this fact, but indicate that there is an optimal temperature, at least for men, that minimizes winners' times. One study collected data on the temperature and winning time for that marathon for each year from 1978 to 1998. A plot of these data for men clearly reveals a nonlinear relationship; winning times improve at cooler temperatures unless it is too cold, and then times increase again.

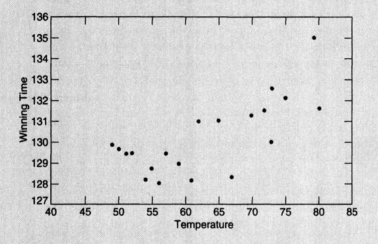

A regression model that includes both the temperature and its square allows for the OLS regression "line" to be a curve. Results from this regression for men confirm the quadratic relationship; temperature measured in actual levels and its square are both significant at least at the 10% level. Applying standard techniques to find the minimum of the curve indicates that the ideal temperature for a marathon for men is 54 degrees.

	Men			Women		
	Coefficient	Standard error	*T* statistic	Coefficient	Standard error	*T* statistic
Intercept	148.51	12.58	11.81	140.25	2.32	60.45
Temperature	−0.71	0.40	1.78	0.119	0.036	3.31
Temperature squared	0.0065	0.0031	2.10			

Interestingly, the relationship for women appears to be linear, with winning times increasing in direct relationship to the temperature. Just think what would happen if they ran the marathon in Oslo!

SOURCE: Martin, David E. and John F. Buoncristiani, "The Effect of Temperature on Marathon Runners' Performance," *Chance*, Vol. 12, No. 4 (Fall 1999), pp. 20–24. Reprinted with permission from *Chance*. Copyright © 1999 by the American Statistical Association. All rights reserved.

case there is an exact linear relationship between X_1 and X_2. In this case our model becomes

$$Y_i = \beta_0 + \beta_1 X_{1i} + \beta_2 \gamma X_{1i} + \varepsilon_i$$
$$= \beta_0 + (\beta_1 + \beta_2 \gamma) X_{1i} + \varepsilon_i$$

We could estimate the slope coefficient in this model $\beta_1 + \beta_2 \gamma$, but we could not estimate β_1 and β_2 separately.

Example

To see this point intuitively, consider the following example. Suppose you are on the swim team. Before many of your swim meets your grandmother takes you out for a terrific pasta dinner and gives you one of her famous pep talks. When you get this special treatment you invariably swim well. Now, would you ever be able to figure out whether it is the pasta dinner or the pep talk that produces this wonderful result? The answer is no. The two things (pasta dinner/pep talk) always happen together. We wouldn't be able to disentangle their separate effects unless we sometimes had the pep talk with no dinner or the dinner with no pep talk. In regression terms, we couldn't figure out the ceteris paribus effects of the two variables since they are perfectly correlated. That is, they always happen together. More specifically, they are perfectly collinear. Figuring out how an explanatory variable affects the dependent variable requires there be some independent variation in that explanatory variable.

In practical terms, when we have perfect multicollinearity as described above, it is not possible to estimate the regression model. To see this, recall that in deriving the estimators for the multiple regression model we would solve $k + 1$ equations for the $k + 1$ unknown parameters. That is, we solve

$$\sum_{i=1}^{n} e_i = 0 \tag{1}$$

$$\sum_{i=1}^{n} e_i X_{1i} = 0 \tag{2}$$

$$\sum_{i=1}^{n} e_i X_{2i} = 0 \tag{3}$$

$$\cdot$$
$$\cdot$$
$$\cdot$$

$$(k + 1) \sum_{i=1}^{n} e_i X_{ki} = 0$$

Now, for example, if X_1 and X_2 are perfectly correlated, then $X_2 = \gamma X_1$ and so equation (3) becomes

$$\sum_{i=1}^{n} e_i X_{2i} = \sum_{i=1}^{n} e_i \gamma X_{1i} = \sum_{i=1}^{n} e_i X_{1i} = 0$$

which is the same as equation (2). That is, there are now only k equations with which to solve for the $k + 1$ unknowns. Clearly, this is not possible. In the presence of perfect multicollinearity, most computer programs are designed to drop any offending variable(s) so as to avoid the problem.

Perfect multicollinearity can arise for a number of different reasons. It will occur if some variable always takes on the same value. Suppose everyone is the same age in your data and age is an explanatory variable. We would not be able to figure out how differences in age affects the dependent variable if age doesn't vary. It will also occur if we have two variables that always sum to a constant. Suppose you include two dummy variables, one identifying whether the observation is for a man, the other identifying if the observation is for a woman. Since the two dummies will always sum to 1, you have perfect multicollinearity.

Multicollinearity is not a failure of the model but rather is simply a failure of having too little variation in your data. That is, it is a data problem. Often, one explanatory variable might be closely, but not perfectly, correlated with some linear combination of one or more other explanatory variables. Indeed, we will define multicollinearity as the existence of an approximate linear relationship between two or more explanatory variables. In this case you don't have perfect multicollinearity, but you do have correlation between your independent variables. This may or may not be a problem. Economic variables are usually correlated and it is to be expected that your explanatory variables will often be correlated to some extent. The big question is whether they are so closely correlated that it becomes difficult to unravel their separate effects. If they are highly correlated it may be difficult to do so. The practical result of this is that the standard errors associated with your coefficients will likely be very high if the explanatory variables are highly correlated. That is, you are unable to estimate their separate effects with any degree of precision. Indeed, the more closely the explanatory variables are correlated, the higher the resulting standard errors for your coefficients. In this case, a variable may be statistically insignificant—that is, we can't reject the null that it doesn't affect the explanatory variable. But, this may be because of the multicollinearity. The t ratio is driven down by large standard error. This highlights the fact that when we say we cannot reject the null that a variable has no effect, we are not saying it has no effect. It could have an effect, but due, for example, to multicollinearity, we are simply unable to detect it.

13.6 MEASUREMENT ERROR

Sometimes the data we want to work with are poor. They may have been recorded in a sloppy fashion. Or, they may not perfectly measure the concept we would ideally like to incorporate into our model. We will refer to these problems as problems of *measurement error*. Again, the question we will confront is whether, and how, our least squares estimates are affected by these problems. As we shall see, errors in our explanatory variable(s) can create a correlation between our explanatory variable(s) and the error term similar to that associated with omitted variable bias. That is, measurement error associated with our explanatory variables can be problematic. On the other hand, measurement error in our dependent variable may not be a problem.

Examples

1. The Keynesian consumption function relates consumption in a given year to income in that year. According to the *permanent income hypothesis,* this model is misspecified. The correct model, it is claimed, should have consumption depending on lifetime income. Accordingly, current income does not properly measure the variable we would ideally like to incorporate into our model.

2. A student is hired as a research assistant to input data into a computer. The student, while typing in the numbers, occasionally types the wrong number.

13.6.1 Probability Limits

To derive the implications of measurement error, it is important to revisit the notion of an estimator being *consistent* and the associated tool of *probability limits.* You should recall that when we say the probability limit of a random variable equals some constant K, we mean that the sampling distribution of that random variable collapses on K as the sample size n approaches infinity. More formally,

$$p \lim \hat{\beta} = K \text{ if } \lim_{n \to \infty} prob(|\hat{\beta} - K| < \delta) = 1$$

where δ is an arbitrarily small number.

Properties of Probability Limits

The following are some of the basic properties of probability limits. We will use some of these properties in showing whether particular estimators are consistent.

1. $p \lim(c) = c$ where c is a constant.
2. $p \lim(\hat{\theta}_1 \hat{\theta}_2) = p \lim(\hat{\theta}_1) p \lim(\hat{\theta}_2)$.
3. $p \lim\left(\dfrac{\hat{\theta}_1}{\hat{\theta}_2}\right) = \dfrac{p \lim(\hat{\theta}_1)}{p \lim(\hat{\theta}_2)}$.
4. $p \lim(g(\hat{\theta}_2)) = g(p \lim(\hat{\theta}_2))$ if g is a continuous function.

You might note that probability limits are much easier to apply than expected values. This is why it is often possible to show that an estimator is consistent, but not be able to show that it is unbiased.

13.6.2 The Classic Errors-in-Variables Model

Suppose we (the fallible researchers) do not observe the true (or conceptually pure or accurately recorded, etc.) value of X and Y, but instead observe a measurement-error-tainted measure.

Let X_i^*, Y_i^* be the true (but unobserved) values.

Let X_i, Y_i be the observed values.

The "classic" errors-in-variables model makes the following assumptions

$$X_i = X_i^* + u_i$$

$$Y_i = Y_i^* + v_i$$

where u and v are error terms. Notice that this model assumes that the observed values are equal to the true values plus an error term that captures the measurement error. In addition, we must make some assumptions about the error terms. In particular, we will assume that $\text{cov}(X,u) = \text{cov}(Y,v) = 0$

$$\text{cov}(X,v) = \text{cov}(Y,u) = 0$$

$$\text{cov}(u,v) = 0$$

$$E(u) = E(v) = 0$$

Thus, the error terms are uncorrelated with the true values, uncorrelated with each other, and have a mean of zero. Now, suppose we run our regression using the data we have— namely, the error-ridden observed values. To simplify the algebra, assume the mean of X and Y are (or have been transformed to be) zero. Thus,

$$\hat{\beta} = \frac{\sum_{i=1}^{n}(X - \bar{X})(Y - \bar{Y})}{\sum_{i=1}^{n}(X - \bar{X})^2} = \frac{\sum_{i=1}^{n}XY}{\sum_{i=1}^{n}X^2}$$

$$= \frac{\sum_{i=1}^{n}(X^* + u)(Y^* + v)}{\sum_{i=1}^{n}(X^* + u)^2} = \frac{\sum_{i=1}^{n}X^*Y^* + \sum_{i=1}^{n}X^*v + \sum_{i=1}^{n}Y^*u + \sum_{i=1}^{n}uv}{\sum_{i=1}^{n}X^{*2} + 2\sum_{i=1}^{n}X^*u + \sum_{i=1}^{n}u^2}$$

Dividing each element by the sample size we have

$$\hat{\beta} = \frac{\dfrac{\sum_{i=1}^{n}X^*Y^*}{n} + \dfrac{\sum_{i=1}^{n}X^*v}{n} + \dfrac{\sum_{i=1}^{n}Y^*u}{n} + \dfrac{\sum_{i=1}^{n}uv}{n}}{\dfrac{\sum_{i=1}^{n}X^{*2}}{n} + \dfrac{2\sum_{i=1}^{n}X^*u}{n} + \dfrac{\sum_{i=1}^{n}u^2}{n}}$$

Then we can take the probability limit of this estimator. That is, we can determine what the parts of the estimator will converge to as $n \to \infty$.

$$p\lim \hat{\beta} = \frac{\text{cov}(X^*,Y^*) + \overbrace{\text{cov}(X^*,v)}^{=0} + \overbrace{\text{cov}(Y^*,u)}^{=0} + \overbrace{\text{cov}(u,v)}^{=0}}{\text{var}(X^*) + \underbrace{2\,\text{cov}(X^*,u)}_{=0} + \text{var}(u)}$$

$$= \frac{\text{cov}(X_i^*, Y_i^*)}{\text{var}(X^*) + \text{var}(u)}$$

$$= \beta \frac{\text{var}(X_i^*)}{\text{var}(X_i^*) + \text{var}(u_i)} = \beta \frac{\text{var}(X_i^*)}{\text{var}(X_i)} < \beta$$

Thus, we can see that measurement error causes the least squares estimator to be biased downward.

Example

To have some intuition for this result, imagine we are in an experimental setting where we have randomly assigned people into a treatment group and a control group. Suppose, for example, our treatment group participates in a skills training program and the control does not. We want to learn the effect of the training program on the participants' wages. Normally, we'd just consider the average treatment effect by comparing the average outcomes of the two groups. Suppose such a program does raise wages. Now, suppose there is measurement error in that when we are tallying the results we accidentally misclassify some of the treatment group members as control group members and some of the control group members as treatment group members. In this case, the average in the treatment group would be lower (because of the presence of the control members who didn't get the beneficial training) and the average in the control group would be higher (because of the presence of the treatment group members who had the beneficial training). This would cause the difference between the groups (i.e., the treatment effect) to be understated.

It is worth noting the following about the impact of measurement error.

1. Measurement error in the dependent variable causes no problem in the classical error-in-variables model. The error in Y is simply captured in the error term. It is measurement error in the explanatory variable(s) that causes our estimator to be biased downward.

Proof.

Suppose only Y is measured with error. That is, $Y_i^* = \beta_0 + \beta_1 X_i^* + \varepsilon_i$ is the true model. We observe Y, X^* where $Y_i = Y_i^* + v_i$. Then, we have $Y_i - v_i = \beta_0 + \beta_1 X_i^* + \varepsilon_i$ or $Y_i = \beta_0 + \beta_1 X_i^* + \varepsilon_i + v_i$. Given the assumptions in the classic errors-in-variables model (in particular that $\text{cov}(Y, v) = 0$), this model would satisfy all of the assumptions of the simple regression model and the least squares estimates would be unbiased. In effect, the error in Y is simply incorporated into the error term.

2. Measurement error in the explantory variable does cause the least squares estimates to be biased. The bias arises because of a resulting correlation between the explanatory variable and the error term.

Proof.

Suppose only X is measured with error. That is, $Y_i^* = \beta_0 + \beta_1 X_i^* + \varepsilon_i$ is the true model. We observe Y^*, X where $X_i = X_i^* + u_i$. Then, we have

$$Y_i^* = \beta_0 + \beta_1 X_i^* + \varepsilon_i$$

$$= \beta_0 + \beta_1 (X_i - u_i) + \varepsilon_i$$

$$= \beta_0 + \beta_1 X_i - \underbrace{\beta_1 u_1 + \varepsilon_i}_{\text{Error term}}$$

Notice that u is correlated with X, which, as we have seen, creates a bias if we use OLS.

3. The size of the bias depends on the size of the variance in the measurement error in X. The ratio

$$\frac{\text{var}(X^*)}{\text{var}(X)}$$

is sometimes called the "signal-to-total-variance ratio." The numerator is the true variance (or signal) whereas the denominator is the total variance (or, if you prefer, signal plus noise, i.e., measurement error).

4. There are several approaches to dealing with measurement error. First, we might simply get better measurements! Second, it may be possible to learn the magnitude of the signal-to-total-variance ratio by conducting additional surveys. That is, if we had a sample in which we were convinced measurement error was not present, then we could compare the variance in this sample to that in the full sample to get the signal-to-total-variance ratio and use it to adjust our estimates. Third, if we have repeated observations on the same variable, we might take the average of these observations. Averaging would reduce the variance of the error (i.e., var(u)). A more general approach is that of using an instrumental variables estimator.

13.6.3   Instrumental Variables

Instrumental variables provide a powerful way of dealing with both issues of measurement error and issues of potential omitted variable bias. In both of these cases we have a situation where a correlation between the explanatory variable(s) and the error term in the regression equation causes the ordinary least squares estimator to be biased.

Assume our regression model is $Y_i = \beta_1 X_i + \varepsilon_i$ but that $\text{cov}(X, \varepsilon) \neq 0$ because of either omitted variables or measurement error (note that for convenience we'll assume that there is no intercept in the model—the mean of X and Y equal zero).

Suppose we could find a variable—call it Z—that satisfies two conditions:

1. Z is correlated with X. That is, $\text{cov}(Z, X) \neq 0$.

2. Z is uncorrelated with the error term in the regression. That is, $\text{cov}(Z, \varepsilon) = 0$.

Such a variable is called an *instrumental variable*.

Now, if $Y_i = \beta_1 X_i + \varepsilon_i$, then we could multiply by Z and sum over all n observations and divide by n, giving us

$$\frac{\sum_{i=1}^{n} Z_i Y_i}{n} = \frac{\beta_1 \sum_{i=1}^{n} Z_i X_i}{n} + \frac{\sum_{i=1}^{n} Z_i \varepsilon_i}{n}$$

As $n \to \infty$ the last term would be the covariance between Z and ε, which (if Z is an instrumental variable) is assumed to be zero. So, as n becomes large we have the *consistent* estimator

$$\hat{\beta}_1 = \frac{\sum\limits_{i=1}^{n} Z_i Y_i}{\sum\limits_{i=1}^{n} Z_i X_i}$$

which is the *instrumental variables estimator*. An instrumental variable works as follows. First, you figure out how a unit change in Z translates into a change in X. Then you figure out how a unit change in Z affects Y. Then you have

$$\frac{dY}{dX} = \frac{\dfrac{dY}{dZ}}{\dfrac{dX}{dZ}}$$

To see this more clearly, notice the instrumental variables estimator

$$\hat{\beta}_1 = \frac{\sum\limits_{i=1}^{n} Z_i Y_i}{\sum\limits_{i=1}^{n} Z_i X_i}$$

If we rewrite it as

$$\hat{\beta}_1 = \frac{\dfrac{\sum\limits_{i=1}^{n} Z_i Y_i}{\sum\limits_{i=1}^{n} Z_i^2}}{\dfrac{\sum\limits_{i=1}^{n} Z_i X_i}{\sum\limits_{i=1}^{n} Z_i^2}}$$

by dividing the top and bottom by

$$\sum\limits_{i=1}^{n} Z_i^2$$

we can see that the numerator is the regression coefficient for a regression of Y on Z, and the denominator is the regression coefficient of a regression of X on Z.

It is probably worth noting that good instrumental variables can be hard to find! And, once you have one, there is no way to prove that the variable is in fact uncorrelated with the error term in the regression. Further, the variance associated with the instrumental variables estimator is larger than that of the ordinary least squares estimator. Thus, we might develop a consistent estimator (which is good) at the expense of having rather imprecise estimates (which is bad!). A particularly good way to think of instrumental variables is that they provide a source of variation in our explanatory variable that is

---

APPLICATION 13.4   *Double the Pleasure, Double the (Econometric) Fun*

As we described in Application 9.3, past research has estimated the return to a year's investment in education by running a regression of log wages on years of education. Some have argued that this approach is misleading because those individuals who are inherently more productive and who would earn more in the labor market will also obtain more education. Therefore, it is the innate ability, not the education, that leads to the higher wage. One approach that has been used in the literature to counter this argument is the analysis of wage differences between identical twins. If one twin happens to acquire more education, any increase in his or her earnings compared to the other twin would not be attributable to differences in innate ability.

One problem with conducting such an analysis is measurement error. Although evidence indicates that individuals report their own education reasonably accurately, they do not do so perfectly. It turns out that this small degree of measurement error does not have a big impact on the standard types of cross-sectional regression results reported in Chapter 9. But for technical reasons it creates bigger problems in the present context, where we are estimating the *difference* in twins' wages brought about by the *difference* in their levels of education.

One research paper uses two approaches to address this particular measurement error problem. First, the authors of this study had available to them two separate reports of an individual's level of education, and the average of the two will be measured with less error than either one individually. Second, they implement an instrumental variables strategy. For each twin pair, each individual reported a value not only for his or her own number of years of schooling, but also for his or her sibling. These authors use the self-reported level of education as an instrument for the level of an individual's education reported by his or her sibling. In both cases, the resulting estimates of the returns to a year of education are comparable to, or maybe even somewhat larger, than the estimates obtained by estimating the simple OLS regression model.

SOURCE: Ashenfelter, Orley and Alan Krueger, "Estimates of the Economic Return to Schooling from a New Sample of Twins," *American Economic Review*, Vol. 84, No. 5 (December 1994), pp. 1157–1173.

(hopefully) uncorrelated with the error term in much the same way that random assignment accomplishes this in an experimental context. Because of this, instrumental variables can be thought of as examples of "natural" or "quasi" experiments. A good instrument will, in effect, provide us with an experiment by which to measure the effect of one variable on another.

APPLICATION 13.5   *Horatio Alger Meets the Data*

According to American mythology, anyone can rise from rags to riches. But do the data support the notion that individuals are likely to improve their standing in the income distribution? One way to examine economic mobility in the United States is to compare the income levels of parents and their children. A strong relationship would indicate that one's economic position is largely accounted for by one's position at birth whereas a weak relationship would suggest that significant mobility exists. Researchers have investigated such a link by relating the earnings of a sample of sons to those of their fathers. That is: $Income_i^{son} = \beta_0 + \beta_1 \cdot Income_i^{father} + \varepsilon_i$. The closer the coefficient β_1 is to 1, the stronger the link in earnings. Early studies reported estimates of β_1 close to .2, suggesting a great deal of mobility occurs.

One difficulty in conducting such an analysis resides in the fact that earnings are not typically observed over the course of an individual's entire lifetime. Data of that type simply do not exist. In its place, researchers often used measures of income for the father and son for a single year. Such a "snapshot" introduces the potential problem of measurement error that could bias the estimate of β_1 downward—suggesting more mobility than in fact exists. To control for such a bias, one study used data for several years for both the fathers and the sons and used an average to estimate lifetime earnings. Such an approach would help mitigate the bias due to measurement error and provide a better estimate of the actual extent of mobility. After such a control for measurement error was implemented, the estimate of β_1 jumped to about 0.4—suggesting less mobility than had previously been believed to exist.

SOURCE: Zimmerman, David J., "Regression Toward Mediocrity in Economic Stature," *American Economic Review,* Vol. 82, No. 3 (June 1992), pp. 409–429.

13.7   PROBLEMS

1. Explain why the following claims might not imply causal relationships and outline how you would test for a causal effect using an experimental methodology with a treatment and control group:
   a. People with larger feet earn more money.
   b. Smokers earn less.
   c. People with college education earn more than people with only high school education.
   d. Children born into families that receive welfare are themselves more likely to receive welfare when they attain adulthood.

2. For observations on investment (Y) and profits (X) for 100 firms it is known that $Y = \alpha + \beta X + \varepsilon$. Suppose every firm in the sample had the same profits. Draw a graph illustrating this situation. What, if any, problem would this create?

3. This problem demonstrates how multiple regression models can be used to measure discrimination in labor markets. The data, taken from the 1991 *Current Population Survey,* contain information on wages, education, years of labor market experience, gender, and union status. These data are available at http://www.wiley.com/college/ashenfelter/ch13q3.dta.
   a. Calculate the mean hourly wage for men and women in this sample. What is the difference in mean wages? Is this evidence of discrimination? Why or why not?

b. Estimate a model relating the log of wage to gender. How do you interpret the coefficient on gender? How does it relate to your answer in part (a)? How do you interpret the other coefficients?

c. Estimate a model relating the log of wage to education, years of labor market experience, gender, and union status. What happens to the coefficient on gender compared to part (b)? Why? Does this suggest discrimination? Why or why not? Suggest other variables you might include in the model.

d. Suppose you could add a series of dummy variables indicating each person's occupation to the model estimated in part (d). What might happen to the coefficient on gender? Is this a legitimate variable to include in the analysis? Why or why not?

4. You would like to test the hypothesis that tariff protection makes companies "less competitive." Suppose you have quarterly data for the Harley-Davidson Corporation both before and after the United States imposed large tariffs on the import of large motorcycles in the early eighties. The data for each quarter consist of the number of Harleys produced, the hours of labor employed, and the value of the capital stock employed. Assume a stochastic Cobb–Douglas production function:

$$Y_t = AL_t^\alpha K_t^\beta \varepsilon_t$$

where $E(\varepsilon_t) = 1$.

How would you test the hypothesis that productivity declined after the imposition of tariffs? Provide *details* of how this could be done using only a computer routine for OLS estimates (there are no data for this problem). What different ways can you think of to test for a change in productivity? What problems would you worry about in your estimation? Give economic rationale for these.

Chapter 14

Heteroskedasticity and Serial Correlation

14.1   INTRODUCTION

In this chapter we consider additional violations to the maintained assumptions of the regression model. In particular, we investigate causes, consequences, and potential solutions to situations where the error terms do not share a common constant variance (i.e., are heteroskedastic) or are not independent of one another (i.e., are serially correlated). We will see that using ordinary least squares in the presence of either heteroskedasticity or serial correlation still yields unbiased estimates. The estimators are, however, no longer the best linear unbiased estimators (BLUE). If we are willing to make some assumptions about the nature of the heteroskedasticity or serial correlation we can do better than OLS.

14.2   HETEROSKEDASTICITY

14.2.1   Definition

Consider the two graphs shown below. How do they differ?

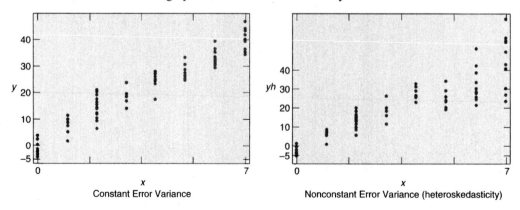

Constant Error Variance   Noncontant Error Variance (heteroskedasticity)

The graph on the left exhibits what is called a constant error variance. Or, in more formal terms, we say the errors are *homoskedastic*. That is, if you look at the dispersion in the observations for different levels of the explanatory variable, the dispersion is about the same. In the graph on the right, we see that the variance in the errors gets larger as the explanatory variable gets larger. This is an example of nonconstant error variance or, in more formal terms, *heteroskedasticity*. In short, heteroskedasticity is the situation of having the variance in our error terms differ across observations. Thus, our model now becomes: $Y_i = \beta_0 + \beta_1 X_i + \varepsilon_i$, with the usual maintained assumptions, except that $\mathrm{var}(\varepsilon_i) = \sigma_i^2$. Notice that the variance of the errors is no longer assumed to be a constant, but can now vary across observations. Again, this can be seen in the graphs above by noting that the variance of the errors is much smaller when $X = 1$ than when $X = 7$. It should be noted that the graphs above show a particular *example* of heteroskedasticity, namely one where the error variance increases with the level of X. An infinite number of other patterns are possible. The error variance might fall with the level of X. Or, it could rise and fall and rise, and so on.

14.2.2 Causes

Why might we observe heteroskedasticity? There are many reasons why the variance around the regression line might be related to the explanatory variable(s).

Examples

1. Suppose, for example, that 100 students enroll in a typing class. Suppose some of the students have typed before, and others have not. After the first class some students are pretty terrible typists. Others are quite good. If we constructed a graph showing the number of typing mistakes made by the students plotted against the number of hours of typing practice, we might well see the dispersion in the errors fall as the explanatory variable (number of hours of typing practice) rose. After the first class there would be a great deal of dispersion. After the final class the difference between the best and worst typists in the class would probably be smaller than at the first class. That is, the error variance would be nonconstant, and, in this case, would fall as X increased (where x is time). This pattern might be observed in any situation involving learning.

2. Suppose we gathered data on the income and food expenditures of a large number of families. If we made a graph relating food expenditures to income we might expect to observe heteroskedasticity. In this case, the dispersion in food expenditures for different levels of income would likely rise as income rose. Those who are poor have less discretion in their level of food expenditures, so for low levels of income we might see very little dispersion in food expenditures across families. For wealthier families, we might observe some families spending a great deal (dining at fancy restaurants every night) and others spending much less.

In practice, heteroskedasticity arises most often in the context of cross-sectional data.

14.2.3 Consequences for OLS Estimates

If we use the ordinary least squares estimators when the errors are heteroskedastic, our estimators are still unbiased. The standard errors are, however, incorrect and OLS is no longer BLUE. Since the standard errors are incorrect, any hypothesis tests conducted using these standard errors could yield erroneous results. This creates some cause for concern.

To see why the estimators are unbiased in the presence of heteroskedasticity, imagine drawing repeated samples from a population where there is heteroskedasticity. As above, suppose the population appears as in the graph below.

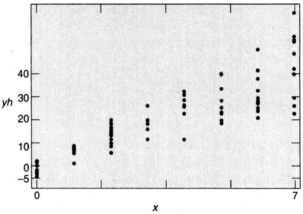

Nonconstant Error Variance (Heteroskedasticity)

For simplicity, suppose our random sample only selected observations where $X = 1$ and $X = 7$. On average, the regression line would pass through the center of these two clusters of observations, just as it would if the error variance was the same at the two levels of X. Thus, our estimator would be unbiased.

Proof. The proof that OLS is still unbiased proceeds in a similar manner to that described in Chapter 10, but here we treat X as a random variable rather than a constant. As in Chapter 10, we apply the notation that $x_i = X_i - \overline{X}$ and we use many of the same algebraic "tricks" to simplify expressions that we did there. Then:

$$E(\hat{\beta}_1) = \sum_{i=1}^{n} E\left(\frac{x_i Y_i}{\sum_{i=1}^{n} x_i^2}\right)$$

$$= \sum_{i=1}^{n} E\left(\frac{x_i(\beta_0 + \beta_1 X_i + \varepsilon)}{\sum_{i=1}^{n} x_i^2}\right)$$

$$= \beta_0 \sum_{i=1}^{n} E\left(\frac{x_i}{\sum_{i=1}^{n} x_i^2}\right) + \beta_1 \sum_{i=1}^{n} E\left(\frac{x_i X_i}{\sum_{i=1}^{n} x_i^2}\right) + \sum_{i=1}^{n} E\left(\frac{x_i \varepsilon_i}{\sum_{i=1}^{n} x_i^2}\right)$$

$$= \beta_1 + \sum_{i=1}^{n} E\left(\frac{x_i \varepsilon_i}{\sum_{i=1}^{n} x_i^2}\right) = \beta_1$$

This proof (see the last line) depends primarily on the covariance between X and ε being zero. The variance of the error term does not enter into the proof.

Now, if we formed the standard error based on the usual formula for the simple linear regression case, we would have

$$\mathrm{var}(\hat{\beta}_1) = \sum_{i=1}^{n} \left(\frac{x_i}{\sum_{i=1}^{n} x_i^2} \right)^2 \mathrm{var}(Y_i)$$

$$= \frac{1}{\left(\sum_{i=1}^{n} x_i^2 \right)^2} \sum_{i=1}^{n} x_i^2 \, \mathrm{var}(Y_i)$$

In our earlier proof (see Chapter 10) we drew on the assumption that $\mathrm{var}(Y_i) = \theta_Y^2$—a constant. This allowed the above expression to be simplified to

$$\mathrm{var}(\hat{\beta}_1) = \frac{\sigma_Y^2}{\sum_{i=1}^{n} x_i^2}$$

If the variance of Y is not a constant, then the proof would have to stop at the expression:

$$\mathrm{var}(\hat{\beta}_1) = \frac{1}{\left(\sum_{i=1}^{n} x_i^2 \right)^2} \sum_{i=1}^{n} x_i^2 \, \mathrm{var}(Y_i)$$

Thus, using the OLS formulas for the standard error is incorrect.

In general, the direction of the error in calculating $\mathrm{var}(\hat{\beta}_1)$ based on the usual formula depends on the pattern of the heteroskedasticity. It is possible, however, to imagine the effect if the pattern was as in the graph above, that is, if the variance in the errors rose with the level of X. In this case, the standard formula would, in effect, use an average (or weighted average) of the variances to form an estimate of σ_Y^2. This estimate would be smaller than the variance when $X = 7$. With this smaller variance, the variance in the sampling distribution of possible slope estimates would be reduced. Thus, when the variance of the errors increases with X, the standard errors for the slope coefficient would be too small. This would bias any hypothesis tests away from the null. In particular, we would be more apt to reject the null that X has no effect on Y. Again, this is not a general result, but rather holds for a particular pattern in the error variance.

14.2.4   Detection

A variety of tests have been proposed to detect the presence of heteroskedasticity. Most of these tests share a similar approach—they look for some association between some function of the errors and some function of the explanatory variable(s). Note first that the OLS estimates are constructed such that there will be no correlation between the errors and the explanatory variables. This suggests we work with some function of the errors.

One approach is to regress e_t^2 on the explanatory variables and all combinations of the explanatory variables. Notice the logic of this approach—we are looking to see if larger values of the error are associated with some function of the explanatory variables. For example, if the variance of the errors rises with X, then the magnitude of the errors (captured by the square of the errors in this approach) would also rise with X. The test would then consider whether any of the coefficients in this model were significant. Alternatively, we could conduct a similar analysis using the absolute value of e rather than the square. The logic of the test is the same.

14.2.5 Weighted Least Squares

If the ordinary least squares estimators are not the best (BLUE) estimators in the presence of heteroskedasticity, what then are the best estimators? Essentially, we can imagine weighting our observations such that more weight is put on observations associated with levels of X having a smaller error variance. For example, if we were given the choice of selecting 5 observations from our graph that shows nonconstant error variance, we would hope to select them from levels of X where the error variance is low. Such observations would simply be more likely to supply us with an estimate of the slope that is closer to the true slope. Observations drawn from, say, $X = 7$, are riskier in that more unusual outcomes are more likely. Using this logic, suppose we transform our model in such a way that the errors no longer exhibit heteroskedasticity. Our basic model with heteroskedasticity is given by $Y_i = \beta_0 + \beta_1 X_i + \varepsilon_i$ and $\text{var}(\varepsilon_i) = \sigma_i^2$.

We transform the model by dividing each observation by the associated standard deviation of the error. That is,

$$\frac{Y_i}{\sigma_i} = \frac{\beta_0}{\sigma_i} + \beta_1 \frac{X_i}{\sigma_i} + \frac{\varepsilon_i}{\sigma_i}$$

The OLS estimators for this transformed model (known as *weighted least squares*) can be shown to be BLUE in the presence of heteroskedasticity (although we do not prove it here because the proof is tedious). Notice that the error term in the transformed model is no longer heteroskedastic. That is,

$$\text{var}\left(\frac{\varepsilon_i}{\sigma_i}\right) = \frac{\text{var}(\varepsilon_i)}{\sigma_i^2} = \frac{\sigma_i^2}{\sigma_i^2} = 1$$

Notice also that we call OLS on the transformed model weighted least squares since each observation is now weighted by the inverse of the standard deviation of the error.

In practice, the major difficulty in estimating weighted least squares is that we don't observe σ_i. There are a variety of ways to estimate σ_i that we will describe in the following sections.

Simple Case

We might be able to estimate the variances of the errors using the data. For example, when our heteroskedasticity appears as below

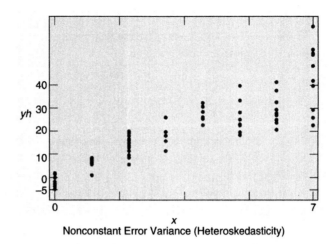

x
Nonconstant Error Variance (Heteroskedasticity)

we might be able to simply estimate the variances of the errors for each level of the explanatory variable. This approach would be plausible if we had enough observations for each level of the explanatory variable. For example, for $X = 7$ we would simply calculate

$$\frac{1}{n}\sum_{i=1}^{n_7} e_i^2$$

where the sum is done for the observations for which $n = 7$. We would do the same for other levels of X. We could then apply weighted least squares using these estimated variances to form the required transformation of the data. Unfortunately, there are often relatively few observations for each level of the explanatory variable, making this approach less likely to be feasible.

Assume σ_i^2 Is a Function of an Explanatory Variable

Suppose the standard deviation of the errors is a function of one of the explanatory variables. That is, $\sigma_i = \gamma X_{ji}$ and so $\sigma_i^2 = \gamma^2 X_{ji}^2$. Thus, the standard deviation of the error rises (or falls) linearly with X_j. In this case, we can implement weighted least squares by dividing each observation by the value of X_{ji}. For example, suppose our model is $Y_i = \beta_0 + \beta_1 X_{1i} + \beta_2 X_{2i} + \varepsilon_i$ and $\text{var}(\varepsilon_i) = \gamma^2 X_{1i}^2$.

Then, we can transform the model as follows:

$$\frac{Y_i}{X_{1i}} = \frac{\beta_0}{X_{1i}} + \beta_1 \frac{X_{1i}}{X_{1i}} + \beta_2 \frac{X_{2i}}{X_{1i}} + \frac{\varepsilon_i}{X_{1i}}$$

$$= \frac{\beta_0}{X_{1i}} + \beta_1 + \beta_2 \frac{X_{2i}}{X_{1i}} + \frac{\varepsilon_i}{X_{1i}}$$

Notice that the error term in the transformed model is now homoskedastic. That is,

$$\text{var}\left(\frac{\varepsilon_i}{X_{1i}}\right) = \frac{\text{var}(\varepsilon_i)}{X_{1i}^2} = \frac{\gamma^2 X_{1i}^2}{X_{1i}^2} = \gamma^2 \text{—a constant}$$

When we run this weighted least squares regression, we must be careful in interpreting our resulting coefficients. Notice that the constant in the regression would be an estimate of β_1 while the coefficient on

$$\frac{1}{X_{1i}}$$

would provide an estimate of the intercept in the original model.

Grouped Data

Suppose that we are using data that represent averages over a certain representative group of people (like state averages from representative samples of a state population, for instance). We know from the Central Limit Theorem that these sample averages will be distributed normally with mean μ and variance σ^2/n. Even if the errors across individuals were homoskedastic, the errors in the averages across states will not be; by the Central Limit Theorem the variance of the mean from the bigger states will be smaller than the variance of the mean from smaller states. A weighted least squares approach should, therefore, place more weight on the estimates from bigger states since the error variance is smaller for those observations.

Under the assumption that the underlying variances for individuals are the same, but the sample sizes used to compute means across groups are not, we can transform the regression model in the following way:

$$\sqrt{n_s} * \overline{Y}_s = \sqrt{n_s} * \alpha + \beta_1 * (\sqrt{n_s} * \overline{X}_s) + \sqrt{n_s} * u_s$$

and estimate the transformed regression model, $Y_s^* = \alpha^* + \beta_1 X_{1s}^* + u_s^*$, where each variable is now multiplied by the square root of the sample size used to form the average. Notice that the error term will now be homoskedastic

$$var(u_s^*) = var(\sqrt{n_s} * u_s) = n_s \, var(u_s) = n_s \frac{\sigma^2}{n_s} = \sigma^2$$

which is a constant.

14.2.6   White Correction

We have seen that OLS is not BLUE when the errors are heteroskedastic. In addition, OLS, while providing unbiased estimates, will provide incorrect standard errors. If we are willing to make some assumptions about the way in which the error variance varies with the explanatory variables (as above), then we can use weighted least squares and generate efficient estimates. Sometimes (often!) we will be unsure how to best characterize the heteroskedasticity. In this case, we might be willing to forgo the efficiency of weighted least squares (and avoid likely misspecification in the process) and instead use OLS with *corrected standard errors*. That is, we will use OLS but generate the standard errors using a formula that is robust to the presence of heteroskedasticity.

APPLICATION 14.1   *Was Welfare Reform Worth the Weight?*

When President Clinton was voted into office in 1992, he promised to "end welfare as we know it." In the following years states were allowed to introduce experimental reforms on their own and then national welfare reform legislation was enacted in 1996. Between 1993 and 2000, the fraction of the population on welfare fell by over half. But welfare reform was not the only thing happening over this period; the national unemployment rate fell to a 30-year low. Did the share of the population on welfare fall because of changes in the law or because the strong labor market enabled potential welfare recipients to find work?

One study used state-level data from the period 1976 to 1996 (prior to national welfare reform) to distinguish between the two competing hypotheses. A regression model with roughly the general form $\ln W_{st} = \beta_0 + \beta_1 \cdot U_{st} + \beta_2 \cdot R_{st} + \beta_3 \cdot X_{st} + \varepsilon_{st}$ was estimated, where W represents the share of the population collecting welfare in state s at time t, U is the unemployment rate, R is a dummy variable indicating whether any state-level reforms had been enacted, and X represents a series of additional variables that characterize other conditions in the state (including state and year fixed effects, as described in Chapter 18). Because the states differ so dramatically in size, one would expect heteroskedasticity to be present with larger error variances in smaller states. Using population weights would correct for this.

The results of the analysis with and without population weights are:

	Without weights	With weights
Unemployment rate	0.036	0.031
	(0.0029)	(0.0026)
State-level reform	−0.063	−0.051
	(0.024)	(0.019)

Note: Standard errors in parentheses.

As expected, the coefficients are largely unchanged but the estimated standard errors are reduced. The results indicate that both the decline in unemployment rates and the introduction of state-level reforms contributed to the decline in the share of the population on welfare. Further analysis indicates that the decline in unemployment had a larger impact, but both played a major role.

SOURCE: Council of Economic Advisers. *Explaining the Decline in the Welfare Caseload, 1993–1996.* Washington, DC: Council of Economic Advisers, May 1997; and authors' calculations.

In influential research, the econometrician Halbert White derived appropriate formulas for the standard errors under heteroskedasticity. In the case of simple linear regression we have seen that the standard errors for the slope coefficient are

$$\text{var}(\hat{\beta}_1) = \frac{1}{\left(\sum\limits_{i=1}^{n} x_i^2\right)^2} \sum\limits_{i=1}^{n} x_i^2 \, \text{var}(Y_i) = \frac{1}{\left(\sum\limits_{i=1}^{n} x_i^2\right)^2} \sum\limits_{i=1}^{n} x_i^2 \sigma_i^2$$

where σ_i^2 is the variance of Y, which equals the variance of the errors. In the place of σ_i^2, White proposed using the square of the least squares residual e_i^2. He has shown that this produces a consistent estimator for the variance of the slope coefficient. These formulas can be accessed easily in some popular statistical software packages.

14.3   SERIAL CORRELATION

14.3.1   Definition

Serial correlation (sometimes called *autocorrelation*) occurs when the errors in the regression model are correlated with each other. For example, consider the two graphs below:

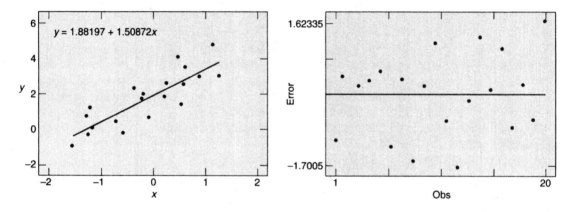

The graph on the left simply shows the scatterplot of *Y* against *X*. The graph on the right shows the errors for the different observations. Notice, there is no obvious pattern in the right graph. The errors seem random. Sometimes, however, the errors follow a pattern. That is, they are correlated across observations. This creates a situation in which our observations are not independent with one another. For example, consider the graphs shown below. The graph on the left shows the scatter plot of unemployment rates against inflation rates for the years 1954–1989. Such data form the basis for estimates of the well-known (and controversial) Phillips Curve.

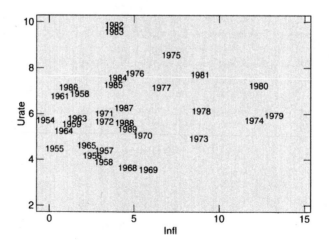

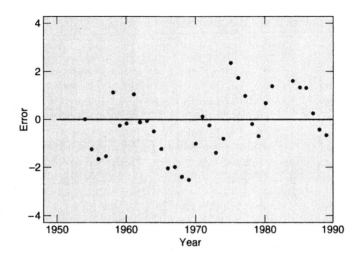

The scatterplot to the right shows the residuals for the different observations (years). Notice that they do not seem to be random, but rather seem to follow something of a pattern.

14.3.2   Causes

Autocorrelation can arise for several reasons. Remember that the error term in the regression captures measurement error (conceptual or recording) as well as omitted variables (that are, hopefully, uncorrelated with the included explanatory variables). Most often, autocorrelation is seen in the context of time series data where an observation is observed at a point in time. In this context, it is frequently seen that factors omitted from the model are correlated over time. That is, they might be correlated across observations.

Example

1. Suppose we have a model relating unemployment and inflation (as above). Some factors that might explain unemployment are relegated to the error term. Some of these variables might themselves be correlated over time. An example would be the oil shocks in the early 1970s. The oil shock would cause us to observe a large positive error. That is, unemployment would be higher than we would expect based on the model (which doesn't control for the oil shock). Further, given the effects of the oil shock do not dissipate immediately, further errors would also be positive. Gradually, the errors would move toward zero; until, perhaps, there is another unanticipated shock.

2. We might observe autocorrelated errors if we try to fit a nonlinear relationship with a linear model. For example, suppose there is in fact a quadratic relation between Y and X but we fit a linear model to the data. In this case, the errors would not be random but would follow a pattern.

As shown in the right-hand graph, the errors would initially be positive, then negative, and then positive again.

14.3.3 Consequences for OLS Estimates

If we use the ordinary least squares estimator when the errors are autocorrelated, our estimators are still unbiased. Again, the proof that the OLS estimators are unbiased does not rely in any way on the errors being independent of one another. The standard errors are estimated incorrectly, however, as they are in the case of heteroskedasticity. Again, if the standard errors produced by the usual formulas are wrong, then any hypothesis tests conducted using these standard errors could yield erroneous results. It is not possible, in general, to show that the standard errors are always overstated or understated. As in the case of heteroskedasticity, it depends on the nature of the autocorrelation. In the special (and quite common) case of the errors being positively correlated across adjacent periods and the explanatory variable increasing over time, it can be shown that the standard errors are biased downward. This suggests that, in that case, the constructed t *ratio* would be overstated, making us more likely to reject the null that the explanatory variable has an effect on the dependent variable.

Finally, OLS is no longer BLUE. This fact flows from the basic observation that there is a pattern in the errors that is ignored when estimating using OLS. This suggests that an estimator that exploited the fact that the errors are correlated would be more efficient.

14.3.4 Correction: Quasi-Differencing

Suppose our model is the following:

$$Y_t = \beta_0 + \beta_1 X_{1t} + \beta_2 X_{2t} + \ldots \beta_k X_{kt} + \varepsilon_t$$

and suppose that

$$\varepsilon_t = \rho \varepsilon_{t-1} + v_t$$

The second equation captures the correlation in the errors across periods (i.e., observations). This model is a model of *first-order serial correlation*. We call it "first order" in that the correlation in the errors is such that the error in any period (i.e., t) is a function of the error in the prior period (i.e., $t-1$). That is, the error depends on the *lagged* error plus an error term v_t that is assumed to satisfy all of our usual assumptions (e.g., mean zero, serially uncorrelated, constant error variance, etc.). The parameter ρ measures the correlation in the error between adjacent observations.

There is a clever way to transform a model that is characterized by first-order serial correlation so that the errors are no longer serially correlated. This transformation is called *quasi-differencing* and works as follows.

Suppose we lag our original model by one period and multiply each variable by ρ. This yields $\rho Y_{t-1} = \rho \beta_0 + \rho \beta_1 X_{1t-1} + \rho \beta_2 X_{2t-1} + \ldots \rho \beta_k X_{kt-1} + \rho \varepsilon_{t-1}$.

Subtracting this from our original model yields (note we are not quite *differencing* but are almost differencing across periods—hence the expression *quasi-differencing*):

$$Y_t - \rho Y_{t-1} = \beta_0 - \rho\beta_0 + \beta_1 X_{1t} - \rho\beta_1 X_{1t-1} + \beta_2 X_{2t} - \rho\beta_2 X_{2t-1} + \ldots \beta_k X_{kt} - \rho\beta_k X_{kt-1} + \underbrace{\varepsilon_t - \rho\varepsilon_{t-1}}_{=v_t}$$

$$= \beta_0(1 - \rho) + \beta_1(X_{1t} - \rho X_{1t-1}) + \beta_2(X_{2t} - \rho X_{2t-1}) + \beta_k(X_{kt} - \rho X_{kt-1}) + v_t$$

Notice that this transformation yields a residual that satisfies our usual requirements. Running the multiple regression (i.e., the *quasi-differenced model*) $Y_t^* = \beta_0^* + \beta_1 X_{it}^* + \beta_2 X_{it}^* + \ldots \beta_k X_{kt}^* + v_t$ where $\beta_0^* = \beta_0(1-\rho)$, $X_{it}^* = X_{1t} - \rho X_{1t-1}$, and so forth will yield estimates of the slope coefficients of the original model. While OLS is not BLUE in the context of first-order serial correlation, OLS on the transformed model is BLUE.

This result is encouraging—at least, if you are willing to believe the model. The practical difficulty of implementing the quasi-differenced model resides in the fact that we don't know ρ. We will consider two of the many ways that have been suggested to estimate ρ.

The Durbin Procedure

Recall that the quasi-difference model was written

$$Y_{it} - \rho Y_{it-1} = \beta_0 - \rho\beta_0 + \beta_1 X_{1t} - \rho\beta_1 X_{1t-1} + \beta_2 X_{2t} - \rho\beta_2 X_{2t-1} + \ldots + \beta_k X_{kt} - \rho\beta_k X_{kt-1} + \varepsilon_t - \rho\varepsilon_{t-1}$$

If we take the lagged dependent variable Y_{t-1} to the right-hand side of this expression, we have

$$Y_t = \rho Y_{t-1} + \beta_0(1-\rho) + \beta_1 X_{1t} - \rho\beta_1 X_{1t-1} + \beta_2 X_{2t} - \rho\beta_2 X_{2t-1} + \ldots \beta_k X_{kt} - \rho\beta_k X_{kt-1} + v_t$$

We could then run a regression of Y_t on $Y_{t-1}, X_{1t}, X_{1t-1}, X_{2t}, X_{2t-1}, \ldots X_{kt}, X_{kt-1}$. The coefficient on Y_{t-1} from this regression would provide an estimate of ρ that might then be used to form the variables used in the quasi-differenced regression.

The Cochrane–Orcutt Procedure

The Cochrane–Orcutt procedure is probably the most popular procedure for estimating the quasi-differenced model. It proceeds by first estimating the original model $Y_t = \beta_0 + \beta_1 X_{1t} + \beta_2 X_{2t} + \ldots \beta_k X_{kt} + \varepsilon_t$. Next, the errors from the model ($\varepsilon_t = Y_t - \hat{Y}_t$) are used to estimate ρ by using $e_t = \hat{\rho} e_{t-1}$, the sample analog of $\varepsilon_t = \rho\varepsilon_{t-1} + v_t$. That is, we regress the errors from the original regression on their lagged values. The slope coefficient of this regression provides an estimate of ρ. Given the estimate, $\hat{\rho}$, it is possible to estimate the quasi-differenced model $Y_t^* = \beta_0^* + \beta_1 X_{1t}^* + \beta_2 X_{2t}^* + \ldots + \beta_k X_{kt}^* + v_t$ where $\beta_0^* = \beta_0(1-\hat{\rho})$, $X_{it}^* = X_{1t} - \hat{\rho} X_{1t-1}$, and so on. Then, using the estimates of the coefficient generated by this estimation (and dividing the intercept $\beta_0(1-\hat{\rho})$ by $(1-\hat{\rho})$ to provide an estimate of the original intercept) it is possible to generate a new set of errors $e_i = Y_i - \hat{Y}_i$. The procedure then iterates, using these new errors to form a new estimate of ρ, using the new estimate of ρ to construct and estimate the quasi-differenced model, using the errors formed from the estimates of the original coefficients as generated by the quasi-differenced model to generate new errors, and so on. The procedure stops when the estimated $\hat{\rho}$ does not change by "much." It is hoped that such a procedure will lead to a minimization of the sum of squared errors in the quasi-differenced equation. Unfortunately, nothing in the procedure assures this will be the case. A better way to ensure the sum of squared errors is minimized would be to do a *grid search* whereby different values (an extremely large number) of ρ are tried in estimating the quasi-differenced equation and the estimates corresponding to the minimum sum of squared errors are selected. But this approach is computationally intensive and time consuming.

14.3.5 Detection: The Durbin–Watson Test

The Durbin–Watson test provides a way to test the null hypothesis that $\rho = 0$. That is, it is a test for the presence of first-order serial correlation. The alternative hypothesis can be $\rho \neq 0$, $\rho > 0$, or $\rho < 0$—the latter two suggesting positive or negative serial correlation, respectively. Most often in economics the likely alternative is positive serial correlation, so we will first consider the hypotheses

$$H_0: \rho = 0$$
$$H_1: \rho > 0$$

To conduct this test, we use the Durbin–Watson statistic, which is defined as

$$d = \frac{\sum_{t=2}^{n}(e_t - e_{t-1})^2}{\sum_{t=1}^{n}e_t^2}$$

where e_t is the residual from the regression $Y_t = \beta_0 + \beta_1 X_{1t} + \beta_2 X_{2t} + \ldots + \beta_k X_{kt} + \varepsilon_t$ and e_{t-1} is the one-period lagged value of e_t. If we expand the expression for d we can see that

$$d = \frac{\sum_{t=2}^{n}e_t^2 - 2\sum_{t=2}^{n}e_t e_{t-1} + \sum_{t=2}^{n}e_{t-1}^2}{\sum_{t=1}^{n}e_t^2}$$

$$\approx 1 - 2\hat{\rho} + 1 = 2(1 - \hat{\rho})$$

Thus, under the null we would expect d to be near 2, and the smaller d, the more plausible the alternative hypothesis. We would then probably imagine testing the hypothesis by rejecting H_0 if d was far enough below 2 that it was unlikely that such a value would happen by chance.

In practice, there is a peculiar difficulty in applying this test in that the sampling distribution of d depends on the values of the explanatory variables. Since every problem has a different set of explanatory variables, Durbin and Watson derived upper and lower limits for the critical value of the test. Accordingly, if we define d^* as the critical value of d (i.e., if $d < d^*$, we reject the null), Durbin and Watson derived upper and lower limits such that $d_l \leq d^* \leq d_u$. With this in hand, they developed the following decision rule:

$$\text{If } \begin{cases} d \leq d_l \rightarrow \text{reject } H_0 \\ d_l < d < d_u \rightarrow \text{test is inconclusive} \\ d \geq d_u \rightarrow \text{do not reject } H_0 \end{cases}$$

Tables of d_u and d_l are in Appendix B.

If we suspect negative serial correlation, the appropriate test becomes

---

APPLICATION 14.2   *Where Is the Inflation?*

Inflation-fighting is a difficult job, especially when one of your simplest tools is letting you down. One that historically helped Federal Reserve officials determine whether inflation was around the corner was the NAIRU (the nonaccelerating inflation rate of unemployment), sometimes referred to as the natural rate of unemployment. If the observed unemployment rate fell below this level, inflation would start to rise at an increasing rate. This offshoot of the Phillips Curve has traditionally provided a useful benchmark to use along with other factors in determining whether to raise interest rates.

But how does one estimate the NAIRU? In its simplest form, it is a component of the relationship

$$\pi_t - \pi_{t-1} = \beta_1 \cdot (u_{t-1} - \bar{u}) + \beta_2 \cdot (u_{t-2} - \bar{u}) + \varepsilon_t$$

where π and u are the inflation and unemployment rates at time t and $\bar{u}$ is the NAIRU. As suggested above, this relationship indicates that if unemployment deviates from the NAIRU in the recent past, it will lead to an acceleration in the inflation rate. To estimate NAIRU, we can use some algebra and rewrite this specification as

$$\pi_t - \pi_{t-1} = \beta_0 + \beta_1 \cdot u_{t-1} + \beta_2 \cdot u_{t-2} + \varepsilon_t$$

where $\bar{u} = -\beta_0/(\beta_1 + \beta_2)$. This is a standard OLS regression and we can use the intercept and the slopes to get the NAIRU. With time series data, however, serial correlation is a potential problem and one would want to test for it and correct it if present.

We estimated this model using annual data from 1948 to 1999 and obtained the following results:

	β_0	β_1	β_2	Durbin–Watson statistic
OLS	0.0025	−0.0075	0.0068	1.18
	(0.0109)	(0.0026)	(0.0026)	
Cochrane–Orcutt	.0121	−0.0106	0.0086	1.93
	(0.0100)	(0.0021)	(0.0020)	

Note: Standard errors in parentheses.

The Durbin-Watson statistic of 1.18 obtained when estimating the model with OLS is below the lower bound critical value of 1.44 with 2 explanatory variables and 46 observations. Therefore, we estimate the model using the Cochrane–Orcutt method, where the standard errors are noticeably smaller (which leads to a more precise estimate of the NAIRU). Based on these estimates, the NAIRU is about 6%. With the unemployment rate hovering around 4% at the time we are writing this, one could ask: Where is the inflation?

Source: Staiger, Douglas, James H. Stock, and Mark W. Watson, "The NAIRU, Unemployment, and Monetary Policy," *Journal of Economic Perspectives*, Vol. 11, No. 1 (Winter 1997), pp. 33–49.

$$H_0: \rho = 0$$
$$H_1: \rho < 0$$

The decision rule for this hypothesis is given by

$$\text{If} \begin{cases} d \geq 4 - d_l \rightarrow \text{reject } H_0 \\ 4 - d_u < d < 4 - d_l \rightarrow \text{test is inconclusive} \\ d \leq 4 - d_u \rightarrow \text{do not reject } H_0 \end{cases}$$

Notice that if $\rho = -1$, then $d \approx 4$.

Finally, if we have no strong prior belief about whether there is positive or negative serial correlation, we can use a two-tailed test:

$$H_0 : \rho = 0$$
$$H_1 : \rho \neq 0$$

The decision rule for this hypothesis is simply a combination of the one-tailed tests given above:

$$\text{If} \begin{cases} d \leq d_l \text{ or } d \geq 4 - d_l \rightarrow \text{reject } H_0 \\ d \geq d_u \text{ or } d \leq 4 - d_u \rightarrow \text{do not reject } H_0 \\ \text{otherwise test is inconclusive} \end{cases}$$

14.4 PROBLEMS

1. When using OLS, we assume that the errors are independent (i.e., not serially correlated) and normally distributed with constant variance (i.e., homoskedastic). These assumptions allow us to use the F and t distributions to perform significance tests on the estimated coefficients in the model. However, we often wish to estimate models in which we doubt the validity of these assumptions. For the following scenarios, explain why these assumptions may fail:

   a. Estimating a model of stock prices as a function of changing market conditions

   b. Estimating one's expenditure on housing as a function of one's income using cross-sectional data

   c. Estimating the effect of median income on the per-capita level of public education spending using data from a sample of 100 cities

2. You are investigating the effect of income on family size in rural India. The relationship

$$\text{Family size} = \beta_0 + \beta_1(\text{Family income}) + \varepsilon$$

   is proposed. The available data come from a survey of 100 villages, but include only village average family size and village average income, not observations of individual families. However, you do know the number of families sampled in each village.

   a. What would be the consequences of using OLS to estimate the above model using the averaged data? (That is, how are your estimated coefficients and standard errors affected compared to the estimates that would be produced if individual family data were available?)

   b. Propose an alternative method for estimating the model, and explain why the alternative is better than OLS.

3. Why are the error terms in cross-sectional data unlikely to be serially correlated? Can you give an example in which serial correlation could be present in a cross-sectional dataset?

4. The dataset for this problem contains three variables: year, unemployment (U_t), and Infl = inflation rate for the years 1951 through 1999. This problem deals with one of the most famous empirical relationships in macroeconomics, the Phillips Curve, which suggests that unemployment is negatively related to inflation. In 1968 Milton Friedman denied the existence of an inflation/unemployment tradeoff in the long-term, saying, "The temporary tradeoff comes not from inflation per se, but from unanticipated inflation, which generally means a rising rate of inflation."

   a. For the period 1951–1970, estimate the model

   $$U_t = a + b\text{Infl}_t + e_t \tag{1}$$

   Can you reject the hypothesis that $b = 0$ at the 10% level? What does this suggest about the existence of an unemployment/inflation tradeoff? Use the Durbin–Watson statistic to test for autocorrelation. If you find the residuals are serially correlated, implement an appropriate technique to correct the problem. What do you conclude now?

   b. Now, estimate model (1) using data through 1980. What would you have concluded about the existence of a tradeoff had you used this sample? Now estimate the model using the full sample. What do you conclude about the existence of a tradeoff based on the full sample?

   c. One way of trying to get at Friedman's temporary tradeoff is to consider the model:

   $$U_t = a + b(\text{Infl}_t - \text{Infl}_{t-1}) + e_t \tag{2}$$

   What sign would Friedman predict for part (b)? What does this assume about inflationary expectations? Estimate (2) using all the data. Do the results support Friedman's prediction?

   d. The more general model

   $$U_t = a + b\text{Infl}_t + c\text{Infl}_{t-1} + e_t \tag{3}$$

   includes both (1) and (2) as special cases. Estimate (3). Test the implied restrictions on (3) to get to (1) and (2). What model would you choose to describe the data?

Chapter 15

Simultaneous Equations

15.1   INTRODUCTION

In previous chapters we focused on issues related to estimation and inference for a single equation. In this chapter we consider the situation where the equation we are interested in estimating is embedded in a system of simultaneous linear equations. Such a situation is very common in economics. Models of supply and demand, for example, determine prices and quantities and are, of course, central to economic analyses. Investment/Savings (IS) and Liquidity/Money (LM) curves are used in macroeconomics to determine equilibrium aggregate income. We will begin the chapter by introducing some terminology used in relation to simultaneous equations. We then demonstrate that the use of ordinary least squares is typically not a desirable estimation strategy in the context of simultaneous equations—leading to (asymptotically) biased estimates of the parameters of interest. Next we turn to the *identification question,* which asks whether it is logically possible to estimate the parameters of the equation of interest. Finally, we introduce appropriate methods for estimating equations that are part of a system of linear equations.

15.2   STRUCTURAL AND REDUCED-FORM EQUATIONS

Consider the following simple Keynesian model for the determination of aggregate income.

$$\left. \begin{array}{l} C_t = \alpha + \beta Y_t + \varepsilon_t \\ Y_t = C_t + I_t \end{array} \right\} \text{Structural equations}$$

(1)

(2)

where:

C_t is consumption expenditures in time period t

Y_t is income in period t

I_t is investment in period t

ε_t is an error term with mean zero and constant variance

α and β are parameters

Notice that this simple model contains two equations. These equations are called *structural equations.* You might think of them, in this example, as providing a *structure* for how the economy functions. Structural equations arise from our theoretical model or introspective reasoning on some economic phenomena. In this example, the first structural equation is a *consumption equation.* It relates consumption spending to income. The coefficient β is familiar to any student of macroeconomics. It indicates the amount that consumption is expected to increase if income rises by one dollar. That is, it is the *marginal propensity to consume.* It is highly useful to have an empirical estimate of the magnitude of β since many policy interventions (e.g., tax cuts) are postulated to exercise their expansionary impacts on income through their effects on consumption. The more sensitive is consumption to changes in income (i.e., the larger is β) the larger the effect of any expansionary measure. The parameters α and β are called (not surprisingly) *structural parameters.* Our goal is to provide estimates and conduct statistical inferences for structural parameters.

It is important to notice that this model contains two dependent variables: C_t and Y_t. These variables are *jointly dependent* in that consumption affects income and income affects consumption. They are, thus, simultaneously determined. We refer to those variables that are determined within the context of our model as *endogenous variables.* Clearly there must be as many equations in our model as there are endogenous variables. Similarly, variables that are determined outside the context of the model are called *exogenous variables.* We do not expect to explain the exogenous variables using our model. In our model, Investment (I_t) is the only exogenous variable.

It is often useful to express our endogenous variables in such a way that they are functions *only* of exogenous variables. Thus, we would like to express C_t and Y_t as functions of I_t. To do this we substitute equation (1) into equation (2) and, similarly, equation (2) into equation (1). These new equations are called the *reduced-form* equations of our model.

$$C_t = \frac{\alpha}{1-\beta} + \frac{\beta}{1-\beta} I_t + \frac{1}{1-\beta} \varepsilon_t \tag{3}$$

$$Y_t = \frac{\alpha}{1-\beta} + \frac{1}{1-\beta} I_t + \frac{1}{1-\beta} \varepsilon_t \tag{4}$$

Reduced-form equations

It can be seen from equation (3) that the coefficient on investment is simply the well-known multiplier. Indeed, the coefficients on reduced-form equations are often called *impact multipliers.* The multiplier in the consumption equation can be easily understood by considering the structural equations (1) and (2). A dollar increase in investment leads to a dollar increase in income. The dollar increase in income, in turn, leads to a β-dollar increase in consumption, which leads to a β-dollar increase in income, which leads to a β^2-dollar increase in consumption. Tracing out the resulting infinite geometric series we see the effects from each "round" being

$$
\begin{aligned}
\beta + \beta^2 &+ \beta^3 + \dots \\
&= \beta(1 + \beta + \beta^2 + \dots) \\
&= \frac{\beta}{1 - \beta}
\end{aligned}
$$

15.3   SIMULTANEOUS EQUATIONS BIAS

Suppose our empirical goal was to estimate the structural coefficients α and β. A natural approach would simply be to estimate these parameters by applying ordinary least squares (OLS) to equation (1). But, is this appropriate? It turns out that it is usually not appropriate to use ordinary least squares in the context of simultaneous equations. This is because, in this example, there is a correlation between the endogenous variable on the right-hand side of the equation and the error term in that equation. That is, $\text{cov}(Y_t, \varepsilon_t) \neq 0$, which violates a maintained assumption of the regression model and would induce a bias were we to employ OLS. To see that such a correlation exists, note that an increase in the error term in equation (1) would cause consumption to rise. The increase in consumption would cause an increase in income (via equation (2)). Thus, income and the error term are correlated.

$$
\varepsilon \uparrow \Rightarrow C \uparrow \Rightarrow Y \uparrow
$$

Using OLS in this context will render biased estimates of α and β. It is possible to measure the direction of the bias in this example. To simplify the notation, we define c_t and y_t to be measured as the deviations of C_t and Y_t from their respective means (i.e., $c_t = C_t - \overline{C}$). Then, using the fact that $C_t = \alpha + \beta Y_t + \varepsilon_t$, so that $c_t = C_t - \overline{C}_t = (\alpha + \beta Y_t + \varepsilon_t) - (\alpha + \beta \overline{Y}_t) = \beta Y_t + \varepsilon_t$, we have

$$
\hat{\beta}_{\text{ols}} = \frac{\displaystyle\sum_{t=1}^{T} c_t y_t}{\displaystyle\sum_{t=1}^{T} y_t^2} = \frac{\displaystyle\sum_{t=1}^{T} (\beta y_t + \varepsilon_t) y_t}{\displaystyle\sum_{t=1}^{T} y_t^2}
$$

$$
= \beta + \frac{\displaystyle\sum_{t=1}^{T} \varepsilon_t y_t}{\displaystyle\sum_{t=1}^{T} y_t^2} = \beta + \frac{\dfrac{\displaystyle\sum_{t=1}^{T} \varepsilon_t y_t}{T}}{\dfrac{\displaystyle\sum_{t=1}^{T} y_t^2}{T}}
$$

But asymptotically,

$$\frac{\sum_{t=1}^{T} \varepsilon_t y_t}{T} = E[y_t \varepsilon_t] = E[(Y_t - \overline{Y}_t)\varepsilon_t] = E[Y_t \varepsilon_t] - \overline{Y}_t E[\varepsilon_t] = E[Y_t \varepsilon_t]$$

where we used the fact that $\overline{Y}_t$ is a constant and $E(\varepsilon_t) = 0$. We can show that the resulting expression is nonzero using equation (4):

$$E[Y_t \varepsilon_t] = \frac{\alpha}{1 - \beta} \underbrace{E[\varepsilon_t]}_{=0} + \frac{1}{1 - \beta} \underbrace{E[I_t \varepsilon_t]}_{=0} + \frac{1}{1 - \beta} \underbrace{E[\varepsilon_t^2]}_{=\sigma_\varepsilon^2}$$

$$= \frac{1}{1 - \beta} \sigma_\varepsilon^2 \neq 0$$

Combining this with the fact that, asymptotically,

$$\frac{\sum_{t=1}^{T} Y_t^2}{T} = \text{var}(Y) = \sigma_y^2$$

yields

$$p \lim \hat{\beta}_{\text{ols}} = \beta + \frac{\left(\dfrac{1}{1 - \beta}\right)\sigma_\varepsilon^2}{\sigma_Y^2} \neq \beta$$

Thus, we have shown that the ordinary least squares estimate of the marginal propensity to consume (β) would be inconsistent (or asymptotically biased). Indeed, since we know from our knowledge of economics that $\beta \in (0,1)$ then we know that $\hat{\beta}_{\text{ols}}$ would be biased upward asymptotically. Such an overestimate of the marginal propensity to consume could, for example, cause overly enthusiastic predictions for the effectiveness of fiscal policy.

Now, suppose rather than estimating equation (1) using OLS we estimate the reduced-form equation (3) using OLS. OLS on this equation would be appropriate since investment and the error term are uncorrelated by the assumption that investment is exogenous.

15.4 IDENTIFICATION

Based on the preceding discussion, one can see that there are advantages to estimating reduced-form models in that OLS will provide unbiased estimates. On the other hand, it does not provide direct estimates of the structural parameters, but functions of them. In fact, only under certain circumstances can one "unscramble" the reduced-form estimates to recover the associated structural parameters. The problem of whether we can solve the reduced-form equations for unique values of the structural equations is called the *identification problem*.

To develop the identification problem more clearly, we will use the following simple two-equation structural model:

$$Y_1 = \beta_1 Y_2 + \beta_2 X_1 + \beta_3 X_2 \atop Y_2 = \gamma_1 Y_1 + \gamma_2 X_1 + \gamma_2 X_2 \Big\} \text{Structural equations}$$

$$(5)$$
$$(6)$$

where Y_1, Y_2 are endogenous and X_1, X_2 are exogenous variables. Notice that equations (5) and (6) do not contain an error term. We have purposely omitted the error term to emphasize the point that the identification problem is *not* statistical in nature; rather it is a logical problem. Identification is an issue that must be resolved logically prior to estimation.

To solve for the reduced-form equations associated with equations (5) and (6) we plug equation (6) into equation (5) and, similarly, plug equation (5) into equation (6), which yields:

$$Y_1 = \frac{\beta_1 \gamma_2 + \beta_2}{1 - \beta_1 \gamma_1} X_1 + \frac{\beta_1 \gamma_3 + \beta_3}{1 - \beta_1 \gamma_1} X_2 \atop Y_2 = \frac{\beta_2 \gamma_1 + \gamma_2}{1 - \beta_1 \gamma_1} X_1 + \frac{\beta_3 \gamma_1 + \gamma_3}{1 - \beta_1 \gamma_1} X_2 \Bigg\} \text{Reduced-form equations}$$

$$(7)$$
$$(8)$$

We usually write the reduced-form equations using the simplified notation:

$$Y_1 = \Pi_{11} X_1 + \Pi_{12} X_2 \atop Y_2 = \Pi_{21} X_1 + \Pi_{22} X_2 \Big\} \text{Reduced-form equations}$$

$$(9)$$
$$(10)$$

where

$$\Pi_{11} = \frac{\beta_1 \gamma_2 + \beta_2}{1 - \beta_1 \gamma_1}, \Pi_{12} = \frac{\beta_1 \gamma_3 + \beta_3}{1 - \beta_1 \gamma_1}$$

and so on.

Now, even if we *knew* the four reduced-form parameters Π_{11}, Π_{12}, Π_{21}, Π_{22}, we should *not* be very optimistic about using these four numbers (Π_{11}, Π_{12}, Π_{21}, Π_{22}) to solve for the six structural parameters (β_1, β_2, β_3, γ_1, γ_2, γ_3) in the structural model; in general one cannot solve four equations for six unknowns. Thus, we might say "We are unable to identify the structural parameters given knowledge of the reduced-form parameters."

We may thus define the identification problem as the question of whether the values of the coefficients of a particular structural equation can be deduced from the reduced-form coefficients. If it is possible to deduce the structural coefficients of an equation from a knowledge of the reduced-form equations, we say that that particular structural equation is *identified*. The process of estimating the reduced-form model and recovering the structural parameters is called *indirect least squares*, which is described in more detail below. It should be clear at this point that if a model is not identified it cannot be estimated by indirect least squares, or any other method.

Let us now look in more detail at how we could determine whether the parameters of a particular structural equation are identified. Suppose we knew Π_{11}, Π_{12}, Π_{21}, Π_{22} from equations (9) and (10). Let's focus on equation (5). If we substitute equations (9) and (10) into equation (5) for Y_1, Y_2 respectively we have

$$\Pi_{11}X_1 + \Pi_{12}X_2 = \beta_1(\Pi_{21}X_1 + \Pi_{22}X_2) + \beta_2 X_1 + \beta_3 X_2$$

Collecting terms we have

$$(\Pi_{11} - \beta_1 \Pi_{21} - \beta_2)X_1 + (\Pi_{12} - \beta_1 \Pi_{22} - \beta_3)X_2 = 0 \qquad (11)$$

Equation (11) must hold for all values of X_1 and X_2. Suppose we set $X_1 = 1$ and $X_2 = 0$. Then equation (11) simplifies to

$$(\Pi_{11} - \beta_1 \Pi_{21} - \beta_2)1 = 0 \qquad (12)$$

Similarly, if we set $X_1 = 0$ and $X_2 = 1$, then

$$(\Pi_{12} - \beta_1 \Pi_{22} - \beta_3)1 = 0 \qquad (13)$$

must hold. Now the question is: Can we solve equations (12) and (13) for the structural parameters in equation (5), that is, β_1, β_2, β_3? Clearly we cannot. We have two equations with three unknowns. On the basis of this way of looking at identification we can now distinguish three cases.

Case 1

In the situation considered we say that structural equation (5) is not identified. This means, in essence, that we have more structural coefficients to determine than we have equations to determine them with. In fact, both equations (5) and (6) (try to show this!) are not identified in their present form.

Case 2

The problem in Case 1 was that there were too many structural parameters to estimate relative to the number of reduced-form parameters. Suppose we could impose more a priori restrictions on the structural model—in effect reducing the number of structural coefficients we need to identify. For example, suppose that we believed that $\beta_3 = 0$. Equations (12) and (13) would then simplify to

$$(\Pi_{11} - \beta_1 \Pi_{21} - \beta_2)1 = 0 \qquad (12')$$

$$(\Pi_{12} - \beta_1 \Pi_{22})1 = 0 \qquad (13')$$

In this case there are two equations with two unknowns (β_1, β_2). Hence, the imposition of the restriction that $\beta_3 = 0$ would allow us to identify the structural parameters in equation (5). In this case we say that equation (5) is just or exactly identified. That is, there is exactly one way to "unscramble" the reduced-form parameters to deduce the structural parameters. From equation (13'), we can show that

$$\beta_1 = \frac{\Pi_{12}}{\Pi_{22}}$$

Substituting into (12'), and solving for β_2 yields:

$$\beta_2 = \Pi_{11} - \frac{\Pi_{12}}{\Pi_{22}}\Pi_{21}$$

Case 3

Now, suppose we impose yet another restriction on our model. Suppose we believed that $\beta_3 = 0$ and $\beta_2 = 0$. Thus, we are saying that equation (5) should really be written as $Y_1 = \beta_1 Y_2$ with just one unknown structural parameter β_1. Equations (12) and (13) now simplify to

$$(\Pi_{11} - \beta_1 \Pi_{21})X_1 = 0 \tag{12''}$$

$$(\Pi_{12} - \beta_1 \Pi_{22})X_2 = 0 \tag{13''}$$

We now have two equations with only one unknown. It is possible to unscramble the reduced-form equations in two different ways to solve for the structural parameter β_1. From equation (12'') we have

$$\beta_1 = \frac{\Pi_{11}}{\Pi_{21}}$$

From equation (13'') we have

$$\beta_1 = \frac{\Pi_{11}}{\Pi_{22}}$$

In this situation we have *more* a priori restrictions on the structural model than we need to identify the structural parameters. In this situation we say that equation (5) is *overidentified*.

15.5   THE ORDER CONDITION

You might have noticed a pattern in the three cases shown above. In Case 1, where equation (5) was not identified, we had fewer exogenous variables excluded from the equation (i.e., the coefficient on the variable was restricted to zero) than endogenous variables included. Indeed, for Case 1 there were no exogenous variables excluded from equation (5) and there was one endogenous variable included on the right-hand side of equation (5). In Case 2, there was one exogenous variable not included in equation (5) (i.e., X_2) and there was one endogenous variable included on the right-hand side of equation (5) (i.e., Y_2). In this case equation (5) was exactly identified. In Case 3 there were two exogenous variables not included in equation (5) (i.e., X_1 and X_2) and there was one endogenous variable included on the right-hand side of equation (5) (i.e., Y_2). In this case equation (5) was overidentified. This pattern suggests a simple rule for deciding whether an equation is identified. This rule is referred to as the *order condition*.

Let X = the number of exogenous variables in the system of equations that are excluded from a particular equation.

Let N = the number of endogenous variables on the right-hand side of a particular equation.

If $X < N$ the equation is not identified.

If $X = N$ the equation is exactly identified.

If $X > N$ the equation is overidentifed.

The order condition is a necessary but not sufficient condition for identification. If the exogenous variables excluded from a particular equation are not perfectly correlated (i.e., collinear), then the condition is also sufficient for identification.

It is worth noting that if an equation is not identified, then it cannot be estimated. We now turn to methods for estimating exactly and overidentified equations.

15.6 ESTIMATION

15.6.1 Exactly Identified Equations: Indirect Least Squares

As we saw above, when an equation is exactly identified there is a one-to-one correspondence between the structural and the reduced-form parameters. Then there is a unique way to unscramble the reduced-form equation to solve for the structural parameters of an equation.

OLS on a reduced-form equation is called *indirect least squares* and gives consistent estimates of the reduced-form parameters. The only difficulty with this approach is that we must be able to solve the reduced-form equations for unique values of the structural parameters. If we can do this, the property of consistency will carry over from the estimated reduced-form parameters to the estimated structural parameters. In our simple example above, the indirect least squares procedure would work. For example, an indirect least squares (i.e., OLS) estimation of equation (3) would yield an estimated coefficient on investment for

$$\frac{\beta}{1 - \beta}$$

Similarly, OLS on equation (4) would yield an estimated coefficient on investment of

$$\frac{1}{1 - \beta}$$

Taking the ratio of these reduced-form coefficients would provide an estimate of β.

15.6.2 Overidentified Equations: Two-Stage Least Squares

Consider the following system of simultaneous linear equations:

$$Y_{1t} = \beta_{10} + \beta_{11}Y_{2t} + \gamma_{11}X_{1t} + \gamma_{21}X_{2t} + u_{1t} \tag{14}$$

$$Y_{2t} = \beta_{20} + \beta_{21}Y_{1t} + u_{2t} \tag{15}$$

Using the order condition we can see that equation (14) is not identified and equation (15) is overidentified. Thus, there is no way to estimate the structural parameters in equation (14) but there are multiple ways to estimate the structural parameters in equation (15).

Now, recall that the reason we cannot use ordinary least squares to estimate equation (15) stems from the correlation between the error term and the right-hand side endogenous variable (i.e., the correlation between Y_{1t} and u_{2t}). This is conceptually the same problem as that faced in the context of omitted variable bias. One possible solution in that context and also in this context is to use an *instrumental variable*. An appropriate instrumental variable

---

APPLICATION 15.1   *Something Smells Fishy*

In perfectly competitive models, the "law of one price" indicates that all consumers should pay the same price for the same good. Testing this proposition is generally a difficult task because one must obtain sufficient data on the prices paid by different types of consumers who are all buying identical products in markets that appear to be perfectly competitive. One example of research that has conducted such an analysis investigated prices paid at the Fulton Fish Market in New York City. The author obtained detailed records on the sale of a particular type of fish to different types of customers, estimated regression models of prices paid as a function of the customers' characteristics, and found that Asian customers paid 7% less for fish than white customers.

The fact that the mostly white merchants charged Asians less rules out an explanation of animus-based discrimination and would lead one to consider price discrimination as a potential reason. In an economic model of (third-degree) price discrimination, firms charge those customers with a higher demand elasticity a lower price. Therefore, a relevant test in the present context is whether Asians have a higher elasticity of demand than whites.

The estimation of demand (and supply) models presents perhaps the most common example in economics of simultaneous equations. As every student who has taken Economics 101 knows, prices are determined by the interaction of supply and demand, so that the equilibrium price and quantity of goods sold (which is all that we can observe in the marketplace) are determined simultaneously. Specifically, an econometric model of the market outcome would take the form

$$\ln Q^d = \beta_0 + \beta_1 \ln P + \beta_2 X + \varepsilon$$

$$\ln P = \gamma_0 + \gamma_1 \ln Q^d + \gamma_2 X' + e$$

When estimated in this double-log form, β_1 represents the demand elasticity (see Chapter 9) and γ_1 represents something called the *inverse demand elasticity*. The unbiased estimation of β_1 requires elements of X' that are not also elements of X to be identified and vice versa for γ_1. In this study of fish prices, weather conditions in the Atlantic Ocean and dummy variables representing different days of the week are included in X, but not X'. Both of these sets of variables would affect the quantity sold in the market independent of price (holding price constant, bad weather means fewer fish are available to purchase and people buy more fish late in the week). These variables provide the identification to obtain unbiased estimates of γ_1. The results suggest that Asians do have more elastic demand than whites, providing some indication that merchants are practicing price discrimination.

Source: Grady, Kathryn, "Testing for Imperfect Competition at the Fulton Fish Market," *Rand Journal of Economics*, Vol. 26, No. 1 (Spring 1995), pp. 75–92.

---

would be (1) correlated with Y_{1t} and (2) uncorrelated with u_{2t}. We have two logical choices for instrumental variables within the system of equations. Notice that X_1 and X_2 are both correlated with Y_{1t} (via equation (14)) and, since they are exogenous by assumption, they are uncorrelated with the error term. Thus, there are two ways to estimate equation (15)—one using X_1 as the instrument and the other using X_2 as the instrument.

We might now ask whether we could combine these instruments somehow to provide a unique estimate of β_{21}. Notice that X_1 and X_2 are viable instruments, in part, because they are correlated with Y_{1t}. Suppose we found a variable that was an optimal linear combination of X_1 and X_2 in the sense that it maximized the correlation with Y_{1t}. Since the ordinary least squares regression of Y_{1t} on X_1 and X_2 would produce the linear combination of the two exogenous variables that maximizes the R^2 (i.e., the goodness of fit), a natural approach would be to proceed in that fashion. This is the logic behind the *two-stage least squares estimator (2SLS)*.

Two-Stage Least Squares

Stage 1: Estimate the reduced-form equations using ordinary least squares and take the predicted values from that estimation (i.e., the linear combination of the exogenous variables maximizing the correlation with the problematic endogenous variable).

Stage 2: Use the predicted value of the endogenous variable in place of the endogenous variable and estimate the resulting equation using ordinary least squares.

Example

To estimate equation (15) using 2SLS we would do the following.

Stage 1: Regress the endogenous right-hand side variable on all of the exogenous variables in the system of equations (i.e., the reduced form for that variable). Form the predicted values from this regression. That is, regress Y_{1t} on X_1 and X_2. Retain the predicted values $\hat{Y}_{1t} = \hat{\Pi}_{10} + \hat{\Pi}_{11}X_{1t} + \hat{\Pi}_{12}X_{2t}$ where the $\hat{\Pi}$ coefficients are the ordinary least squares estimates of the reduced-form coefficients.

Stage 2: Use the predicted value of the right-hand side endogenous variable in place of the original variable and estimate the resulting equation using ordinary least squares; that is, estimate the model $Y_{2t} = \beta_{20} + \beta_{21}\hat{Y}_{1t} + u_{2t}$. The resulting estimate of $\hat{\beta}_{21}$ supplies a consistent estimate of this structural parameter.

Notice that estimation of 2SLS would not be possible if the equation was not identified. In this case the predicted value of the endogenous variable would be perfectly multicollinear with the exogenous variables in the structural equation. To see this, consider equation (14) above. The first stage of 2SLS would regress Y_{2t} on X_1 and X_2. The second stage would regress Y_{1t} on $\hat{Y}_{2t}$, X_1 and X_2. But, $\hat{Y}_{2t}$ would, by nature of its construction, be perfectly collinear with X_1 and X_2. Thus, estimation would be impossible. Two other facts are worth noting. First, it can be shown that estimates provided by 2SLS will be identical to those provided by indirect least squares when the equation is exactly identified. Second, it can be shown that the standard errors calculated for the structural coefficients using 2SLS as described above would be incorrect. Standard statistical packages correct for this problem.

APPLICATION 15.2 | *Will Spending an Extra Dime Help Reduce the Rate of Crime?*

One solution traditionally proposed to help reduce the crime rate is to hire additional police. But do these additional expenditures accomplish their intended goal? Are they "worth it"? Estimating the relationship between the number of police and the crime rate is complicated by the fact that police employment is endogenous; communities tend to hire more police when crime is a more serious problem.

One recent study used a two-stage least squares approach to solve this econometric issue. The author takes advantage of the fact that lawmakers tend to hire more police in election years in an attempt to look "tough on crime." Therefore, election years are used as an instrumental variable that is used to help predict the number of police on the street at a point in time; the timing of an election is correlated with the number of police, but should be uncorrelated with the residual in a crime equation.

The results of this analysis indicate that the number of police do indeed increase during gubernatorial and mayoral election years. Using this information to provide exogenous variation in the number of police, the author then finds that a larger police force does lead to less violent crime, but has little impact on property crime.

SOURCE: Levitt, Steven D., "Using Electoral Cycles in Police Hiring to Estimate the Effect of Police on Crime," *American Economic Review*, Vol. 87, No. 3 (June 1997), pp. 270–90.

15.6.3 Hausman Specification Test

Suppose we suspect that a right-hand side variable in an equation is endogenous. How might we test whether this is the case? A general approach suggested by Hausman compares two estimators for which both of the estimators are consistent if the right-hand side variable being considered is exogenous, but for which only one of the estimators is consistent if the variable is endogenous. We might then ask whether the difference between the two estimators is large enough to suggest that endogeneity is a problem. To see this more clearly, consider the following table:

	Right-hand side variable is:	
Estimator	*Endogenous*	*Exogenous*
OLS	Inconsistent estimates	Consistent and efficient estimates
Instrumental variable	Consistent estimates	Consistent but inefficient estimates

Then, if the suspected right-hand side variable is endogenous, it should be the case that the ordinary least squares estimates should be similar (but with smaller standard errors) to the instrumental variables estimator. If, however, the suspected variable is endogenous, then the two estimators should yield different estimates. In this section we outline a precise way to implement this approach in practice.

Consider the following model:

$$Y_i = \beta X_i + \varepsilon_i \tag{16}$$

APPLICATION 15.3   *When Your Number Comes Up*

Does military service improve the wages of veterans when they reenter civilian life? One could imagine that the armed forces provide those who serve with the training and motivation that are valued in the labor market, leading to greater compensation. In fact, definitive evidence of such an effect would offer a valuable enticement to potential recruits (although advertising for the military alludes to this effect even without the evidence!).

The difficulty in estimating the relationship between military service and subsequent wages in the labor market is that those who serve in the armed forces tend to be different from those who do not. An OLS regression approach can control for those factors that can be measured, but many of these differences (work ethic, innate intelligence, etc.) cannot possibly be observed. These omitted factors create a correlation between the dummy variable for military service and the error term in a wage equation and will lead to biased estimates.

To address this problem, one study adopts a two-stage least squares approach, taking advantage of a unique event in military manpower policy. During the Vietnam war, a draft was in effect. To improve the equity in the draft procedure, all age-eligible men were assigned a lottery number based on the month and day they were born. If the number assigned to your birthday was 1, you certainly would be drafted, if it was 365 you almost certainly would not, and you would be uncertain if your lottery number based on your birthday was in the middle. Importantly, the ordering of birthdays from 1 to 365 was done randomly.

In this one study, conceptually the author uses the draft lottery to define a first-stage equation where the dependent variable is a dummy variable indicating military service and the independent variable is the individual's lottery number (Chapter 16 provides a more detailed examination of models in which the dependent variable is a dummy variable). In the second-stage equation, the dependent variable represents the individual's wage many years after leaving the service and the independent variable of interest is the predicted value of his or her military service obtained from the first stage. Importantly, this prediction of military service will be a function of the random lottery number and unrelated to unobservable individual characteristics. Results from this analysis indicate that a white male Vietnam war veteran actually earned 15% *less* than a comparable white male who did not serve. Apparently, exposure to the war had a detrimental labor market effect on the soldiers who fought in it.

SOURCE: Angrist, Joshua D., "Lifetime Earnings and the Vietnam Era Draft Lottery: Evidence from Social Security Administrative Records," *American Economic Review*, Vol. 80, No. 3 (June 1990), pp. 313–336.

We want to test the hypotheses:

$$H_0 : \text{cov}(X_i, \varepsilon_i) = 0$$
$$H_1 : \text{cov}(X_i, \varepsilon_i) \neq 0$$

That is, we want to test whether the right-hand variable X is exogenous. The null hypothesis H_0 specifies the situation where there is no simultaneity. The alternative hypothesis indicates the existence of a correlation between the right-hand side variable and the error term. You might note that this framework could also be used to test for the presence of measurement error as discussed in Chapter 13 since both endogeneity and measurement error create a correlation of this sort.

Now, suppose we have an instrumental variable Z. By definition $\text{cov}(Z,\varepsilon)=0$. Regressing X on Z yields $X_i = \hat{X}_i + e_i$, where e is a vector of residuals from regression of X on Z. Note: $\text{cov}(\hat{X},e)=0$ since $\hat{X}$ is a linear combination of Z which, by definition, is uncorrelated with e. If we substitute this into (16) we have

$$Y_i = (\hat{X}_i + e_i)\beta + \varepsilon_i$$

or

$$Y_i = \beta\hat{X}_i + \beta e_i + \varepsilon_i$$

Now, run the regression:

$$Y_i = \beta\hat{X}_i + \delta e_i + \varepsilon_i \tag{17}$$

Recall, $\text{cov}(\hat{X},\varepsilon) = 0$ under both the null and alternative hypotheses (it is a linear combination of Z, which is orthogonal to ε). Furthermore, $\text{cov}(\hat{X},e) = 0$ by construction. Thus, the least squares regression coefficient on $\hat{X}$ is consistent under both hypotheses. The estimate of δ should only be the same as this under the null hypothesis where $\text{cov}(X,\varepsilon) = 0$. Thus, we might test whether they are indeed equal.

Add and subtract βe from (17):

$$
\begin{aligned}
Y &= \beta\hat{X}_i + \delta e_i + \varepsilon_i \\
&= \beta\hat{X}_i + \delta e_i + \varepsilon + \beta e_i - \beta e_i \\
&= \beta(\hat{X}_i + e_i) + e_i(\delta - \beta) + \varepsilon_i \\
Y &= \beta X_i + \alpha e_i + \varepsilon_i; \alpha = \delta - \beta
\end{aligned}
$$

Thus, the test is whether $\alpha = 0$. That is, the null hypothesis implies $\delta = \beta$ or, equivalently, $\alpha = 0$. We can thus use a simple t test to test this hypothesis.

To summarize, to apply the Hausman test for endogeneity we simply run a multiple regression model of our dependent variable on X and the error term from a regression of X on an instrumental variable. We then test whether the coefficient on the error term variable is zero. If we can reject its being zero, we conclude that endogeneity is a problem.

15.7 PROBLEMS

1. Explain the identification problem in the context of a simple supply-and-demand model of price determination. Under what conditions could we identify the supply curve or the demand curve?

2. Consider the following simultaneous equations model:

$$Y_{1i} = \beta_0 + \beta_1 Y_{2i} + \beta_2 X_{1i} + \beta_3 X_{2i} + \beta_4 X_{3i} + u_{1i} \tag{1}$$

$$Y_{2i} = \alpha_0 + \alpha_1 Y_{1i} + \alpha_2 X_{1i} + \alpha_3 X_{2i} + \alpha_4 X_{3i} + u_{2i} \tag{2}$$

a. Explain what is meant by the "identification problem."

b. Explain why it would be inappropriate to use ordinary least squares to estimate the structural coefficients in this model (no proofs required).

c. For each of the following cases determine whether equation (1) or equation (2) is identified:

 i. The model is as above.

 ii. $\beta_2 = 0$ and $\alpha_2 = 0$.

 iii. $\beta_3 = 0$ and $\alpha_3 = 0$.

d. Suppose $\beta_3 = 0$ and $\beta_4 = 0$. Explain exactly how you would estimate equation (1) using two-stage least squares. Could you use the same procedure to estimate equation (2)? Why or why not?

3. Consider the following two-equation simultaneous model for the agricultural labor market in the United States:

$$\text{Ln}(L_i) = b_0 + b_1\text{ln}(W_i) + b_2\text{ln}(\text{Land}_i) + b_3\text{ln}(\text{RE}_i) + b_4\text{ln}(\text{Othexp}_i) + b_5\text{ln}(\text{Sch}_i) + e_1 \tag{1}$$

$$\text{Ln}(W_i) = \alpha_0 + a_1\text{ln}(L_i) + a_2\text{ln}(\text{Sch}_i) + a_3\text{ln}(\text{Othwag}_i) + e_2 \tag{2}$$

where:

 Labor = labor (total person days of farm labor by state)

 Wage = wage (annual average composite farm wage per hour)

 RE = research and extension service expenditures (a proxy for innovations)

 Land = value of stock of farmland

 Othexp = nonlabor operating expenses

 Sch = median years of formal schooling of rural males

 Othwag = alternative wage (weighted average) for craftsmen, foremen, etc.

This data is found at http://www.wiley.com/college/ashenfelter.

a. Which variables are exogenous? Which variables are endogenous?

b. Solve analytically (i.e., do the algebra) for the two reduced-form equations.

c. Using the order condition, show that equation (1) is exactly identified while equation (2) is overidentified.

d. Estimate (1) and (2) using OLS. Also estimate (1) and (2) using two-stage least squares. Compare the results. Do you think OLS is an inappropriate method of estimation for this problem?

4. Consider two structural models given by the following system of equations:

Model I:
$$Y_1 = \alpha_1 + \alpha_2 Y_2 + \alpha_3 X_1 + \alpha_4 X_2 + u_1$$
$$Y_2 = \beta_1 + \beta_2 Y_3 + \beta_3 X_2 + u_2$$
$$Y_3 = \gamma_1 + \gamma_2 Y_2 + u_3$$

Model II:
$$Y_1 = \alpha_0 + \alpha_1 Y_2 + \alpha_2 X_2 + u_1$$
$$Y_2 = \beta_0 + \beta_1 X_1 + \beta_2 X_2 + \beta_3 X_3 + u_2$$

For each system:

a. Determine which equations are underidentified, just identified, and overidentified.

b. Explain how you would estimate the identified equations.

5. Consider a market in which q is the quantity of good Q, p is its price, and z is the price of good Z, a related good. We assume that z enters both the supply and demand equations for Q. For example, Z might be a crop that is purchased by consumers instead of Q if z falls relative to p, and/or farmers may choose to grow more Z and less Q if the price z rises relative to the price p. This suggests the following structural model:

$$q_d = \alpha_0 + \alpha_1 p + \alpha_2 z + u_1 \qquad \text{(demand)}$$

$$q_s = \beta_0 + \beta_1 p + \beta_2 z + u_2 \qquad \text{(supply)}$$

$$q_d = q_s \qquad \text{(equilibrium)}$$

a. Discuss the identifiability of the demand and supply equations under the following conditions:

    i. as written

    ii. if $\beta_2 = 0$

    iii. if $\alpha_2 = \beta_2 = 0$

b. Obtain the reduced form of the model and discuss the restrictions implied by the reduced form under the following conditions:

    i. as written

    ii. if $\beta_2 = 0$

    iii. if $\alpha_2 = \beta_2 = 0$

Chapter **16**

Dummy Dependent Variable Models

16.1 INTRODUCTION

In this chapter we introduce models that are designed to deal with situations in which our dependent variable is a dummy variable. That is, it assumes either the value 0 or the value 1. Such models are very useful in that they allow us to address questions for which there is a "yes or no" answer.

Examples

1. A labor economist is studying factors that influence whether people complete high school. In this case, the dependent variable assumes the value 1 if the person graduates from high school and 0 otherwise. The explanatory variables might include family income, attributes of the school (e.g., student–teacher ratio, teacher salaries), characteristics of the neighborhood (e.g., mean income), gender, race, and so on.

2. To measure whether there is racial bias in the application of capital punishment, a researcher defines the dependent variable to be 1 if a murderer receives the death penalty and 0 otherwise. Explanatory variables include the race of the defendant, race of the victim, characteristics of the crime (e.g., was the victim a stranger, a child?, etc.), and so on.

Notice that in these cases the data on the dependent variable will be a list containing zeros and ones (i.e., is a dummy variable). The explanatory variables my be either continuous or dummy variables. We will consider three ways of estimating these models.

16.2 LINEAR PROBABILITY MODEL

In the case of a dummy dependent variable model we have:

$$Y_i = \beta_0 + \beta_1 X_{1i} + \beta_2 X_{2i} + \beta_3 X_{3i} + \ldots + \beta_k X_{ki} + \varepsilon_i$$

where $Y_i = 0$ or 1 and $E(\varepsilon_i) = 0$.

What would happen if we simply estimated the slope coefficients of this model using OLS? What would the coefficients mean? Would they be unbiased? Are they efficient?

A regression model in the situation where the dependent variable takes on the two values 0 or 1 is called a *linear probability model*. To see its properties note the following.

1. Since the mean error is zero, we know that $E(Y_i) = \beta_0 + \beta_1 X_{1i} + \beta_2 X_{2i} + \beta_3 X_{3i} + \ldots + \beta_k X_{ki}$.

2. Now, if we define $P_i = \text{Prob}(Y_i = 1)$ and $1 - P_i = \text{Prob}(Y_i = 0)$, then $E(Y_i) = 1 \cdot P_i + 0 \cdot (1 - P_i) = P_i$. Thus, our model is $P_i = \beta_0 + \beta_1 X_{1i} + \beta_2 X_{2i} + \beta_3 X_{3i} + \ldots + \beta_k X_{ki}$ and the estimated slope coefficients would tell us the impact of a unit change in that explanatory variable on the probability that $Y = 1$.

3. The predicted values from the regression model $\hat{P}_i = \hat{\beta}_0 + \hat{\beta}_1 X_{1i} + \hat{\beta}_2 X_{2i} + \hat{\beta}_3 X_{3i} + \ldots + \hat{\beta}_k X_{ki}$ would provide predictions, based on some chosen values for the explanatory variables, for the probability that $Y = 1$. There is, however, nothing in the estimation strategy that would constrain the resulting predictions from being negative or larger than 1—clearly an unfortunate characteristic of the approach.

4. Since $E(\varepsilon_i) = 0$ and uncorrelated with the explantory variables (by assumption), it is easy to show that the OLS estimators are unbiased. The errors, however, are heteroskedastic. A simple way to see this is to consider an example. Suppose that the dependent variable takes the value 1 if the individual buys a Rolex watch and 0 otherwise. Also, suppose the explanatory variable is income. For low level of income it is likely that *all* of the observations are zeros. In this case, there would be no scatter around the line. For higher levels of income there would be some zeros and some ones. That is, there would be some scatter around the line. Thus, the errors would be heteroskedastic. To see this more formally, note that:

$$Y_i = 0 \Rightarrow \varepsilon_i = -(\beta_0 + \beta_1 X_{1i} + \beta_2 X_{2i} + \beta_3 X_{3i} + \ldots + \beta_k X_{ki}) = -P_i$$

with probability $1 - P_i$ and

$$Y_i = 1 \Rightarrow \varepsilon_i = 1 - (\beta_0 + \beta_1 X_{1i} + \beta_2 X_{2i} + \beta_3 X_{3i} + \ldots + \beta_k X_{ki}) = 1 - P_i$$

with probability P_i. Thus,

$$
\begin{aligned}
\text{var}(\varepsilon_i) = E(\varepsilon_i^2) &= (1 - P_i)E[\varepsilon_i^2/y_i = 0] + P_i E[\varepsilon_i^2/y_i = 1] \\
&= (1 - P_i)(-P_i)^2 + P_i(1 - P_i)^2 \\
&= P_i^2(1 - P_i) + P_i(1 - P_i)(1 - P_i) \\
&= P_i^2(1 - P_i) + P_i(1 - P_i) - P_i^2(1 - P_i) \\
&= P_i(1 - P_i) \\
&= E(Y_i) \cdot (1 - E(Y_i))
\end{aligned}
$$

Thus, since $E(Y_i)$ varies with the explanatory variables, we have heteroskedasticity. For example, if $E(Y_i) = 0$ or 1, then the variance in the errors would be zero. If $E(Y_i) = .5$ then the variance would be .25.

This suggests two empirical strategies. First, we know that the OLS estimators are unbiased but would yield the incorrect standard errors. We might simply use OLS and then use the White correction to produce correct standard errors. Alternatively, we could use weighted least squares.

16.3   LOGIT AND PROBIT MODELS

One potential criticism of the linear probability model (beyond those mentioned above) is that the model assumes that the probability that $Y_i = 1$ is *linearly* related to the explanatory variables. We might, however, expect the relation to be nonlinear. For example, increasing the income of the very poor or the very rich will probably have little effect on whether they buy an automobile. It could, however, have a nonzero effect on other income groups.

Two models that are nonlinear, yet provide predicted probabilities between 0 and 1, are the *logit* and *probit* models. The difference between the linear probability model and the nonlinear logit and probit models is depicted in the figure below.

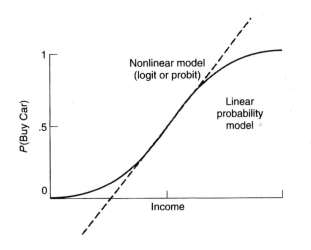

To motivate these models, suppose that our underlying dummy dependent variable depends on an unobserved ("latent") utility index Y^*. For example, if the variable Y is discrete, taking on the values 0 or 1 if someone buys a car, then we can imagine a continuous variable Y^* that reflects a person's desire to buy the car. It seems reasonable that Y^* would vary continuously with some explanatory variable like income. More formally, suppose

$$Y_i^* = \beta_0 + \beta_1 X_{1i} + \varepsilon_i$$

and

$$Y_i = 1 \text{ if } Y_i^* \geq 0 \text{ (i.e., the utility index is "high enough")}$$
$$Y_i = 0 \text{ if } Y_i^* < 0 \text{ (i.e., the utility index is not "high enough")}$$

Then:

$$P_i = \text{Prob}(Y_i = 1)$$
$$= \text{Prob}(Y_i^* \geq 0)$$
$$= \text{Prob}(\beta_0 + \beta_1 X_{1i} + \varepsilon_i \geq 0)$$
$$= \text{Prob}(\varepsilon_i \geq -\beta_0 - \beta_1 X_{1i})$$
$$= 1 - F(-\beta_0 - \beta_1 X_{1i}) \text{ where } F \text{ is the c.d.f. for } \varepsilon$$
$$= F(\beta_0 + \beta_1 X_{1i}) \text{ if } F \text{ is symmetric}$$

Given this, our basic problem is selecting F—the cumulative density function for the error term. It is here where the logit and probit models differ. As a practical matter, we are likely interested in estimating the β's in the model. This is typically done using a maximum likelihood estimator (MLE). To outline the MLE in this context, recognize that each outcome Y_i has the density function $f(Y_i) = P_i^{Y_i}(1 - P_i)^{1-Y_i}$. That is, each Y_i takes on either the value of 0 or 1 with probability $f(0) = (1 - P_i)$ and $f(1) = P_i$. Then the likelihood function is:

$$\ell = f(Y_1, Y_2, \ldots Y_n)$$
$$= f(Y_1)f(Y_2)\ldots f(Y_n)$$
$$= P_1^{Y_1}(1 - P_1)^{1-Y_1}P_2^{Y_2}(1 - P_2)^{1-Y_2}\ldots P_n^{Y_n}(1 - P_n)^{1-Y_n}$$
$$= \prod_{i=1}^{n} P_i^{Y_i}(1 - P_i)^{1-Y_i}$$

and

$$\ln \ell = \sum_{i=1}^{n} Y_i \ln P_i + (1 - Y_i)\ln(1 - P_i)$$

which, given $P_i = F(\beta_0 + \beta_1 X_{1i})$, becomes

$$\ln \ell = \sum_{i=1}^{n} Y_i \ln F(\beta_0 + \beta_1 X_{1i}) + (1 - Y_i)\ln(1 - F(\beta_0 + \beta_1 X_{1i}))$$

Analytically, the next step would be to take the partial derivatives of the likelihood function with respect to the β's, set them equal to zero, and solve for the MLEs. This could be a very messy calculation depending on the functional form of F. In practice, the computer will solve this problem for us.

16.3.1 Logit Model

For the logit model we specify

$$\text{Prob}(Y_i = 1) = F(\beta_0 + \beta_1 X_{1i}) = \frac{1}{1 + e^{-(\beta_0 + \beta_1 X_{1i})}}$$

It can be seen that $\text{Prob}(Y_i = 1) \to 0$ as $\beta_0 + \beta_1 X_{1i} \to -\infty$. Similarly, $\text{Prob}(Y_i = 1) \to 1$ as

$\beta_0 + \beta_1 X_{1i} \to \infty$. Thus, unlike the linear probability model, probabilities from the logit model will be between 0 and 1. A complication arises in interpreting the estimated β's. In the case of a linear probability model, a $\hat{\beta}$ measures the ceteris paribus effect of a change in the explanatory variable on the probability Y equals 1. In the logit model we can see that

$$\frac{\partial \text{Prob}(Y_i = 1)}{\partial X_1} = \frac{\partial F(\hat{\beta}_0 + \hat{\beta}_1 X_{1i})}{\partial X_1} \hat{\beta}_1$$

$$= \frac{\hat{\beta}_1 e^{-(\beta_0 + \beta_1 X_{1i})}}{[1 + e^{-(\beta_0 + \beta_1 X_{1i})}]^2}$$

Notice that the derivative is nonlinear and depends on the value of X. It is common to evaluate the derivative at the mean of X so that a single derivative can be presented.

16.3.2   Probit Model

In the case of the probit model, we assume that the $\varepsilon_i \sim N(0, \sigma^2)$. That is, we assume the error in the utility index model is normally distributed. In this case,

$$\text{Prob}(Y_i = 1) = F\left(\frac{\beta_0 + \beta_1 X_{1i}}{\sigma}\right)$$

where F is the standard normal cumulative density function. That is,

$$\text{Prob}(Y_i = 1) = F\left(\frac{\beta_0 + \beta_1 X_{1i}}{\sigma}\right) = \int_{-\infty}^{\frac{\beta_0 + \beta_1 X_{1i}}{\sigma}} \frac{1}{\sqrt{2\pi}} e^{-\frac{t^2}{2}} dt$$

In practice, the c.d.f. of the logit and the probit look quite similar to one another. Once again, calculating the derivative is moderately complicated. In this case,

$$\frac{\partial \text{Prob}(Y_i = 1)}{\partial X_1} = \frac{\partial F\left(\frac{\beta_0 + \beta_1 X_{1i}}{\sigma}\right)}{\partial X_1} = f\left(\frac{\beta_0 + \beta_1 X_{1i}}{\sigma}\right)\beta_1$$

where f is the density function of the normal distribution. As in the logit case, the derivative is nonlinear and is often evaluated at the mean of the explanatory variables. In the case of dummy explanatory variables, it is common to estimate the derivative as the probability $Y = 1$ when the dummy variable is 1 (other variables set to their mean) minus the probability $Y = 1$ when the dummy variable is 0 (other variables set to their mean). That is, you simply calculate how the predicted probability changes when the dummy variable of interest switches from 0 to 1.

16.3.3   Which Is Better? Logit or Probit?

Fortunately, from an empirical standpoint, logits and probits typically yield very similar estimates of the relevant derivatives. This is because the cumulative distribution functions for the logit and probit are similar, differing slightly only in the tails of their respective

---

| APPLICATION 16.1 | *Do Banks Discriminate in Giving Out Mortgage Loans?* |

The decision by a bank to make a loan should solely be a function of the borrower's ability to repay it. Other characteristics of the borrower should not be taken into account; if they do, it would represent discrimination. From an economic standpoint, that discrimination may be profit-maximizing from the bank's perspective. If the bank is unable to obtain complete information regarding the ability to repay, it may take advantage of additional group characteristics that may help improve its projected repayment probability. Alternatively, the discrimination may represent the tastes of the bank officers. From a legal standpoint, however, such a distinction is irrelevant; the behavior is illegal.

How does one determine whether a bank's lending practices are discriminatory? One may consider using data regarding the bank's lending decision as a function of characteristics of the applicants that hold constant creditworthiness along with a series of dummy variables that represent an applicant's group affiliation, such as race or sex. If any of the race or sex variables are statistically significant, then we could conclude that the bank discriminates. Importantly, however, the procedure must control for all differences in an individual applicant's creditworthiness. If not, omitted-variable bias may result if any of the omitted measures are correlated with an applicant's demographic characteristics, unfairly leading to charges of discrimination.

One recent study implemented just such a research design. These authors obtained data on a large number of applications for mortgages in the Boston area. Along with information on the outcome of the application, they also had access to much of the same information that the banks had in order to assess an applicants' creditworthiness. They estimated logit models of the probability of a rejection including these creditworthiness measures along with the applicant's race/ethnicity and sex. Without controlling for creditworthiness, they found that, in particular, Blacks were 18 percentage points more likely to have been denied. Even after controlling for differences in creditworthiness, this differential was still 8 percentage points. Unfortunately, the possibility always remains that omitted-variable bias explains why this differential by race exists. Otherwise, this study would provide evidence that blacks were being discriminated against in obtaining a mortgage in Boston in the early 1990s.

SOURCE: Munnell, Alicia H., Geoffrey M.B. Tootell, Lynn E. Browne, and James McEneaney, "Mortgage Lending in Boston: Interpreting HMDA Data," *American Economic Review*, Vol. 86, No. 1 (March 1996), pp. 25–53.

distributions. Thus, the derivatives are different only if there are enough observations in the tail of the distribution. While the derivatives are usually similar, it is important to remember that the parameter estimates associated with logit and probit models are not. A simple approximation suggests that multiplying the logit estimates by .625 makes the logit estimates comparable to the probit estimates.

16.4 CENSORED REGRESSION MODEL

We have now seen models where the dependent variable is continuous (i.e., the classic regression model) and models where the dependent variable is constrained to take on only the values 0 or 1 (i.e., the logit and probit models). Often, however, the dependent variable is constrained such that it takes on a positive value for some observations and takes on the value zero for other observations. The data are not continuous because there is a large cluster of observations at zero. In cases like this we say our dependent variable is *censored.* Using ordinary least squares will lead to biased estimates of the parameters if used in this context.

Examples

1. Suppose we have a data set containing information on the number of hours people worked last week along with their age. Some people will have worked a positive number of hours (e.g., 40 or 30, etc.). Others will not have worked at all and will report working zero hours.

2. Suppose we have data on families' expenditures on new automobile purchases during a particular year. Some families spend a positive amount, while others, who do not purchase a car that year, report spending nothing.

Now, recall for the probit and logit we defined a latent variable $Y_i^* = \beta X_i + u_i$ with

$$Y_i = 1 \text{ if } Y_i^* > 0$$
$$= 0 \text{ if } Y_i^* \leq 0$$

Suppose now that Y_i is not a binary (0/1) variable but rather is observed as Y_i^* if $Y_i^* > 0$ and is not observed for $Y_i^* \leq 0$. For example, Y_i^* may represent a family's dollar expenditure on a car. Then:

$$Y_i = Y_i^* = \beta X_i + u_i \text{ if } Y_i^* > 0$$
$$= 0 \text{ otherwise}$$

and u is assumed to follow the normal distribution with mean 0 and variance σ_2. This is called the *Tobit model*—named for its originator, James Tobin—and is also known as the *censored regression model.*

To estimate this model, we specify the likelihood function for this problem and generate the maximum likelihood estimator. Procedures to estimate such models are now commonplace in standard statistical programs. The (log) likelihood for the Tobit model is given by

$$\log L = \sum_{Y_i>0} -\frac{1}{2}\left[\log(2\pi) + \log \sigma^2 + \frac{(Y_i - \beta X_i)^2}{\sigma^2} \right] + \sum_{Y_i=0} \log\left[1 - F\left(\frac{\beta X_i}{\sigma}\right) \right]$$

where F is the cumulative density function for the normal distribution. Notice that the likelihood function has two parts: one for the uncensored observations and one for the observations censored at zero. To obtain a consistent estimator, we would maximize the likelihood function with respect to β.

16.4.1 Heckman Two-Step Estimator

James Heckman has developed a relatively simple two-step estimation procedure as an alternative to estimation of the Tobit model using maximum likelihood methods. Heckman's approach yields consistent estimates of the parameters of interest.

As before, suppose that the model we are trying to estimate takes the form

---

APPLICATION 16.2 | *Lotto Fever: Does it Make Economic Sense?*

From an economic perspective, buying a lottery ticket is a classic example of decision making under uncertainty. Since the expected payout from a typical state-sponsored lottery is less than half the purchase price of a ticket, only strongly risk-preferring economic agents should purchase tickets. Nevertheless, it is unambiguous that the demand for tickets should rise with the expected payout.

Yet estimating this demand relationship is complicated by two facts. First, for a particular lottery system the expected payout generally does not vary, and comparing across lottery systems (i.e., different states or countries) introduces the possibility that other differences exist that may be related to the expected payout and ticket sales (i.e., omitted-variable bias). Second, a large fraction of the population does not participate in the lottery at all, indicating that the relationship between sales and the expected payout is not linear.

One recent study circumvents both of these problems. The authors take advantage of "rollovers," in which no one won in a particular week so the jackpot rolled over into the next week's purse. Expected payouts are higher when rollovers occur. Second, a Tobit model is estimated that specifically takes into account the fact that many individuals do not buy lottery tickets. Specifically, the authors define a model of the form

$$t_{it}^* = \beta_0 + \beta_1 EP_t + \beta_2 X_{it} + \varepsilon_{it} \quad \text{where } t_i = \begin{cases} t_i^* \text{ if } t_i^* > 0 \\ 0 \text{ if } t_i^* < 0 \end{cases}$$

where t, EP, and X represent ticket sales, the expected payout, and a set of other control variables, respectively, for individual i at time t. The expected payout is only a function of the week the individual purchased the ticket, and not of any of his or her own personal characteristics. The results of this study show that ticket sales are quite responsive to the expected payout. For every 10-percentage-point rise in the expected payout, ticket sales were estimated to rise by 26%.

In addition to estimating the responsiveness to the expected payout, this study also estimated the responsiveness of the number of tickets purchased to changes in individuals' income levels. The results indicate that a 10% increase in income leads to a 5-percentage-point increase in ticket sales. This finding confirms that the lottery represents a regressive tax in that those at lower income levels purchase proportionally more tickets, and therefore provide more revenue to the state, than those at higher income levels.

SOURCE: Farrell, Lisa and Ian Walker, "The Welfare Effects of Lotto: Evidence from the UK," *Journal of Public Economics*, Vol. 72, No. 1 (April 1999), pp. 99–120.

$$Y_i = Y_i^* = \beta X_i + u_i \text{ if } Y_i^* > 0$$
$$= 0 \text{ otherwise}$$

Then, the mean value of Y, conditional upon it being greater than zero, may be written as

$$E[Y_i / Y_i > 0] = \beta X_i + E[u_i / u_i > 0] = BX_i + E[u_i / u_i > -Bx_i]$$

Although beyond the scope of this book, it can be shown that

$$E[u_i / u_i > - \beta x_i] = \frac{\sigma f(\beta X_i)}{F(\beta X_i)} \equiv \sigma \lambda$$

where

$$\lambda = \frac{f(\beta X_i)}{F(\beta X_i)}$$

and f is the normal density function and F is the normal cumulative density function. Also, λ is called the *inverse Mills ratio* or, sometimes, the *hazard rate*. Thus, we may write: $E[Y_i / Y_i > 0] = \beta X_i + \sigma \lambda$.

If we simply regressed the positive values of Y_i on X_i we would suffer omitted-variable bias (i.e., we would exclude λ from the model). If we could get an estimate of λ we could run ordinary least squares on X and λ. Heckman proposes the following:

1. Define

$$I_i = 1 \text{ if } Y_i > 0$$
$$= 0 \text{ otherwise}$$

Thus, I is simply a dummy variable taking on the value 1 for the positive values of Y and 0 otherwise.

2. Estimate $\hat{\lambda}$ by estimating a probit model of I_i on X. That is, since the probit model specifies $\text{Prob}(Y = 1) = F(\beta X_i)$, we can get estimates of β by estimating the probit model. We can then use the estimates of β to form

$$\hat{\lambda} = \frac{f(\hat{\beta} X_i)}{F(\hat{\beta} X_i)}$$

Note: Typically the probit equation would contain variables other than the explanatory variables (i.e., X) found in the Tobit model. Without the inclusion of such variables the estimated $\hat{\lambda}$ would simply be a nonlinear function of the explanatory variables in the Tobit model. Although the nonlinearity of the prediction of $\hat{\lambda}$ would avoid the problem of perfect multicollinearity, it is preferable to include these additional variables in the probit step of Heckman's two-step model.

3. Using the positive values of Y, run ordinary least squares on $X, \hat{\lambda}$. This will yield consistent estimates of β.

Note: As in the linear probability model case, the errors generated by this procedure are heteroskedastic. Thus, the reported (ordinary least squares) t-statistics are wrong. Many statistical packages will provide "corrected" standard errors in their output.

16.5 PROBLEMS

1. Give examples of three policy analyses that might employ a dummy dependent variable model.

2. Why must we exercise caution in using OLS to estimate the parameters of a dummy dependent variable model?

3. "It is often the case that parameter estimates using OLS are very similar to the derivatives associated with a logit or probit model." Why might this be the case?

4. It is sometimes asserted that the welfare system creates a form of intergenerational "dependency." That is, children born into households that receive welfare will themselves become more apt to receive welfare when they attain adulthood. The data found at http://www.wiley.com/college/ashenfelter provide information on the following variables:

   Recwelfm = 1 if the mother received welfare.

   Recwelfd = 1 if the mother's daughter received welfare when she attained adulthood.

   lnFaminc = the log income of the mother's family.

   a. What percentage of daughters received welfare? What is the percentage among daughters whose mothers received/did not receive welfare? Do the raw data suggest grounds for a "dependency" effect?

   b. Estimate the model $Recwelfd_i = \beta_0 + \beta_1 Recwelfm_i + \varepsilon_i$ using OLS. What is the effect of maternal receipt on her daughter's welfare receipt in adulthood?

   c. Now, estimate a probit model relating the daughter's welfare receipt to her mother's welfare receipt. Calculate the effect of maternal welfare receipt on the probability the daughter receives welfare as an adult using the estimated coefficients.

   d. Repeat (b) and (c) including Faminc in the model. What do you conclude?

5. It has often been claimed that the death penalty is applied in a racially discriminatory fashion. This problem uses data from a classic study by David Baldus (Reprinted by permission from Michael O. Finkelstein and Bruce Levin, *Statistics for Lawyers*, pp. 453–455. Copyright © 1990. Springer-Verlag New York, Inc.) that investigates this issue. Data were provided by the Georgia Parole Board, the Georgia Supreme Court, lawyers involved in the cases, and so forth, on the following variables:

   obsnum = observation number.

   death = 1 if got death penalty; 0 otherwise.

   blkdef = 1 if black defendant; 0 otherwise.

   whtvict = 1 if white victim; 0 otherwise.

   aggcirc = number of aggravating circumstances.

   fevict = 1 if female victim; 0 otherwise.

   stranger = 1 if stranger victim; 0 otherwise.

   multvic = 1 if 2 or more victims; 0 otherwise.

   multstab = 1 if multiple stabs; 0 otherwise.

   yngvict = 1 if victim 12 or younger; 0 otherwise.

   The data can be found in http://www.wiley.com/college/ashenfelter.

   a. Run a linear probability model using death as the dependent variable and the other variables as explanatory variables. What do you find?

   b. Now, estimate the same model with the probit estimator. What are the advantages of this estimator? What can we tell by looking at the coefficients? If your statistical package allows you to easily estimate probit derivatives (like the dprobit command in Stata), estimate these derivatives. Are the results similar to the linear probability model?

   c. Using the model estimated in part (a), what is the predicted probability of the death penalty for a black defendant who kills a white (female) victim who is a stranger, with aggravating circumstances, multiple victims and stabs, younger than 12 years of age? What would the prediction be if all that changed was that the defendant was not black?

Chapter 17

Analysis of Time Series Data

17.1   INTRODUCTION

The linear models presented so far have centered on finding the relationship between a dependent variable and a set of explanatory variables. Models of this sort are typically aimed at finding a causal relationship between the dependent and explanatory variables. Time series models often have a different goal, attempting to relate movements in the dependent variable to its own past values and a set of potentially correlated error terms. Such models have proven to be quite effective in making short-run forecasts.

Moreover, up to this point virtually the entire treatment of econometric analysis has proceeded with the implicit assumption that the data being used came from a cross-section (serial correlation, described in Chapter 14, is the main exception). Yet for many purposes, time series data possess certain features that require the researcher to use somewhat different techniques than one would use with data from a cross-section. In a cross-section we typically have individual observations that represent random draws from the same underlying population. Notions of sampling distributions and statistical inference, for instance, seem reasonably intuitive in such a situation.

Time series data, however, do not necessarily possess this property. At a particular point in time we are able to observe the value for the entire population (i.e., GDP in a particular year or the closing value of a stock market index on a particular day). Yet, one can think of that value as the *realization* of a random variable that has a particular distribution. The exact outcome on a given day simply represents a draw from that distribution that may have been affected by a variety of factors that we may never be able to fully understand or explain, so that we may attribute its specific value as the result of chance. A time series data set, therefore, contains a multitude of such observations, each representing realizations of random variables from different time periods. *If* (and this is a crucial condition) each of those random variables has the same distribution, then the time series data could be thought of analogously to that from the cross-section. The purpose of this chapter is to explore the unique statistical issues that are brought about by the use of time series data.

17.2 DESCRIBING TIME SERIES PROCESSES

A time series is a set of time-ordered observations $\{y_1, y_2, y_3 \ldots y_T\}$. For example, we might observe interest rates, or Gross Domestic Product (GDP), or unemployment rates over time. We are often interested in forecasting future observations for such variables. These observations are usefully viewed as being realizations of a series of jointly distributed random variables $\{Y_1, Y_2, Y_3 \ldots Y_T\}$ which could, ideally, be characterized by a joint probability density function $f\{Y_1, Y_2, Y_3 \ldots Y_T\}$. If we could specify such a function we could characterize possible future outcomes and their associated probabilities. This, unfortunately, is typically too difficult to accomplish. Instead, we often utilize models that are, in effect, approximations to such a general model but have the virtue of being simpler and possible to estimate. The usefulness of such an approximation might be judged by how well it helps us forecast future outcomes for the time series.

Our first task will be to describe how the relationship between a particular realization in a time series relates to past realizations. Although, in a cross-section, we typically assumed there was no relationship between different observations, such an assumption seems unrealistic in the context of a time series. In many instances it seems reasonable that historical developments may have important implications for present outcomes. This section will present some of the ways in which we can describe movements in outcomes over time.

17.2.1 Moving Average Models

In a *moving average* (MA) model, we assume that there are random shocks (sometimes called *innovations*) that affect a particular outcome and that shocks from past periods affect outcomes in current periods. For instance, we may write a model of the form

$$y_t = \beta_0 + \varepsilon_t + \delta_1 \varepsilon_{t-1} + \delta_2 \varepsilon_{t-2} + \ldots + \delta_m \varepsilon_{t-m}$$

In this model, ε_t represents a random shock that occurred at time t to the outcome y_t. If there are no shocks, then the outcome would equal a constant, β_0, which would represent the steady state. Shocks going back m periods affect present outcomes, but the influences of shocks in different periods are assumed to have differential impacts. It may seem natural, for instance, for shocks that occurred longer ago to have less influence than a present shock. We say that this specification is a moving average process of order m: MA(m). If, for instance, we let $m = 1$, we would have a first-order moving average, MA(1):

$$y_t = \beta_0 + \varepsilon_t + \delta_1 \varepsilon_{t-1}$$

Suppose we were interested in tracing the impact of a shock on the values of future realizations of an outcome. Consider, for instance, an MA(1) in which a shock occurred in period t, but there had been no shocks in the periods preceding that and none in the following periods. We would then have:

$$y_{t-1} = \beta_0$$

$$y_t = \beta_0 + \varepsilon_t$$

$$y_{t+1} = \beta_0 + \delta_1\varepsilon_t$$

$$y_{t+2} = \beta_0$$

Assuming that $\delta_1 < 1$, this process would graphically appear as:

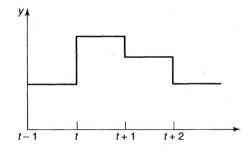

More generally, in MA models of order m, the impact of the shock fully dissipates after $m + 1$ periods and the outcome returns to steady state.

17.2.2 Autoregressive Models

In an *autoregressive* (*AR*) model, the realization of today's outcome is a function of past outcomes. More formally, we write an autoregressive model of order m, or AR(m), as

$$y_t = \alpha_0 + \phi_1 y_{t-1} + \phi_2 y_{t-2} + \ldots + \phi_m y_{t-m} + \varepsilon_t$$

In this model, the outcomes in the past m periods have a direct impact on the outcome today. As a specific example, consider an AR(1), or first-order autoregressive process:

$$y_t = \alpha_0 + \phi_1 y_{t-1} + \varepsilon_t$$

Here the outcome in period $t - 1$ directly affects today's outcome. But this model actually has a longer memory than one would infer from this statement. To see this, suppose that $\alpha_0 = 0$ and that for several periods there is no shock to the series (i.e., $\varepsilon_0, \varepsilon_1, \varepsilon_2, \ldots = 0$). For all periods after the first, we would have $y^s = \phi_1 y_{t-1} = 0$, where y^s represents the steady-state outcome.

Now suppose that in period t a shock occurs, so that $\varepsilon_t \neq 0$, but that no shocks occur after that (i.e., $\varepsilon_{t+1}, \varepsilon_{t+2}, \varepsilon_{t+3}, \ldots = 0$). Then we would have

$$y_{t-1} = \phi_1 y_{t-2} + \varepsilon_{t-1} = 0$$

$$y_t = \phi_1 y_{t-1} + \varepsilon_t = \varepsilon_t$$

$$y_{t+1} = \phi_1 y_t = \phi_1 \varepsilon_t$$

$$y_{t+2} = \phi_1 y_{t+1} = \phi_1^2 y_t = \phi_1^2 \varepsilon_t$$

$$y_{t+3} = \phi_1 y_{t+2} = \phi_1^3 y_t = \phi_1^3 \varepsilon_t$$

.

.

.

Therefore, one can see that the shock in one period will have a lasting impact for several subsequent periods. In fact, for $\phi < 1$, one can see that outcomes in subsequent periods will converge back to the steady state. The rate of convergence will depend upon the value of ϕ: As shown in the following figure, the closer it is to unity, the slower the rate of convergence. In fact, serious problems result if $\phi = 1$, as we will discuss shortly.

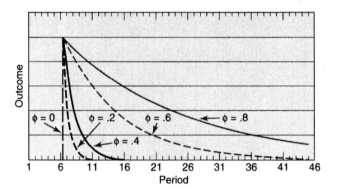

17.2.3 ARMA Models

Autoregressive and moving average processes are not mutually exclusive, however, and a time series may exhibit both properties. Processes that do so are labeled (perhaps not surprisingly) autoregressive moving average (or ARMA) models. Formally, an ARMA model is specified as

$$y_t = \alpha_0 + \phi_1 y_{t-1} + \phi_2 y_{t-2} + \ldots + \phi_m y_{t-m} + \varepsilon_t + \delta_1 \varepsilon_{t-1} + \delta_2 \varepsilon_{t-2} + \ldots + \delta_k \varepsilon_{t-k}$$

where this general version includes an autoregressive component of order m, AR(m), and a moving average component of order k, MA(k) and, hence, we say that this model is an ARMA(m,k). As an example, an ARMA(1,1) would take the form

$$y_t = \alpha_0 + \phi_1 y_{t-1} + \varepsilon_t + \delta_1 \varepsilon_{t-1}$$

We will discuss models related to this one later in the chapter.

17.2.4 Unit Roots and Random Walks

Let us return to the simplified AR(1) example we examined in Section 17.2.2 that took the form

$$y_t = \phi_1 y_{t-1} + \varepsilon_t$$

In that section, we showed how a shock to the series would result in a convergence back to the steady state so long as ϕ was less than 1. But suppose that $\phi = 1$. The resulting model $y_t = y_{t-1} + \varepsilon_t$ is called a *random* walk or, alternatively, when $\phi = 1$ the AR(1) model is said to have a *unit root*. In such a model, any shock to the series will have permanent effects. From our earlier example, where we considered a series where there were no shocks from period zero through period $t - 1$, then a shock in period t, and no shocks following that, we can see that:

$$y_{t-1} = \phi_1 y_{t-2} + \varepsilon_{t-1} = 0$$
$$y_t = \phi_1 y_{t-1} + \varepsilon_t = \varepsilon_t$$
$$y_{t+1} = \phi_1 y_t = \phi_1 \varepsilon_t = \varepsilon_t$$
$$y_{t+2} = \phi_1 y_{t+1} = \phi_1^2 y_t = \phi_1^2 \varepsilon_t = \varepsilon_t$$
$$y_{t+3} = \phi_1 y_{t+2} = \phi_1^3 y_t = \phi_1^3 \varepsilon_t = \varepsilon_t$$
$$\vdots$$

If, say, GDP followed a pattern like this, and a shock to the economy (such as an oil shock) led to a reduction in GDP, the economy would permanently operate at a lower level. Therefore, the existence of a unit root has very significant implications for the evolution of a time series process. It is also worth noting that in situations where $\phi_1 > 1$, the process "explodes" in the sense that the y will grow without bound.

The stylized example just described was instructive, but it is very limiting in several important dimensions. Perhaps foremost among them is that it only allows there to be one shock over the entire course of history. Of course, time series processes are subject to shocks every period and we need to incorporate this possibility into our thinking about the evolution of a time series.

More generally, consider the same basic model that exhibits a unit root, $y_t = y_{t-1} + \varepsilon_t$, where each period a random shock occurs, but this shock is assumed to have mean zero. Now suppose at time zero we have the realization y_0. In period 1 a shock occurs of magnitude ε_1 so that $y_1 = y_0 + \varepsilon_1$. From this point forward, future shocks will be expected to occur and the series will regularly deviate from y_1. But because future shocks have mean zero, the expectation of any future value of this series will remain at y_1. To see this, note that

$$E(y_2) = E(y_1 + \varepsilon_2) = y_1$$
$$E(y_3) = E(y_2 + \varepsilon_3) = y_1$$
$$E(y_4) = E(y_3 + \varepsilon_4) = y_1$$
$$\vdots$$

After the second period, the same property will hold and the expectation of all future values after the realization in period 2 will be y_2. Analogous to the stylized example provided earlier, all shocks are expected to have permanent effects if the series is characterized by a unit root. A series that exhibits this property is said to follow a *random walk*. In any subsequent period the movement from one location to the next is purely random; once you get to the next point the following move is purely random as well. Therefore, your best guess of where you will end up is where you started from.

A second limitation of our stylized example is that it does not allow for any trend over time. It seems reasonable that many time series, and particularly those of an economic nature, may exhibit some "normal" rate of growth or decline. For instance, GDP has grown at an average rate of 3.4% over the past century in the United States, and we may be interested in the deviation from that normal rate. A straightforward extension of the preceding model can incorporate a trend like this that will enable us to examine the deviations from trend. Suppose we considered a model of the form

$$y_t = \alpha_0 + y_{t-1} + \varepsilon_t$$

In this model, ignoring shocks, today's value will equal last period's outcome plus an additional constant, α_0, which represents the trend. Note that this model still exhibits a unit root in that we have implicitly assumed that $\phi = 1$. Therefore, any shock to the series will still have permanent effects, but in this case it will lead to a discrete shift in the trend line. Subsequent shocks will lead to additional deviations, but at a point in time the expectation is that the process will stay on the new trend line. A model such as this is said to exhibit a *random walk with drift*. In any subsequent period the movement from one location to the next is purely random beyond the traditional drift in one direction.

17.2.5   Stationarity

In the introduction to this chapter, we indicated that the principal difference between the analysis of time series and cross-sectional data is that each time series observation represents a realization from a particular random variable that may change over time. Observations from a cross-section are more naturally thought of as random draws from a fixed distribution. Therefore, an important consideration in the analysis of time series data is whether all time series observations are drawn as random variables from the same underlying distribution. If they are, then the typical methods described for cross-sectional data earlier in this text will apply directly. As we will describe in the following section of this chapter, if they are not, then alternatives may be needed.

If the time series observations are drawn from the same underlying distribution, we say that the time series process is *stationary*. More generally, the process is *stationary* if the joint probability density function $f(Y_1,Y_2,Y_3 \ldots Y_T)$ characterizing the process is invariant to any displacement in time. That is, $f(Y_t,Y_{t+1},Y_{t+2} \ldots Y_{t+k}) = f(Y_{t+m}, \ldots ,Y_{t+m+k})$ for all m and k. In this case, for example, the relationship between the 3rd and 4th obervations is the same as that between the 203rd and 204th observations. More often we require a less onerous form of stationarity. Specifically, we define a process to be *weakly stationary* if

1. $E(Y_t) = \mu$: the mean of Y_t is a constant over time,
2. $\text{var}(Y_t) = E[(Y_t - \mu)^2] = \sigma^2$: the variance of Y_t is constant over time, and

3. $Cov(Y_t, Y_{t+k}) = E[(Y_t - \mu)(Y_{t+k} - \mu)] = \pi_k$: the covariance of Y_t and Y_{t+k} is only a function of k, the length of time between periods, and not t, the particular period itself.

Any process that is stationary satisfies the conditions required for weak stationarity.

Importantly, if a time series process has a unit root or, equivalently, exhibits a random walk, then it is not stationary. To see this, consider the model described earlier, $y_t = y_{t-1} + \varepsilon_1$, where we now formally assume that ε_t is stationary with constant mean, μ, and variance, σ^2. If we assume that $y_0 = 0$, then we can write y_t as the sum of all past shocks:

$$y_t = \sum_{i=1}^{t} \varepsilon_i$$

If ε_t is stationary with mean, μ, then

$$E(Y_t) = \sum_{i=1}^{t} E(\varepsilon_t) = \sum_{i=1}^{t} \mu = t\mu$$

Only if $\mu = 0$ would this satisfy the conditions for stationarity. The variance of Y_t will never be constant, however:

$$var(Y_t) = \sum_{i=1}^{t} var(\varepsilon_t) = \sum_{i=1}^{t} \sigma^2 = t\sigma^2$$

Therefore, a variable that follows a random walk (with or without drift) is nonstationary.

Even if a time series process itself is not stationary, sometimes its first difference would be. For instance, consider a random walk where $y_t = y_{t-1} + \varepsilon_t$. In this case, the first difference would be $Y_t - Y_{t-1} = \varepsilon_t$, which we defined to be stationary. In this case, we say that the variable follows a *difference stationary* process.

17.2.6 ARIMA Models

As we saw above, an ARMA model is specified as $y_t = \alpha_0 + \phi_1 y_{t-1} + \phi_2 y_{t-2} + \ldots + \phi_m y_{t-m} + \varepsilon_t + \delta_1 \varepsilon_{t-1} + \delta_2 \varepsilon_{t-2} + \ldots + \delta_k \varepsilon_{t-k}$. We say an ARMA model is an *integrated process of order d* if differencing the series d times results in a stationary series. The stationarity of the series depends only on the autoregressive part of the model. Such a model is then called an ARIMA(m,k,d), indicating it is an *autoregressive moving average model* with m lags in the autoregressive component and k lags in the moving average component, and is stationary when differenced d times. Thus, an ARIMA model embeds within it both stationary and nonstationary, autoregressive and moving average models as special cases.

17.3 ESTIMATING THE RELATIONSHIP BETWEEN TWO VARIABLES

Suppose you have two time series variables and want to estimate a simple regression model of the relationship between them. The regression would take the form $y_t = \beta_0 + \beta_1 x_t + \varepsilon_t$. This section of the chapter considers estimation of this relationship, taking into consideration the possibility that the two time series variables may be nonstationary.

APPLICATION 17.1   *Should You Use Darts to Pick Your Stocks?*

Perhaps one of the most controversial hypotheses in economics is the notion that the stock market is "efficient." If the market was efficient, then all known information that is available to investors is already incorporated into the price of individual stocks, so that movements in stock prices are either random or generated by previously unknown information. Under these conditions, it would be impossible to hold an investment portfolio that could consistently outperform the overall trend in the market. Since movements in the market are either unanticipated or random, mutual funds that outperform the market over one period are just lucky and they have no greater likelihood of outperforming the market in subsequent periods than any other fund. Investing in index funds, that, in effect, purchase shares of every stock in the market, would then be a desireable strategy because the investor would obtain the average market return and pay lower transactions fees and administrative expenses for operating the fund.

As one might expect, individual investors (and the financial services sector!) have quite a stake in understanding whether it is really possible to beat the market. Tests of the efficient market hypothesis have generally focused on whether overall movements in the market follow a random walk. If so, then stock market movements would be appropriately characterized by the relationship $s_t = \alpha_0 + s_{t-1} + \varepsilon_1$; importantly, no additional information would be useful in predicting its future value beyond its past value plus an additional term representing a trend change and a random element.

Past research has uncovered that a random walk may not be a bad approximation of stock market movements, but that some factors beyond the last period's price do seem to contribute to a better prediction. For instance, stocks seem to move in regular patterns over days of the week or months of the year, violating the efficient market hypothesis. For investors, however, one would need to profit sufficiently from owning an actively managed account to compensate the investor for the additional costs of operating such an account. It is still difficult to determine the extent to which this is possible based on the available evidence.

SOURCES: Malkiel, Burton G. *A Random Walk Down Wall Street*. New York: Norton, 1999; Lo, Andrew W. and Craig Mackinlay. *A Non-Random Walk Down Wall Street*. Princeton, NJ: Princeton University Press, 1999.

17.3.1   Spurious Regression

Variables that follow a random walk have a peculiar property in that they have the tendency to appear to follow a trend. To demonstrate this, we conducted the following exercise. We defined a random walk of the form $y_t = y_{t-1} + \varepsilon_t$, set $y_0 = 0$, and specified ε_t to have a standard normal distribution, so that $\varepsilon_t \sim N(0,1)$. Then we created 20 samples with 50 time series observations, where we allowed a random number generator to assign specific values for the error terms. Graphs for each of the resulting series are provided below. It is clear from these graphs that many of the series exhibit obvious trends. In fact, we estimated simple regression models of the form $y_t = \beta_0 + \beta_1 t + \varepsilon_t$ to provide estimates of the trend. Results from these regressions show that eight have negative coefficients that are significantly different from zero, seven have positive coefficients that are statistically different from zero, and five have coefficients that are not significantly different from zero. Now these particular findings are obviously specific to the exact values of the random numbers generated in these limited numbers of samples. Nevertheless, this example clarifies the point that time series processes that exhibit a random walk are prone to appear to trend over time.

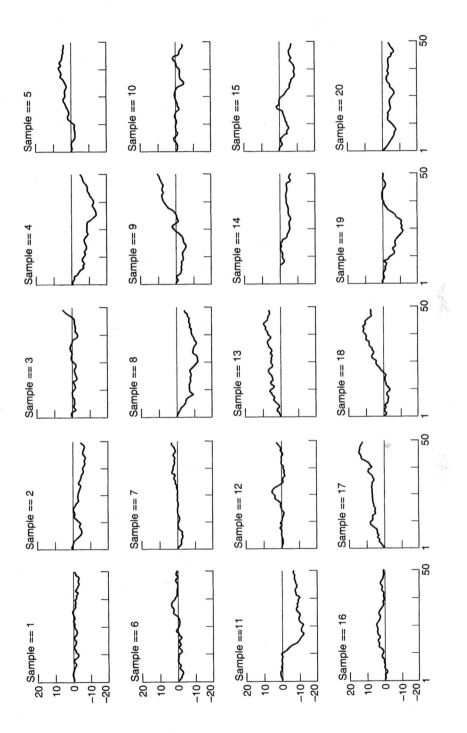

The problem with this is that if we run a regression of the form $y_t = \beta_0 + \beta_1 x_t + \varepsilon_t$, and both variables have unit roots, they will both have a tendency to trend. Even if they are completely unrelated, if they happen to trend together (apart), then we will estimate a positive (negative) relationship between them that may even appear to be quite strong. Such a finding would be purely spurious. Therefore, in conducting an exercise such as this, it is very important to identify whether the variables in question are stationary.

17.3.2 Dickey–Fuller Tests

An intuitive test of stationarity for a particular variable, y_t, in the present context would be to estimate a regression model of the form $y_t = \beta_0 + \beta_1 y_{t-1} + \varepsilon_t$. If the model has a unit root, then β_1 would equal 1. If so, whether or not β_0 equals zero would determine whether the series follows a random walk with or without drift.

The main limitation to this approach, of course, is that estimates from a regression model are themselves random variables and even if, in fact, β_1 is equal to unity, its estimate, $\hat{\beta}_1$, may not be. One would have to conduct a hypothesis test to determine whether we could reject the null hypothesis that $\beta_1 = 1$ based on the available estimate, $\hat{\beta}_1$.

Methods for conducting tests similar to this one were described in Chapter 10; one would think a standard t test would be applicable here. In that approach, we would specify null and alternative hypotheses, which in this case would be

$$H_0 : \beta_1 = 1$$
$$H_1 : \beta_1 < 1$$

In this case, the appropriate alternative hypothesis is defined to be $\beta_1 < 1$, because a time series with this property would behave like the AR(1) models presented earlier in this chapter where a shock would lead to a slow convergence back to the steady state. If $\beta_1 > 1$, a shock would yield an explosive process that would continually deviate further and further from the steady state, and that seems less likely. Based on our earlier discussion, once we define our null and alternative hypotheses, we would compute a t statistic. For the present purposes, however, we replace the notation t with a τ (called *tau*—we do this for reasons that will become clear shortly) and estimate a test statistic of the form

$$|\tau| = \left| \frac{\hat{\beta}_1 - 1}{s_{\hat{\beta}_1}^2} \right|$$

We would then compare this t statistic to the chosen critical value from the t distribution and, based on this comparison, we would determine whether to reject the null hypothesis.

Three problems with this approach arise in the present context. First, if the null hypothesis is true, the tau-statistic will not follow a student's t distribution even in large samples. The detailed reason for this is beyond the scope of this book, but involves the fact that the application of the Central Limit Theorem is invalid if a time series of random variables is nonstationary. As a result, this particular hypothesis test, the *Dickey–Fuller test*, has been named after the two economists who estimated the form of the distribution. The testing procedure is identical to a t test in that one computes the tau-statistic and compares it to some critical value to determine whether to reject the null hypothesis. In this particular case, however, the critical values are different from (and, in fact, larger than) those obtained from a t distribution. For sufficiently large samples, these critical values (in absolute value) are 2.57, 2.86, and 3.43 at the 10%, 5%, and 1% levels of significance. These compare to 1.28, 1.645, and 2.326 at the same levels of significance for one-sided t tests.

The second problem with this testing procedure involves the potential for serial correlation in the error term. The Dickey–Fuller test just described assumes that the residual is not serially correlated, and we know from our earlier discussion in Chapter 14 that serial correlation of the error term is of great concern with time series data. If serial correlation is present, the distribution of the tau-statistic used in the Dickey–Fuller test would be inaccurate and bias the results of the test. To address this problem, one would conduct an *augmented Dickey–Fuller test*. This test is virtually identical to that described earlier, but the regression model specified to provide an estimate of β_1 would take the form

$$y_t = \beta_0 + \beta_1 y_{t-1} + \sum_{i=1}^{m} (y_{t-i} - y_{t-i-1}) + \varepsilon_t$$

The lagged first differences of y_t are included so that the residuals are no longer serially correlated. A determination of how many lags to include (m in the notation used in this model) is generally made by the econometrician based on empirical results. If the residuals are no longer serially correlated, the same critical values used in the standard Dickey–Fuller test are appropriate here as well.

The final problem inherent in these testing procedures is that the best one can do is to reject the null hypothesis; we may never accept the null. In the present context, the null hypothesis is that a unit root is present, indicating the existence of a nonstationary process, which, among other things, leads to potential problems if such variables are included in a regression model. If our testing procedures reject the null hypothesis, then we are reasonably certain that the process is stationary. On the other hand, if we fail to reject, it is not necessarily true that the process is nonstationary. With some potentially significant probability, we may not be rejecting a process that is stationary. This is the problem of limited power that was discussed in Chapter 8; unfortunately we often have little at our disposal to circumvent this problem.

17.3.3 Regression in First Differences

One potential solution to the problem of spurious regression in the case of nonstationary variables is to estimate regression models in first differences. Suppose, for example, that we want to estimate a regression model of the form $y_t = \beta_0 + \beta_1 x_t + \varepsilon_t$, but both x_t and y_t are nonstationary ($y_t = y_{t-1} + \varepsilon_t$ and $x_t = x_{t-1} + \varepsilon_t$) so that we are worried about estimating a spurious relationship between the two. Now consider the one-period lag of this regression model: $y_{t-1} = \beta_0 + \beta_1 x_{t-1} + \varepsilon_{t-1}$. If we subtracted the lagged left and right sides of this equation from the corresponding contemporaneous equation, we would have

$$y_t - y_{t-1} = \beta_1(x_t - x_{t-1}) + (\varepsilon_t - \varepsilon_{t-1}) \Rightarrow \Delta y_t = \beta_1 \Delta x_t + \Delta \varepsilon_t$$

This approach has the advantage of still being able to provide an estimate of β_1, which, generally, is the parameter of interest.

17.3.4   Cointegration

Suppose that we are interested in estimating the relationship between two variables that are both nonstationary in levels, but are both difference stationary (i.e., integrated of degree 1). Earlier we learned that a regression of the form $y_t = \beta_0 + \beta_1 x_t + \varepsilon_t$ is subject to the problem of spurious regression. Because both y_t and x_t follow a random walk, they have a tendency to appear to trend over time and if they both tend to move in the same (opposite) direction, regression estimates will find the two variables to be positively (negatively) related even though no such relationship exists.

But consider two time series variables that may follow random walks, but their apparent trends really are related. For instance, consider two alternative types of investment instruments that offer different degrees of risk. Standard models of finance suggest that the riskier investment should always offer a greater return than the safer investment. Now suppose that the returns on each of the two investments follow a random walk so that shocks that affect them actually occur periodically and are not expected to dissipate over time. But suppose that the shock to one form of investment is greater than the shock to the other. This would increase the difference between rates of return and may create arbitrage opportunities for investors who would be drawn to the above-average relative return on one of the investments. This process would return the difference in the rates of return to its steady state. In this example, the trending relationship between the two variables reflects the fact that an increase in one return actually is related to an increase in the other return and is not spurious.

Under what circumstances can we expect a regression of one nonstationary random variable on another to yield something other than a spurious relationship? The answer has to do with the concept of *cointegration*. Earlier in the chapter we defined the degree of integration of a time series process to indicate the length of differencing required to make a process stationary. It turns out that it is possible that if we have two processes that are, say, integrated of degree 1 (i.e., difference stationary), then a linear combination of those series may be integrated of degree 0, or stationary. If so, we say that the two series are cointegrated. More formally, if y_t and x_t are both I(1) and $\varepsilon_t = y_t - \beta_1 x_t$ is I(0), then y_t and x_t are cointegrated. In this case, β_1 is called the *cointegrating factor*. If the two variables are cointegrated, a regression of one on the other does not yield a spurious regression, but indicates an estimate of the true relationship between them. In the investment example, the two investment vehicles are cointegrated with $\beta_1 = 1$.

The intuition for testing whether two variables are cointegrated is straightforward based on our earlier discussion of tests for stationarity. In theory, all we would need to do is to conduct a Dickey–Fuller or augmented Dickey–Fuller test for stationarity on the residual, $\varepsilon_t = y_t - \beta_1 x_t$. In practice, an additional difficulty is encountered because, in fact, we do not know the value of β_1. It must be estimated first from the regression model, $y_t = \beta_0 + \beta_1 x_t + \varepsilon_t$ and substituted in to calculate the estimated residuals $\hat{\varepsilon}_t = y_t - \hat{\beta}_1 x_t$ before tests for nonstationarity can be conducted. Because of this additional step, the shape of the underlying distribution of the tau-statistic is different than in the standard Dickey–Fuller test leading to alternative critical values. For sufficiently large samples, these critical values (in absolute value) are 3.04, 3.59, and 3.90 at the 10%, 5%, and 1% levels of significance. These compare to 2.57, 2.86, and 3.43 at the same levels of significance in the standard test.

17.4 ESTIMATION AND FORECASTING

The ultimate use of the time series models developed in section 17.2 often is to forecast future values for some variable of interest. We might, for example, want to forecast interest rates or stock prices or the rate of inflation.

To generalize the discussion, consider the following ARIMA model:

$$y_t = \alpha_0 + \phi_1 y_{t-1} + \phi_2 y_{t-2} + \ldots + \phi_m y_{t-m} + \varepsilon_t + \delta_1 \varepsilon_{t-1} + \delta_2 \varepsilon_{t-2} + \ldots + \delta_k \varepsilon_{t-k}$$

This model embeds within it the various models introduced above.

Examples

1. If $\phi_2 = \phi_3 \ldots = \phi_m = \delta_1 = \delta_2 \ldots = \delta_k = 0$ and the series is stationary, then the general ARIMA model simplifies to an AR(1) model: $y_t = \alpha_0 + \phi_1 y_{t-1} + \varepsilon_t$.

2. If $\phi_2 = \phi_3 \ldots = \phi_m = \delta_2 = \delta_3 \ldots = \delta_k = 0$ and the series is stationary, then the general ARIMA model simplifies to an ARMA(1,1) model: $y_t = \alpha_0 + \phi_1 y_{t-1} + \varepsilon_t + \delta_1 \varepsilon_{t-1}$.

Once we have estimated an ARMA (or ARIMA) model we often want to use it to produce forecasts. Our objective would be to predict future values for the time series and to do so as accurately as possible. Suppose we had generated parameter estimates for the model. The estimated model is given by

$$\hat{y}_t = \hat{\alpha}_0 + \hat{\phi}_1 y_{t-1} + \hat{\phi}_2 y_{t-2} + \ldots + \hat{\phi}_m y_{t-m} + \varepsilon_t + \hat{\delta}_1 \varepsilon_{t-1} + \hat{\delta}_2 \varepsilon_{t-2} + \ldots + \hat{\delta}_k \varepsilon_{t-k}$$

Then, a one-period forward estimate would be

$$\hat{y}_{t+1} = \hat{\alpha}_0 + \hat{\phi}_1 y_t + \hat{\phi}_2 y_{t-1} + \ldots + \hat{\phi}_m y_{t+1-m} + \varepsilon_{t+1} + \hat{\delta}_1 \varepsilon_t + \hat{\delta}_2 \varepsilon_{t-1} + \ldots + \hat{\delta}_k \varepsilon_{t+1-k}$$

where we typically assume the future shock ε_{t+1} to be zero.

A two-period forecast would be

$$\hat{y}_{t+2} = \hat{\alpha}_0 + \hat{\phi}_1 y_{t+1} + \hat{\phi}_2 y_t + \ldots + \hat{\phi}_m y_{t+2-m} + \varepsilon_{t+2} + \hat{\delta}_1 \varepsilon_{t+1} + \hat{\delta}_2 \varepsilon_t + \ldots + \hat{\delta}_k \varepsilon_{t+2-k}$$

where we would assume ε_{t+1} and ε_{t+2} are zero and the prediction for y_{t+1} would come from the one-period forward forecast. Thus, future forcasts are computed recursively by using earlier forecasts as inputs to later predictions.

To actually conduct the forecast we would, of course, need estimates of the parameters of the model. Estimating an ARMA (or ARIMA) model proceeds in two steps. First, estimation requires us to specify the values for m, k, and d. That is, we must specify the number of lags associated with the autoregressive and moving average variables along with the number of times the equation must be differenced to become stationary. Once m, k, and d have been specified we can estimate the paramaters associated with the autoregressive and moving average components of the time series process.

To identify any necessary adjustments required to make the series stationary we can simply plot the series. If, for example, the series trends upward we could difference it. If it trends upward in an exponential fashion we might take logarithms and then difference. If the plot of the differenced series still trends upward we could difference a second time. Most economic time series become stationary if differenced once or twice.

The *autocorrelation function* and the *correlogram* are useful tools in selecting the values for m and k. The *autocorrelation function* calculates the correlation between observations at different points in time and is defined as:

$$\rho(y_t, y_{t-s}) = \frac{\text{Cov}(y_t, y_{t-s})}{\text{Var}(y_t)} = \frac{E(y_t y_{t-s})}{E(y_t^2)}$$

where we assume that the observations are expressed as deviations from their mean value. The *correlogram* is simply a graph of the correlation function for different values of s. For example, for an AR(1) process we have

$$\begin{aligned} y_t &= \phi_1 y_{t-1} + \varepsilon_t \\ &= \phi_1(\phi_1 y_{t-2} + \varepsilon_{t-1}) + \varepsilon_t \end{aligned}$$

which, by repeated substitution yields

$$\begin{aligned} &= \dots \\ &= \varepsilon_t + \phi_1 \varepsilon_{t-1} + \phi_1^2 \varepsilon_{t-2} + \dots \end{aligned}$$

Then, applying the definition for the autocorrelation function we have

$$\begin{aligned} \rho(Y_t, Y_{t-s}) &= \frac{E(Y_t Y_{t-s})}{E(Y_t^2)} \\ &= \frac{E((\varepsilon_t + \phi_1 \varepsilon_{t-1} + \phi_1^2 \varepsilon_{t-2} + \dots \phi_1^{s-1} \varepsilon_{t-s-1} + \phi_1^s \varepsilon_{t-s} + \dots)(\varepsilon_{t-s} + \phi_1 \varepsilon_{t-s-1} + \phi_1^2 \varepsilon_{t-s-2} + \dots))}{E((\varepsilon_t + \phi_1 \varepsilon_{t-1} + \phi_1^2 \varepsilon_{t-2} + \dots)^2)} \end{aligned}$$

Given the independence of the error terms, all of the cross products (i.e., the covariance between errors in different time periods) would be zero, and the equation would simplify to

$$\rho(y_t, y_{t-s}) = \frac{\phi_1^s \sigma_\varepsilon^2 (1 + \phi_1^2 + \phi_1^4 + \dots)}{\sigma_\varepsilon^2 (1 + \phi_1^2 + \phi_1^4 + \dots)} = \phi_1^s$$

Notice that for $\phi_1 < 1$ the correlation between observations declines geometrically. Thus, the time series process exhibits an *infinite memory* in the sense that current values are affected by all previous values—though the importance of previous values declines over time. For an MA(k) process it is easy to show that autocorrelation function takes on the value zero for all lags greater than k. Thus, if the autocorrelation function approaches zero after k^* lags, then a reasonable choice for k would be k^*.

To estimate m we make use of the *partial autocorrelation function* and the *partial correlogram*. First, we estimate a simple AR(1) model using OLS. This gives an estimate of ϕ_1. We then estimate an AR(2) model. This gives us an estimate of ϕ_2—the effect of a two-period lag *holding the one-period lag constant*. Similarly, we can estimate an AR(3) model to find the ceteris (or *partial*) effect of a three-period lag (i.e., ϕ_3). Continuing in this fashion we generate the values of the partial autocorrelation function. Graphing these values gives us the partial correlogram, which shows us the correlation between the current observation and each lag holding other lags constant. At some point the partial autocorrelation will become close to zero. Or, equivalently, the partial correlogram will approach the horizontal axis. The point at which this occurs gives us a useful guideline for the number of lags to include with the autoregressive part of the model. Thus, if $\phi_{m^*} = 0$, then we use m^* as our value for m.

Now, suppose we have *specified* the values for m, k, and d for an ARIMA model and we wish to estimate the parameters of the model:

$$y_t = \alpha_0 + \phi_1 y_{t-1} + \phi_2 y_{t-2} + \ldots + \phi_m y_{t-m} + \varepsilon_t + \delta_1 \varepsilon_{t-1} + \delta_2 \varepsilon_{t-2} + \ldots + \delta_k \varepsilon_{t-k}$$

Let's assume that the model is stationary or has already been differenced. Then, if the model does not contain a moving average component (i.e., $\delta_1 = \delta_2 = \delta_3 \ldots = \delta_k = 0$), we may estimate the parameters α, ϕ_1, $\ldots$, ϕ_m using ordinary least squares. In this case, the error term satisfies all of the usual assumptions underlying the classic regression model. It has a mean of zero, is serially uncorrelated, and so on. As usual, if you include too many lags of the dependent variable on the right-hand side, you will generate inefficient estimates. Similarly, if you don't include enough lags your estimates will be biased and inconsistent. If, however, the model *does* contain a moving average component, then the model becomes nonlinear and ordinary least squares will not yield consistent estimators. In this context we employ a maximum likelihood estimation strategy. A variety of software programs can estimate such models, though the procedure for doing so is quite complicated.

17.5   VECTOR AUTOREGRESSION (VAR)

In the 1950s and 1960s, large-scale simultaneous equation models—often containing several hundred equations—were developed to help forecast key variables in the economy. These equations were *structural* in the sense that they were built on a set of assumptions about human behavior. These models, unfortunately, were open to a variety of attacks. First, the theory underlying the specification of the equations could be challenged. Second, the parameters in these models might themselves be dependent on the state of economic policy and would change when policy changed. These concerns, and others, gave rise to an alternative approach to forecasting the macroeconomy. The *vector autoregression model* (VAR) makes minimal assumptions about the structure underlying the model. Indeed, the model simply relates a set of endogenous variables to lags of those same variables and other exogenous variables. The researcher does not have to impose assumptions about the lag structure of the model. Thus, the VAR model takes the form

$$y_{1t} = \alpha_{01} + \sum_{j=1}^{m} \beta_{11j} y_{1t-j} + \sum_{j=1}^{m} \beta_{12j} y_{2t-j} + \sum_{j=1}^{m} \beta_{13j} y_{3t-j} + \ldots \sum_{j=1}^{m} \beta_{1nj} y_{nt-j} + \ldots \sum_{j=1}^{l} \gamma_{11j} Z_{1t-j}$$

$$+ \ldots \sum_{j=1}^{l} \gamma_{1rj} Z_{rt-j} + \varepsilon_{1t}$$

.
.
.

$$y_{nt} = \alpha_{0n} + \sum_{j=1}^{m} \beta_{n1j} y_{1t-j} + \sum_{j=1}^{m} \beta_{n2j} y_{2t-j} + \sum_{j=1}^{m} \beta_{n3j} y_{3t-j} + \ldots \sum_{j=1}^{m} \beta_{nnj} y_{nt-j} + \ldots \sum_{j=1}^{l} \gamma_{n1j} Z_{1t-j} + \ldots \sum_{j=1}^{l} \gamma_{nrj} Z_{rt-j} + \varepsilon_{nt}$$

APPLICATION 17.2 *Frustration in Forecasting Inflation*

The importance of forecasting the rate of inflation in the future cannot be underestimated. Given the lags associated with the impact of changes in interest rates, the Federal Reserve policy decisions today are based upon the rate of inflation at some future time. Unnecessarily raising interest rates may lead to a recession, reducing the economic well-being of the nation. Doing nothing in an inflationary environment may lead to spiraling prices that would subsequently require very strict policies that may lead to even greater hardship down the road. Therefore, getting the forecast of inflation right is very beneficial.

With that in mind, it would be nice if forecasting inflation was uncontroversial, but unfortunately that is not the case. In particular, what variables should be used to predict inflation is somewhat uncertain. Some have proposed using commodity prices (oil, precious metals, etc.), financial indicators (exchange rates, measures of money supply, etc.), and other economic measures (unemployment rate, manufacturing activity, etc.). Does the addition of any of these variables individually improve on a forecast just based on past time series movements in prices?

One recent study argues that none of these indicators, in isolation, improves forecasts of inflation. To test this proposition, the authors use quarterly data on the consumer price index (CPI) beginning in 1975 through, say, 1988, and estimate an AR(4) model of the form

$$\Delta CPI_t = \beta_0 + \sum_{i=1}^{4} \beta_i \cdot CPI_{t-i} + \varepsilon_t$$

and use the results to forecast inflation for, say, 1989 and 1990. These forecasts are then compared to those in which the same model augmented with one of the additional indicators (IND) lagged one period:

$$\Delta CPI_t = \beta_0 + \sum_{i=1}^{4} \beta_i \cdot CPI_{t-i} + IND_{t-1} + \varepsilon_t$$

The results indicate that the forecasts for the more complicated models often were no better, and sometimes worse, than the ones from the simpler model. Another recent study, however, shows that adding a sophisticated aggregation of these other indices to the model does outperform simpler methods. While the debate rages, the Fed still goes about its work!

SOURCES: Cecchetti, Stephen G., Rita S. Chu, and Charles Steindel, "The Unreliability of Inflation Indicators," *Current Issues in Economics and Finance* (a publication of the Federal Reserve Bank of New York), Vol. 6, No. 4 (April 2000); Stock, James H. and Mark W. Watson, "Forecasting Inflation," *Journal of Monetary Economics*, Vol. 44, No. 2 (October 1999), pp. 293–335.

This system of equations allows for an arbitrary set of lags for each variable in the model. Researchers can include as many lags as they like—bearing in mind that the degrees of freedom fall as additional variables are included. It is appropriate to estimate each equation using ordinary least squares, since each equation has only lagged endogenous variables and exogenous variables on the right-hand side and the error terms are assumed to be uncorrelated.

A useful way to describe the dynamic characteristics of the VAR model is to use an *impulse response function*. The impulse response function describes the response of each endogenous variable to a shock to the model. If, for example, the error term in the first equation increases unexpectedly for one period (the "impulse"), we can trace the effects on all of the endogenous variables in the system. Some of the variables may exhibit an immediate change. Others, due to the lag structure in the VAR, may not exhibit changes until several periods have passed. We could graph the value for each variable against time to see the dynamic effects arising from the shock and could conduct a similar exercise for shocks to each equation in the model.

17.6 PROBLEMS

1. Define each of the following: random walk, ARMA, stationarity, unit root.
2. Show how for an MA(2) model any shocks will dissipate after 3 periods.
3. Suppose $y_t = \alpha_0 + \phi_1 y_{t-1} + \varepsilon_t$. Graph the value of y against t for 10 periods for $\varepsilon_1 = .2$ and $\phi_1 = .8$ and $\alpha_0 = 0$.
4. The data provided in http://www.wiley.com/college/ashenfelter contain information on the unemployment rate (monthly and seasonally adjusted) from 1951 through 1999 with a year variable.

   a. Estimate an AR(1) model. Test for first-order serial correlation. Conduct the estimation excluding the three most recent years. Using the models parameter estimates, perform an "insample" prediction for those three periods. How well does the model do?

   b. Repeat part (a) using an AR(2) model. Which model do you prefer?

Chapter 18

Panel Data Models

18.1   INTRODUCTION

Our discussion of regression analysis so far has concentrated on two particular types of data. Mostly we have considered cross-sectional data, where a unit of observation may represent some entity (typically an individual) at a particular point in time. In essence, the cross-section represents a "slice" of the population. In some instances, we have also considered the specific problems associated with time series data, in which information for a particular entity (like a country) is followed over time. Chapter 17 provided a detailed examination of some of the problems associated with using time series data and the problem of serial correlation, discussed in Chapter 14, is another example.

In practice, one other type of data is sometimes available to the researcher that requires additional considerations, and, under particular assumptions, offers certain advantages. Panel data provide information for particular entities (like individuals, countries, or others) over a period of time. In this chapter, we will describe the methods that provide these advantages along with the assumptions they require.

18.2   UNOBSERVABLE HETEROGENEITY AND PANEL DATA

18.2.1   What Is Unobservable Heterogeneity?

An important consideration in our discussion of regression analysis has been the problem of omitted-variable bias. Recall from Chapter 13 that OLS is biased if a variable is omitted that is related to the dependent variable and is related to an included explanatory variable. If a properly specified model takes the form

$$Y_i = \beta_0 + \beta_1 X_{1i} + \beta_2 X_{2i} + \varepsilon_i$$

but instead, we estimate the model

$$Y_i = \tilde{\beta}_0 + \tilde{\beta}_1 X_{1i} + \tilde{\varepsilon}_i$$

we showed that the expected value of the OLS estimate of β_1 is $E(\hat{\beta}_1) = \beta_1 + \beta_2 b_{12}$, where b_{12} indicates the impact of X_1 on X_2. The second term in this expression represents the bias and is equal to 0 if $b_{12} = 0$; that is, X_1 and X_2 are not related to each other. The obvious solution to this problem is to be sure to include X_2 when specifying the regression model.

The problem with this is that X_2 may be a variable that we cannot observe. It is possible that we cannot observe X_2 either because it is unavailable in the dataset to which we have access or it may be inherently unobservable. Regardless, if it is not included in the regression model and if it is both related to Y and to X_1 it will introduce bias. This problem is called *unobservable heterogeneity*.

Example

As in Chapter 13, suppose we want to test the impact of cigarette smoking on the incidence of cancer. If we omit any variables that are related to both smoking and cancer, our estimate of the impact of smoking will be biased. In reality, many factors are likely to be related to both of these variables. Smoking and drinking are highly correlated, and drinking may have an impact on cancer incidence. If the data at our disposal does not include drinking information, omitted-variable bias may result. But smoking may be correlated with other lifestyle choices as well, like poor diet, that may themselves be the main culprit in causing cancer. Identifying all of these factors and collecting data on all of them may be virtually impossible.

18.2.2   The Role of Panel Data

The availability of panel data provides us with techniques that allow us to formally recognize the possible existence of unobservable heterogeneity in our model. To see this, suppose that we have data on N individuals over a period of T years, so that our complete dataset includes $N \times T$ observations. Furthermore, suppose that we want to estimate a standard regression model of Y on a number (k) of X variables, but that there exists an individual-specific component that cannot be controlled for because it is not observed. Under these circumstances, we can specify the model to take the form

$$Y_{it} = \beta_0 + \gamma_i + \beta_1 X_{1it} + \beta_2 X_{2it} + \beta_3 X_{3it} + \ldots + \beta_k X_{kit} + \varepsilon_{it}$$

where, for instance, Y_{it} represents the value of the dependent variable for individual i at time t and the remainder of the notation is analogous. The term, γ_i, represents the individual-specific component. The attributes of this model will depend on the particular manner in which we treat this individual-specific component. If it is treated as a constant, then we have a fixed effects model. If it is treated as a random variable, then we have a random effects model. The remainder of this chapter will consider each of these types of models in turn.

18.3 FIXED EFFECTS MODELS

The key assumption in a fixed effect model is that any characteristics of the individual that cannot be observed are predetermined. In other words, there are unique attributes of individuals that are not the result of random variation but represent fixed, longstanding differences. If this assumption is accurate, the availability of panel data enables us to estimate unbiased slope coefficients for those variables that are included in the model. In other words, methods can be introduced using panel data that eliminate the potential bias brought about by unobservable heterogeneity.

In this model, the fixed effect acts like a dummy variable, shifting the intercept up or down for each person in the sample. Without the availability of panel data, it is clearly impossible to estimate this model because it requires us to estimate one collective intercept, k slope coefficients, and one value of the intercept shifter, γ_i, for all but one person in the data. In other words, if our cross-sectional sample contains N observations, the OLS normal equations would require us to solve for $N + k$ unknowns, which cannot be done. Such a model could only be estimated if we had multiple observations per person. Panel data provide us with just this sort of data and will therefore allow us to estimate models with fixed effects. Procedures for doing so are discussed subsequently.

18.3.1 First Differences

The first approach uses data from two separate periods for the same individuals. In this model, we could specify two separate regression models for each period:

$$Y_{i,t-1} = \beta_0 + \gamma_i + \beta_1 X_{1i,t-1} + \beta_2 X_{2i,t-1} + \beta_3 X_{3i,t-1} + \ldots + \beta_k X_{ki,t-1} + \varepsilon_{i,t-1}$$

$$Y_{it} = \beta_0 + \gamma_i + \beta_1 X_{1it} + \beta_2 X_{2it} + \beta_3 X_{3it} + \ldots + \beta_k X_{kit} + \varepsilon_{it}$$

Notice that all variables in the first and second equations contain the time subscripts, $t - 1$ and t, respectively, except for the individual fixed effect, which is assumed to be time invariant. It captures all such characteristics of the individual regardless of whether they are observed. Subtracting the second equation from the first yields

$$\Delta Y_i = \beta_1 \Delta X_{1i} + \beta_2 \Delta X_{2i} + \beta_3 \Delta X_{3i} + \ldots + \beta_k \Delta X_{ki} + \Delta \varepsilon_i$$

where $\Delta Y_i = Y_{it} - Y_{i,t-1}$, and the remainder of the notation is analogous. Because we are taking the difference in variables between one period and the next, this method is called *first differences*. It solves the unobservable heterogeneity problem because the characteristics of individuals that are fixed over time, regardless of whether they are observed, disappear in this equation. Hence, the remaining slope coefficients will not be subject to omitted-variable bias when the assumptions of this model hold.

18.3.2 Deviations from Means

A second approach uses data from multiple periods for the same individual. In this model, we start with the same basic regression equation

$$Y_{it} = \beta_0 + \gamma_i + \beta_1 X_{1it} + \beta_2 X_{2it} + \beta_3 X_{3it} + \ldots + \beta_k X_{kit} + \varepsilon_{it}$$

APPLICATION 18.1 *Getting Your Monet's Worth*

One would think that constructing an index of the price of a particular commodity would be simple enough; all you have to do is track its selling price over time. For some commodities, however, an important problem emerges in that it may not be exactly the same good being sold from one year to the next. The housing market is a prime example. Suppose in one year most sales are to young home buyers purchasing their first home, but in a subsequent year most sales are to those in middle age who are "buying up." Transacted prices certainly would have risen a great deal, but that does not necessarily indicate that excess demand drove them up.

One way that researchers have circumvented this problem is to construct a price index focusing exclusively on those houses that have been sold more than once. Consider a simple model of the sales price of housing in years t and $t + 1$:

$$\ln P_{ht} = \ln P_t + \ln P_h$$

$$\ln P_{k,t+1} = \ln P_{t+1} + \ln P_k$$

In this model, the observed selling price (in logs) is a function of the strength of the real estate market in a particular year (in logs), P_t and P_{t+1}, and the specific characteristics, valued in log dollars, of the homes being sold in a particular year, P_h and P_k. An accurate home price index should provide the value of $\ln P_{t+1} - \ln P_t$, but the simple difference in observed selling prices of all houses, $\ln P_{t,k+1} - \ln P_{ht}$, does not capture this if the characteristics of the houses have changed (i.e., $P_h \neq P_k$). If, however, we used only those properties where there have been repeated sales, then $P_h = P_k$, and the characteristics of the home act as a fixed effect. The difference in transacted prices will difference out the fixed effect and solely identify the change in prices brought about by changes in market conditions.

A similar problem exists in the art market. Figuring out the extent to which your Monet has appreciated is difficult if each year at auction different Monets are being sold. Using a repeat sales index will hold constant any variation in the value of the art that is brought about because of its different characteristics. Results from this research indicates that "investments" in art yield very low rates of return; it may be better to think about those purchases as consumption!

Sources: Case, Karl E., and Robert J. Shiller, "The Efficiency of the Market for Single-Family Homes." *American Economic Review*, Vol. 79, No. 1 (March 1989), pp. 125–137; and Pesando, James E. "Art as an Investment: The Market for Modern Prints." *American Economic Review*, Vol. 83, No. 5 (December 1993), pp. 1075–89.

and modify it by taking the mean value of each variable:

$$\bar{Y}_i = \beta_0 + \gamma_i + \beta_1\bar{X}_{1i} + \beta_2\bar{X}_{2i} + \beta_3\bar{X}_{3i} + \ldots + \beta_k\bar{X}_{ki} + \bar{\varepsilon}_i$$

Notice that the second equation contains the same individual fixed effect, γ_i, because the mean of a constant is a constant. A similar differencing technique to that used earlier can then be employed to eliminate the fixed effect. Subtracting the second equation from the first yields

$$Y_{it} - \bar{Y}_i = \beta_1(X_{1it} - \bar{X}_{1i}) + \beta_2(X_{2it} - \bar{X}_{2i}) + \beta_3(X_{3it} - \bar{X}_{3i}) + \ldots + \beta_k(X_{kit} - \bar{X}_{ki}) + (\varepsilon_{it} - \bar{\varepsilon}_i)$$

Estimates of the parameters of this model can be obtained with no omitted-variable bias provided that it is valid to assume that all individual characteristics that are not explicitly included are constant over time.

18.3.3 Individual Dummy Variables

Perhaps conceptually, the simplest solution to estimating models with fixed effects is to include a dummy variable for each individual in the sample. In theory, as long as there are multiple observations per individual, such a model can be estimated. In practice, however, computer limitations would make it impossible to do this if the number of individuals is very large. Luckily, one can show that this approach is identical to the deviations from means approach, just described, so that when the number of individuals is large, that technique may be employed.

18.4 POOLED CROSS-SECTION, TIME SERIES DATA

The discussion regarding fixed effects models so far has proceeded assuming that the panel nature of the data takes the form of repeated observations of particular entities, like individuals. It turns out that some panels of data take an alternative form in that they represent several cross-sections of data taken at different points in time. Data of this form do not represent repeated observations on exactly the same entities, but rather different samples drawn over time from the same entities. Suppose, for instance, that a nationally representative sample was drawn and state-level means were computed for a particular point in time, and that this procedure was repeated for several years. The panel would not include data on exactly the same respondents in the different surveys, but it would include repeated observations of means within states over time. In other words, the panel would consist of average state characteristics over time.

18.4.1 Fixed Effects Methods with Pooled Cross-Section, Time-Series Data

Problems of unobservable heterogeneity in data of this type may exist as well. In particular, suppose that we had pooled cross-section, time series data for all states over a period of years and wanted to estimate the relationship between the average characteristics of inhabitants of a state and their average outcomes. We may specify such a model as

$$Y_{st} = \beta_0 + \beta_1 X_{1st} + \beta_2 X_{2st} + \beta_3 X_{3st} + \ldots + \beta_k X_{kst} + \varepsilon_{st}$$

where Y_{st} represents the average outcome for respondents in state s at time t and the remainder of the notation is analogous. Unobservable heterogeneity may impose bias on parameter estimates from this model in much the same way that it would in the models described earlier. Some characteristics of residents in particular states may be different from those in other states and we may not have access to variables that characterize those differences or we never may be able to observe them. If those omitted characteristics are also related to the included explanatory variables, bias will result.

Under the appropriate assumptions, this problem may be addressed using fixed effect methods analogous to those described earlier. One could alternatively specify a model of the following form:

$$Y_{st} = \beta_0 + \gamma_s + \beta_1 X_{1st} + \beta_2 X_{2st} + \beta_3 X_{3st} + \ldots + \beta_k X_{kst} + \varepsilon_{st}$$

In this specification, γ_s represents a state fixed effect. It incorporates differences across states that are assumed to be fixed over time. All three approaches described earlier for estimating fixed effects models can be utilized here as well.

One additional consideration that often comes into play in models using data of this sort is the concern that there may be some time-specific component to the outcome that may exist as well and that may not be observed. For instance, some national change in attitudes may affect the dependent variable and we would not be able to control for it directly. If this change affects the entire nation equally so that it is fixed across states, we can augment the preceding model with an additional term, γ_t, that represents year fixed effects:

$$Y_{st} = \beta_0 + \gamma_s + \gamma_t + \beta_1 X_{1st} + \beta_2 X_{2st} + \beta_3 X_{3st} + \ldots + \beta_k X_{kst} + \varepsilon_{st}$$

The easiest way to control for both state and year fixed effects in the same model is simply to include dummy variables for each of them. In this manner, omitted-variable bias brought about by this particular form of unobservable heterogeneity can be eliminated.

Example

Suppose one wanted to estimate the impact of gun control laws on the murder rate using data from the 50 states and the District of Columbia over a 10-year period. Historically, residents of many Southern and Mountain states have traditionally expressed greater opposition to gun control. With relatively few of the nation's largest metropolitan areas, murder rates have been historically lower in those locations as well, although it would be difficult to attribute causality to this relationship on this basis alone. Including state fixed effects would enable us to control for the longstanding differences across states in their attitudes toward guns to see whether a state that enacts new gun control legislation experiences a decline in murder rates. But suppose that murder rates happen to be falling anyway (as they had been in the 1990s) and it happens that gun control laws are becoming more popular (after incidents like the Columbine High School shooting tragedy, for instance). Including year fixed effects would enable us to control for changes in national attitudes toward gun control that may be spuriously correlated with a falling murder rate. A model with both state and year fixed effects would enable us to detect whether changes in the murder rate are actually brought about by changes in gun control laws.

18.4.2   Quasi-Experiments in Theory

In some instances, estimating models using pooled cross-section, time series data may have an interpretation similar to that of a controlled experiment. Recall that a controlled experiment randomly assigns participants to control and treatment groups. Members of the treatment group would, in some way, be treated differently while nothing would change for the control group. If random assignment is carried out perfectly, the two groups will be statistically identical a priori and any difference in outcomes can be causally attributed to the treatment.

Models using pooled cross-section, time series data can be interpreted in a similar fashion under particular assumptions if the exercise is focused on estimating the impact of a change in a discrete explanatory variable, such as a policy change. Suppose, for instance, that a subset of states enacted new legislation in a particular year and others did not. One could then create pseudotreatment and control groups (where the prefix *pseudo* is used to clarify that no formal random assignment has taken place) and compare them to determine the impact of the treatment. Researchers use the expressions *quasi-experiments* or, sometimes, *natural experiments* to indicate the existence of such a pseudoexperimental design.

With a quasi-experiment one could simply compare outcomes in the two sets of states after the policy change took place and claim to have determined the impact of the policy. Alternatively, one could just look at the states that implemented the policy and see if the relevant outcome changed over time. But one could still be concerned about the types of problems of unobservable heterogeneity previously described. For instance, the set of states that instituted the policy may have been different in many ways from those that did not. Moreover, trends may have been occurring over time that would bias the results of an analysis that just looked at changes in outcomes within those states implementing the policy change. In other words, we may be worried about the existence of state and year fixed effects that may be correlated with the treatment status.

However, quasi-experimental methods can help us circumvent these problems. To simplify the problem, suppose that we defined a model of the outcomes in which there are two types of states (treatment and control) and two time periods (before and after the policy change). The state and year fixed effects γ_s and γ_t represent the unobservable difference between the two types of states and between the two periods, respectively. Define the variable P_{st} to be a dummy variable equal to 1 in the states and years in which the policy is in effect and 0 otherwise. Then we can specify a model of the outcome in state s at time t to be

$$O_{st} = \beta_0 + \gamma_s + \gamma_t + \delta_1 P_{st} + \varepsilon_{st}$$

As shown in the following chart, comparing the changes in outcomes over time between the treatment and control groups of states provides an estimate of the impact of the policy change, δ_1. An estimator of this type is sometimes called a *difference-in-difference* estimator.

Group	Period	Expected outcome in state/period	Difference	Difference-in-difference
Pseudo-treatment	After policy change	$\overline{O}_{st} = \beta_0 + \gamma_s + \gamma_t + \delta_1$	$\Delta O^T = \gamma_t + \delta_1$	
	Before	$\overline{O}_{st} = \beta_0 + \gamma_s$		$\Delta O^T - \Delta O^C = \delta_1$
Pseudo-control	After	$O_{st} = \beta_0 + \gamma_t$	$\Delta O^C = \gamma_t$	
	Before	$O_{st} = \beta_0$		

18.4.3   Quasi-Experiments in Practice

Although the intuition provided in the previous section is invaluable in interpreting the results of quasi-experimental techniques, the stylized model presented is rarely replicated in practice. The main limitation of that framework is that it assumes that no changes took place in the two sets of states besides the policy change. In practice, to the extent that we can observe these other changes, they can be controlled for in a regression framework by including these other factors in the model. We could then specify an alternative model of the form

$$O_{st} = \beta_0 + \gamma_s + \gamma_t + \delta_1 P_{st} + \beta_1 X_{1st} + \beta_2 X_{2st} + \beta_3 X_{3st} + \ldots + \beta_k X_{kst} + \varepsilon_{st}$$

This model is identical in form to that specified in our earlier discussion of pooled cross-section, time-series data and indicates that models of that form may be interpreted within this quasi-experimental framework.

Of course, this model can control for those factors changing across states over time only if they are available in a particular dataset or can be observed at all. Changing attitudes over time that may differ across states is a typical example of this problem. In other words, we have not completely eliminated the problem of unobservable heterogeneity. These techniques are only effective at eliminating the bias brought about when the differences across states are constant over time or when the differences over time are constant across states. If these conditions are not met, quasi-experimental estimates may still be plagued by omitted-variable bias. It is for this reason that the prefix *quasi* is used in naming this method.

Example

Consider the earlier example of estimating the impact of gun control legislation on murder rates. If a subset of states instituted the laws at one point in time and nothing else changed between the two sets of states, the difference-in-difference technique described earlier could be employed directly to evaluate the results of this quasi-experiment. A comparable regression-based technique could also be employed that includes other observable factors changing over time along with both state and year fixed effects. In this model, the effect of the law change is still determined by the ceteris paribus comparison of changes over time in murder rates in those states that enacted gun control laws with the changes over time in those states with no law change. It therefore shares this quasi-experimental interpretation.

18.5   RANDOM EFFECTS MODELS

The key assumption in the fixed effect model described in Section 18.3 is that the entity-specific (which we will continue to assume is individual-specific) component, γ_i, is a constant. In the earlier model, individual fixed effects simply shifted the intercept of the regression line in a deterministic manner. By assumption, some individuals always have outcomes that differ from others in a specific way (even after controlling for other observable factors), which is captured by the individual fixed effect.

One might propose an alternative framework to characterize differences across individuals, however. Suppose that the individual-specific component was not a constant, but was each individual's realization of a random variable that was specific to him or her. As such, it may more appropriately be thought of as an element of the model's residual in addition to the standard error term in the regression model. Within this framework, the residual for a particular individual would take the form $\gamma_i + \varepsilon_{it}$ and we would write the regression model as

$$Y_{it} = \beta_0 + \beta_1 X_{1it} + \beta_2 X_{2it} + \beta_3 X_{3it} + \ldots + \beta_k X_{kit} + \gamma_i + \varepsilon_{it}$$

This form of this specification is identical to that reported earlier in Section 18.3 regarding fixed effects, except that in this model the individual-specific component, γ_i, is treated as a random variable rather than a constant. One could still interpret this effect as shifts in the intercept for different individuals, but the difference in this model is that those shifts are randomly distributed across individuals. A straightforward extension of this model could also include a random time component, γ_s, but we omit this here to simplify the discussion.

APPLICATION 18.2   *How Much Does Legal Abortion Reduce Births?*

Birth rates (births per 1000 women between the ages of 15 and 44) in the United States had been trending downward relatively rapidly in the late 1960s and 1970s. But what impact did the legalization of abortion, which took place during this period, have on childbearing patterns? The historical pattern of abortion legalization across states provides an opportunity to use quasi-experimental methods to estimate the impact. In 1970, California, New York, and a few other states legalized abortion ahead of the January 1973 Supreme Court ruling in Roe v. Wade that legalized it in the remainder of the country. That means that women living in those states had easier access to abortion than women in the rest of the country *only* during the 1971 to 1973 period (note that there is roughly a 9 month delay until the policy change can have any effect—that's biology, not economics!). If legalized abortion led to changes in birth rates, then births should have fallen in New York, California, and the other early legalizers relative to the rest of the country during this period and then that difference should have been eliminated afterwards.

An important difficulty in implementing this test is the influence of state- and time-specific factors. California and New York may have longstanding differences in demographic composition, culture, institutions, and the like that may affect their birth rates relative to the rest of the country. Moreover, many other important changes were taking place in society during the period of abortion legalization (changing women's roles, the Vietnam war, etc.) that also may have contributed to declining births. To control for these factors, one can include state and year fixed effects, setting up a quasi-experimental design. In fact, in the context of abortion legalization, two quasi-experiments are being conducted. In the first, following the 1970 changes, the early legalizers act as the treatment group and the remaining states represent the controls. In the second, the experimental roles of the states reverse following Roe v. Wade. Researchers using this approach have concluded that abortion legalization led to a 5 to 10 percent decline in births.

SOURCE: Levine, Phillip B., Douglas Staiger, Thomas J. Kane, and David J. Zimmerman, "Roe v. Wade and American Fertility." *American Journal of Public Health*, February 1999, pp. 199–203.

In such models, it is commonly assumed that this part of the residual has a constant variance for different individuals, so that $\text{var}(\gamma_i) = \sigma_\gamma$ for all i, but that the covariance of these residuals across individuals is zero: $\text{Cov}(\gamma_i, \gamma_{j'}) = 0 \; \forall \; i \neq j$. In addition, we assume that the individual component of the residual is uncorrelated with any of the included explanatory variables: $\text{cov}(\gamma_i, X_{jt}) = 0 \; \forall \; i, j$, and t.

Under these assumptions, OLS is not biased because the residual for the model is uncorrelated with any of the explanatory variables; that is, $\text{cov}(\gamma_i + \varepsilon_{it}, X_{jt}) = 0 \; \forall \; i, j$, and t. In other words, despite the presence of unobservable heterogeneity brought about by this individual-specific component, OLS remains unbiased because it is uncorrelated with any of the included explanatory variables.

APPLICATION 18.3 *If It Wasn't a Franchise, Would They Ask If You Wanted Fries?*

In the fast food industry, some establishments are owned by the company and others are franchised, in which a local owner/operator purchases the right to run the unit from the company. An interesting economic question is the relationship between the wages paid to workers at the two types of establishments. In franchised operations, the owner/operator is on-site and can directly oversee the behavior of his/her employees. In company-owned units, however, the "owner" has no direct oversight, placing a manager in charge who does not have as strong an incentive to make sure his/her workers do a good job. This is called an agency problem; theoretical models suggest that it can be solved by paying workers at corporate-owned units a wage above the market clearing level (called an "efficiency wage") to prevent them from shirking.

One research paper has tested this hypothesis in the fast food industry using data on wages paid to employees at corporate-owned and franchised units of several well-known fast food restaurants. A natural approach to conduct this test would be to estimate a regression model of the form:

$$\ln W_{ij} = \beta_0 + \beta_1 \cdot C_{ij} + \beta_2 \cdot X_{ij} + \varepsilon_i$$

where the log of wages (W) are regressed against a dummy variable (C) indicating whether the establishment is company-owned (versus franchised) and a set of other worker- and establishment-specific characteristics (X) for worker j at restaurant i. In this specification, the hypothesis would be supported if $\beta_1 > 0$; wages would be higher at corporate-owned compared to franchised units after holding constant other differences.

One problem with this approach in the present context is that several employees from each specific restaurant are included in the dataset. Therefore, one might expect any of the random elements affecting a worker's wage to be comprised of two components, one affecting all workers at a particular establishment and one affecting the individual worker. Specifically, it may be the case that $\varepsilon_{ij} = \alpha_i + e_{ij}$ where α_i and ε_{ij} represent the restaurant-specific and individual-specific random error components of individual's wages. This specification defines a random effects model and the author of this study estimates this model to test his hypothesis. Results indicate that, indeed, corporate-owned establishments pay wages up to 9 percent higher than those paid at units that are franchised.

SOURCE: Krueger, Alan B, "Ownership, Agency, and Wages: An Examination of Franchising in the Fast Food Industry." *Quarterly Journal of Economics*, Vol. 106, No. 1 (February 1991), pp. 75–101.

The problem that does arise is serial correlation. In particular, for the N observations for each individual in the sample, there is a nonzero correlation in the residuals, that is, $\text{cov}(\gamma_i + \varepsilon_{it}, \gamma_i + \varepsilon_{is}) \neq 0$ for $s \neq t$. As a result, OLS is no longer BLUE, and OLS formulas for computing standard errors of regression coefficients yield incorrect estimates that influence hypothesis testing.

The solution to this problem involves an estimation procedure, generalized least squares (GLS), that is beyond the scope of this book. Conceptually, however, one can think about the solution as being similar to the quasi–first differencing technique that was described in Chapter 14 to solve a different type of serial correlation problem, first-order serial correlation in time series data. An appropriate transformation of the model yields a modified residual that does not exhibit serial correlation. As with quasi–first differencing, where the correlation coefficient, ρ, is needed to perform the transformation, but is unknown and requires estimation, a similar issue arises in random effects models where the variance of the two terms in the residual, σ_γ and σ_ε, requires estimation. Most modern, sophisticated statistical software provides the means to perform this estimation and make the appropriate transformation to estimate the model.

18.6 FIXED EFFECTS OR RANDOM EFFECTS?

The fixed effects and random effects models make very different assumptions about the individual-specific component, γ_i. In choosing between fixed and random effects models, it is important to recognize the advantages and disadvantages of the two types of models. The main disadvantage of the fixed effects model is that it requires estimation of a separate parameter for all N individuals in the sample (estimating these models using deviations from the mean is computationally easier, but is otherwise identical to the dummy variable approach). This causes problems because much of the variation that exists in the data is used up estimating these dummy variables. As a result, it may be difficult to precisely estimate the coefficients on the other included explanatory variables. To see this more clearly, consider the deviations from means approach to estimating fixed effects models. In this approach, the parameters of the model are estimated using the deviations between an individual's characteristics at a point in time and his or her long-run average characteristics. For many people, their characteristics may have changed little over time so these observations essentially would be eliminated from the analysis.

A random effects model incorporates different limitations. Perhaps chief among them is that its assumptions are rather strict, particularly the assumption that the random effect is uncorrelated with all of the X variables. This is problematic precisely because of the omitted-variable bias problem discussed earlier in this chapter. It seems quite plausible that there may be characteristics of individuals that are not included in the regression model that may also be related to some of the included characteristics. This would violate the assumptions of the random effects model, and estimates resulting from this model would be biased.

In fact, one potential method for determining which method is the right one to use could proceed by testing whether the model's estimated residuals are correlated with any of the explanatory models. Tests of this form do indeed exist, but the validity of these tests requires that some specific assumptions hold.

Alternatively, many researchers simply use their intuition regarding whether it makes sense to model the entity-specific components as fixed or random. The immediately preceding discussion has treated this component as being individual-specific, but the particular entity could be states (as described earlier in the chapter) or other forms. When we have data on all states in the country, for instance, it seems intuitive to think of the differences that exist across them to be fixed in nature and not the result of a random draw. As such, our intuition tells us that a fixed effects specification probably is sensible.

Making such a determination with individual data is more difficult, however. In a relatively small sample of the population, it may seem reasonable to assume that the differences across the specific individuals who happen to have been chosen may be the result of random variation, so a random effects specification might seem natural. On the other hand, the concern over omitted-variable bias and unobservable heterogeneity remains an important one, limiting the appeal of such an approach. In such instances, the discretion of the researcher comes into play and often leads to great debate.

18.7 PROBLEMS

1. Suppose we have data on individuals over time and that the regression model is properly specified with individual fixed effects in the following manner:

$$Y_{it} = \beta_0 + \gamma_i + \beta_1 X_{1it} + \beta_2 X_{2it} + \beta_3 X_{3it} + \ldots + \beta_k X_{kit} + \varepsilon_{it}$$

Rather than estimating this model, we neglect to control for the fixed effect and instead we estimate

$$Y_{it} = \beta_0 + \beta_1 X_{1it} + \beta_2 X_{2it} + \beta_3 X_{3it} + \ldots + \beta_k X_{kit} + \varepsilon_{it}$$

What impact could this omission have on the estimated coefficients? What impact could it have on the standard errors of the estimated coefficients? In your answer, consider the relationship between the error term for observations of the same person at different points in time.

2. In March 1994, California instituted a "three strikes and you're out" policy that requires a mandatory 25-years-to-life sentence for any criminal convicted of a third felony offense, regardless of the degree of that offense. You have been hired to evaluate the effectiveness of this policy, measured by subsequent reductions in crime. Describe your evaluation, including the following:

   a. The difficulties of identifying the causal impact of the policy

   b. How your evaluation would overcome these difficulties

   c. The econometric models you would estimate

   d. The types of data you would use (assuming that you can get all of these data)

   e. How you would interpret the results of your analysis

3. A number of public policies related to alcohol consumption have been instituted over the past couple of decades in an attempt to limit the number of alcohol-related traffic fatalities. These policies include:

   • Increasing taxes on beer.

   • Raising the minimum legal drinking age (MLDA).

   • Automatically suspending driver's licenses of drunk drivers ("per se law").

   • Automatically suspending licenses of drivers who refuse to take a blood alcohol test ("implied consent law").

- Permitting those injured by drunk drivers to sue those who served alcohol to the driver ("dram shop law").

The data found in http://www.wiley.com/college/ashenfelter represent a dataset constructed by Christopher Ruhm for his paper, "Alcohol Policies and Highway Vehicle Fatalities" (*Journal of Health Economics*, Vol. 15, No. 4 (August 1996), pp. 435–454). The author has graciously provided these data for use here. It contains data for the vehicle fatality rate in each of the 48 contiguous United States (i.e., excluding Alaska and Hawaii) in each year between 1982 and 1988, along with each of the policies listed above and other factors that may influence accident rates.

a. Estimate an OLS regression model of the vehicle fatality rate on each of the policy variables along with: the unemployment rate, the percentage of drivers between the ages of 15 to 24, per capita income, the average miles driven, and a dummy variable for each year of the sample (excluding 1). Interpret the results of this regression.

b. Estimate the same regression model, but now include state fixed effects. Conduct an *F* test to determine whether you can reject the null hypothesis that these state fixed effects are jointly equal to zero.

c. Compare the coefficient estimates in this model compared to that in the OLS regression. Provide an explanation for any differences that emerged.

d. Which model do you prefer? Why?

e. Based on the evidence you have compiled, what policy recommendations would you make regarding approaches to reduce alcohol-related traffic fatalities?

Appendix A

Review of Probability and Statistics

A.1 INTRODUCTION

A.2 BASIC PROBABILITY THEORY

A.3 DESCRIPTIVE STATISTICS

A.4 CALCULATING PROBABILITIES FROM A NORMAL DISTRIBUTION

A.5 THE DISTRIBUTION OF THE SAMPLE MEAN

A.6 HYPOTHESIS TESTING

A.7 THE t DISTRIBUTION VERSUS THE STANDARD NORMAL DISTRIBUTION

A.8 MEASURES OF ASSOCIATION

A.1 INTRODUCTION

Chapters 1 through 8 of this book provide a detailed discussion of the methods of probability and statistics that is designed for a one-semester undergraduate course in econometrics. At many institutions, the undergraduate econometrics curriculum is spread across an entire year in which the first semester deals exclusively with the concepts of probability and statistics and the second semester examines multivariable methods, typically beginning with simple regression models. In those second-semester courses, students are held responsible for the material covered in the first-semester probability and statistics course, even though the two courses may have been taken months or even years apart.

This appendix is designed for students at institutions that have adopted a two-semester econometrics sequence and who need to have their memories refreshed regarding the key concepts of probability and statistics. It is specifically designed to provide a concise review of the particular topics that will certainly come into play, either directly or indirectly, in second-semester courses and is not intended to be exhaustive. It naturally precedes the discussion that begins in Chapter 9 and continues for the remainder of the book regarding multivariate econometric methods. Those instructors whose courses begin at this point should assign this appendix as supplemental reading in the first week of the course.

A.2 BASIC PROBABILITY THEORY

A.2.1 Properties of Probabilities

Let's start right from the beginning with a definition of what we mean by a probability. We can define a probability as a measure of how likely it is that an outcome will occur (i.e., probability of getting a head in the toss of a fair coin is 50%). How do you know this? One way to think about it is that if you repeated the event an infinite number of times, that is the fraction of heads you would get.

Some important properties of probabilities include:

1. All events (A) have some probability of occurring or, at worst, a zero probability of occurring. Therefore, all probabilities are nonnegative:

$$P(A \geq 0)$$

2. If there are n events that are possible (denoted by $A_1, \ldots, A_n$), one of them must occur:

$$\sum_{i=1}^{n} P(A_i) = 1$$

A.2.2 Random Variables

The formal definition of a random variable pertains to the mapping of a set of outcomes to particular numeric variables. Intuitively, however, it is simpler to think about a random variable as being an event that has an unknown outcome. Examples of random variables include: (1) the outcome of a coin toss; (2) the number of rainy days in a week; or (3) amount of rain in a week. A random variable that takes on a limited number of distinct values is called a *discrete random variable*. A random variable that takes on an infinite number of values over a continuous distribution is called a *continuous random variable*. In most applications in the remainder of the book we will examine continuous random variables, so the rest of this discussion will focus on them.

A.2.3 Continuous Probability Distributions

Continuous random variables pose a difficulty that is not faced by discrete random variables in that the probability that any particular value is observed is very small. Therefore, we cannot assign probabilities for particular values of the outcome, but only for ranges of values. To do this, we utilize a function, denoted by $f(x)$, that has the property that the area under the graph of the function between two values u and v is the probability that X assumes a value in that interval. In notation, we write that

$$P(u \leq X \leq v) = \int_u^v f(x)dx$$

We refer to $f(x)$ as the *probability density function* for the random variable X. Some important properties of continuous probability distributions include:

1. The probability that a value within a particular range of the distribution as observed is positive or, at worst, zero:

$$P(u \le X \le v) = \int_u^v f(x)dx \ge 0$$

2. Over the entire range of possible outcomes, it is certain that one of the values must be observed. In other words, the probability of observing one of the possible values is 1:

$$P(-\infty \le X \le \infty) = \int_{-\infty}^{\infty} f(x)dx = 1$$

Both of these properties merely reflect the basic properties of probabilities written specifically for continuous random variables.

A *cumulative distribution function* (CDF) is a function F that states the probability that a random variable X will assume a value less than or equal to a specified number. Mathematically, we write that

$$F(x) = P(X \le x) = \int_{-\infty}^{x} f(t)dt$$

Some of the properties of the CDF include:

1. The probability of X assuming a value below negative infinity is 0: $F(-\infty) = 0$.
2. The probability of X assuming a value below positive infinity is 1: $F(\infty) = 1$.
3. The probability that X assumes a value above u is 1 minus the probability that X assumes a value below u: $P(X \ge u) = 1 - F(u)$.
4. The probability that X is between u and v is the probability that X is below u less the probability X is below v: $P(u \le X \ge v) = F(v) - F(u)$.

A.3 DESCRIPTIVE STATISTICS

While probability distributions provide us with a tremendous amount of information, sometimes it would be useful if we had a simpler characterization of the data. Rather than knowing the whole distribution, we may be satisfied knowing some of its basic characteristics, like its "middle" (central tendency) and how spread out it is (dispersion).

A.3.1 Measures of Central Tendency

The two most common measures of central tendency are the *median* and the mean. The *median* is the value for which half the observations are bigger and half the observations are smaller. It is used relatively infrequently (if at all) in the multivariate described in Chapters 9 through 18 of this book. The mean, on the other hand, is used extensively and we will discuss it here in detail.

We define the *mean* to be

$$E(X) = \sum_{all\ x} x_i P(x_i)$$

if X is a discrete random variable. Note that if all values of x have an equal probability of occurring, then we have

$$E(X) = \sum_{i=1}^{n} x_i,$$

which is a formula quite familiar to students computing average grades. If the probabilities are not equal then the expected value reflects a weighted average.

The expected value has several important properties:

1. The expected value of a constant is the constant itself, $E(a) = a$. If you get the same grade on every exam, your average would be that grade.

2. The expected value of a constant times a random variable is the constant times the expected value of the random variable: $E(bX) = bE(X)$. If you multiplied each exam score by 2, your average would be twice as high.

3. For any random variable X and any constants, a and b, $E(a + bX) = a + bE(X)$.

A.3.2 Measures of Dispersion

Although the central tendency tells us something of where the middle of the distribution is, it does not tell us anything about how dispersed the distribution is. Two common measures of dispersion are the variance and standard deviation of a variable. The *variance* of a random variable X is denoted by var(X) or σ_x^2 and is given by var(X) = $E[(X - E(X))^2]$. We estimate this as the average squared deviation from the mean rather than the average deviation because the average deviation would be zero. Some values are above the mean and some are below and these would cancel each other out, giving an average deviation of zero.

The *standard deviation* is the square root of the variance. The reason for taking the square root is that the variance is measuring everything in squared units and that typically does not have a lot of intuition. If we take the square root of the variance, that allows us to interpret a measure as something like the average distance away from the mean. We denote the standard deviation of the random variable X as σ_x:

$$\sigma_x = \sqrt{\text{var}(X)}$$

Some of the important properties of the variance and standard deviation include:

1. var(a) = 0 if a is a constant. Constants do not vary!
2. var(bX) = b^2var(X) ==> s.d.(bX) = $b\sigma_x$.
3. If $Y = a + bX$, then var(Y) = b^2var(X).

A.4 CALCULATING PROBABILITIES FROM A NORMAL DISTRIBUTION

The normal distribution is a continuous probability distribution that is completely characterized by its mean and variance. Therefore, we write $X \sim N(\mu_X, \sigma_X^2)$ and say that X is distributed normally with mean μ_X and variance σ_X^2. Because it is a symmetric distribution, the probability on each side of the mean equals 0.5 and the mean equals the median. To calculate probabilities from the normal distribution, we need to convert the normally distributed variable, $X \sim N(\mu_X, \sigma_X^2)$, into a variable Z that has a standard normal distribution that has zero mean and unit variance: $Z \sim N(0, 1)$. The way that we do that is to subtract off the mean and divide through by the standard deviation:

$$Z = \frac{X - \mu_X}{\sigma_X}$$

Once you've computed the Z statistic, you can look up its value appendix table B.1 in Appendix B, Table B.1. The table shows the probability that Z is less than any particular value, z, (i.e., $P(Z \leq a)$) in the standard normal distribution.

We can use this to calculate several types of probabilities using some of the properties of probability that were introduced earlier:

1. $P(a \leq Z \leq b) = F(b) - F(a)$. The probability that Z is between a and b equals the probability that Z is below b minus the probability that Z is below a.
2. $P(Z \geq b) = 1 - F(b)$. The probability that Z is greater than b is 1 minus the probability that Z is below b.
3. $P(Z \leq -a) = P(Z \geq a)$. This is true since $f(Z)$ is symmetric.

Although one can determine probabilities from the standard normal distribution for all possible values of Z, a number of these probabilities appear frequently and it may be expedient to commit them to memory: These probabilities include:

1. $P(Z \leq 0) = 0.5$
2. $P(Z \leq 1.96) = 0.975$
3. $P(Z \geq 1.96) = 0.025$
4. $P(0 \leq Z \leq 1.96) = .975 - .5 = .475$
5. $P(-1.96 \leq Z \leq 1.96) = 0.975 - 0.025 = 0.95$
6. $P(-1.645 \leq Z \leq 1.645) = 0.90$
7. $P(-2.576 \leq Z \leq 2.576) = 0.99$

A.5   THE DISTRIBUTION OF THE SAMPLE MEAN

The sample mean,

$$\overline{X} = \frac{1}{n} \sum_{i=1}^{n} x_i$$

is an important descriptive statistic and is frequently used to estimate the mean of a particular population. One important limitation of the sample mean, however, is that it is a random variable. If we drew different samples of the population and constructed sample means from each sample, we would get different answers each time. Therefore, the sample mean is not a constant, but has a distribution.

Fortunately, the *Central Limit Theorem* tells us precisely the form of that distribution under certain assumptions. This theorem states that for large enough sample sizes

$$\bar{X} \sim N\left(\mu_x, \frac{\sigma_x^2}{n}\right)$$

where n is the sample size. Alternatively, the random variable

$$\frac{\bar{X} - \mu_x}{\sqrt{\dfrac{\sigma_x^2}{n}}}$$

has an approximately standard normal distribution (mean 0 and variance 1). The approximation increases as n increases.

A.6   HYPOTHESIS TESTING

The fact that we typically have only samples and can compute statistics like the sample mean based only on these samples leads to difficulties in terms of interpreting the results of any statistical analysis. Suppose you estimate a sample mean and find that $\bar{X} = 5$. Is the true population mean really 5? Not necessarily, because we know this is just an estimate based on the sample that we have drawn. It could be bigger or smaller than five. In fact, it is not even clear whether the true mean is even a positive number. What we need is a methodology for making statements about what we think is true given the underlying constraint that we have only an estimate of the truth. The approach that we use to do this is called *hypothesis testing*.

A.6.1   Setting Up the Test

The first step in the process is defining a null hypothesis (H_0) and an alternative hypothesis (H_A). The null hypothesis is what you are testing against: "Is the true value of the population parameter equal to some number?" The alternative hypothesis is what is true if the null is incorrect. For example, in a test regarding the value of the sample mean, we may establish a null and an alternative hypothesis of the form

$$H_0 : \mu_x = a$$
$$H_A : \mu_x \neq a$$

This test states that the true value of the population mean is α. We estimated the sample mean and did not get α, but we understand that because this statistic was just estimated from a sample of the population, the probability of getting a sample mean of exactly α was very small. The alternative hypothesis just states that the true population mean is not α.

A.6.2   Intuition of the Test

The intuition behind our testing procedure is as follows: We first ask ourselves what is the probability that we would have obtained a sample mean of $\bar{X}$ if the true population mean is α. If that probability is very, very small, then we can reasonably confidently reject the null hypothesis that the true population mean really is α. If that probability is not so small, then it is not clear what we should think. While it still may not be true, we may not be willing to reject the null hypothesis. Under these circumstances, what we typically say is that we have failed to reject the null hypothesis. Note that at no time are we ever willing to conclude that the null hypothesis is true (accepting the null). The best we can do is to fail to reject the null.

A.6.3   Procedure for a Sample Mean

Hypothesis tests for the value of the sample mean provide one important example of why the Central Limit Theorem is very useful. It is from the Central Limit Theorem that we know that the statistic

$$\frac{\overline{X} - \mu_x}{\sqrt{\dfrac{\sigma_x^2}{n}}}$$

has the standard normal distribution. If the true value of the mean is α, we can then calculate the probability of observing a sample mean of $\overline{X}$. If that probability is very small, we can reject the null hypothesis that the true population mean really is α. Traditionally, "very small" means 1%, 5%, or 10% of the time, with 5% being the most common definition. From our earlier discussion about calculating probabilities from the standard normal distribution, you will recall that we can tell this by seeing if Z is greater than or equal to the absolute value of 1.645, 1.96, or 2.576. By far, a 5% cutoff is the most common, so usually 1.96 is the relevant critical value. To simplify, sometimes people just talk about the statistic being greater than or equal to 2 in absolute value.

A.7   THE t DISTRIBUTION VERSUS THE STANDARD NORMAL DISTRIBUTION

One limitation of these testing procedures using the normal distribution is that they require that you know the population variance. But typically we do not know that value either. In most instances, however, this turns out not to be a significant problem. Rather than compute a Z statistic in these circumstances, we can compute a t statistic, which is comparable except that it includes a value of the variance that is estimated from the sample. We would then compare the value of the t statistic to a critical value from the t distribution. For large enough samples (on the order of 50 to 100 observations), the t distribution and the standard normal distribution are virtually identical and we can use them interchangeably.

A.8   MEASURES OF ASSOCIATION

Up to this point, we have focused the discussion on the analysis of a single random variable. Statistical measures of association between two random variables also play an important role in the development of a broader econometric methodology and are reviewed here. The two key concepts to be reviewed are covariance and correlation. Both provide information regarding the relationship between movements in one variable and movements in the other. If the two variables move together, so that an increase in one variable goes along with an increase in the other variable, then the two variables are positively related. Alternatively, if an increase in one variable goes along with a decrease in the other variable, then they are negatively related. Covariance and correlation simply provide a formal way to express the extent of those relationships.

A.8.1   Covariance

The *covariance* between two random variables X and Y, denoted by (X,Y), is given by

$$cov(X,Y) = E[(X - E(X))(Y - E(Y))]$$

The sign $(+, -, 0)$ of the covariance indicates whether the random variables are positively, negatively, or not related. It is capable of providing an indication of only the direction of any relationship between the two variables, not its magnitude. This is because the covariance depends on the units in which X and Y are measured: Changing the units would change the covariance. Therefore, it provides a measure of the direction of association, but caution must be used in employing it as a measure of the strength of that association.

Some important properties of covariance include:

1. $cov(X,Y) = E(XY) - E(X)E(Y)$
2. If X and Y are statistically independent, then $cov(X,Y) = 0$.
3. If $Y = X$, then $cov(X,X) = E[(X - E(X))(X - E(X))] = var(X)$.
4. If X and Y are two random variables, then:

    a. $var(X + Y) = var(X) + var(Y) + 2\ cov(X,Y)$
    b. $var(X - Y) = var(X) + var(Y) - 2\ cov(X,Y)$

More generally, if $X_1, X_2, X_3, \ldots, X_N$ are N random variables, then:

    c. $var\left(\sum_{i=1}^{N} X_i\right) = \sum_{i=1}^{N} var(X_i) + 2\sum_{j<k} cov(X_j, X_k)$

    d. $var\left(\sum_{i=1}^{N} X_i\right) = \sum_{i=1}^{N} var(X_i) - 2\sum_{j<k} cov(X_j, X_k)$

A.8.2   Correlation

The *correlation* between two random variables X and Y is denoted by $corr(X,Y)$ or by ρ_{XY} and is given by

$$corr(X,Y) = E\left[\left(\frac{X - E(X)}{\sigma_X}\right)\left(\frac{Y - E(Y)}{\sigma_Y}\right)\right]$$
$$= \frac{cov(X,Y)}{\sigma_X \sigma_Y}$$

The correlation measure of association has an advantage over the covariance in that it is unit free and provides a measure of the *degree* of linear association between the two random variables that is not influenced by the units used to measure the variables.

Some important properties of correlation include:

1. The correlation between two variables is bounded by -1 and 1: $-1 \leq \rho_{XY} \leq 1$.

2. $|\rho_{XY}| = 1$ if and only if $Y = a + bX$. Thus, the correlation between two variables will equal 1 in absolute value only if there is a perfect linear relationship between the two variables.

3. Correlation does not imply causality. Two variables may move together but not be causally related.

Appendix B

Statistical Tables

Table B.1 Cumulative Areas Under the Standard Normal Distribution

z	0	1	2	3	4	5	6	7	8	9
−3.0	0.0013	0.0013	0.0013	0.0012	0.0012	0.0011	0.0011	0.0011	0.0010	0.0010
−2.9	0.0019	0.0018	0.0018	0.0017	0.0016	0.0016	0.0015	0.0015	0.0014	0.0014
−2.8	0.0026	0.0025	0.0024	0.0023	0.0023	0.0022	0.0021	0.0021	0.0020	0.0019
−2.7	0.0035	0.0034	0.0033	0.0032	0.0031	0.0030	0.0029	0.0028	0.0027	0.0026
−2.6	0.0047	0.0045	0.0044	0.0043	0.0041	0.0040	0.0039	0.0038	0.0037	0.0036
−2.5	0.0062	0.0060	0.0059	0.0057	0.0055	0.0054	0.0052	0.0051	0.0049	0.0048
−2.4	0.0082	0.0080	0.0078	0.0075	0.0073	0.0071	0.0069	0.0068	0.0066	0.0064
−2.3	0.0107	0.0104	0.0102	0.0099	0.0096	0.0094	0.0091	0.0089	0.0087	0.0084
−2.2	0.0139	0.0136	0.0132	0.0129	0.0125	0.0122	0.0119	0.0116	0.0113	0.0110
−2.1	0.0179	0.0174	0.0170	0.0166	0.0162	0.0158	0.0154	0.0150	0.0146	0.0143
−2.0	0.0228	0.0222	0.0217	0.0212	0.0207	0.0202	0.0197	0.0192	0.0188	0.0183
−1.9	0.0287	0.0281	0.0274	0.0268	0.0262	0.0256	0.0250	0.0244	0.0239	0.0233
−1.8	0.0359	0.0351	0.0344	0.0336	0.0329	0.0322	0.0314	0.0307	0.0301	0.0294
−1.7	0.0446	0.0436	0.0427	0.0418	0.0409	0.0401	0.0392	0.0384	0.0375	0.0367
−1.6	0.0548	0.0537	0.0526	0.0516	0.0505	0.0495	0.0485	0.0475	0.0465	0.0455
−1.5	0.0668	0.0655	0.0643	0.0630	0.0618	0.0606	0.0594	0.0582	0.0571	0.0559
−1.4	0.0808	0.0793	0.0778	0.0764	0.0749	0.0735	0.0721	0.0708	0.0694	0.0681
−1.3	0.0968	0.0951	0.0934	0.0918	0.0901	0.0885	0.0869	0.0853	0.0838	0.0823
−1.2	0.1151	0.1131	0.1112	0.1093	0.1075	0.1056	0.1038	0.1020	0.1003	0.0985
−1.1	0.1357	0.1335	0.1314	0.1292	0.1271	0.1251	0.1230	0.1210	0.1190	0.1170
−1.0	0.1587	0.1562	0.1539	0.1515	0.1492	0.1469	0.1446	0.1423	0.1401	0.1379
−0.9	0.1841	0.1814	0.1788	0.1762	0.1736	0.1711	0.1685	0.1660	0.1635	0.1611
−0.8	0.2119	0.2090	0.2061	0.2033	0.2005	0.1977	0.1949	0.1922	0.1894	0.1867
−0.7	0.2420	0.2389	0.2358	0.2327	0.2296	0.2266	0.2236	0.2206	0.2177	0.2148
−0.6	0.2743	0.2709	0.2676	0.2643	0.2611	0.2578	0.2546	0.2514	0.2483	0.2451
−0.5	0.3085	0.3050	0.3015	0.2981	0.2946	0.2912	0.2877	0.2843	0.2810	0.2776
−0.4	0.3446	0.3409	0.3372	0.3336	0.3300	0.3264	0.3228	0.3192	0.3156	0.3121
−0.3	0.3821	0.3783	0.3745	0.3707	0.3669	0.3632	0.3594	0.3557	0.3520	0.3483
−0.2	0.4207	0.4168	0.4129	0.4090	0.4052	0.4013	0.3974	0.3936	0.3897	0.3859
−0.1	0.4602	0.4562	0.4522	0.4483	0.4443	0.4404	0.4364	0.4325	0.4286	0.4247
−0.0	0.5000	0.4960	0.4920	0.4880	0.4840	0.4801	0.4761	0.4721	0.4681	0.4641
0.0	0.5000	0.5040	0.5080	0.5120	0.5160	0.5199	0.5239	0.5279	0.5319	0.5359

0.1	0.5398	0.5438	0.5478	0.5517	0.5557	0.5596	0.5636	0.5675	0.5714	0.5753
0.2	0.5793	0.5832	0.5871	0.5910	0.5948	0.5987	0.6026	0.6064	0.6103	0.6141
0.3	0.6179	0.6217	0.6255	0.6293	0.6331	0.6368	0.6406	0.6443	0.6480	0.6517
0.4	0.6554	0.6591	0.6628	0.6664	0.6700	0.6736	0.6772	0.6808	0.6844	0.6879
0.5	0.6915	0.6950	0.6985	0.7019	0.7054	0.7088	0.7123	0.7157	0.7190	0.7224
0.6	0.7257	0.7291	0.7324	0.7357	0.7389	0.7422	0.7454	0.7486	0.7517	0.7549
0.7	0.7580	0.7611	0.7642	0.7673	0.7704	0.7734	0.7764	0.7794	0.7823	0.7852
0.8	0.7881	0.7910	0.7939	0.7967	0.7995	0.8023	0.8051	0.8078	0.8106	0.8133
0.9	0.8159	0.8186	0.8212	08238	0.8264	0.8289	0.8315	0.8340	0.8365	0.8389
1.0	0.8413	0.8438	0.8461	0.8485	0.8508	0.8531	0.8554	0.8577	0.8599	0.8621
1.1	0.8643	0.8665	0.8686	0.8708	0.8729	0.8749	0.8770	0.8790	0.8810	0.8830
1.2	0.8849	0.8869	0.8888	0.8907	0.8925	0.8944	0.8962	0.8980	0.8997	0.9015
1.3	0.9032	0.9049	0.9066	0.9082	0.9099	0.9115	0.9131	0.9147	0.9162	0.9177
1.4	0.9192	0.9207	0.9222	0.9236	0.9251	0.9265	0.9279	0.9292	0.9306	0.9319
1.5	0.9332	0.9345	0.9357	0.9370	0.9382	0.9394	0.9406	0.9418	0.9429	0.9441
1.6	0.9452	0.9463	0.9474	0.9484	0.9495	0.9505	0.9515	0.9525	0.9535	0.9545
1.7	0.9554	0.9564	0.9573	0.9582	0.9591	0.9599	0.9608	0.9616	0.9625	0.9633
1.8	0.9641	0.9649	0.9656	0.9664	0.9671	0.9678	0.9686	0.9693	0.9699	0.9706
1.9	0.9713	0.9719	0.9726	0.9732	0.9738	0.9744	0.9750	0.9756	0.9761	0.9767
2.0	0.9772	0.9778	0.9783	0.9788	0.9793	0.9798	0.9803	0.9808	0.9812	0.9817
2.1	0.9821	0.9826	0.9830	0.9834	0.9838	0.9842	0.9846	0.9850	0.9854	0.9857
2.2	0.9861	0.9864	0.9868	0.9871	0.9875	0.9878	0.9881	0.9884	0.9887	0.9890
2.3	0.9893	0.9896	0.9898	0.9901	0.9904	0.9906	0.9909	0.9911	0.9913	0.9916
2.4	0.9918	0.9920	0.9922	0.9925	0.9927	0.9929	0.9931	0.9932	0.9934	0.9936
2.5	0.9938	0.9940	0.9941	0.9943	0.9945	0.9946	0.9948	0.9949	0.9951	0.9952
2.6	0.9953	0.9955	0.9956	0.9957	0.9959	0.9960	0.9961	0.9962	0.9963	0.9964
2.7	0.9965	0.9966	0.9967	0.9968	0.9969	0.9970	0.9971	0.9972	0.9973	0.9974
2.8	0.9974	0.9975	0.9976	0.9977	0.9977	0.9978	0.9979	0.9979	0.9980	0.9981
2.9	0.9981	0.9982	0.9982	0.9983	0.9984	0.9984	0.9985	0.9985	0.9986	0.9986
3.0	0.9987	0.9987	0.9987	0.9988	0.9988	0.9989	0.9989	0.9989	0.9990	0.9990

Examples: If $Z \sim$ Normal $(0,1)$ then $P(Z \leq -1.24) = .1075$ and $P(Z \leq 1.53) = .9370$.

Source: This table was generated using the Stata® function normd.

Table B.2 Critical Values of the *t* Distribution

		Significance level				
1-Tailed:		.10	.05	.025	.01	.005
2-Tailed:		.20	.10	.05	.02	.01
	1	3.078	6.314	12.706	31.821	63.657
	2	1.886	2.920	4.303	6.965	9.925
	3	1.638	2.353	3.182	4.541	5.841
	4	1.533	2.132	2.776	3.747	4.604
	5	1.476	2.015	2.571	3.365	4.032
	6	1.440	1.943	2.447	3.143	3.707
D	7	1.415	1.895	2.365	2.998	3.499
e	8	1.397	1.860	2.306	2.896	3.355
g	9	1.383	1.833	2.262	2.821	3.250
r	10	1.372	1.812	2.228	2.764	3.169
e	11	1.363	1.796	2.201	2.718	3.106
e	12	1.356	1.782	2.179	2.681	3.055
s	13	1.350	1.771	2.160	2.650	3.012
	14	1.345	1.761	2.145	2.624	2.977
	15	1.341	1.753	2.131	2.602	2.947
o	16	1.337	1.746	2.120	2.583	2.921
f	17	1.333	1.740	2.110	2.567	2.898
	18	1.330	1.734	2.101	2.552	2.878
F	19	1.328	1.729	2.093	2.539	2.861
r	20	1.325	1.725	2.086	2.528	2.845
e	21	1323	1.721	2.080	2.518	2.831
e	22	1.321	1.717	2.074	2.508	2.819
d	23	1.319	1.714	2.069	2.500	2.807
o	24	1.318	1.711	2.064	2.492	2.797
m	25	1.316	1.708	2.060	2.485	2.787
	26	1.315	1.706	2.056	2.479	2.779
	27	1.314	1.703	2.052	2.473	2.771
	28	1.313	1.701	2.048	2.467	2.763
	29	1.311	1.699	2.045	2.462	2.756
	30	1.310	1.697	2.042	2.457	2.750
	40	1.303	1.684	2.021	2.423	2.704
	60	1.296	1.671	2.000	2.390	2.660
	90	1.291	1.662	1.987	2.368	2.632
	120	1.289	1.658	1.980	2.358	2.617
	∞	1.282	1.645	1.960	2.326	2.576

Examples: The 5% critical value for a two-tailed test with 15 *df* is 2.131. The 5% critical for a two-tailed test with large (> 120) *df* is 1.96.

Source: This table was generated using the Stata® function invt.

Table B.3a   10% Critical Values of the F Distribution

		1	2	3	4	5	6	7	8	9	10
						Numerator degrees of freedom					
D	10	3.29	2.92	2.73	2.61	2.52	2.46	2.41	2.38	2.35	2.32
e	11	3.23	2.86	2.66	2.54	2.45	2.39	2.34	2.30	2.27	2.25
n	12	3.18	2.81	2.61	2.48	2.39	2.33	2.28	2.24	2.21	2.19
o	13	3.14	2.76	2.56	2.43	2.35	2.28	2.23	2.20	2.16	2.14
m	14	3.10	2.73	2.52	2.39	2.31	2.24	2.19	2.15	2.12	2.10
i	15	3.07	2.70	2.49	2.36	2.27	2.21	2.16	2.12	2.09	2.06
n	16	3.05	2.67	2.46	2.33	2.24	2.18	2.13	2.09	2.06	2.03
a	17	3.03	2.64	2.44	2.31	2.22	2.15	2.10	2.06	2.03	2.00
t	18	3.01	2.62	2.42	2.29	2.20	2.13	2.08	2.04	2.00	1.98
o	19	2.99	2.61	2.40	2.27	2.18	2.11	2.06	2.02	1.98	1.96
r	20	2.97	2.59	2.38	2.25	2.16	2.09	2.04	2.00	1.96	1.94
D	21	2.96	2.57	2.36	2.23	2.14	2.08	2.02	1.98	1.95	1.92
e	22	2.95	2.56	2.35	2.22	2.13	2.06	2.01	1.97	1.93	1.90
g	23	2.94	2.55	2.34	2.21	2.11	2.05	1.99	1.95	1.92	1.89
r	24	2.93	2.54	2.33	2.19	2.10	2.04	1.98	1.94	1.91	1.88
e	25	2.92	2.53	2.32	2.18	2.09	2.02	1.97	1.93	1.89	1.87
e	26	2.91	2.52	2.31	2.17	2.08	2.01	1.96	1.92	1.88	1.86
s	27	2.90	2.51	2.30	2.17	2.07	2.00	1.95	1.91	1.87	1.85
o	28	2.89	2.50	2.29	2.16	2.06	2.00	1.94	1.90	1.87	1.84
f	29	2.89	2.50	2.28	2.15	2.06	1.99	1.93	1.89	1.86	1.83
F	30	2.88	2.49	2.28	2.14	2.05	1.98	1.93	1.88	1.85	1.82
r	40	2.84	2.44	2.23	2.09	2.00	1.93	1.87	1.83	1.79	1.76
e	60	2.79	2.39	2.18	2.04	1.95	1.87	1.82	1.77	1.74	1.71
e	90	2.76	2.36	2.15	2.01	1.91	1.84	1.78	1.74	1.70	1.67
d	120	2.75	2.35	2.13	1.99	1.90	1.82	1.77	1.72	1.68	1.65
o	∞	2.71	2.30	2.08	1.94	1.85	1.77	1.72	1.67	1.63	1.60
m											

Example: The 10% critical value for numerator $df = 5$ and denominator $df = 30$ is 2.05.

Source: This table was generated using the Stata® function invfprob.

Table B.3b   5% Critical Values of the F Distribution

| | | \multicolumn{10}{c}{**Numerator degrees of freedom**} | | | | | | | | | |
		1	2	3	4	5	6	7	8	9	10
D	10	4.96	4.10	3.71	3.48	3.33	3.22	3.14	3.07	3.02	2.98
e	11	4.84	3.98	3.59	3.36	3.20	3.09	3.01	2.95	2.90	2.85
n	12	4.75	3.89	3.49	3.26	3.11	3.00	2.91	2.85	2.80	2.75
o	13	4.67	3.81	3.41	3.18	3.03	2.92	2.83	2.77	2.71	2.67
m	14	4.60	3.74	3.34	3.11	2.96	2.85	2.76	2.70	2.65	2.60
i	15	4.54	3.68	3.29	3.06	2.90	2.79	2.71	2.64	2.59	2.54
n	16	4.49	3.63	3.24	3.01	2.85	2.74	2.66	2.59	2.54	2.49
a	17	4.45	3.59	3.20	2.96	2.81	2.70	2.61	2.55	2.49	2.45
t	18	4.41	3.55	3.16	2.93	2.77	2.66	2.58	2.51	2.46	2.41
o	19	4.38	3.52	3.13	2.90	2.74	2.63	2.54	2.48	2.42	2.38
r	20	4.35	3.49	3.10	2.87	2.71	2.60	2.51	2.45	2.39	2.35
D	21	4.32	3.47	3.07	2.84	2.68	2.57	2.49	2.42	2.37	2.32
e	22	4.30	3.44	3.05	2.82	2.66	2.55	2.46	2.40	2.34	2.30
g	23	4.28	3.42	3.03	2.80	2.64	2.53	2.44	2.37	2.32	2.27
r	24	4.26	3.40	3.01	2.78	2.62	2.51	2.42	2.36	2.30	2.25
e	25	4.24	3.39	2.99	2.76	2.60	2.49	2.40	2.34	2.28	2.24
e	26	4.23	3.37	2.98	2.74	2.59	2.47	2.39	2.32	2.27	2.22
s	27	4.21	3.35	2.96	2.73	2.57	2.46	2.37	2.31	2.25	2.20
o	28	4.20	3.34	2.95	2.71	2.56	2.45	2.36	2.29	2.24	2.19
f	29	4.18	3.33	2.93	2.70	2.55	2.43	2.35	2.28	2.22	2.18
F	30	4.17	3.32	2.92	2.69	2.53	2.42	2.33	2.27	2.21	2.16
r	40	4.08	3.23	2.84	2.61	2.45	2.34	2.25	2.18	2.12	2.08
e	60	4.00	3.15	2.76	2.53	2.37	2.25	2.17	2.10	2.04	1.99
e	90	3.95	3.10	2.71	2.47	2.32	2.20	2.11	2.04	1.99	1.94
d	120	3.92	3.07	2.68	2.45	2.29	2.17	2.09	2.02	1.96	1.91
o	∞	3.84	3.00	2.60	2.37	2.21	2.10	2.01	1.94	1.88	1.83

Example: The 5% critical value for numerator $df = 2$ and denominator $df = 40$ is 3.23.
Source: This table was generated using the Stata® function invfprob.

Table B.3c   1% Critical Values of the *F* Distribution

		Numerator degrees of freedom									
		1	2	3	4	5	6	7	8	9	10
D	10	10.04	7.56	6.55	5.99	5.64	5.39	5.20	5.06	4.94	4.85
e	11	9.65	7.21	6.22	5.67	5.32	5.07	4.89	4.74	4.63	4.54
n	12	9.33	6.93	5.95	5.41	5.06	4.82	4.64	4.50	4.39	4.30
o	13	9.07	6.70	5.74	5.21	4.86	4.62	4.44	4.30	4.19	4.10
m	14	8.86	6.51	5.56	5.04	4.69	4.46	4.28	4.14	4.03	3.94
i	15	8.68	6.36	5.42	4.89	4.56	4.32	4.14	4.00	3.89	3.80
n	16	8.53	6.23	5.29	4.77	4.44	4.20	4.03	3.89	3.78	3.69
a	17	8.40	6.11	5.18	4.67	4.34	4.10	3.93	3.79	3.68	3.59
t	18	8.29	6.01	5.09	4.58	4.25	4.01	3.84	3.71	3.60	3.51
o	19	8.18	5.93	5.01	4.50	4.17	3.94	3.77	3.63	3.52	3.43
r	20	8.10	5.85	4.94	4.43	4.10	3.87	3.70	3.56	3.46	3.37
D	21	8.02	5.78	4.87	4.37	4.04	3.81	3.64	3.51	3.40	3.31
e	22	7.95	5.72	4.82	4.31	3.99	3.76	3.59	3.45	3.35	3.26
g	23	7.88	5.66	4.76	4.26	3.94	3.71	3.54	3.41	3.30	3.21
r	24	7.82	5.61	4.72	4.22	3.90	3.67	3.50	3.36	3.26	3.17
e	25	7.77	5.57	4.68	4.18	3.85	3.63	3.46	3.32	3.22	3.13
e	26	7.72	5.53	4.64	4.14	3.82	3.59	3.42	3.29	3.18	3.09
s	27	7.68	5.49	4.60	4.11	3.78	3.56	3.39	3.26	3.15	3.06
o	28	7.64	5.45	4.57	4.07	3.75	3.53	3.36	3.23	3.12	3.03
f	29	7.60	5.42	4.54	4.04	3.73	3.50	3.33	3.20	3.09	3.00
F	30	7.56	5.39	4.51	4.02	3.70	3.47	3.30	3.17	3.07	2.98
r	40	7.31	5.18	4.31	3.83	3.51	3.29	3.12	2.99	2.89	2.80
e	60	7.08	4.98	4.13	3.65	3.34	3.12	2.95	2.82	2.72	2.63
e	90	6.93	4.85	4.01	3.54	3.23	3.01	2.84	2.72	2.61	2.52
d	120	6.85	4.79	3.95	3.48	3.17	2.96	2.79	2.66	2.56	2.47
o **m**	∞	6.63	4.61	3.78	3.32	3.02	2.80	2.64	2.51	2.41	2.32

Example: The 1% critical value for numerator $df = 4$ and denominator $df = \infty$ is 3.32.
Source: This table was generated using the Stata® function invfprob.

Table B.4 Critical Values of the Chi-Square Distribution

		Significance level		
		.10	.05	.01
	1	2.71	3.84	6.63
	2	4.61	5.99	9.21
	3	6.25	7.81	11.34
	4	7.78	9.49	13.28
	5	9.24	11.07	15.09
D	6	10.64	12.59	16.81
	7	12.02	14.07	18.48
e	8	13.36	15.51	20.09
g	9	14.68	16.92	21.67
r	10	15.99	18.31	23.21
e	11	17.28	19.68	24.72
e	12	18.55	21.03	26.22
s	13	19.81	22.36	27.69
	14	21.06	23.68	29.14
o	15	22.31	25.00	30.58
f	16	23.54	26.30	32.00
	17	24.77	27.59	33.41
F	18	25.99	28.87	34.81
r	19	27.20	30.14	36.19
e	20	28.41	31.41	37.57
e	21	29.62	32.67	38.93
d	22	30.81	33.92	40.29
	23	32.01	35.17	41.64
o	24	33.20	36.42	42.98
m	25	34.38	37.65	44.31
	26	35.56	38.89	45.64
	27	36.74	40.11	46.96
	28	37.92	41.34	48.28
	29	39.09	42.56	49.59
	30	40.26	43.77	50.89

Example: The 10% critical value with $df = 16$ is 23.54.
Source: This table was generated using the Stata® function invchi.

Table B.5   Durbin–Watson d Statistic: Significance Points of d_L and d_U at 0.05 Level of Significance

	$k^1 = 1$		$k^1 = 2$		$k^1 = 3$		$k^1 = 4$		$k^1 = 5$		$k^1 = 6$		$k^1 = 7$		$k^1 = 8$		$k^1 = 9$		$k^1 = 10$	
n	d_L	d_U	d_L	d_U	d_L	d_U	d_L	d_U	d_L	d_U	d_L	d_U	d_L	d_U	d_L	d_U	d_L	d_U	d_L	d_U
6	0.610	1.400	—	—	—	—	—	—	—	—	—	—	—	—	—	—	—	—	—	—
7	0.700	1.356	0.467	1.896	—	—	—	—	—	—	—	—	—	—	—	—	—	—	—	—
8	0.763	1.332	0559	1.777	0.368	2.287	—	—	—	—	—	—	—	—	—	—	—	—	—	—
9	0.824	1.320	0.629	1.699	0.455	2.128	0.296	2.588	—	—	—	—	—	—	—	—	—	—	—	—
10	0.879	1.320	0.697	1.641	0.525	2.016	0.376	2.414	0.243	2.822	—	—	—	—	—	—	—	—	—	—
11	0.927	1.324	0.658	1.604	0.595	1.928	0.444	2.283	0.316	2.645	0.203	3.005	—	—	—	—	—	—	—	—
12	0.971	1.331	0.812	1.579	0.658	1.864	0.512	2.177	0.379	2.506	0.268	2.832	0.171	3.149	—	—	—	—	—	—
13	1.010	1.340	0.861	1.562	0.715	1.816	0.574	2.094	0.445	2.390	0.328	2.692	0.230	2.985	0.147	3.266	—	—	—	—
14	1.045	1.350	0.905	1.551	0.767	1.779	0.632	2.030	0.505	2.296	0.389	2.572	0.286	2.848	0.200	3.111	0.127	3.360	—	—
15	1.077	1.361	0.946	1.543	0.814	1.750	0.685	1.977	0.562	2.220	0.447	2.472	0.343	2.727	0.251	2.979	0.175	3.216	0.111	3.438
16	1.106	1.371	0.982	1.539	0.857	1.728	0.734	1.935	0.615	2.157	0.502	2.388	0.398	2.624	0.304	2.860	0.222	3.090	0.155	3.304
17	1.133	1.381	1.015	1.536	0.897	1.710	0.779	1.900	0.664	2.104	0.554	2.318	0.451	2.537	0.356	2.757	0.272	2.975	0.198	3.184
18	1.158	1.391	1.046	1.535	0.933	1.696	0.820	1.872	0.710	2.060	0.603	2.257	0.502	2.461	0.407	2.667	0.321	2.873	0.244	3.073
19	1.180	1.401	1.074	1.536	0.967	1.685	0.859	1.848	0.752	2.023	0.649	2.206	0.549	2.396	0.456	2.589	0.369	2.783	0.290	2.974
20	1.201	1.411	1.100	1.537	0.998	1.676	0.894	1.828	0.792	1.991	0.692	2.162	0.595	2.339	0.502	2.521	0.416	2.704	0.336	2.885
21	1.221	1.420	1.125	1.538	1.026	1.669	0.927	1.812	0.829	1.964	0.732	2.124	0.637	2.290	0.547	2.460	0.461	2.633	0.380	2.806
22	1.239	1.429	1.147	1.541	1.053	1.664	0.958	1.797	0.863	1.940	0.769	2.090	0.677	2.246	0.588	2.407	0.504	2.571	0.424	2.734
23	1.257	1.437	1.168	1.543	1.078	1.660	0.986	1.785	0.895	1.920	0.804	2.061	0.715	2.208	0.628	2.360	0.545	2.514	0.465	2.670
24	1.273	1.446	1.188	1.546	1.101	1.656	1.013	1.775	0.925	1.902	0.837	2.035	0.751	2.174	0.666	2.318	0.584	2.464	0.506	2.613
25	1.288	1.454	1.206	1.550	1.123	1.654	1.038	1.767	0.953	1.886	0.868	2.012	0.784	2.144	0.702	2.280	0.621	2.419	0.544	2.560
26	1.302	1.461	1.224	1.553	1.143	1.652	1.062	1.759	0.979	1.873	0.897	1.992	0.816	2.117	0.735	2.246	0.657	2.379	0.581	2.513
27	1.316	1.469	1.240	1.556	1.162	1.651	1.084	1.753	1.004	1.861	0.925	1.974	0.845	2.093	0.767	2.216	0.691	2.342	0.616	2.470
28	1.328	1.476	1.255	1.560	1.181	1.650	1.104	1.747	1.028	1.850	0.951	1.958	0.874	2.071	0.798	2.188	0.723	2.309	0.650	2.431
29	1.341	1.483	1.270	1.563	1.198	1.650	1.124	1.743	1.050	1.841	0.975	1.944	0.900	2.052	0.826	2.164	0.753	2.278	0.682	2.396
30	1.352	1.489	1.284	1.567	1.214	1.650	1.143	1.739	1.071	1.833	0.998	1.931	0.926	2.034	0.854	2.141	0.782	2.251	0.712	2.363
31	1.363	1.496	1.297	1.570	1.229	1.650	1.160	1.735	1.090	1.825	1.020	1.920	0.950	2.018	0.879	2.120	0.810	2.226	0.741	2.333
32	1.373	1.502	1.309	1.574	1.244	1.650	1.177	1.732	1.109	1.819	1.041	1.909	0.972	2.004	0.904	2.102	0.836	2.203	0.769	2.306
33	1.383	1.508	1.321	1.577	1.258	1.651	1.193	1.730	1.127	1.813	1.061	1.900	0.994	1.991	0.927	2.085	0.861	2.181	0.795	2.281
34	1.393	1.514	1.333	1.580	1.271	1.652	1.208	1.728	1.144	1.808	1.080	1.891	1.015	1.979	0.950	2.069	0.885	2.162	0.821	2.257
35	1.402	1.519	1.343	1.584	1.283	1.653	1.222	1.726	1.160	1.803	1.097	1.884	1.034	1.967	0.971	2.054	0.908	2.144	0.845	2.236
36	1.411	1.525	1.354	1.587	1.295	1.654	1.236	1.724	1.175	1.799	1.114	1.877	1.053	1.957	0.991	2.041	0.930	2.127	0.868	2.216
37	1.419	1.530	1.364	1.590	1.307	1.655	1.249	1.723	1.190	1.795	1.131	1.870	1.071	1.948	1.011	2.029	0.951	2.112	0.891	2.198
38	1.427	1.535	1.373	1.594	1.318	1.656	1.261	1.722	1.204	1.792	1.146	1.864	1.088	1.939	1.029	2.017	0.970	2.098	0.912	2.180
39	1.435	1.540	1.382	1.597	1.328	1.658	1.273	1.722	1.218	1.789	1.161	1.859	1.104	1.932	1.047	2.007	0.990	2.085	0.932	2.164
40	1.442	1.544	1.391	1.600	1.338	1.659	1.285	1.721	1.230	1.786	1.175	1.854	1.120	1.924	1.064	1.997	1.008	2.072	0.952	2.149
45	1.475	1.566	1.430	1.615	1.383	1.666	1.336	1.720	1.287	1.776	1.238	1.835	1.189	1.895	1.139	1.958	1.089	2.022	1.038	2.088
50	1.503	1.585	1.462	1.628	1.421	1.674	1.378	1.721	1.335	1.771	1.291	1.822	1.246	1.875	1.201	1.930	1.156	1.986	1.110	2.044
55	1.528	1.601	1.490	1.641	1.452	1.681	1.414	1.724	1.374	1.768	1.334	1.814	1.294	1.861	1.253	1.909	1.212	1.959	1.170	2.010
60	1.549	1.616	1.514	1.652	1.480	1.689	1.444	1.727	1.408	1.767	1.372	1.808	1.335	1.850	1.298	1.894	1.260	1.939	1.222	1.984
65	1.567	1.629	1.536	1.662	1.503	1.696	1.471	1.731	1.438	1.767	1.404	1.805	1.370	1.843	1.336	1.882	1.301	1.923	1.266	1.964
70	1.583	1.641	1.554	1.672	1.525	1.703	1.494	1.735	1.464	1.768	1.433	1.802	1.401	1.837	1.369	1.873	1.337	1.910	1.305	1.948
75	1.598	1.652	1.571	1.680	1.543	1.709	1.515	1.739	1.487	1.770	1.458	1.801	1.428	1.834	1.399	1.867	1.369	1.901	1.339	1.935
80	1.611	1.662	1.586	1.688	1.560	1.715	1.534	1.743	1.507	1.772	1.480	1.801	1.453	1.831	1.425	1.861	1.397	1.893	1.369	1.925
85	1.624	1.671	1.600	1.696	1.575	1.721	1.550	1.747	1.525	1.774	1.500	1.801	1.474	1.829	1.448	1.857	1.422	1.886	1.396	1.916
90	1.635	1.679	1.612	1.703	1.589	1.726	1.566	1.751	1.542	1.776	1.518	1.801	1.494	1.827	1.469	1.854	1.445	1.881	1.420	1.909
95	1.645	1.687	1.623	1.709	1.602	1.732	1.579	1.755	1.557	1.778	1.535	1.802	1.512	1.827	1.489	1.852	1.465	1.877	1.442	1.903
100	1.654	1.694	1.634	1.715	1.613	1.736	1.592	1.758	1.571	1.780	1.550	1.803	1.528	1.826	1.506	1.850	1.484	1.874	1.462	1.898
150	1.720	1.746	1.706	1.760	1.693	1.774	1.679	1.788	1.665	1.802	1.651	1.817	1.637	1.832	1.622	1.847	1.608	1.862	1.594	1.877
200	1.758	1.778	1.748	1.789	1.738	1.799	1.728	1.810	1.718	1.820	1.707	1.831	1.697	1.841	1.686	1.852	1.675	1.863	1.665	1.874

n	$k^1 = 11$ d_L	d_U	$k^1 = 12$ d_L	d_U	$k^1 = 13$ d_L	d_U	$k^1 = 14$ d_L	d_U	$k^1 = 15$ d_L	d_U	$k^1 = 16$ d_L	d_U	$k^1 = 17$ d_L	d_U	$k^1 = 18$ d_L	d_U	$k^1 = 19$ d_L	d_U	$k^1 = 20$ d_L	d_U
16	0.098	3.503	—	—	·		—	—	—	—	—	—	—	—	—	—	—	—	—	—
17	0.138	3.378	0.087	3.557	—	—	—	—	—	—	—	—	—	—	—	—	—	—	—	—
18	0.177	3.265	0.123	3.441	0.078	3.603	—	—	—	—	—	—	—	—	—	—	—	—	—	—
19	0.220	3.159	0.160	3.335	0.111	3.496	0.070	3.642	—	—	—	—	—	—	—	—	—	—	—	—
20	0.263	3.063	0.200	3.234	0.145	3.395	0.100	3.542	0.063	3.676	—	—	—	—	—	—	—	—	—	—
21	0.307	2.976	0.240	3.141	0.182	3.300	0.132	3.448	0.091	3.583	0.058	3.705	—	—	—	—	—	—	—	—
22	0.349	2.897	0.281	3.057	0.220	3.211	0.166	3.358	0.120	3.495	0.083	3.619	0.052	3.731	—	—	—	—	—	—
23	0.391	2.826	0.322	2.979	0.259	3.128	0.202	3.272	0.153	3.409	0.110	3.535	0.076	3.650	0.048	3.753	—	—	—	—
24	0.431	2.761	0.362	2.908	0.297	3.053	0.239	3.193	0.186	3.327	0.141	3.454	0.101	3.572	0.070	3.678	0.044	3.773	—	—
25	0.470	2.702	0.400	2.844	0.335	2.983	0.275	3.119	0.221	3.251	0.172	3.376	0.130	3.494	0.094	3.604	0.065	3.702	0.041	3.790
26	0.508	2.649	0.438	2.784	0.373	2.919	0.312	3.051	0.256	3.179	0.205	3.303	0.160	3.420	0.120	3.531	0.087	3.632	0.060	3.724
27	0.544	2.600	0.475	2.730	0.409	2.859	0.348	2.987	0.291	3.112	0.238	3.233	0.191	3.349	0.149	3.460	0.112	3.563	0.081	3.658
28	0.578	2.555	0.510	2.680	0.445	2.805	0.383	2.928	0.325	3.050	0.271	3.168	0.222	3.283	0.178	3.392	0.138	3.495	0.104	3.592
29	0.612	2.515	0.544	2.634	0.479	2.755	0.418	2.874	0.359	2.992	0.305	3.107	0.254	3.219	0.208	3.327	0.166	3.431	0.129	3.528
30	0.643	2.477	0.577	2.592	0.512	2.708	0.451	2.823	0.392	2.937	0.337	3.050	0.286	3.160	0.238	3.266	0.195	3.368	0.156	3.465
31	0.674	2.443	0.608	2.553	0.545	2.665	0.484	2.776	0.425	2.887	0.370	2.996	0.317	3.103	0.269	3.208	0.224	3.309	0.183	3.406
32	0.703	2.411	0.638	2.517	0.576	2.625	0.515	2.733	0.457	2.840	0.401	2.946	0.349	3.050	0.299	3.153	0.253	3.252	0.211	3.348
33	0.731	2.382	0.668	2.484	0.606	2.588	0.546	2.692	0.488	2.796	0.432	2.899	0.379	3.000	0.329	3.100	0.283	3.198	0.239	3.293
34	0.758	2.355	0.695	2.454	0.634	2.554	0.575	2.654	0.518	2.754	0.462	2.854	0.409	2.954	0.359	3.051	0.312	3.147	0.267	3.240
35	0.783	2.330	0.722	2.425	0.662	2.521	0.604	2.619	0.547	2.716	0.492	2.813	0.439	2.910	0.388	3.005	0.340	3.099	0.295	3.190
36	0.808	2.306	0.748	2.398	0.689	2.492	0.631	2.586	0.575	2.680	0.520	2.774	0.467	2.868	0.417	2.961	0.369	3.053	0.323	3.142
37	0.831	2.285	0.772	2.374	0.714	2.464	0.657	2.555	0.602	2.646	0.548	2.738	0.495	2.829	0.445	2.920	0.397	3.009	0.351	3.097
38	0.854	2.265	0.796	2.351	0.739	2.438	0.683	2.526	0.628	2.614	0.575	2.703	0.522	2.792	0.472	2.880	0.424	2.968	0.378	3.054
39	0.875	2.246	0.819	2.329	0.763	2.413	0.707	2.499	0.653	2.585	0.600	2.671	0.549	2.757	0.499	2.843	0.451	2.929	0.404	3.013
40	0.896	2.228	0.840	2.309	0.785	2.391	0.731	2.473	0.678	2.557	0.626	2.641	0.575	2.724	0.525	2.808	0.477	2.892	0.430	2.974
45	0.988	2.156	0.938	2.225	0.887	2.296	0.838	2.367	0.788	2.439	0.740	2.512	0.692	2.586	0.644	2.659	0.598	2.733	0.553	2.807
50	1.064	2.103	1.019	2.163	0.973	2.225	0.927	2.287	0.882	2.350	0.836	2.414	0.792	2.479	0.747	2.544	0.703	2.610	0.660	2.675
55	1.129	2.062	1.087	2.116	1.045	2.170	1.003	2.225	0.961	2.281	0.919	2.338	0.877	2.396	0.836	2.454	0.795	2.512	0.754	2.571
60	1.184	2.031	1.145	2.079	1.106	2.127	1.068	2.177	1.029	2.227	0.990	2.278	0.951	2.330	0.913	2.382	0.874	2.434	0.836	2.487
65	1.231	2.006	1.195	2.049	1.160	2.093	1.124	2.138	1.088	2.183	1.052	2.229	1.016	2.276	0.980	2.323	0.944	2.371	0.908	2.419
70	1.272	1.986	1.239	2.026	1.206	2.066	1.172	2.106	1.139	2.148	1.105	2.189	1.072	2.232	1.038	2.275	1.005	2.318	0.971	2.362
75	1.308	1.970	1.277	2.006	1.247	2.043	1.215	2.080	1.184	2.118	1.153	2.156	1.121	2.195	1.090	2.235	1.058	2.275	1.027	2.315
80	1.340	1.957	1.311	1.991	1.283	2.024	1.253	2.059	1.224	2.093	1.195	2.129	1.165	2.165	1.136	2.201	1.106	2.238	1.076	2.275
85	1.369	1.946	1.342	1.977	1.315	2.009	1.287	2.040	1.260	2.073	1.232	2.105	1.205	2.139	1.177	2.172	1.149	2.206	1.121	2.241
90	1.395	1.937	1.369	1.966	1.344	1.995	1.318	2.025	1.292	2.055	1.266	2.085	1.240	2.116	1.213	2.148	1.187	2.179	1.160	2.211
95	1.418	1.929	1.394	1.956	1.370	1.984	1.345	2.012	1.321	2.040	1.296	2.068	1.271	2.097	1.247	2.126	1.222	2.156	1.197	2.186
100	1.439	1.923	1.416	1.948	1.393	1.974	1.371	2.000	1.347	2.026	1.324	2.053	1.301	2.080	1.277	2.108	1.253	2.135	1.229	2.164
150	1.579	1.892	1.564	1.908	1.550	1.924	1.535	1.940	1.519	1.956	1.504	1.972	1.489	1.989	1.474	2.006	1.458	2.023	1.443	2.040
200	1.654	1.885	1.643	1.896	1.632	1.908	1.621	1.919	1.610	1.931	1.599	1.943	1.588	1.955	1.576	1.967	1.565	1.979	1.554	1.991

Source: This table is an extension of the original Durbin-Watson table and is reproduced from N. E. Savin and K. J. White. "The Durbin-Watson Test for Serial Correlation with Extreme Small Samples or Many Regressors." *Econometrica*, vol. 45, November 1977, pp. 1989–96 and as corrected by R. W. Farebrother, *Econometrica*, vol. 48, September 1980, p. 1554. Reprinted by permission of the Econometric Society.

Note: n = number of observations, k^1 = number of explanatory variables excluding the constant term.

Example. If $n = 60$ and $k^1 = 3$, $d_L = 1.480$ and $d_u = 1.689$. If a computed d value is less than 1.480, there is evidence of positive first-order serial correlation; if it is greater than 1.689, there is no evidence of positive first-order serial correlation; but if d lies between the lower and the upper limit, there is inconclusive evidence regarding the presence or absence of positive first-order serial correlation.

Index